Artemis Cooper is the author of a number of books including *Cairo in the War, 1939–1945*, *Writing at the Kitchen Table: The Authorized Biography of Elizabeth David* and, most recently, *Patrick Leigh Fermor: An Adventure*. With her husband, Antony Beevor, she wrote *Paris After the Liberation, 1945–1949*. She has edited two collections of letters as well as *Words of Mercury*, an anthology of the work of Patrick Leigh Fermor; and, with Colin Thubron, she edited *The Broken Road*, the final volume of Leigh Fermor's European trilogy.

Praise for Elizabeth Jane Howard

'An unexpected treasure . . . It is as compelling and unified as a novel, while recounting a full, messy, complex human story . . . Cooper is respectful but never sycophantic, clear-eyed but never mocking. Familiar stories are retold but also reconsidered, and set in context. And the book pays the literary biography's ultimate compliment – it will send even the most familiar with the novels back to the bookshelves to revisit them' *Financial Times*

'In this fascinating biography, Artemis Cooper paints a picture of a complex and tricky woman' *Sunday Express*

'I inhaled every blissful word. A sad, revelatory, brilliantly written account of one remarkable woman's life . . . An unexpected triumph' Rachel Johnson, *Daily Mail*

'Elizabeth Jane Howard's life was long, messy and ultimately unhappy, and Cooper records its vicissitudes and achievements with sympathy and practised skill . . . her warmth and engagement are compelling' *Literary Review*

'This is no ordinary biography . . . a fitting tribute to one of our greatest writers' *Lady*

'Riveting . . . ill[d's] was a dangerous innoc[   ]nd a scintillating
read' *Cou[*

C334080463

Elizabeth Jane Howard

A Dangerous Innocence

ARTEMIS COOPER

JOHN MURRAY

First published in Great Britain in 2016 by John Murray (Publishers)
An Hachette UK Company

First published in paperback in 2017

1

A CIP catalogue record for this title is available from the British Library

ISBN 978-1-84854-926-5
Ebook ISBN 978-1-84854-928-9

Typeset in Bembo MT by Hewer Text UK Ltd

Printed and bound by Clays Ltd, St Ives plc

John Murray policy is to use papers that are natural, renewable and
recyclable products and made from wood grown in sustainable forests.
The logging and manufacturing processes are expected to conform
to the environmental regulations of the country of origin.

John Murray (Publishers)
Carmelite House
50 Victoria Embankment
London EC4Y 0DZ

www.johnmurray.co.uk

For my mother, with love

Contents

I

Dancing with the Ballets Russes

A FEW DAYS BEFORE Christmas 1919 a young English ballet dancer took the boat train to Paris to embark on the greatest adventure of her life. Her name was Katharine (known as Kit) Somervell, and in five years' time she would be the mother of Elizabeth Jane Howard; but as she leaned over the deck rail with a cloche hat rammed over her hair, motherhood was the last thing on her mind. She had taken up dancing relatively late, in her mid-teens, but such was her passion and determination that she had secured an eight-month contract to dance in the corps de ballet of the most celebrated dance company in Europe, the Ballets Russes.

On the advice of her ballet teacher, Professor Enrico Cecchetti, she took a room at 25 Boulevard des Capucines in Paris: a boarding house on five floors filled with actors and dancers, just a few minutes' walk from the Opéra de Paris where rehearsals took place. The theatre was vast, with rooms of breathtaking magnificence linked by miles of dim passages; but 'there are only a few taps in the corridors for washing,' she told her parents, 'where one takes towels and soap.'[1] Kit's first rehearsal, for *Prince Igor*, was on 23 December. She was one of the dancers in Russian dress, and she hoped to be on stage within a few days. Kit was lucky to have Professor Cecchetti to guide her through the chaos of Russian and French dancers, set-makers, choreographers, trainers, designers and costume-makers; but then, it was he who had first brought her to the attention of Sergei Diaghilev.

At the end of his career as a solo dancer in St Petersburg Enrico Cecchetti had joined the Ballets Russes as a teacher and trainer, where his students had included Anna Pavlova, Tamara Karsavina and Vaslav Nijinsky – but the glory days of the company were over. The Russian Revolution of 1917 had impoverished the rich Russians on whom Diaghilev relied to fund the Ballets Russes. The company went on tour much more than it used to, and held regular seasons in London. Cecchetti, while maintaining his ties with Diaghilev, set up a ballet school in Shaftesbury Avenue towards the end of the Great War.

Kit was among his first students, along with Marie Rambert and Ninette de Valois. Most dancers begin their training before puberty, when the body is still soft and pliable. But Kit, starting in her mid-teens, had to force herself to maintain those unnatural twists of knee and ankle; and by the time she joined Cecchetti's classes some five years later, she had developed that strength of character on which all dancers depend. Ballet demands a hyper-vigilant self-criticism awake to the slightest lapse, a formidable endurance and a willingness to push the body beyond pain. This goes especially for female dancers, for whom hours of practice on point leave the toes mashed, bruised and bleeding: few other arts require such a degree of self-punishment.

Kit had been studying with Cecchetti for about a year when Diaghilev appeared in the studio. He was looking for one young dancer to join the corps de ballet, and out of Cecchetti's class of sixteen students, he chose Kit. She kept a copy of her contract, signed by Diaghilev, which engaged her to dance with the company from 22 December 1919 to August 1920. 'I shall be able to live quite easily as we planned,' she wrote, 'with one good restaurant meal a day and breakfast and supper of my own making – it isn't expensive just to buy eggs and bacon, and macaroni.'[2]

This would not be her first time on the stage: earlier in 1919 she had a small part as a nanny in a play called *Home and Beauty* by Somerset Maugham, starring Gladys Cooper and Charles Hawtrey, and she may have understudied or taken other bit parts as well.[3] But while she had appeared on the London stage under her own name, in the Ballets Russes all names had to sound either Russian or French. Kit danced as Jane Forestier.

Kit Somervell had been born in 1898, the second daughter of the composer Arthur (later Sir Arthur) and Edith Somervell. The Somervells were from Windermere. In her memoir Jane described how her grandfather Arthur's family were of such modest means that only one of the children had piano lessons – and that was not Arthur. But so keen was he to learn that he would hide in the room as the lesson was being given, and then practise what he had heard. Not all the family were badly off. One branch of the Somervells had founded a successful shoe-making business in Kendal, which became known nationwide as K Shoes.

Arthur Somervell gained a scholarship to the Royal School of Music, where he became a teacher; and he is now remembered for his five song cycles of poems by Tennyson, Housman and Browning. He might have risen further as a composer had he not been such a champion of musical education. He pioneered the establishment of music as a recognized subject in schools, and developed the system of grades in musical proficiency that is still in use today. In 1890 he married an aesthetic and egocentric beauty called Edith Collett, and they had four children. Antonia was the eldest, then came Kit, and she was followed by twin brothers, Hubert and Ronald.

At a time when women were defined by their marriageable qualities, Kit (unlike her elder sister) was neither sweet-tempered nor classically beautiful, although she did have the small, neat body of a dancer. Her abundant chestnut hair had been so long she could sit on it, until she had it bobbed; and there was a challenge in her dark eyes and heavy eyebrows. In this very musical family, everyone played the piano; but Kit was the most musically responsive of all the Somervell children, and clever with her hands too: she enjoyed sewing and knitting, dressmaking, embroidery and book-binding. For her mother she made a little manuscript volume of Shakespeare's sonnets, on vellum with jewel-like decoration and capitals in gold leaf. Yet these were just pastimes: she had only one real passion, and that was ballet.

Her father had always encouraged her dancing, although her mother fretted that such single-minded dedication might affect her marriage prospects. After all, before the war it had been almost unthinkable for a well-brought-up girl to perform on a public stage. But Kit had worked very hard for this opportunity to dance with the Ballets Russes, and she was not going to miss it. However, she had also found a highly eligible suitor.

Every young woman who came of age just after the First World War knew that finding a husband was not going to be easy. Most of the hundreds of thousands of Englishmen who had died in the mud of Flanders had not had time to find a wife, and the attrition rate among young officers was far higher even than for private soldiers. Kit and her parents could hardly have escaped reading about the

'Surplus Women Problem', which had the press wringing its hands over the fate of all those middle-class spinsters who had been robbed by the war of husband, children, status and everything they had been brought up to expect. Yet despite the odds, Kit had caught the attention of a tall, good-looking man who had come back from the war not only alive, but with a rank and a medal his family could be proud of; and he was, at least superficially, undamaged.

David Liddon Howard, the second son of a prosperous timber merchant, had been seventeen when the war broke out. Excited by the prospect, he tried to join his older brother Alexander, always known as Geoff, who had been given a commission in the Coldstream Guards. The regiment turned David down for being a year too young so he approached the Machine Gun Corps, lied about his age and was accepted. Years later, he told his daughter that he had once saved a gun from overheating by peeing on it. Also that when he saw his brother Geoff for the first time in fourteen months, it was their horses who had recognized each other first, while they were still over a hundred yards apart.

By 1918 David Howard was a major with the Military Cross and bar, but he had not escaped the effects of war. His lungs had been weakened by living in gas-filled trenches, and of all the officers in his company he had been the only one to survive. For the rest of his life he kept a photograph of those dead friends on his dressing table; but, like almost everyone who had been through the horror of the Great War, he never talked about it.

His daughter Jane felt that he coped by refusing to grow up: 'The schoolboy who went to France and did his best there for four years returned to England as if he were a schoolboy embarking on the holidays,'[4] she wrote, and that sense of release touched everything. Survivor guilt is a well-known phenomenon, but David Howard displayed the other side of the coin – survivor celebration. He spent money lavishly; and when ordering champagne or buying huge boxes of chocolates on the spur of the moment, he would say, 'It's my birthday.' He also had a spontaneous charm that beguiled everyone. 'Commissionaires would eagerly hail taxis, waiters would escort him to the best tables . . . the barmen in theatres always seemed to serve him first . . . girls in restaurants always looked at him, looked away and then watched him covertly.'[5]

David Howard had no trouble attracting women and was spoilt for choice. But Kit's sharp wits, her strength and humour and intelligence made other girls look vapid. Together she and David were like flints sparking off each other, and they both loved dancing, skiing, sailing, tennis and riding. In the infinitely subtle gradations of the English class system his family's solid prosperity was matched by her cultural credentials, and he too had been brought up in a family that took music seriously. He played the violin, while his mother's piano-playing was good enough for her to play duets with her friend, the celebrated pianist Myra Hess.

David and Kit must have met and fallen in love before she left for Paris, because he appears in the letters she wrote back to her parents. Her first mention of him is in a letter of 20 January 1920: 'Give heaps of love to my dearest dearest David. I think so much of him and *long* to be with him, and I'm sure things will come right for us. I want to write to him so dreadfully sometimes – one can't send long messages somehow can one – I use the lovely little pencil he gave me a dozen times a day and think of him whenever I see it.'[6]

Presumably what she wanted to 'come right for us' was that they would eventually marry, and from that it follows that they were not yet formally engaged. If they had been, there could be no reason for not writing to each other. But at a time when engagement carried serious obligations, David's family might have urged him not to make such a commitment – at least not yet. Heaven knows what might happen to Kit in Paris, that dangerously seductive city; and when she left England in December 1919, her excitement at joining the Ballets Russes had clearly far outweighed the prospect of marrying David.

Decades later, Kit's daughter explored that part of her mother's life in an abandoned novel; and she too imagines that Kit's feelings for David are more equivocal than those expressed in her letters to her parents.

She picked up the little gold pencil that had 'Kit' inscribed on it. Of course it reminded her of him, but since being in Paris, she had neither the time nor the energy to long to be with him. Once or twice she had longed to write to him, but the agreement was that they should neither meet nor communicate until she had finished her tour, and although she would never have admitted to him or to her family that this arrangement actually suited her, that was in fact the case. Being irrevocably in love with [David] carried with it a whole weight of implications that she was simply unwilling – possibly unable to face.[7]

There was certainly little room for anything but work, as she told her mother when she had been with the company for about a month.

There is an *awful lot* to learn of it and it's frightfully hard to plunge in when everyone else knows it. This morning *Thalmar* which wasn't so hard – I was lucky in having awfully nice men for partners . . . who weren't cross and nasty as some can be at having a new person. The amount of toe-work in *Boutique* [*La Boutique Fantasque*] is appalling, though nothing really hard – just on and on for ages and never off the toes . . . I do hope I shall go on to Italy because as it is I never get a chance of dancing my best, learning everything in about an hour and a half for each ballet and then being supposed to go on in anyone's place if they are ill![8]

She still wasn't dancing as much as she would have liked, because the person she was supposed to have replaced didn't leave the company after all. But on stage or off, everyone in the corps de ballet had to attend rehearsals; and rather than sit in the stalls with nothing to do, Kit brought her knitting. She described one very stressful day when 'Stravinsky *lui-même* attended the *Rossignol* rehearsal, and of course revolutionized all the tempi and banged about on the piano and sang and shouted and the ballet was a gorgeous mess by the time he'd done.'[9]

That spring, Kit's mother Edith joined her in Rome for the start of the Ballets Russes's Italian tour. 'Mind you see my dearest David again before you come [to Italy],' Kit had written. 'I do so long to write to him – I *can't* send messages through other letters to him. That's why I so seldom write about him, as there is nothing to say – I *love* to get all the news of him there is.'[10] She learned *The Three-Cornered Hat* in a day, and danced it the next. She was also one of the nurses in *Petrouchka*, and her Russian was improving with help from the Russians in the company.

Mother and daughter were in Rome for about a month with the Ballets Russes, 'having a ripping time together';[11] then Kit went on with the company to Milan, Florence and Monte Carlo. She was back in London with her family in June, a few weeks before her contract ran out. The adventure was over. She was twenty-two, and the time had come to settle down.

*

For six months she had been a part of a professional ballet company, but even had she continued it is unlikely that she would have ever been considered for the role of soloist or principal. David Howard was still waiting for her, but there was no question of her pursuing her career once they were married.

And if she had turned him down to go on dancing, what could she have expected? Ballet dancers usually retire in their thirties, so she would have had another ten years on stage at most, by which time every man she knew would be married to someone else. Her own family were not rich, and she would have had to support herself on the meagre earnings of a ballet teacher, while knowing that Mrs David Howard (whoever she might be by then) enjoyed the security of a well-to-do family and a fine social position. So unless Kit wanted to dash all her parents' hopes as well as her own, giving up the ballet was inevitable and she did so with a good grace.

She and David were married on 12 May 1921; and it was only then that Kit discovered that while she had to give up some things, she was also expected to submit to others. The aesthetic sublimation of sex in ballet had left her quite unprepared for the real thing. She knew that refusing one's husband led to trouble, so she did not resist David's attentions; but her dislike for the sexual act meant that sooner or later he would look for more easy-going female companionship. In *The Light Years*, Jane described the parabola of her mother's married life through the character of Viola Cazalet, who had given up her ballet career on marriage:

> That this decision was the most momentous of her life had not struck her at the time; then, when she thought about it, it seemed that she was giving up not very much for everything. But over the years of pain and distaste for what her mother called 'the horrid side of married life', of lonely days filled with aimless pursuits or downright boredom, of pregnancies, nurses, servants and the ordering of endless meals, it had come to seem as though she had given up everything for not very much.[12]

2

Family Life

THE NEWLY MARRIED Howards settled in Bedford Gardens, Kensington, where Kit's parents also lived, and every morning David went to work in his chauffeur-driven Bentley to the offices of W.W. Howard Brothers in Trinity Square, overlooking the Tower of London. The firm had been founded in 1876 by his grandfather William Walters Howard, who came from Hunton Bridge in Hertfordshire. As the business grew he brought in two of his four brothers, of whom the youngest – Alexander, father of Geoff and David – succeeded him as chairman on William's retirement in 1916. When Geoff and David came home from the war, they were made managing directors.

The firm, which was divided into Hardwoods, Softwoods and Veneers, employed about a hundred men who worked in two wharves with sawmills and drying-kilns on the River Lea in the East End of London. In the early 1900s Howard Brothers set up another wharf at Southampton. Here massive logs from the Far East, Africa, Australia and the Americas were unloaded, seasoned and cut; and then delivered, in pale blue Howard Brothers carts or lorries (until 1936, they were also using dray horses), to craftsmen and contractors all over the country. During the First World War, the staff of Howard Brothers worked day and night shifts to provide hutments, shell battens and boxwood implements for pushing the powder into shells for the army; while the Air Ministry established a depot at one of their London wharves to store Sitka spruce for aeroplane manufacture.

By 1918, the exhaustion of supplies of the most commonly used hardwoods paved the way for the introduction of many species new to the timber trade. Howard Brothers began to import jarrah and karri from Western Australia, and in 1920 the Secretary of State for India asked Alexander Howard to advise him on the best way to exploit the forests of India, Burma and the Andaman Islands. Howard

Brothers had supplied the Australian jarrah wood for the pier at Worthing, and from the piles of the old Waterloo Bridge (salvaged in 1935) they made a beautiful panelling of silver-grey elm.[1]

Alexander Howard's knowledge and love of his trade produced three books, including *A Manual of the Timbers of the World* (1920) which he continued to enlarge and update – the third edition was finished just before his death in 1946. Another of his books was on the identification of timbers, and his granddaughter Jane recalled the wood samples that covered her grandfather's desk, 'of every colour from the palest skin, to the darkest animal fur; they were striped, whorled and figured'.[2]

Within his family Alexander Howard was known as the Brig, because he had never had the experience of war; and by a similar feat of non-analogy, David's mother was known as the Witch, or Witchy, because she was so beautiful and un-witchlike. Her real name was Florence, and she was one of the seven daughters of an eminent crystallographer called Christopher Barlow. The senior Howards lived in the rural folds of the Sussex Weald, at Home Place: a modestly comfortable house set amid woods and fields near the village of Whatlington, surrounded by orchards and paddocks, stables, a tennis court and plenty of servants. So far only two of their children have been mentioned, Geoff and David, but there were two more, John and Ruth. John was too young to have served in the war, and he did not want to join the family firm. To his parents' dismay he became a painter, taught art at Oundle, and married an Irish-American wife called Kathleen. As for Ruth, she developed a close relationship with a violinist called Marjorie Gunn. Had she been born in a later age, perhaps Ruth and Marjorie might have lived together. As it was, Ruth took it for granted that she would look after her ageing parents.

David and Kit would often drive down to Home Place for weekends and holidays. Kit got on well with the Brig and the Witchy, with whom she played the piano; and she was also close to her brother-in-law Geoff and his American wife, Helen. Helen had been brought up a Quaker and like Kit she was a woman of austere tastes. The two became very close, particularly as their children were growing up, and their intimacy was perhaps too well established for them to fully welcome John's wife Kathleen a few years later; although for the sake of family harmony they rubbed along well enough.

Kit seemed to need few friends outside the large circle afforded by the Howards and the Somervells. They admired her thriftiness and her iron self-discipline (although she was a heavy smoker), and she liked the Howards' predilection for strong drink, plain food and cold houses: Jane said that the feeblest fire in any room had them rushing to hurl open the windows. Kit did not keep up her ballet: in fact, she seems to have locked the door on that part of herself, which is perhaps an indication of how much she missed it. Instead, she made a point of filling her day with piano practice, needlework, spinning, weaving and reading, though none of these things ever filled the void. She still enjoyed sailing and skiing, tennis and riding – all of which she did superbly well. But she had trained her mind to overcome the body and its weaknesses, and to tolerate nothing less than perfection – perhaps not the best preparation for domesticity and motherhood.

Kit's first child was a girl, called Jane. She died soon after birth, but Kit loved the name – it reflected the part of her that was still Jane Forestier the dancer. She gave it to her second daughter who was born on 26 March 1923, and christened Elizabeth Jane Howard, though she would always be known as Jane. 'She was a very neat little baby with distinct features and a great deal of mouse-coloured hair . . . She would give tiny little cries in her sleep without opening her mouth. She had rather long fingers, beautifully formed.'[3]

As was usual for well-off middle-class children, Jane spent most of her waking and sleeping hours in the nursery with Nanny Wilshire, who came as a maternity nurse when Jane was five weeks old and stayed for five years. Jane loved Nanny, but she adored her parents and especially her mother with a passionate anxiety. She became ill when they went abroad for three weeks in the summer of 1924, and her mother was shocked at the change in the child on her return. 'All her merriness [was] gone,' wrote Kit, 'and she would sit silent with a little puckered forehead fiddling with small toys.'[4]

But with her mother home Jane soon returned to normal, and Kit was enchanted by her little daughter: 'She sometimes had tea tête-a-tête with me, sat on her own little drawing room chair and eating very carefully toast and butter, frequently pausing to borrow my handkerchief to wipe her fingers and blow her nose, and making conversation such as "Fire there", or "'ts nice, isn't it?" '[5]

It was nice. Jane had her mother's undivided attention, and Kit made sporadic entries in the exercise book that she kept to record her child's progress. Jane enjoyed music on the gramophone from an early age, and had a touching desire to share her pleasures with those around her: 'Travelling with her this September [of 1924], she pressed gratuities from my purse on all her fellow travellers. A flower has to be carried round and smelt rapturously by everyone and a cake is also offered in turn.'[6]

On 12 August 1925, when she was two and a half, Jane's brother Robin was born. From a difficult baby he grew into a cheerful and sturdy toddler, while Jane's doings (she was now aged four) were still worth recording. In March 1927 Kit wrote: 'Playing at going to bed in the drawing room she and David were discovered by the parlour-maid under a rug on the floor. Jane looked up and said, "I'm Mrs Cox in bed with Daddy!" '[7]

That scene might have raised a modern mother's eyebrow, but Kit was serenely unconcerned. '[Jane] can sew, skip a bit, write several letters, use a knife and fork . . . and improvise a tolerably plausible fairy tale without undue plagiarism. This is in the nature of a record, not a boast, for I do not think any of these are at all advanced for an eldest child, but it will be of interest to compare with Robin's progress.'[8]

Not boasting was a virtue much prized in the Howard family, who thought that children should be praised as little as possible, and Jane felt that every little childhood triumph was put down. She comes back again and again to the fact that her mother was constantly criticizing and finding fault with everything she did. She was slow at learning to read, and to Kit's irritation she seemed unwilling to practise. Early lessons with her mother began well, but Jane soon lost interest – or perhaps lost heart, for she needed frequent applause and reassurance while Robin was catching up with her on every front.

'And what can I not say of my darling Robin who grows so steadily in strength of character and smiles the livelong day?' wrote Kit. 'About the middle of September, 1929 [when Jane was six and Robin four] he began having lessons with me four mornings a week, and learnt in about 6 weeks what Janie took 18 months to learn, and can now read slowly from a first primer.'[9] Soon after that, Robin began writing a book. Jane thought that 'writing a book' meant taking one down from the shelf and copying it out in block capitals. This is what she did, and very tedious it was too; but she persevered, hoping it would earn her the encouragement she craved.

Robin's book was called *Percy Rainsbull Edwards, the Adventures of a Pig*. Like all good novels it had been torture to write: Robin trembled with fear as he chronicled the ordeals of his hero. Once completed, his book was enthusiastically received, typed up, illustrated by the author, read aloud, and bound by their mother in soft red leather. Jane's effort was, of course, forgotten. From her mother she was absorbing the fact that she was never going to be as good as Robin, who basked in his mother's love and approval in a way that Jane felt she never could.

Given their mother's feelings it is hardly surprising that Jane grew up increasingly unsure of herself, while Robin had total confidence and an innate grasp of how the world worked. Once, when they were discussing what they would most like to be, Jane assumed a saintly tone and said that she wanted to be kind and brave. Robin gave her a pitying look and said he would rather be rich and pretty.

Jane's fear of being abandoned was as strong as ever; and when Kit did go on holiday one can hardly blame her for making a fast exit, rather than endure days of tearful pleading from her daughter before departure. Jane, aged six or seven, remembered her anguish when her parents had gone off skiing on Christmas Day. For Jane, the up-heaval was completely unexpected. 'She had left, quite suddenly, after Christmas lunch, and the whole day was ashes and despair – the presents were useless, and I was left trying to count the hours till her return.'[10]

Her growing lack of confidence expressed itself physically too. 'Jane is rather lanky and untidy in her movements,' wrote Kit, who had sent both children to a Swedish gym. Kit thought that ballet might improve her coordination, and tried to teach her. Jane remembered agonizing mornings holding on to the bath rail, while Kit hit her bare legs with a riding crop; but her mother soon gave up. 'Her feet are too narrow,' wrote Kit, 'and she looks like being too tall for it to be worth undergoing the drudgery of dancing technique.'[11]

Kit had finished with ballet, but on one occasion it rose spontaneously to the surface. Jane and her mother were at home, and the waltz by Delibes from *Coppélia* was playing on the gramophone. Kit rose from her chair, kicked off her shoes and danced, while Jane watched in amazement; and the moment the music stopped she sat down, put on her shoes and resumed whatever she'd been doing. The incident was never mentioned again.[12]

3

Lessons

ONCE JANE LEARNED to read there was no stopping her. When she was about seven or eight the family moved from Bedford Gardens to Lansdowne Road in Notting Hill, and there – curled up in a large and ugly leather chair – she plunged into Andrew Lang's *Coloured Fairy Books*. Another escape was a particular patterned square on the eiderdown of her bed, which became her very own desert island. It had a river running down to a sandy beach, and on it lived tigers and cheetahs and a small elephant who could all talk. She loved stories about animals and longed to have a dog – but since this was not allowed she had to make do with worms and caterpillars, or pocket-money pets like goldfish.

In London a Miss Kettle was engaged to oversee Jane's basic education, and Robin joined her classes when he was five. They also had piano lessons, and here again Robin triumphed. To their mother's delight, 'he had the ear and could play [the piano] before he could read.'[1] Jane's feelings of inadequacy were expressed by a deep-rooted homesickness. This was not so much a yearning for home as a terror of being outside it, making even children's parties an ordeal.

Yet she was not utterly consumed by anxiety. Active and gregarious, she loved the family holidays with her cousins in Sussex. The three Howard brothers eventually produced ten children between them, born between 1923 and 1934: Dana (a boy who was given his mother's surname, pronounced Dayna), Geoff, Audrey and Penelope were Geoff's children; Jane, Robin and Colin were David's; and Rob, Judy and Bill were John's. When Home Place became too small to accommodate them and their parents, Alexander Howard bought a large and rather spartan house three and a half miles away at Staplecross, called the Beacon. Here the children rode and played tennis and rambled over the countryside, gathered blackberries and cobnuts, swapped secrets and played games and put on plays. Alliances were made and fell apart, quarrels raged and then blew out. They took turns to drive the Very, Very Old Car which sat gently rusting in a field, and squealed with delight at the thought of a day by the sea at Bexhill or Hastings. All her life Jane enjoyed that sense of belonging that comes with being in a big family group, and the feeling of never being alone unless you wanted to be. When she wanted to be solitary there were window-seats and apple trees to curl up in, to read E. Nesbit and Captain Marryat and R.M. Ballantyne – she had a great desire to be shipwrecked.

When she was about eight or nine, her brother Robin was sent to prep school. He had been her closest friend, and when he went away Jane was left desolate. 'We did everything together, so it was awful when he went . . . I spent about a year hoping I'd turn into a boy so that I could join him. I couldn't bear to sleep in the room we'd shared.' What made the separation even more painful was that when Robin came home for the holidays, he made it very clear that their child-hood companionship was over. 'He didn't want to play with girls. That's what happens when boys go away to school.'[2]

Yet despite the loss of Robin, those cousin-crowded days at the Beacon were among the happiest of her existence, and the ability to see with a child's perception is something she never lost. Often in her novels it is a child who sees things as they really are, while the adults are lost and blinded by their own concerns.

In 1932, when Jane was nine years old, she was sent to Francis Holland School in Graham Terrace near Sloane Square. Miss Kettle had been a good teacher, which meant she was ahead of most of the girls in her form; but when Jane was moved up a year she was merci-lessly bullied. The ringleaders would lock her in the lavatory to make her late for lessons, stole her textbooks, twisted her wrist so she couldn't write, scattered salt over her lunch to make it inedible, and her tentative confidence was eroded by their mockery. Her only escape was in illness; and since she was prone to sore throats and often went without lunch, this was not hard to achieve.

It was decided that she should skip the summer term which was to be spent at the Beacon, where she arrived at the end of a sun-drenched afternoon. She immediately ran out into the meadow, filled with the flowers of early summer. 'I lay down in it; the whole sensation of being in this richly embroidered place, with the minute buzzing and ticking and whirring of its many insect inhabitants, gave me intense feelings of pleasure . . . I can shut my eyes now, over seventy years later, and go back to it. It was then that I began to love the country.'[3]

That September (1933) she went back to Francis Holland, where her second year proved easier than the first. The school performed Gluck's *Orpheus*, and she was chosen for the choir; she enjoyed the rehearsals, not least because they got her off games. She made a friend, a South African girl called Tony Imre who was two years older, and who stood up to the bullies who had been tormenting Jane the year before. Her grandfather Somervell came to examine the pianists in her form, and Jane came second. Everyone said it was favouritism: but Jane knew he had erred on the stern side in judging her performance, for he was as keen to avoid the slur as she was.

Jane became ill again that winter, and perhaps it wasn't just school that was to blame: 1934 was a year of changes. Her mother Kit was pregnant again, and Jane and Robin's nanny – to whom they were devoted – had left from one day to the next: Kit gave her no opportunity to say goodbye to the children for fear it would upset them, but of course it had the opposite effect and made Jane feel more frightened of life than ever. She had no one with whom she could share all her anxieties: Kit had little patience with her daughter's fretfulness, and Jane's only friend Tony Imre had gone home to South Africa.

Jane had made her mother promise that she would be the first in the family to see the new baby, and she was looking forward to that moment with great excitement. She was invited to spend the day and night of her eleventh birthday, 26 March, with her paternal grandparents who lived in Chester Terrace, Regent's Park; and on the morning after, there was a telephone call. Glowing with smiles, Aunt Ruth told Jane that she now had another brother.

It was a moment of utter betrayal: how could Jane be the first to see him now? She recalled storming down the stairs, but her aunt caught her before she had torn open the front door. Jane worked herself up into such a paroxysm of tearful rage and despair that she was taken home at once in a taxi.

She loved Colin on sight and he was to become one of the most important people in her life; but he could not be her friend for a few years yet, and Robin was at prep school. Jane felt isolated and bereft. When she finally left Francis Holland after another unsatisfactory term she felt a complete failure, and was afraid of people her own age. Luckily, she was about to meet one of the best teachers she would ever have in her life.

Miss Eleanor Meredith Cobham had been governess to Kit, so she must have been in her fifties when she came to tutor Jane. Jane described her as 'one of the ugliest women I have ever seen in my life – large, fat, almost blind but infinitely gentle'.[4] She had a broad knowledge of literature, art, history, geography, science and mathematics, and gave Jane all the patience and encouragement she needed. Her pupil's one regret was that Miss Cobham, incapable of being stern, did not make Jane apply herself to the subjects she found difficult. Instead they began working their way through the whole of Shakespeare, which inspired Jane's early determination to become an actress.

After a year of having her lessons alone Jane was joined by two more pupils, Carol Beddington and Penelope Fletcher, and her enthusiasm for acting infected them too. Together they acted plays and pieces they wrote themselves knowing that they had, in Miss Cobham, a warm and appreciative audience. Jane also began to write a succession of short stories, cautionary tales, poetry and, eventually, plays. Her first story, inspired by *Black Beauty*, was an interminable tale about a horse at which she plugged away for months until even she was bored with it. At the age of fourteen she wrote her first play, *Our Little Life* – a domestic comedy which had Miss Cobham in stitches; and a later story recounted the events of the Nativity as seen through the eyes of the innkeeper. For once, Kit was so delighted with this effort of Jane's that she sent it to Lady Somervell, known to her grandchildren as Grannia (Jane's grandmother). Grannia wrote a wonderfully Edwardian letter back, describing how she had summoned the servants and read the story aloud to them. They were very amused, and left the drawing room 'laughing and wondering at "how clever Miss Jane is" '.[5]

Jane's resolve to become an actress may have had some support from Miss Cobham, but her parents were discouraging and the only plays she was allowed to see were Christmas pantomimes or Shakespeare. She was mad about Gielgud, and had seen him playing

Hamlet in 1934; and two years later, she saw him playing Romeo at the New Theatre (he was alternating the roles of Romeo and Mercutio with Laurence Olivier), with Peggy Ashcroft as Juliet. This was a role that Jane strongly identified with, and knew almost by heart. Kit maintained that her daughter had played Juliet to perfection, aged fourteen, and never acted so well again.

A succession of French governesses failed to teach Jane French. She had drawing lessons and riding lessons, and Great-Aunt May taught her needlework two afternoons a week: 'She was always making something, and whenever she rose – with difficulty – out of her chair, she left a nest of little balls of wool or silk, which I came to believe she must have laid, like a chicken.'[6] Jane enjoyed every form of needlework, and was still knitting and doing petit-point into her ninetieth year. In this department, at least, Kit was not disappointed – but music was more important, and Jane claimed that she was an indifferent piano player.

Her piano teacher, Miss Luker, was exasperated by her lack of progress: and to see if Jane's playing might be improved, Kit sought the advice of a friend called Harold Craxton, who was one of the most celebrated piano teachers and accompanists of his day. Craxton saw immediately that Jane's confidence had been shattered by Miss Luker's harshness, and that she needed far gentler handling if she was ever to get any better. But why would such a celebrated teacher, most of whose pupils went on to become professional musicians, take on a schoolgirl? Perhaps he was swayed by his friendship for Kit, or the Somervell name, or perhaps by her emerging beauty – but the most likely reason was pure kindness. He wanted to give her back her pleasure in music and whether she played well or not, he wanted her to enjoy it. Craxton decided he could spare her half an hour a week: too short for a proper lesson, but enough time in which to dispense a little encouragement.

Like so many of Craxton's students, Jane became a welcome guest at his house, Acomb Lodge in Grove End Road, St John's Wood. Here Harold and Essie Craxton lived with their five sons, one daughter and a stream of students and visitors. For Jane, brought up with Edwardian standards of punctuality and order, the cheerful chaos of Acomb Lodge was a revelation. The hall was full of bicycles and the sound of piano practice was never far away. Meals were haphazard and irregular, and outside the kitchen stood a trolley bearing the remains of ancient puddings and jellies should anyone feel hungry. Clothes that needed washing or mending were left about in heaps, and on the upstairs landings Jane remembered pails of socks soaking in grey water, waiting for Essie to wash them.

Her closest contemporary among the Craxtons was John, fourth of the five Craxton boys and later a celebrated painter. Six months older than Jane, John joined the lessons with Miss Cobham at Lansdowne Road (possibly in exchange for the piano tuition), but all he wanted to do was draw and paint, and look for things that appealed to his eyes and imagination. Jane joined him for early morning shopping trips to the Caledonian Road market, where they would buy Turkish knives and bits of embroidery. Every Christmas the Craxtons put on a panto-mime, and one year it was *Ali Baba and the Forty Thieves*. John made and painted all the scenery, and for weeks he – and Jane, who had begged to be included – went round in turbans, long robes and elaborate beards that were held on with spirit gum.

Yet it was not John but his father Harold whom Jane loved, 'with that helpless, tearing love that can occur when you are fourteen and have never been in love before'. Craxton was then in his early fifties, and at the drop of a hat he would do his imitations of Dame Clara Butt (whose accompanist he was on several international tours), and play 'Three Blind Mice' in the style of any composer one cared to mention. His ascetic, scholarly looks reminded her of Holbein's draw-ings of Erasmus. 'He taught me something about how to learn,' she went on, 'how to take the trouble and go on taking it; and above all, how to listen to what I was doing.'[7]

Craxton dedicated Five Impromptus of his own composition to the Howard family, one each for Jane, Robin, Colin, David and Kit. And as he would never have dedicated a piece to Jane that she could not play, I hoped that the music would give me some idea of her proficiency. Not being a piano player, I asked the musician Julian Berkeley to play it for me. The tempo is *allegretto leggero*, fairly quick and light; but Julian observed that 'if you were at Grade 3 or 4 and not quite up to that speed, the music would still make sense if you took it slower.'

Jane also liked to spend time at Acomb Lodge because of tensions at home. Her grandfather, Sir Arthur Somervell, died in May 1937.

She missed his quavery voice, his gentleness, the way the tears streamed down his face as he laughed at his own jokes and the smell of sweet briar that clung about him. Kit was left desolate, for she too had not had much love from her mother. After her father's death she became more withdrawn and brittle, and she and David seemed to be moving away from each other. Jane noticed her father's effect on the women who came to dinner or bridge parties: how they flirted with him, how their eyes followed him round the room.

Kit displayed no interest in or sympathy with what Jane was feeling as her body matured, but that was hardly unusual. Many mothers of her generation would have thought such conversations best avoided, since they could only encourage an unhealthy self-absorption. Jane grew fast – she was bigger-boned than her mother, and Kit found her clumsiness exasperating. And she was not pleased when Jane burst into the drawing room one day when Kit had a visitor, to announce she was bleeding.

Kit, who didn't waste money on sanitary towels, gave her some pins and rags from the linen cupboard and told her that it would happen every month. There was no further discussion; Kit believed in overcoming the body, not giving in to it. Or, as Jane saw it, 'My mother made it plain that everything to do with bodies was disgusting.'[8] It was sad that they were temperamentally such opposites. Kit was as hard on herself as she was on others, and despised every weakness. She could not understand Jane's anxiety, her tendency to cling and her pleading eyes.

Things were much easier with her father, who never made her feel plain or clumsy or stupid the way her mother did. One weekend, as a special treat, he took her sailing on the thirty-foot yawl he kept on the River Hamble. As they sailed towards the Isle of Wight Jane became more and more queasy and miserable; when David asked her what was the matter, she burst into tears and admitted she hated sailing. David was instantly sympathetic and set about making things better. As soon as they put in to Cowes he took her on a shopping spree, followed (we assume she was no longer feeling sick) by a lavish tea.

For her fourteenth birthday he gave her a beautiful crimson velvet cloak, and when Kit had her Red Cross evenings they would dine 'in state' together with candles and wine (Jane was expected to take an interest in its name and vintage). When David took her to a musical there was dinner afterwards at the Ivy, and she glowed with pride at how splendid he looked in his dinner jacket, how he smiled at her with his easy confidence. She sparkled in the light of his attention, and felt deliciously grown-up and feminine.

And then, around her fifteenth birthday, her emotional stability was rocked when her father began to want more from Jane than a goodnight hug and a peck on the cheek. In his eyes she had become something different, something sexual – and he began making advances she found terrifying.

'I can't remember the exact circumstances of his first assault,' she wrote in *Slipstream*. 'We must have been alone and it was evening. Anyway, one moment he was remarking on how fast I was growing up and the next minute I was caught in his arms, one hand hurting my breast, and stifled by what I afterwards learned was a French kiss.'[9] She pulled away and fled; but she had to endure his groping hands and lips a few more times before she learned never to be alone with him.

Jane had no context or language that could explain what happened, and she had neither read nor experienced anything that might make sense of it. And yet her feelings were probably more complicated than she could admit. Yes, the assault had been frightening and horrible; but she had also felt the dark undertow of her own attraction to a predatory male, and that was even more alarming. She felt scared, betrayed, and at the same time too ashamed to tell anyone about it.

Jane turned in on herself, became sullen and moody. One evening, when the family went to the Gargoyle Club for dinner and dancing, she refused point-blank to dance with her father. Kit was furious: how could she be so graceless, so ungrateful, so hurtful? And of course Jane could do nothing but stare at the ground in shame and misery. Her father's pounces also explain why she fell so deeply for Harold Craxton, to whom she transferred all the love she no longer dared give her father.

The damage David had caused his daughter left deep scars, but Jane's assessment of his behaviour is forgiving. Over time she understood 'that he had suffered shocks [during the war] when he was not much older than I was then, and that as a consequence he had never, in some senses, grown up. He loved me, and when I ceased to be a little girl he simply added another dimension to his love. This was irresponsible and selfish, but it wasn't wicked.'[10]

Kit knew or at least suspected that David was seeing other women, and her humiliation was matched by her disgust at his sexual appetite; but it is unlikely that she noticed any change in his attitude to Jane, and she certainly can't be blamed for his conduct. Yet children who have been abused often find it harder to forgive the parent who 'let it happen', than the parent who assaulted them. Throughout her memoir, Jane often reiterates that she was never good enough for her over-critical mother. There is no doubt that she believed this to be true, and there is much in Kit's character to bear it out. Kay Howard, who married into the family, recalled that Kit 'had a look in her eye that made you feel that you'd never match up to her expectations'.[11]

And yet there is another testimony that casts Kit in rather a different light. Helen Howard, Kit's sister-in-law, was very fond of her: they brought up their children together and remained close all their lives. Yet Helen told her daughter-in-law, Kay, that she never approved of the way that Kit and David lavished praise on Jane in front of the family, admiring her looks or clapping wildly as she acted in charades or played the piano. That is not to deny, however, that there was all too little of it in private.

In her mid to late teens it seems as if Jane's emotional development got stuck, like a record going round and round, as she tried to make sense of her rage and shame, and her own awakening sexuality. She could no longer trust her father and could not confide in her mother, who didn't love her or even like her very much – certainly far less than her brothers. She felt constantly on trial, and incapable of earning her mother's approval.

This is why, like her father, a part of Jane 'never grew up' – another constant refrain in her memoir. She would grow into a beautiful and brilliant woman, who married and had a child and wrote books and made her own way in the world. New experiences overlaid the old grooves of the record; but on some emotional level she remained immature, unconfident, seeing herself as a victim because her mother had not loved and cherished her.

4

Ambitions, Courtship and War

WHILE YOUNG JANE was grappling with her parental demons, the rest of the world was moving towards a Second World War. By the time she turned fifteen in March 1938, Austria had been annexed to the Third Reich. She did not follow the news very closely but she had read a book called *Vain Glory*, an anthology of soldiers' experiences put together by Guy Chapman M.C. after the last global conflict. The book confirmed her worst fears that if there were another war, they would all be bombed or gassed to death.

The threat of imminent destruction was dispelled at the end of September 1938, when Neville Chamberlain returned from his meeting with Hitler in Munich to announce that he had secured 'peace for our time'. Jane was profoundly relieved and tried to forget all about it, which was not very hard: the family had no wireless and newspapers were exclusively for the grown-ups.

Her fifteenth year was the last she spent with Miss Cobham; but Jane never forgot her, and years later she became Miss Milliment, one of the most poignant characters in the Cazalet Chronicle. Jane was now bent on becoming an actress. Her mother considered this a very selfish and frivolous aim for the sombre times ahead. But the idea that war might rob her of a brilliant career in the theatre filled Jane with such indignation, that it displaced her terror of gas and bombs and the threat of invasion.

Before she could think about acting school, she knew that she would have to get over her homesickness: an anxiety so intense that it could bring on stomach cramps, nausea and headaches. She made herself spend a couple of weekends in the country with Carol Beddington's family, and survived the ordeal. Now, in May 1939, Carol was going to do a course in domestic science at Seer Green, near Beaconsfield in Buckinghamshire. With her parents' blessing, Jane decided to join her. She had no particular interest in the course but with Carol there she might be able to reduce her homesickness to manageable levels.

Jane had always dreaded going to boarding school, which her parents had occasionally used as a threat; but there were no uniforms at Seer Green and its routines were hardly oppressive. The forty girls on the course took it in turns to be cooks, housemaids or laundresses, and Jane learned 'how to turn out a room, goffer a surplice, make pastry, bread, pies, tarts and soufflés, how to order appropriate cuts of meat from the butcher, lay a table properly and interview a servant – beginning with, "What is your religion?" '.[1] The stress of homesickness was overwhelming at first and resulted in several broken pudding basins, but gradually it began to recede.

Her fellow students she found both dull and baffling – perhaps because most of them had been to boarding school and knew how to behave in a pack. To Jane they seemed very sophisticated, yet she was astonished by their lack of interest in music or art or the theatre. Their subjects of conversation were clothes, hair, make-up and men. 'But what will you *do*?' Jane would ask earnestly, thinking of the glittering career that awaited her on stage. The summit of achievement for most of these girls was a little travelling, followed by a season in London.

Jane admitted that she must have been an insufferable prig at the time. She pushed successfully for a party from Seer Green to go up to London to see John Gielgud play Hamlet at the Lyceum in June. The headmistress was enthusiastic, and asked Jane to give a résumé of the play before they went – which increased her reputation for brainy eccentricity among the girls.

Two weekends of that first term were spent at home; and when Jane returned to Lansdowne Road, she was surprised to find that a girl a year older than her had joined the family. Her name was Dosia Cropper, and she came from Westmorland where her family knew the Somervells. When Dosia won a place at the Royal School of Music in London, the Somervells suggested that she should lodge with David and Kit Howard. Kit thought that Jane would be jealous and difficult about the new arrival, which makes one wonder why she didn't send her daughter a letter in advance to prepare her; but, in the event, Jane was delighted with Dosia. 'She was funny, full of life, [and she] also played the piano extremely well . . . Not beautiful, she was intensely attractive, and she had a dashing personality that I very much wished I had myself.'²

Jane spent the last summer of peace in Sussex, where the growing children and the need to separate the sexes meant that the Beacon was no longer big enough to house them all. The overflow were accommodated in a converted barn and a small cottage with an outdoor privy. Jane played endless games of squash with her cousin Dana, and tennis with her aunts and uncles. She was too old for children's games, but still enjoyed the expeditions to pick blackberries and mushrooms, and days on the beach. Harold and Essie Craxton came down on two separate occasions. Jane had started to knit Harold a jumper, and he made her play 'The Arrival of the Queen of Sheba' with him on the piano.

She now had an allowance of £42 a year for her clothes and she dined with the grown-ups, for which occasions she would change into an aquamarine housecoat made of furnishing brocade. Some of Seer Green's preoccupations had rubbed off on her, for she worried about her hair and slept in huge uncomfortable rollers. She also experimented with Tangee lipstick – which was orange in the stick, but stained lips to 'the perfect shade for you' when applied.

After the invasion of Czechoslovakia in March and the declaration of the Nazi–Soviet Non-Aggression Pact in August, it became evident that Hitler was going to invade Poland sooner or later; and when that happened, Britain would be obliged to make a move. The Germans advanced into Poland on 1 September 1939; but Jane, recalling the reprieve of the previous year, confidently expected that Mr Chamberlain would pop over to Munich again and sort things out.

Others were not so hopeful. Her Aunt Ruth, who ran a charity for unwanted babies called the Babies' Hotel with the help of student nurses who wanted to become nannies, prepared to move the whole establishment from Clapham to Sussex. Ruth's father, the Brig, had suggested that the barn could house the babies, while the student nurses moved into the squash court. The Brig also bought a wireless, so that he and the adults of the family could hear the result of Britain's ultimatum to Germany. It was broadcast at 11.15 a.m. on Sunday, 3 September. There was a long moment of silence after the prime minister had finished; and Jane remembered how her grandfather got to his feet and kissed all three of his sons, which had never happened before. Within the hour, the first air-raid warning sounded. All her fear of bombs and gas returned, made worse because her cat was in London. She knew cats weren't going to be issued with gas masks.

The British Army was well under strength in both officers and men; but in the weeks following the declaration of war, 158,000 men were sent to northern France. The Howard brothers were too old for service at the front, but civilians were needed in military administration to release officers for active duty. It was decided that the two younger ones, David and John, would join the services while the eldest, Geoff, would be left to run the firm with the Brig, who was now almost completely blind. Jane's father David joined the air force and was given the job of defending Hendon aerodrome, while her Uncle John joined the army.

At the end of that summer Jane returned to Seer Green, alone: Carol Beddington's parents wanted her to do war work, for which she needed more than a qualification in domestic science. Jane stayed on at Seer Green during which time she became (briefly) very religious, inspired by a woman crippled with rheumatoid arthritis whom she would wheel to church. Back in Sussex for the Christmas holidays, she also helped her Aunt Ruth with the evacuated babies of the Babies' Hotel, learning how to bathe and feed them. At the same time, she realized that she was not the stuff of which saints and nuns are made. Early in 1940, during her last term at Seer Green, she and several of the students caught measles. The worst part about those endless weeks was not being able to read, while her few letters home were baked in an oven before being sent so as not to spread the infection.

Following her recovery she rejoined her family in London, where the government had decreed that all theatres and concert halls should be closed for the duration of the war. After the first few weeks people began to complain about this 'cultural blackout', which the wireless was doing little to address. In between its news bulletins, the BBC broadcast a series of 'interminable emergency programmes featuring Sandy McPherson at the theatre organ, alternating with monotonous sequences of gramophone recordings, interrupted by frequent notices about gas masks'.[3]

An even drearier spectacle, according to its director Kenneth Clark, was the National Gallery, now nothing more than a huge empty shell since all its treasures had been moved to safety. He was delighted when, in the autumn of 1939, the pianist Myra Hess suggested that the gallery should be used for a series of daily lunchtime concerts, which became hugely popular and ran for the whole of the war.

It was at one of these concerts in the spring of 1940 that Kit Howard, accompanied by Jane, renewed her acquaintance with Lady Kennet, in whose studio she had danced during the First World War. Lady Kennet was a celebrated sculptor, who had trained at the Slade School of Art and had known Auguste Rodin in Paris. Her first husband had been Captain Robert Falcon Scott, the explorer, who had died in the icy wastes of Antarctica in 1912. He had achieved his mission to reach the South Pole; but his Norwegian rival, Roald Amundsen, had reached it a month before.

Kathleen's grief for her first husband was forged into a fierce exalt-ation of his heroic death. He would never be forgotten; and she would raise their son Peter, who was two when he lost his father, to be worthy of the Scott name and legend. A decade after Scott's death she married the writer, politician and financier Edward Hilton Young, who became Lord Kennet on his retirement from politics in 1935.

The Kennets had one son, Wayland, who was then sixteen. According to him, the reason for meeting up with Kit Howard was that 'my mother suddenly decided that it was time there should be a girl friend in my life'. Kathleen didn't know any girls, but then remembered that Kit Howard had a daughter who ought to be about the right age. 'Thus it came about that we all went to a concert at the National Gallery. I thought you were wonderfully beautiful, but how should I ever make out with someone who was taller than me?'[4]

Undeterred by the girl's height, Lady Kennet suggested that Jane should 'come and play with Wayland' during the Easter holidays, at their house in Norfolk. Jane resisted the idea hard. She did not know the Kennets and was too grown-up to 'play' with anybody. When the invitation came, she refused to go unless her brother Robin came too but that was easily arranged, so she had no choice but to accept.

She looked forward with far greater anticipation to her audition at the London Mask Theatre School. Her parents were not happy about this but Jane had completed the course at Seer Green, and had persuaded them to agree that if she were accepted at the theatre school, she could go. The school was housed in a studio in Ebury Street and run by John Fernald, an actor-teacher who eventually became principal of the Royal Academy of Dramatic Art (RADA). Applicants were told to prepare two pieces for their audition, one of which was to be a speech from Shakespeare. Jane decided to perform Juliet's speech that begins 'The clock struck nine when I did send the nurse',[5] and follow it with a comic sketch of a lady conducting a children's dancing class. She was accepted.

This came as no surprise. With the absolute confidence of the untried, Jane knew she could act, and she knew she could make people laugh; in every other respect she was thoroughly dissatisfied with herself. Her hair was too straight, her nose too big, her forehead too low, her widow's peak off-centre and her legs were not as shapely as fashion demanded. She was also clumsy, gawky and ill-educated. The prospect of ten days with the Kennets brought on sickening waves of apprehension.

After two weeks with their parents on the Norfolk Broads in early May, Robin and Jane were taken to Fritton Hithe: a long, heavily thatched house overlooking Fritton Lake. The Howards were ushered into a drawing room where Lady Kennet sat by the fire with some embroidery, while Wayland played the piano (his mother dreamed of him becoming a composer) and a stocky man dabbed at a canvas on an easel. He was introduced as 'my older son Peter, who is on sick leave'. Lady Kennet insisted they should call her K (although she will be called Kathleen in this narrative, so as not to confuse her with Kit), while Lord Kennet was introduced as Bill. He had lost his right arm in the First World War, and Jane described him as 'one of the most noble and completely civilized men I have ever met'.[6]

To her great surprise, Jane found herself enchanted by this family. 'Whatever we all did – walks in the woods, sailing on the lake, silly word games at meals and charades after dinner – it took place in the sunny climate of mutual admiration. For one who had been brought up with the puritan ethic that nobody could be publicly acknowledged to be good at anything, this atmosphere of confidence and triumph was intoxicating.'[7] She also noticed that Kathleen and Bill's relationship held none of the dark, icy undertones she had felt between her parents at home. They seemed to be on first-name terms with the most illustrious authors, playwrights, politicians, actors and painters of the day, and knew they would leave their mark on the world. By comparison, the Howards' ambitions seemed limited to keeping the family firm ticking over.

On the second day, Peter Scott asked if he could draw Jane, and she was deeply flattered. Peter was then thirty-one, and had lived up to most of his mother's high expectations – even though he had dismayed her by scraping a degree at Cambridge, and dropping out of his course at the Royal Academy of Art. She had been particularly keen to honour Captain Scott's wish that their son be brought up with a love of nature, and sure enough the boy had grown into a passionate natur-alist. He was already an authority on the *Anatidae* family which includes ducks, geese and swans, and had bought a lighthouse at Sutton Bridge on the Wash where he lived and established a refuge for wildfowl. Painting wild birds was how he earned his living, and he had had seven successful exhibitions at the Ackermann Gallery in London before 1939. In addition, Peter was a championship-level skater, and an expert sailor in the small dinghy class who had twice won the Prince of Wales Cup. He had joined the Royal Naval Volunteer Reserve as soon as he could, and in February 1940 he began his first spell of duty as a sub-lieutenant in the destroyer HMS *Broke*.

On board a destroyer at last he looked forward to some dangerous and exciting times, only to find himself stricken by seasickness. 'It had never troubled him in small boats,' wrote his biographer Elspeth Huxley, 'but in rough Atlantic storms the destroyer pitched and rolled so savagely that he soon succumbed. The Captain ordered a bucket to be lashed to the gun-director on the bridge and Peter made frequent use of it, but got no better.'[8] He became so ill and run-down that he developed jaundice, and was given a month's sick leave – which was why he was recuperating at Fritton.

Jane was overawed that someone so glamorous and impressive should be paying her attention; 'Lovely, lovely,' he breathed as he drew her; but when she saw the finished drawing, she felt it looked embarrassingly idealized. They were still at Fritton on 10 May,[9] when Hitler's Panzer Divisions overwhelmed the Low Countries and plunged into France. Chamberlain resigned, exhausted and depressed, and Winston Churchill became prime minister.

For the last week of Peter's leave, when Jane was back in London and spending her days at the Mask School, he took her out every night – to restaurants and theatres and dancing, where to her mortification she found he was a far better dancer than she was. Kathleen rang Jane's mother and told her to warn her daughter that Peter 'had broken many hearts'; but even after he had taken her down to the banks of the Serpentine and kissed her in the dark, Jane felt nothing but a kind of gratitude. Her head had been turned, she wrote, but her heart remained untouched.

This could be because she was also attracted to Peter's half-brother. She had originally been invited as company for him, and she was closer to Wayland in more than just years: he shared her interest in books and the arts, while Jane never caught Peter's enthusiasm for boats and birds. This bond between them was recognized to the extent that Peter sometimes found himself looking over his shoulder, hoping that his younger brother didn't mind him paying court to Jane.

Ten days after their lightning invasion of France, the Germans had trapped the British Expeditionary Force and large numbers of French and Belgian troops in the area around Dunkirk. An operation was mounted to rescue as many men as possible, but it was painfully slow. The coastal waters around the port were so shallow that destroyers could not come in close, so soldiers had to wade out to the ships and wait for hours in the water – knowing that the troops defending the town would not be able to hold the Germans back for much longer. On 27 May the Ministry of Shipping put out a call for all shallow-draughted boats to join in the effort, and the response was so inspiring that 'the spirit of Dunkirk' became a rallying cry throughout the war. By 3 June when the evacuation was called off, over 300,000 men had been rescued.

The war was suddenly very close, not least for Jane's friend Dosia who had left her music studies to become a nurse. Jane wrote to Peter that

Her hospital has had 250 men from Dunkirk, nearly all off their heads having had *no attention* for five days. Dosia is rather shaken I think, because she wrote to me at midnight after her first day in a very wild and miserable way. I have tried to make Mummy let me join her, because they are short-handed but she says they'd find out I wasn't eighteen. It isn't just a question of feeling I ought to now, I want to . . . it's just grotesque to go on acting when people are needing nurses and there is such an agony of suffering.[10]

Peter took no part in the rescue operations at Dunkirk because his ship was undergoing repairs; and by the time she was back in service, the Germans had overrun northern France. The French government abandoned Paris to the enemy on 11 June, and all the roads to the south and west were clogged with cars, trucks, animals and thousands of refugees trying to escape the enemy.

On 9 June Peter was put in charge of an operation to evacuate eighty British wounded from the village of Saint-Valéry-en-Caux, north-east of Le Havre. The operation went smoothly. But while he was on shore he learned, from the chief of staff of the 51st Highland Division, that there were over 8,000 British troops close by, all of whom would be taken prisoner if they were not rescued within the next forty-eight hours. Peter promised that HMS *Broke* would return; and as soon as they had put in to Portsmouth with the wounded, he and his captain requested permission to go back to France and evacuate as many men as they could. To their dismay, the idea was turned down. Enemy air superiority round the French coast was now too strong to risk any more destroyers on rescue missions, and HMS *Broke* was told to await further orders.

Peter blamed himself bitterly for not having evacuated as many as he could of the 51st Division there and then, while he was in Saint-Valéry, without applying to a higher authority. 'I missed a tremendous chance of doing great service by being too ordinary,' he wrote to his mother. 'With real initiative I could have saved 6,000 British troops . . . If I had . . . I should have been court-martialled. But what is a court-martial when an Expeditionary force is at stake?'[11] Anyone in his position would have agonized over abandoning all those men to the enemy, even under orders; but the incident does reveal just how much Peter Scott wanted to be a hero, to the point of self-immolation.

A little later in the month he was able to prove his valour in Brittany. In the course of five separate landings near Brest, often under enemy fire, he and the shore party under his command rescued

250 people and blew up a great deal of industrial equipment, including a 150-ton crane.

'Darling Peter,' wrote Jane, 'your mother rang up and told me about you. You *couldn't* have done better Peter could you? It was *marvellous*.'[12] Jane and Peter had only known each other a few weeks; but while the letters on both sides were becoming more passionate and intense, Peter often warned her of the dangers of a courtship based on letters. At the same time, writing to her took his mind off the harsh realities of his life at sea: terror as the ship bucked and rolled in seventy-foot waves; the discomfort of everything being wet; the lack of privacy; the anguish of pulling the living, dead and injured from torpedoed vessels; and always the leaden weight of knowing that, at any moment, he might be dead or appallingly injured himself.

His mother too was living on an emotional knife-edge for her first-born son, who had been her ambition and her life's work. Kathleen had had several proposals in her youth; but her aim in looking for a husband was not money or status or even love, but to find the man who would give her the perfect child. She found him in Captain Robert Falcon Scott, and they married in 1908; yet until Peter was born the following year, she wrote, her husband had been 'a probationer, a means to an end. Now my aim, my desire, had been abundantly accomplished. I worshipped the two of them as one, father and son.'[13]

Against all the odds, Peter had survived her messianic devotion with his common sense and easy-going charm intact. But Kathleen was acutely aware that he might not live long, and it was vital that the Scott genes be preserved. She had been steering and organizing Peter's life ever since he was born, and now she (and Peter, of course) had to find a woman who could give him a son. Kathleen's telephone call to the seventeen-year-old Jane implies that she was acquiring significance as a potential bride. She had hoped that her son would find someone a few years older and steadier, but for the moment Jane – originally earmarked as company for Wayland – would have to do.

By mid-July Hitler's plan for the invasion of Britain was under way, and the battles in the skies above southern England had begun. The Brig declared that the Beacon should be camouflaged, although the only paints available were sky blue, salmon pink and pea green. The effect was dazzling, and 'we must . . . have provided a most comforting land-mark for the [German] bombers as they made their way to London'.[14] At the same time, Peter was conducting some more effective experiments in camouflage, particularly of smaller destroyers and torpedo boats. To conceal them at night, when most of the hunting and being hunted took place, he suggested that they should be painted in very pale tones that were almost white; an idea so successful that he was awarded an MBE in the King's Birthday Honours of 1942.[15]

Jane spent much of the summer at the Beacon writing her second play, called *Outrageous Fortune*. This was about a ballet dancer faced with the choice so many women have to make, between career and marriage. In the first act, the young dancer is on the brink of professional success, but she knows she will have to give it all up if she accepts her rich suitor's proposal. In the second act she pursues her career, yet in renouncing love she loses hope and ends up killing herself. In the third act she makes the alternative choice, and abandons dancing for a husband and a family; but does this leave her fulfilled, or merely dull and diminished? The play leaves everything in balance, providing no answer. It was of course based on her mother; but Jane said that in writing the play she was more preoccupied with wrestling with the structure than exploring the theme.

She was also watching the dogfights in the sky, and regularly commuting to the Mask School in London. At one point her train was machine-gunned; and a few days after that she told Peter how 'a German bomber very hard hit *grazed* our chimney pots, righted itself and crashed in a field further on. It then started burning and the bombs in it blew up – very noisy. There were about 100 planes above us and a lot of machine gunning, three other planes came down but none so near.'[16]

The bombing of London began towards the end of August; and a month later, during a night in which over 200 incendiaries were dropped, two of the Howard Brothers' timber wharves were burned to the ground and the third partially destroyed. It was a devastating blow for the business; and although there were no casualties, the livelihoods of many of the firm's employees went up in smoke with the wharves.[17] To Peter she wrote that 'The wharves are a terrible sight, but all the family seem to be very calm about them but very pessimistic. They all say things like only the beginning and thin end of the wedge, but apart from photographing them madly they don't seem to do much. And we continue to live here in gentle squalor . . .'¹⁸

Jane had her first taste of acting in a real theatre, the Westminster, as Alice Dearth in J.M. Barrie's *Dear Brutus*; but the directors of the London Mask School felt unable to continue, amid falling glass from the studio roof and the myriad difficulties thrown up by wartime London. When the school closed at the end of the summer, two of its staff decided to start a student repertory company in Devon to play at the Garden Theatre in Bideford. They were Eileen Thorndike, an actress like her more famous sister Sybil; and Herbert (Bertie) Scott, a singer from Northern Ireland who specialized in voice training. Jane had a difficult time persuading her parents to let her go. They wanted her to do a shorthand and typing course, so that she might make herself useful in the war effort. But Jane was one of the students to whom the Scott-Thorndike Repertory Company, as it was called, offered a scholarship, so her parents would not have to pay for her tuition. Grudgingly they gave in, and she left for Devon in mid-October 1940.

The students of the Scott-Thorndike Repertory Company were lodged in the village of Instow, at Instow House. This was a draughty and dilapidated Edwardian pile overlooking the estuary of the rivers Taw and Torridge, and in fine weather the grey shape of Lundy Island appeared on the horizon. Jane shared a freezing cold room with two of the four girl students, while Eileen Thorndike shared another big room with her three daughters who were then in their early to mid teens. There was also an elderly Romanian actress who was getting over a painful love affair, and a Canadian actress who must have been paying a good rent because her room had better furniture and a coal fire. Also in the house were two of the company's three male actors: a young Paul Scofield and a strange young man with yellow hair called Seth Holt.

Every morning they would take the bus or, to save the pennies, hitch a lift into Bideford, which lay three and a half miles to the south on the west bank of the River Torridge. (Jane and her friends found that one of the best ways to bring a car to a stop was to lie down in the road, as if in a faint.) The Garden Theatre itself was glacial, smelled faintly of gas and had dressing rooms like prison cells. Much of Jane's initial confidence was undermined by Bertie Scott, who could not understand why she found it so hard to locate her diaphragm; but he did teach her how to project her voice, how to use its lower registers without strain, and how to 'follow-through' after a line of speech. She far preferred rehearsals with the rest of the cast. Her first parts were Katherine in *The Taming of the Shrew*, and Anne of Bohemia in *Richard of Bordeaux* by Gordon Daviot (the psudonym of Elizabeth Mackintosh, who also wrote historical novels as Josephine Tey). As there were twice as many women to men in the company everyone had to take turns, while Paul Scofield and Seth Holt alternated as Petruchio and Richard.

They thought themselves terribly sophisticated. The girls wore slacks, the boys baggy trousers, patched jackets and brightly coloured scarves. They said 'fuck' a lot in loud voices and everyone smoked. Jane did not tell Peter that everyone at Instow was a proclaimed pacifist; nor that during one party she had won a prize for who could wear the least – using some bits of stamp edging and a powder puff: a daring piece of exhibitionism (later used in her novel *Marking Time*) which indicates that Jane wasn't quite as shy as she sometimes made out. She did tell him that they were always hungry and cold, but by the time the company gathered for their evening meal round the kitchen table (a joint of mutton with potatoes and cabbage, and there was never a scrap left) the air was thick with ambitions. They talked endlessly about their favourite parts and who they wanted to play opposite, which made Jane feel 'rather swamped and very helpless. Only about one of us will ever reach the top, and yet to see them all burning with excitement makes it very heartbreaking.'[19]

At some point that winter, Peter had a week's leave and asked Jane if she would come and stay with him at Fritton; and since she was not in a play at the time, she agreed. With their generous appreciation of herself and of each other, being with the Kennets was a joy – as were the regular meals, after weeks of being hungry. Early one morning Peter took her wildfowling, but sitting on a muddy marsh in a freezing wind for hours on end watching birds was not Jane's idea of fun. He called her Jenny, and kissed her on their winter walks. It was not as exciting as she had hoped, although she longed to be in love with this brilliant man whom everyone said was so attractive.

What Peter felt about her seemed to pull him in different directions. He was drawn to her beauty, awed by her youth and creative ambition; and perhaps it was inevitable, given the age gap between them, that the tone of his letters veered between that of a lover and that of a protective uncle: 'Jenny – d'you know I'm still rather scared of you! I am really though – there's so much in you trying to burst out that I'm terrified by it all. And at the same time thrilled and proud.'[20] She loved his faith in her talent: 'I know that you're an artist,' he wrote. 'You want to be great and you can be. You *should* do all the things you do. You *won't* become a dillettante. You must always create. It may be ages before you discover how you can create best. You *must* give everything a chance. It's right – it's right – I know it.'[21]

At the same time Jane was also drawn to Seth Holt, the young actor who played opposite her in *Richard of Bordeaux*. She admired his cultivated cynicism, and the way he knew so much more than her about almost everything – even though they were the same age. Seth said he had been born in Palestine and run away from his parents, and had travelled over most of Europe and beyond since he was fourteen. He told her she was beautiful, and that she was the only student there who knew how to act. She was clever enough to doubt him, and vain enough to lap it all up.

They became friends. They cuddled up in his bed because it was so cold, and he talked to her about modern poetry. He said he was in love with her, and she enjoyed his caresses, which were very gentle. And then, inevitably, there came a night when Seth wanted more from Jane than she was prepared to give.

Jane left three versions of what happened next. Two were in letters to Peter, the first written in the winter of 1940. 'Last night was a nightmare,' she begins, 'only equalled by the one you know about' – which implies that she had confided in him about her father's assaults. Jane is upset, and very frightened; but she distances herself from the drama by posing as the narrator, and whatever Seth did happened to another girl: 'She said that Richard [Seth] was insane and had twice tried to kill her and she had screamed for me and had finally pushed him on the floor and rushed to the door and escaped, but she still thought anything might happen.'[22]

After this ordeal Jane became very ill and stayed in her room for days. When she got better she kept out of Seth's way, but he did not stay much longer at Instow: Eileen Thorndike got wind of what had happened and told him to leave.★

The third and longest version of the story covers some thirty pages of typescript, written in early 1944. Here Seth, still called 'Richard', is portrayed as someone who enjoys emotionally controlling and breaking women. When she refuses to make love with him he bites her till she bleeds and burns her hand with a lighted cigarette. Then he almost strangles her before breaking down, admitting he'd been abused as a child and threatening to kill himself. Now instead of trying to escape she's terrified of leaving him alone, for fear he'll attempt suicide; but when she reveals her concern he has the last laugh: he had been acting all along.[23]

Jane's letters about her experience with Seth do not seem to have troubled Peter much. Compared to the students at Instow, Peter's existence carried real responsibilities and dangers, and he saw the whole episode as a silly game that had got out of hand. 'I did love getting your wonderful letter,' he wrote.

> Poor dear what a time you've been having, but if you are like me you will be enjoying the very fact that your life is full. It is always so much the more fun for being that even when some of the things are not good . . . But you must *not* think that the curing of Richard's nervous ailments is a principal objective. Take it in your stride by all means but your objectives are much more important than that, so don't lose sight of them.[24]

Jane's mother had also got wind of Jane's imbroglio, and wrote to Peter about it.

> I hate that place [Instow] for her in many ways, but the most nauseating piece of work there [Seth] has been removed now, thank goodness, and if that comes back Jane will be removed,

★ Seth Holt (1924–71) went on to become a film director: first for Ealing Studios, and then for Hammer Films. His most notable movies are *Taste of Fear* (1961) and *The Nanny* (1965) with Bette Davis – who called Holt 'the most ruthless director I have ever worked with outside of William Wyler'. He died aged forty-eight, his health wrecked by drugs and alcohol.

without fail. She has also got her values into a little better perspective . . . and does see that being grown up isn't solely a matter of
late nights and late mornings and lunchless days, bless her, and
reading pacifist novels . . . I do like the way you make her think.
It is lovely for her to have your views among all those silly little
half-baked egoists.[25]

Peter was far more upset by the end of the most important friendship of his life, with a man called John Winter. He and Winter had
met at Cambridge in 1927, and Winter shared his passion for small
boats. Together they had pioneered new techniques in both sailing
and boat-building, they had both competed for and won the Prince
of Wales Cup, they often went wildfowling together and had many
friends in common. So it came as a complete shock to Peter when
John suddenly announced that he was going to marry, without even
consulting his closest friend. This was probably because John knew
that Peter would not like the girl, but nonetheless Peter felt he had
been cut out of his friend's life.

Under intense pressure from Peter, Winter broke off with his fian-
cée; but in the spring of 1941 he became engaged to someone else.
This time, Peter approved of his choice and could raise no objection;
but things would never be the same again, and for Peter this was a
death of the heart. Their friendship, as he explained to Jane, 'could
not now survive . . . because he wouldn't be dependent on me, and I
would have to learn not to be dependent on him'.[26]

He talked to Jane a lot about John, and how much he missed their
intimacy – despite the fact that John was 'not at all clever and not at
all artistic, and not at all imaginative . . . and yet the person whom for
so many years I have been happiest to be with'.

That there was a homo-erotic element to their friendship is obvious, but whether they were lovers is impossible to tell. His future
sister-in-law described Peter as 'a bit ambi [bisexual] – not completely,
but a bit'.[27] One also wonders how his ever vigilant mother saw Peter's
friendship with John. She certainly had homosexual friends with
whom she was very close; but given that Peter had healthy relationships with women too, she was probably unconcerned. She would
have seen it as a friendship in the Greek heroic mode, like that of
Achilles and Patroclus.

Jane encouraged his confidences: 'Pete I love you to talk about John as much as you want, it helps me to understand,' she wrote.[28] Peter was touched by her emotional generosity, and the fact that she was willing to sympathize with his grief made her all the more precious. On 16 February 1941 he had written to Jane from Belfast:

Quite suddenly and unexpectedly I've fallen in love and it's awfully exciting and fresh and it's with the memory of you – and I want to see you more than ever before . . . Jenny I *do* so want to see you again and find out if you're as sweet as I remember you, as I know I shall, and discover that you're twice as sweet . . . Are you still going to be great? Oh *please* send me those plays – I can't wait. I'll send them back awfully quick. Do you know it's nearly a year since you came to Fritton . . .[29]

Peter was trying very hard to attach himself emotionally to Jane, but all that year he was grieving for his lost friend; and while Jane was always invited to Fritton when he came on leave, he seemed strangely indifferent to her presence. In May 1941 his mother Kathleen observed that 'He confined his whole attention to me and scarcely spoke to her at all until after I had gone to bed . . . If that is being in love, the condition has greatly altered since I was young.'[30]

As late as October, Peter told Jane that 'John still aches a bit so life is poor and dull and grey.'[31] He frequently asked his mother whether she thought he should marry Jane but she refused to give an opinion. 'I tell him I will not advise. He keeps asking me . . . A man of thirty-one should not be interfered with even at his own request.'[32]

At Instow Jane met Ronald Jeans, a playwright who had worked with Noël Coward; and in the spring of 1941 both her plays were under scrutiny. Peter and Jeans both felt that *Outrageous Fortune* needed a great deal of work before it was any good; and Eileen Thorndike was reading *Our Little Life*, the domestic comedy she had written aged fourteen. It seems an unlikely choice from the start, since there were too many male roles and not enough men in the company. Eileen kept putting it off, hoping some men would appear; but Jane did get the starring role of Margaret in *Granite*, a melodrama by Clemence Dane. 'It was my great chance, a huge part and the heroine not off the stage for more than ten minutes. I was no good in it.'[33] She was also hurt by the fact that while many of the company had the pleasure of seeing their parents in the audience, hers never came to Bideford – even when she had a starring role.

Jane's relationship with Eileen Thorndike came under strain in the spring of 1941, as she became increasingly worried about the health of one of her fellow students, Joan Heale, who was in bed with an agonizingly sore throat. Eileen Thorndike refused to call a doctor and was outraged when Jane suggested it; so Jane alerted the girl's parents who hastened to Bideford. The doctor they summoned sent their daughter to hospital immediately; she was in the critical stages of diphtheria.

Eileen resented Jane for showing her up, and from then on a great frost descended between them – in contrast to the weather. The last part of June was warm and balmy. Jane and the rest of the company sunbathed as they learned their lines, and went swimming at midnight when they came back from the theatre.

She came home to the Beacon in July, knowing the Instow days were over: Eileen Thorndike was taking the company to Cambridge, and Jane had not been asked to join them. She was under a lot of pressure from her parents to stop acting and do the shorthand course that would qualify her for war work, but she had other plans. Through an ex-actress called Lesley Waring, a friend of her father's, she had received an offer to join the company of the Shakespeare Memorial Theatre at Stratford-upon-Avon for their upcoming winter season. At the same time she took on a three-week stand-in job as an actor/reader at the BBC, for which she was paid £11.

Peter came to visit her at the Beacon in August 1941, when he had a weekend's leave. In the course of a long walk he said how much he wanted to make love to her, but he was reluctant because she was so very young. Jane was irritated by the way Peter and his mother harped on about her youth, but however much she liked to think of herself as sophisticated, she was not. Kathleen described Jane as 'very very pretty, very sweet, fairly nice mannered, very childish and ignorant, and quite egotistic . . . If she turns out well she *might* become a very interesting person.'[34]

That night, Jane crept down the corridor to Peter's room after her parents had gone to bed. Losing her virginity was 'surprising, but Pete had been very affectionate and gentle. It hadn't hurt very much and he'd repeatedly told me how lovely I was and how much he enjoyed it. Somehow I thought I'd enjoy it too, but nothing was said about that. This, I concluded, was because women . . . did it for love, and if you loved somebody, you must want to please them.'[35]

The morning after, her mother drove them to the airfield at Lympne, from where Peter was going to participate in a bombing raid on Germany. Although he had been serving in a destroyer and was liable to be blown up at any moment, there was a mundane quality to his day-to-day life at sea. But in a plane, all the drama is concentrated into a few hours – and Jane had seen at first-hand what happened to planes when they were brought down. For the first time she felt that aching anxiety that grips the heart like a vice, and makes it impossible to do anything else but wait. He returned from the mission safely, but their relationship – at least to Jane – had reached a tipping-point from which there was no turning back.

Both of them explored the idea of marriage in their letters, with varying degrees of playfulness, excitement, love and doubt. At one point Peter also wrote to Wayland, who years later recalled the moment at Jane's request when she was preparing her memoir.

Was I still at Stowe [School]? I left there in May 1941. At any rate that is where I remember myself sitting in my study . . . there arrived a letter asking whether I would mind if he asked you to marry him. I wrote at once, saying I would not, and he should not let the thought of me stand in his way. Go right ahead. I found it difficult to write.[36]

Jane moved to Stratford-upon-Avon in September 1941, where the Shakespeare Memorial Theatre's season was to open with George Bernard Shaw's *The Doctor's Dilemma*. Yet even when she saw the handbill and read her name under that of the leading lady Margaretta Scott, she could not get very excited about it. 'I keep saying this is what you've wanted for twelve years, now it's happening, you're playing with a real company in a real theatre, but at the moment it doesn't do the slightest good,' she wrote to Peter.[37] Over the next few days, the sense of anticlimax didn't lift. She judged the company second-rate; 'there isn't anything like enough enthusiasm and therefore the standard of acting is low'.[38]

Part of the trouble was that most of the young male players were involved in the war, and the average age of their replacements was well over sixty. The plays that winter were chosen to accommodate them, and with the exception of the Shaw, Jane thought they were all terrible – especially one called *His Excellency the Governor* by Robert Marshall. In this work she played the young ingénue with whom the elderly Governor falls in love. 'Did I tell you that at the end I cast myself into Michael's arms and say "My soldier husband!" and he in the second act say [*sic*] "Cheer up *Ethel*, it's glorious to take up arms for your darling" and rushes out heroically.'[39]

When not acting, Jane's life in Stratford was cold and cheerless. Food was scarce, and she faced a long walk home through dark, wet streets after evening performances. When one of the old actors offered to walk her home she was usually groped, and if she walked alone there was the danger of coming across Czech soldiers, who were rumoured to prowl around in pairs looking for girls to molest. Her landlady was friendly, but she shared the house with a drunk and violent father. Jane became ill as she often was in the winter, with bad colds and sore throats. Days were spent in bed; and when she dragged herself back to the theatre, she was sacked for missing rehearsals.

That was the end of Jane's life as a professional actress, but she had had a very ambitious idea for a play which she discussed with Ronnie Jeans. It was called *Triple Harness*: a work in which the players were not characters, but different aspects of one person. Jeans was far more enthusiastic about this than he was about the last play she had shown him, *Outrageous Fortune*, and he suggested they collaborate. He and Jane wrote and rewrote it throughout the winter of 1941; sometimes in his flat in Hallam Street (Jane was renting a room nearby), or at his house in Walberswick, Suffolk, but the play never came right.

That Christmas, Jane found herself under renewed pressure from her family to join the war effort. She applied for a place with the Wrens, but they had no use for someone with no languages and no secretarial skills, who hadn't even passed the School Certificate. It was decided that she would do an intensive course in shorthand and typing with her friend Dosia, who found a flat for them in Warrington Crescent, Maida Vale.

The few weeks in early 1942 that Jane spent with Dosia were among the happiest and most carefree of her youth; and one wishes for Jane's sake that they had lasted longer, that she had been allowed to enjoy them without wishing she was older or being overwhelmed with responsibilities she wasn't ready for.

Jane tended to see her young self as bewildered by the world and unready for it; but in an interview given in 1987, her friend Dosia recalled someone far more positive and energetic: 'She was so extraordinary and exciting as a person, and looks wise, she had no problems, everything fell her way . . . You couldn't not notice her . . . not just her looks, but she seemed to be very happy. She always walked down the street alone singing and jumping about, just because her spirits were high.'

They had a furnished basement flat which came with a piano. '[Jane] christened it Mon Débris because it was fairly squalid, and she invented a butler called Chortle who was never in, and always to blame for everything that went wrong. We never had a boring evening, staying in and and mending our clothes.' Since both she and Dosia were so cheerful and gregarious, there was no shortage of people with whom to go to the cinema, or eat with at little Cypriot restaurants, or invite to their dinner parties of frozen cod and stewed rhubarb. They bicycled all over London, tried to invade the all-male clubs of St James's to see how far they could get, and 'we used to pick up anyone who looked interesting and say come and have a cup of coffee . . . [Jane] needed lots of other people around'.[40]

Once again Jane went to Fritton when Peter was on leave, and Kathleen had another opportunity to observe them together – but the high spirits that Dosia noticed in Jane were not much in evidence. 'Peter has got up at four a.m. each day in order to be on the right marsh before dawn,' wrote his mother.

> There he lies in ecstasy under a white sheet in the snow, then perhaps creeps on his tummy for half a mile or so, then perhaps shoots a duck or two, and returns in time for a hot bath before lunch. He was usually out for eight and sometimes nine hours . . . The rest of the day he painted. He didn't take much notice of poor little Jane, who poured out her woes to me after he had gone to bed.[41]

In a letter to her husband Bill, she wrote that 'I think Pete may likely marry this child, but I do not think he's in love with her, he does not disturb his pastimes at all to have her society. Every morning

I had her from breakfast till lunch, and from 9 to 11 pm . . . If any young man had treated me like that, I would have said "Go to hell", and not fawned upon him on his return.'[42]

Kathleen understood that Peter needed to reconnect with the wild when he was on leave, if only to taste the solitude that can never be found on a ship packed close with the same people for weeks on end. Where that left Jane was hard to say, but Kathleen was right about his intentions.

Peter came to London in late March and Jane and Dosia had a dinner party for him, using up their entire meat ration for the month to make a shepherd's pie. He stayed the night with Jane, and proposed: if she accepted, they could be married when he had three weeks' leave in April. 'I had not thought about marriage at all,'[43] she wrote in her memoir, as if his proposal had been a bolt from the blue. But in early 1942 it was Jane who had set her heart on the marriage, and talked about it to her friends (this got back to Kathleen, who was not best pleased). She wanted with all her heart to be Mrs Peter Scott – although she too could be clear-eyed about her uncertainties. A few weeks before their wedding, she wrote:

> I have many thoughts of you, of us, sometimes a panic, that we are mad, that we know nothing of each other except the easy immediate things, that the war is working its will on us, that for you I am a reaction, that for me you are complex beyond my understanding, that you haven't had time to think or I to live . . . And then I feel we do know each other and that our love is great enough to withstand all material difficulties that the war presents.[44]

Both families were delighted by the engagement, or at least pretended to be. On 2 April, Kathleen wrote in her diary that 'Pete has just rung up to say he will do this deed . . . I shall have to be happy and excited. If she ever hurts him I will kill her.'[45] Only two people were not happy: Jane's eight-year-old brother Colin, one of the few people who never liked Peter; and Ronald Jeans. He sent her a furious letter to say that she was far too young to get married, and in doing so she was throwing away a promising career. He also sent a Revelation suitcase with her initials on it.

Kit insisted that Jane should come home because there was so much to do before the wedding, so she never finished the typing and shorthand course at Pitmans. Instead her days were filled with lists of guests, fittings for her trousseau, and planning the music. In this she was helped by her friend Geraint Jones, an organist who did much to promote baroque music in the post-war years.

The wedding dress was made by Kit's friend Christabel, Lady Ampthill, whose marital relations had been the talk of London in the early 1920s. In the paternity suit filed by Lord Ampthill after their divorce, he claimed that although he had never had sex with his wife, she was adamant that the son she had borne was his – her explanation being that insemination had occurred when she used his sponge in the bath. The speculation surrounding this baffling case of partheno-genesis still continues; but it did no harm to Christabel's dressmaking business, which occupied discreetly opulent premises in Curzon Street. Jane's dress was of white lace, one of the few materials that had not been rationed, and Lady Ampthill also designed her a soft turquoise dress with a short-sleeved jacket to match.

Bill Kennet gave her a gold wristwatch, while Kathleen gave her forty clothes coupons and £100, on condition that she try to give up smoking. She also gave Peter a turquoise and diamond ring for him to give his bride: Jane felt rather sad he had not chosen it himself. But Peter was not ungenerous: he made her an allowance of £15 a month, more money than she had ever had before.

They were married on 28 April 1942 at Christ Church, Lancaster Gate. 'The singing was poor,' wrote Kathleen in her diary, 'the organ mediocre, the flowers rotten, but Jane looked divinely beautiful, Peter tired and diffident . . . My sweet Pete, I think now he is in love with her and will be more so.'[46] The service was followed by a reception for 300 given by the Howards at Claridge's, which Kathleen thought ostentatiously extravagant for wartime.

At this point, Jane was triumphantly happy and very much in love. She was free of her mother, and she would soon have her own house. 'I'd cook and give parties for Pete and one day the war would be over and I'd be married to a painter and he wouldn't talk about guns any longer.'[47] And being together would surely give her more of his time and attention. Until now she had always been hovering on the edges, waiting to be summoned when he had leave, waiting till he came back from wildfowling or painting. Jane believed that in marrying Peter, she would naturally become the centre of his existence.

5

Mrs Peter Scott

THEY SPENT THEIR honeymoon at the Lacket, a cottage near Marlborough in Wiltshire that belonged to Peter's stepfather Bill. 'Our world is flooded with happiness,' Peter wrote. 'In the wind and sun Jane looks like a wild child and then in the firelight in her beautiful white gown with a blue feather pattern on it she looks like a grown-up dignified princess. And always, hour by hour, she grows lovelier and lovelier.'[1] They talked incessantly, he told his mother, jumping from one subject to the next; while Jane told Kathleen that she had 'the most perfect and wonderful and darling person who has ever existed for your son'.[2]

But even on honeymoon, mother and son could not be separated. Peter never asked his bride whether she wanted to spend the last week of this intimate time at Fritton with Kathleen. He took it for granted she would fall in with his plans. Jane was dismayed but tried not to show it. He told her repeatedly what a wonderful girl she was and she played up to being wonderful, to doing what she thought was expected of her.

It was also expected that she should conceive a child as soon as possible. In a letter to Peter written a few months before he had even proposed, Kathleen confronted the baby question head-on. 'I want a grandson, and [Jane] promised me there would be no shirking there and pointed to Sybil Thorndike's four children! We all think she is very sweet and very pretty, and she comes from a very vigorous stock. Which probably you think unimportant in comparison with love but it really isn't.'

Jane knew she was not ready for children yet, and had written a play about a woman's choice between family and career based on her mother's experience. But for a young wife to say she did not want children was far harder then than it is now, and she was so keen to please and eager for praise that she muffled her reservations. Anyway, no one took her doubts very seriously. Once she was pregnant, they said, nature would take over and she would feel nothing but joy and fulfilment. That had certainly been Kathleen's experience, and she was one of the rare women of her time who had managed to combine being a devoted mother with a career. By 1942, however, heart problems and a bad back had obliged her to turn from sculpture to free-hand embroidery.

Her letter to Peter continued: 'I don't think a lass's art or career or whatever we call it, need suffer from matrimony if the call is strong enough. When Jane tells how her mother gave up her dancing because of marrying, she didn't know and I hadn't the heart to tell her . . . that Kitty was a very bad dancer. It used to make me hot and abashed when she would do "turns" in my studio in the middle of an ordinary dance.'[3] But Kit had been good enough for the Ballets Russes, and she had had to give up dancing professionally. A solitary occupation is easier to accommodate in a marriage than one that involves constant rehearsals and late nights.

Honeymoon over, Peter was itching to get back to work. At that stage he was participating in the development of a new sort of vessel, the steam gun boat or SGB. This was in effect a mini-destroyer designed to hunt down German E-boats, with a crew of around thirty men and three officers. Peter was overseeing the trials of SGB 9, which had been built on the Isle of Wight. He was as fascinated by boat-building and naval gunnery as he was by ducks and geese; and everything Peter did was done with a single-minded focus that left very little room for anything else.

Peter and Jane moved into the Gloster Hotel in Cowes. Apart from the night before their wedding Jane had never stayed in a hotel, so the first evening was rather exciting. It was only when Peter jumped out of bed at seven o'clock the next morning to be at the boatyard by eight that she realized that she would be alone for the rest of the day – and every day for weeks after that. ' "How do I have lunch?" I asked. "Darling, just go downstairs and ask for it. May be back for dinner." '[4]

She was the only naval wife in the hotel. In the lobby there were a few old magazines, and there was nothing to do except sink into homesickness and apathy as the hours crawled by. In an interview years later she recalled: 'I just wanted to go home.'[5] The streets of the town were packed with soldiers and sailors so when Jane tried to go for a walk she was assailed by catcalls, wolf-whistles, raucous whispers and ribald laughter. Sometimes Peter came back for dinner, and sometimes he did not. She wrote letters and tried to sound happier than she was.

Things improved when she found some work with the Missions to Seamen, 'making thousands of dirty bunks and washing up, and looking after the books and all that – it's much better to have a job. Some of Pete's crew are there and so I get to know them, which is a Good Thing . . . I will write soon, and as dully, and as long. One day they will be interestinger [sic] but now everything is rather dream-like and I hardly feel me at all. I feel I have been here for 100 years.'[6]

The Scotts went to Fritton for a day or so in May. She had her period at the time which must have come as a relief, but although she had told Peter of her reluctance to have children, she had not dared confess it to her mother-in-law and might even have given the opposite impression: 'Jane is in bed with her little pain,' Kathleen reported to Bill. 'She is disappointed poor little lass as she wanted a Peterkinlet [sic] at once!'[7]

Although Jane admired Kathleen and needed her approval, the tensions between them were never far below the surface. Jane was often nagged about her smoking, which Kathleen saw as an inhibitor of fertility; and she felt that her mother-in-law 'loved Peter too much to let anyone else love him'.[8] In fact there was something in Kathleen's very closeness to Peter that Jane found unsettling.

On one occasion, when she was at Fritton on her own, Jane came down to breakfast late to see that Peter's most recent letter to her had already been torn open and read by Kathleen. Jane was furious, but too nervous to stage a confrontation. But when she told Peter of this outrage, he thought nothing of it. His mother always enjoyed his letters no matter who they were addressed to, and he didn't mind her opening them. Then there was the time when she and Peter were in their room, he already asleep. 'The bedroom door opened noiselessly and, silhouetted against the light in the passage, I saw K. standing motionless. I waited to see whether she would speak, but after a few moments she retired, and the door was shut again. I remember I actually felt frightened of her.'[9]

A month later Jane fainted while out shopping in Cowes. When Peter heard of it he was delighted – he was sure she was pregnant, and the doctor confirmed his guess. Jane's mother, usually so repressed on the subject of bodily functions, was suddenly full of obstetric recommendations: 'I'm sorry, but I can't help giving you advice, because if I had had some I should have had a larger family now so here goes . . . When you rest, rest with your feet up, because in that position he gets nourishment more easily.' She also suggested that Jane practise relaxing every part of her body, 'particularly all his territory . . . Don't let him get you constipated and don't have very hot baths.'[10] Meanwhile Kathleen advised a pillow under the knees after sex, which Peter would tenderly arrange for her.

If only Jane could have told them what she felt about having a baby. In a letter to Peter written two years later she said:

> I was incoherent about it . . . I told you that day we walked up Berkeley Street, that I wanted to get used to being married first, but mostly I didn't feel old enough. I hadn't felt the need to have [a child] and I am sure one should before one begins. I never *did* admit it, hardly even to myself because it seemed so terrible not to want one, so wicked of me and I tried to tell myself to be grateful because a lot of people couldn't . . . and I knew you wanted one badly.[11]

So she repressed what she saw as shameful and unnatural feelings, and in her letters tried to play the happily expectant young mother. She talked about the baby as a boy, who would be called Falcon after his grandfather. In a letter to Kathleen she described eating bread and jam with Peter in bed,

> and [we] thought how lovely Falcon would be. What do you think he'll look like. Like Pete I hope and taller in case he wants to marry a telegraph post of even more imposing length than myself. Of course there might be two of him. Or he might be a girl . . . Pete would be such a good father there ought to be an arrangement so that we could be sure of twins.[12]

Behind this superficial gaiety, Jane was suffering from dreadful morning sickness and Peter suggested she spend a few weeks at home, for which she'd secretly been pining. The shabby austerity of the Beacon where nothing had changed came as a deep comfort, although it felt smaller and emptier.

The only members of the family living there then were her mother and her younger brother Colin, who was already exhibiting a brilliant eccentricity. He had been fascinated by electronics since before he could talk, although it didn't arouse much interest at his prep school, Summerfields, where he was miserable. The last time Jane had seen him he was laid up with a broken bone after falling down the stairs of the squash court. She found him sitting up in bed, 'knitting an incredibly intricate and hideous scarf and talking aggressively about electricity'.[13]

His fellow pupils called him Monkey because of his big ears, and Colin embraced this new identity, even if it had begun as a tease. He preferred it to his given name, and was known as Monkey to friends and family for the rest of his life. His name for Jane was Wog, because as a child she had short hair and when washed it stood out all over her head like a gollywog's. For the rest of this book, Colin will be called Monkey because that was what he called himself. Wog, having been noted, will disappear.

Jane was given a bare little room of her own, and wanted to furnish it with the things she had left in her room in London. But the house in Lansdowne Road had been cleared, and her mother told her that she had got rid of everything: her collection of theatre programmes, her gymkhana cups, her Delft candlesticks – only a few books remained. 'The feeling that all, or nearly all, of my childhood had been stripped away without any consultation kindled an urgent need in me that still lasts now, to make the places that I live in wholly mine.'[14]

But if Jane was angry with her mother, she also found her far easier to get on with. Kit even welcomed the shoe-box filled with forty-odd elephant hawk moth caterpillars (only half their original number, the rest having escaped on the train) that Peter had given Jane to take care of. Being about to pupate they required a great deal of food, which would entail a great many cuttings from the Beacon's supply of fuchsias.

Jane knitted matinée jackets for the baby, and her mother taught her how to do smocking over yards of white Viyella. 'Falcon is going to have small friendly ducks on his coats. Pete is going to draw them.

He said . . . "I might embroider them really, I've never done it but still —" I suppose he might be so clever that he could.'[15]

In July, she and Peter moved to a hotel in Weymouth. Peter was in a state of suppressed excitement, for the flotilla of four steam gun boats (the only ones ready so far) was gearing up to take part in a big operation. He worked long hours and brought officers and technicians home in the evenings, with whom he talked well into the night. 'I loved you almost bitterly,' wrote Jane,

> because I seemed so unnecessary, evening after evening. I became a little mad . . . and if that sounds dramatic, add up the pathetic, absurd reasons why. Because I had nothing to do except mind if you were half an hour late. Because I felt ill. Because I could not understand myself, why one could be so unhappy when one was married . . . I became obsessed by the war and the personal messes it was making . . . and we had those arguments in which I became more unbearable. Through all this you were perfectly reasonable but it did not touch you at all.[16]

The plan to attack the German-occupied port of Dieppe took place on 19 August 1942. It involved over 200 vessels and over 6,000 men, of whom 5,000 were Canadian. The idea was that they should land under cover of darkness, hold the port for as long as they could, gain much needed intelligence and then withdraw, blowing up everything behind them. In the event they ran into a German convoy, which immediately gave the alert. From then on the landings stood no chance, despite support from the RAF. Almost 60 per cent of the men who managed to land on the Dieppe beaches were killed, wounded or taken prisoner. Being in a support role, there was little the SGBs could do to alleviate the massacre on the beaches, so they concentrated on the rescue of those shipwrecked and shot down. For his 'gallantry, daring and skill', Peter was again mentioned in dispatches.

In planning the subsequent Allied landings in Sicily and Normandy, the authorities claimed that much had been learned from what happened at Dieppe; but in the summer of 1942 the catastrophe merely showed that the Allies would not be ready to establish a bridgehead in occupied France for a long time.

The pressure of work eased off after the Dieppe raid. The Admiralty decided that the SGBs needed more armoured protection, and for a while Peter could spend more time with Jane. They took a house at Seaford near Newhaven. Number 3 West Down Road was small, dark and over-furnished but it was their first married home, and Jane's cousin Audrey Tuck (the daughter of Kit's elder sister Antonia) came to stay. Audrey's cheerful presence made life much easier for Jane. 'I think that was the happiest time,' Jane wrote to Peter, 'we did have six weeks and Audrey was a darling . . . Dieppe was over and there was no immediate danger for you.'[17] Then one evening Peter came home with the news that his flotilla was being moved again, and he could not even stay for dinner. Jane burst into tears, and Peter found it difficult to be patient with her incontinent emotions; the war was demanding a great deal of everyone, not just her.

Jane spent most of that winter in Sussex with her mother, and made occasional visits to London. She went to Harrods to buy the baby a teddy bear – it was toffee-coloured, she remembered, 'with a reliable expression'. She also bought a little suitcase. 'What initials, madam?' asked the assistant, and since madam didn't yet know, she replied, 'F. or N. Scott.' F was for Falcon; but if the baby was a girl, Jane had decided that she would be called Nicola – a name inspired by the beautiful Nicola Maude, a character who provokes love and envy in Rosamond Lehmann's *Invitation to the Waltz* (1932) and *The Weather in the Streets* (1936).

Thanks to her mother, Jane found somewhere for the new family to live. Her grandmother Lady Somervell started to develop dementia after the death of her husband; and when she could no longer live alone, her daughters Kit and Antonia moved her into a nursing home in Sussex. Since the house was now empty, Kit suggested that Jane and Peter rent it for £2 a week.

Number 105 Clifton Hill was a detached Gothic villa in St John's Wood, with three bedrooms, a bathroom, a dining room and a large drawing room, as well as attics and a basement. Jane moved in after Christmas, and she and her mother (these challenging situations brought out the best in Kit) embarked on a frenzy of painting and cleaning and moving furniture. Kit arranged for a cook and a cleaner, and Dosia was going to live with the new ménage. This raised Jane's spirits considerably. With Dosia in the house, they might revive some of the happy times at Mon Débris – in anticipation of which, 105 Clifton Hill was to be known as the Villa Vengeance.

Jane's baby was due around the middle of February, but her contractions began on the first of the month. Peter took her into the nursing home in Kensington that had been booked for the birth, and left her at the reception desk. Since the staff were not expecting her for another two weeks she was given a small, freezing room on the top floor and a sleeping pill. When she woke, she was horrified to find the sheet covered in blood, and Jane thought the baby had died. She shouted and rang the bell in a panic. When a nurse finally appeared she said nothing was wrong, just her labour beginning. Jane was cleaned up, and a sour-looking elderly nurse made herself comfortable in a chair at the end of the room.

These days most pregnant women in Britain attend ante-natal classes and have been informed about everything from relaxation techniques to pain relief options, so it is hard to imagine just how ignorant Jane was about childbirth. The novels and plays she had read left her none the wiser, and the only thing her mother had told her was, 'People of our sort never make any fuss or noise when they are having a baby.'[18] While contractions became more and more intense, the sour-looking nurse sat reading her paper. After what seemed like hours of agony Jane asked how long it was going to go on – to which the nurse replied that she was sick of people asking that question.

Jane's only child, Nicola, was born at 10.30 a.m. on 2 February 1943. Jane described the birth as an appalling ordeal but an old friend and contemporary of hers, the novelist Penelope Lively, observed that Jane's labour was no better or worse than that of most mothers in the 1940s. When Peter came to the nursing home he was told that she had had an easy time of it, and perhaps she had. Yet what had been hardest to bear was not the pain but the isolation: the feeling that Peter had abandoned her, and the lack of any human warmth or reassurance during an experience that can be terrifying in its intensity.

For Jane the exhaustion of giving birth was followed not by radiant joy, which is what everyone had told her to expect, but by a long bout of what would now be called post-natal depression. 'I cried for two days, and to begin with, they said things like cheer up, it's all right now, and then they got angry with me for crying, but I couldn't stop. Peter came to see the baby and said he was going to Norfolk to spend the rest of his leave with his mother. He never brought me a flower and I felt he was abandoning me *again*.'[19]

She could tell he was irritated by her constant tears; and she read this as disappointment that she had not borne a son. Nicola was kept from her and only brought in at four-hourly intervals, by which time her breasts felt like cannon balls and the baby was howling with hunger. In the 1940s 'bonding with the baby' was an irrelevance. The goal was to establish a fixed feeding routine, and this regimentation continued when Jane returned to Clifton Hill accompanied by a starchy monthly nurse. 'Alone with [Nicola] I'd say things like "I do like you, and I do want us to be friends." But I felt guilty about her, as I'd never felt about anything else in my life.'[20] Her guilt was not about the rigid nursery protocols of the time, but about her own lack of delight in her daughter.

The monthly nurse was succeeded by a young nanny who had been trained at her Aunt Ruth's Babies' Hotel. She was the same age as Jane, and much more sympathetic. Kathleen, on the other hand, always in tune with her son, had picked up Peter's impatience with his wife. She could not understand Jane's misery, her baffled hopelessness when it came to mothering; to Kathleen it seemed little more than self-pity. And she had produced a girl, a disappointment Kathleen did her best to overcome. 'It's a girl, well so is Jane and so was I and Pete loves us a bit, so I guess he'll love his daughter.'[21] Nevertheless, Jane should set about producing the required male as soon as possible.

She also needed to get more organized. It was just as well that Kathleen arrived early for Nicola's christening, which took place that spring on board Captain Scott's ship, HMS *Discovery*. 'Poor little Jane, she is an incapable bairn,' she wrote to Bill.

Arriving at *Discovery* I found a distracted Captain, he had been told 'a baptism' and nothing else – he had no idea how or where. However we put our heads together, put a table on deck, covered it with the Antarctic flag, got a pail, wrapped a union jack round it, put the *Discovery* bell inverted into it, and a jug of warm water under the table, and a big Bible to give tone! At 12.05 no parson, no Jane, no Nicola, no Pete – I thought I must have made a mistake. When they arrived Jane [was] looking as though she had slept under a hedge all night. The parson was carrying a suitcase, from which he drew *gorgeous* pink stoles, copes, smatherididdles [*sic*] – quite preposterous.[22]

That summer at Fritton, Jane recalled a walk in the woods with her mother-in-law. Kathleen remarked that Peter only married her because he wanted a son, and Jane was presumably aware of the fact. Jane replied that no, she was not aware, 'but my heart began to pound. She looked me straight in the eye and then said, "If you ever made Pete unhappy I should want to stab you. I should enjoy doing it." '[23] It was a horrible thing to say, but being so anxious and miserable Jane took it more seriously than it deserved. Kathleen's son Wayland remarked that 'she was always threatening to kill me',[24] and it was a light word in her vocabulary.

Peter was having what was called 'a good war'. In November 1942 he had been promoted from lieutenant to lieutenant commander, and a month after Nicola's birth he was appointed senior officer of the SGB flotilla. Thanks to his lobbying, the steam gun boats were fitted with heavier guns, and shortly after that he went into action again.

SGB 6, commanded by Peter and accompanied by two smaller motor gun boats, penetrated the Baie de la Seine to look for enemy shipping on the night of 15–16 April 1943 and destroyed a large and well-armed trawler. 'I consider that Lt-Commander Scott showed skill in the handling of his force,' reported C-in-C Portsmouth, 'and great determination in his engagement, pursuit, and re-engagement of the enemy.'[25] Peter was recommended for an award, and received the Distinguished Service Cross.

Kathleen loved hearing about his life on board ship, and encouraged him to talk about his battles in the narrow seas around the French coast. But Jane was not only bored by his stories, she resented them. They reminded her that guns and boats were the centre of his life, not her, and she sulked when people wanted to hear about them.

Peter was well aware of her feelings. 'There is a sadness to me that you do not share my appetite for adventure or care about my adventures, with the result that when for example I return from an adventurous time in France I have no encouragement to tell you about it because you are not interested. I long to tell you about it all, and share all of it with you, but if I begin to tell you I feel that you are slightly bored and slightly disapproving.'[26]

When Jane first came to know the Kennets, she had been enchanted by the way they eagerly listened to each other and cheered each other on – but in this case, she preferred her family's reticence. 'I know that

I am no good with you about the adventures,' she wrote. 'You have been spoilt about that, people have listened [to you] *too* avidly, and I have been spoilt in that I have never been forced to listen to anything, our family do not go in for accounts of doings as you know and if they did they'd probably get snubbed.'[27]

For the rest of that summer and into the autumn he was at sea two or three times a week with his steam gun boats, harrying the enemy. There were some notable successes, but sometimes the damage to his boats and men was greater than the damage they could inflict on their foes; and it was Peter who had to write to the families of the dead, a job he never took lightly. In the course of these months he was mentioned in dispatches yet again, and a bar was added to his DSC.

6

Guilt and Betrayal

ALL THIS TIME, Jane was living with Dosia in Clifton Hill. Nicola was now in the care of the sensible, affectionate and experienced Nanny Buss, who was to be the centre of Nicola's world for years; and around the four of them there ebbed and flowed a constant stream of friends, family, guests and lodgers. They included Jane's cousin Audrey, and Peter's half-brother Wayland. Wayland was seventeen when he went up to Cambridge to read music; but in July 1942, after four terms, he received his call-up papers. He joined the navy and for the first few months of 1943 he had been with the motor gun boats, protecting British coastal shipping; but his lungs were not strong and he was often ill.

Jane had always seen him as an ally, especially since the rest of his family were so much older. He took her side at Fritton, when Kathleen's tight little remarks underlined what a hopeless mother she was. He was also a sympathetic listener when Jane chewed over her difficulties with Peter and Kathleen. Wayland was always welcome at Clifton Hill, as were his friends. There was Denis Pipe-Wolferstan, who was to marry a friend of Dosia's; Peter Tranchell, who on being told that Wayland was not there sat down and waited for him for days; and Wyndham Goodden the poet. Sir Arthur Somervell's piano, still in the drawing room, was in frequent use, played by Jane, Dosia, Wayland, Peter Tranchell and a professional pianist, Denis Matthews, who had been a pupil of Harold Craxton's.

Music ebbed and flowed in and out of Jane's life, but at this point it was very important to her. She was surrounded by musical friends and the music she heard, and played, at this time was for ever associated with happiness and companionship. She was particularly drawn to the composers of the eighteenth century – Scarlatti, Bach, Haydn and Mozart – although her former teacher Harold Craxton was still trying to broaden her range.

Years later when arthritis had made her give up the piano, Jane gave all her sheet music to her friend and literary agent Ann Clowes. As well as the Beethoven Sonatas and Bach Preludes and Fugues that all piano players are familiar with, there was a beautifully bound set of Chopin Nocturnes and two pieces by Ravel, gifts from Harold Craxton. 'I think he wanted to bring her further forward, particularly with the Ravel,' she wrote. 'I'm also sure that she was a pretty good pianist, because Craxton wouldn't have continued to give her fairly difficult music unless she was capable of playing it.'[1]

Jane and Dosia became air-raid wardens, which 'consisted of wearing an immensely hairy dark blue trouser suit and a tin hat'.[2] They counted people in and out of air-raid shelters, and gave lectures on precautionary measures. On the one occasion that a bomb fell a hundred yards away from Clifton Hill, Jane was not on duty but seized her tin hat and went to help. There she had to stop an old lady rushing up the stairs of her bomb-blasted house to find the photograph of her son.

That summer, Peter's half-brother Wayland was given a job at the Admiralty and from then on he was often at Clifton Hill, where everyone seemed to be in love. Dosia met Barry Craig, a painter who had been with Jane's Uncle John at the Slade. Audrey had fallen for a man called John Rideout, a Chinese scholar; and Jane found herself falling in love with her half-brother Wayland. They were not alone much at first, being part of a group of friends walking on Hampstead Heath, going to a play at the Arts Club or spending a rainy afternoon at the cinema; but there was a kind of inevitability about it, and they found more and more excuses to be alone.

She would bicycle down to the Admiralty at lunchtime with sandwiches, which they would eat in St James's Park. He came to the house more frequently, while everyone else turned a blind eye. He rented a boat on the Thames just outside London, and sometimes they would spend the weekends there – with only Monkey, then aged nine, to maintain the proprieties.

'The first time [Wayland] kissed me I discovered what physical desire meant,' wrote Jane.[3] He also provided a level of attention and affection that her husband, at that stage, seemed unable to give. Peter never seemed to mind leaving Jane to go back to his all-absorbing work, but his absence upset her very much. 'Something hard and fierce and selfish in me said, "You can't go on minding at that rate, you must have a life too . . . You can't afford to be so sharply unhappy."'[4] She also knew that Peter had never aroused her sexually, and was not going to waste time turning himself into a skilful lover. Sex was not only more reciprocal with Wayland; there was also a dark edge to it, something that was willing to break taboos and look betrayal in the eye. As she wrote to Peter: 'I can only describe it as a violent reaction, that summer I mean, to the year before. I did love Wayland very much, he made me very happy.'[5]

But Jane and Wayland began to feel guilty, and soon this became so suffocating that they decided they must tell Peter. It took time to summon up the courage to do so, and Peter did not come on leave very often. When they finally told him, it was almost Christmas.

'Pete treated us as though we were unspeakably disloyal children; he was breezy as well as furious. We should be ashamed of ourselves and it must all stop at once. The scene went on for hours, until Pete said he was going out to dinner and that Wayland must leave the house with him.'[6] This is how a cuckolded husband should behave; but Wayland, writing to Jane many years later as she was preparing her memoir, recalled a rather different scene:

> I was in bed early in the morning at Clifton Hill . . . and Peter came in to shave at the basin: there was no hot water anywhere else . . . He talked to me as it were through the mirror. Perhaps he had been wrong in coming between you and me. Perhaps he should not have married you after all. Perhaps he should now leave the field free? How much did I mind about it all? I made light of it, saying that he should not think of any such thing. Inwardly I wondered what I should do if we did – how should I be with a sister-in-law-wife and a niece-step-daughter? In the main I thought I was still too young for this anyhow. Not for love: only for its results. Neither of my parents ever said a word about it.[7]

By late 1943, the Admiralty had decided that they would not build any more steam gun boats. Peter too had had enough – he had been at sea for almost two years, and was suffering from 'operational fatigue'.[8] He still hoped to be given command of a destroyer, but in the meantime he had been posted to Holyhead, just off the north coast of the Isle of Anglesey, as an instructor on HMS *Bee*, the Coastal Forces training base.

Jane, in disgrace, was to accompany him to Holyhead at the end of his Christmas leave, leaving Nicola and Nanny Buss in London. She was not to try to telephone Wayland, nor write to him, ever again. Peter was not by nature jealous. He could see that Jane felt neglected, although that had been inevitable because his work was paramount; but he could not understand her disloyalty. 'How could I do that to him, how could I be so wickedly disloyal? I didn't know, and said so. There were more tears . . . I said again and again that I knew it had been wrong and that I was very sorry. But sleepless in the dark, I thought he didn't love me as I knew Wayland did.'[9]

They moved into the Station Hotel, and Jane was once again left alone in a small town where she knew no one. When Peter came back in the evenings, 'he was still very angry. He bedded me doggedly every single night, which I found more and more unbearable.'[10] Yet if he thought he was going to get her pregnant, he was mistaken. Jane had a sympathetic doctor who knew how depressed she had been after Nicola's birth, and she had been introduced to birth control.

Jane started a morning job making camouflage nets but otherwise she had nothing to do but pine for Wayland and keep her resentment against Peter at a steady simmer.

One night he came back to the hotel to say that someone he knew had a young wife who had just given birth. She was ill and so was her baby, and her husband had to leave her for a night to attend to some business. Would Jane keep her company? Jane said she would. The grateful husband came to pick her up in his car, and they drove for miles inland to a small isolated cottage.

His wife, who was called Myfanwy, was lying upstairs exhausted, feverish and desperately anxious about her baby who would not take the breast. Jane came into her own at moments like these. She made Myfanwy comfortable, gave her a couple of aspirin to help her sleep and took the baby into a little room that had been set up as a nursery. Jane got into the narrow bed, took off her shirt and jumper and held the baby next to her body – skin to skin – for the rest of the night to keep him warm. Occasionally the baby woke, mewing softly, and she managed to give him cooled boiled water from a bottle; but Jane herself did not dare go to sleep. She was still awake when the midwife came the following morning, and the baby was alive.

This was a moment of great significance for Jane. She was just as good as Peter at telling herself that she was wicked and disloyal – perhaps she didn't deserve love, couldn't even give it any more because she was so miserable and selfish. But that long night, much of it spent looking into that tiny trustful face, had proved that love and generosity had not left her altogether.

She had to borrow a bicycle to get back to Holyhead, and by the time she reached the hotel she was wet through and exhausted. She fell ill and once she had recovered, the camouflage netting job had come to an end. Casting about for something to do, she asked the Ports Amenities Liaison Officer whether she might produce a play with the navy. He agreed at once. The local convent consented to lend their hall for performances, and the play selected was *The Importance of Being Earnest* by Oscar Wilde.

Jane could not resist giving herself the part of Gwendoline. A pretty young Wren took the part of Cecily, and there was no trouble finding a Lady Bracknell, one of the most enjoyable comic parts ever written for an older woman. The part of Jack was taken by a friend of Peter's called Jack Lambert, while Algernon was a handsome man called Philip Lee. Rehearsals had to be worked round people's duties, and at the last minute Jack Lambert's boat was sent to Lowestoft. They found another Jack who did his best, but he barely had enough time to learn the part. Nevertheless the play was well attended and applauded, and Peter was happy for Jane that it had been a success.

But after it was over Jane was still on her own, still bored and resentful and aching for Wayland – despite knowing that she could never have a life with him, and that sooner or later he would find someone else. Which was why she did not object when Philip Lee, who had played Algernon, began showing up at the hotel for tea or drinks. He said that he had noticed two things about her: that she was very unhappy and that she didn't wear a bra. That might have set alarm bells ringing had she wanted to steer clear of trouble, but she didn't.

One day he came by and said he had the afternoon off. They walked west out of town, and climbed high into the folds of Holyhead Mountain where they had sex. Jane said it was 'thrillingly romantic', and she decided she was in love again. 'It was balm to be wanted, approved of, to have someone to talk to about books and ideas.'[11] Being 'wanted and approved of' was at the core of fulfilment for Jane: this was what released her sexual energy, far more than desire for a man's body. One wonders how much they talked about books and ideas. Peter found out, but decided to say nothing.

It was also in Holyhead that she began to write again. Her subject was her melodramatic night with Seth, which she now shaped into an extended dialogue (see p.36). The most interesting thing about it is not the biting and burns, but the battle of wills; and how easy it is for a man to toy with the mind of a young girl tied down by ignorance, good manners and chronic lack of confidence. Peter showed it to Jack Lambert, who wasn't very impressed; and Jane, thirsting for encouragement, asked Peter if he would send it to Wayland. Wayland's response was, 'What a hectic, subtle mind she has.'[12]

Peter's job at Holyhead came to an end in March 1944 and he was sent to Portsmouth, to join a group headed by his friend Christopher Dreyer, who was coordinating the deployment of all Coastal Forces craft that were to be involved in the Normandy landings. Jane moved back to Clifton Hill, still home to a floating population – many of whom were getting married, including Dosia and the painter Barry Craig. By the spring of 1944, Jane's relationship with Peter had dwindled into 'a kind of affability – wary on my part, breezy on his'.[13] But their letters to each other are still very loving, and both declare that the crisis in their marriage had only made it stronger. The only difference was that while Peter really meant it, Jane was trying to persuade herself it was true: the alternatives were too frightening to contemplate yet.

For her birthday Peter sent her a collection of Haydn Sonatas, beautifully bound. 'I have been reading them madly as they are nearly all new ground,' she wrote. 'It was a lovely idea.'[14] She also gave him regular, detailed updates on Nicola's progress – her pet name was Popper, and in April she was fourteen months old. Jane was touched that on her return from Holyhead, Nicola 'kissed me firmly and remembers me perfectly. Nanny says she is the best-tempered baby she has ever had.'[15]

But while Peter and Jane seemed to have recovered from the affair with Wayland, it marked a turning-point in their marriage. From then on Jane is pulling back from Peter, while his love deepens as he fears he will lose her. Their letters do not reflect this shift, at least not at first. Peter's letters had always been more affectionate than he was when they were together. Jane, on the other hand, was alarmed by her feelings of bitterness and withdrawal. Her letters to Peter are an exercise in trying to write herself back into a more comfortable and affectionate frame of mind.

She started looking for work in films and plays as soon as she was back in London. She failed to get a part in Terence Rattigan's *While the Sun Shines*, but through Wyndham Goodden she was introduced to the novelist Norman Collins, who was also a producer for the BBC. Collins gave her a job as a continuity announcer, and being the latest recruit she was given the night shift. She was not based at Broadcasting House but in the Peter Robinson building on Oxford Circus, where – four floors underground – she had to read news bulletins, announce live concerts, and select and play gramophone records.

She was shown the ropes by another continuity announcer, a young woman with dark hair and white skin called Jill Balcon. She had been working at the BBC for two years and before that she had trained as an actress, so they had much to talk about. Jane and Jill got on well, and made each other laugh. But although Jill became a friend, Jane saw little of her during working hours when she was alone, separated from two technicians by a glass screen.

The most important thing, she was told, was never to allow more than fifteen seconds of silence or 'dead air time', since that would give the Germans the opportunity to take over the frequency. This does not sound very hard but sometimes a live concert had to be stopped in mid-bar because of an air raid, and Jane had to scramble for a record to plug the gap. And often the news bulletin, which arrived only a few seconds before it had to be read, was bristling with unpronounceable names. Her shift ended in the early hours of the morning, when the platforms of Oxford Circus Tube station were still full of sleeping bodies, wrapped in blankets and overcoats. They seemed oblivious to the trains, and she noticed that while women slept in their curlers and bedroom slippers, men slept in their boots or shoes.

Jill Balcon put Jane in touch with her father, Michael (later Sir Michael) Balcon, who was then the head of Ealing Studios. He took her on as an extra in a film called *Fiddlers Three* (1944), starring the comic Tommy Trinder. Tommy and two friends take shelter one stormy night on the altar of Stonehenge, and a flash of lightning transports them back in time to Nero's Rome. Various capers follow along with some hanky-panky with Poppaea, Nero's wife, before Nero throws the time travellers to the lions – at which point they find themselves suddenly whisked back to Stonehenge. Jane played one of Poppaea's slave girls in thick make-up and false eyelashes, wearing a yellow satin bra and a mini-skirt with a gold fringe. There was a great deal of waiting around; but she treasured the moment when she found Tommy Trinder in a dark corner taking his very short toga up and down, saying, 'Now you see it, now you don't.'

She was still seeing Philip Lee, the man she had met in Holyhead, although he could not get to London very often. Dosia and Barry liked him, and Barry would lend the lovers his studio for their trysts. Philip managed to get down and spend a night with Jane just before D-Day, in June 1944; and told her that when he got some leave, they might go away together for a few days. Jane looked forward to it eagerly; but one evening a few weeks later a new continuity girl said, 'You know Philip Lee, don't you?' Jane admitted that she did. 'Isn't he charming?' The girl had met him when he came to pick up her flatmate, and they were off on holiday to Westmorland.[16] Jane was left stunned, cheapened and humiliated. Her imagination had made something wonderful out of her affair with Philip, but evidently she had meant very little to him.

When Peter and Jane went to visit his mother that summer, she found that whispers about her unfaithfulness had got back to Kathleen, most probably through Jack Lambert when he was in Lowestoft. The subject was not raised while Peter was in the house, but the moment he went out Kathleen challenged Jane about Philip Lee; and when she said non-committally that he had been good in *The Importance of Being Earnest*, Kathleen called her a little liar. For days she followed Jane from room to room, taunting and berating her, trying to force her into a tearful confession and pleas for forgiveness. In retrospect Jane thought that she knew about the affair with Wayland too, but couldn't bring herself to mention it.

That September, Jane wrote Peter a long letter about their marriage and where it had gone wrong. 'I know you say with some justification that I was chiefly responsible for our marriage . . . When you asked me to marry you (rather uncertainly, you were quite rightly none too sure of it) I only thought now I shall have the right to be with him instead of the intolerable position of belonging and not being allowed to possess in return . . . you didn't know how *desperately* I loved you.'[17]

In his reply, Peter too was willing to admit his mistakes. 'I know I was terribly wrong to persuade you against your will to have Nicky,' he wrote. 'There came a sort of urgency which depended on the apparent nearness of death.' As for the Wayland affair: 'To me it came as a staggering blow – just that – staggering and when you are staggering it is difficult to give support . . . It was the discovery that I had failed to make you happy when I thought pathetically that I was . . . it was that discovery that made the blow so heavy.'[18] He does not mention Philip Lee.

Both Jane and Peter ended their letters saying they wanted to give their marriage another chance. But while Jane seethes with restlessness and ill feeling, one cannot doubt Peter's love. He was even prepared to defend her against his mother. Jane had hurt him, and for that Kathleen would never forgive her. According to Peter's biographer, this was the first time that mother and son had been at such loggerheads, and bitter words were exchanged; after which Peter wrote her a letter, begging her to support him in trying to save his marriage:

I have married, I believe, somebody very strange and rare and outstanding. I really believe this; so any attempt to make me believe otherwise is unhelpful. I do not, nor ever did, suppose that it will be easy to be married to that sort of person. I was, and still am, prepared to meet all these difficulties for the sake of the good things that come out of being married to anyone so stimulating and exciting . . .

When our first trouble [Wayland] arose a year ago I took a wrong course which put Jane and me much further apart than we need have been, and prepared the way for the next trouble [Philip Lee], which is now also over, and which might never have arisen had we not been so far apart. The attitude, which was my mistake the first time, is the attitude you have taken in your talks with Jane both then and on this second occasion, which leaves her with no one to turn to.

Now the point, darling, is this. I am taking a definite course . . . best described as taming my wild animal and not caging it . . . Whether you agree or not, you must let me give it a fair chance . . . It is essential for her that she should have confidence, for example in her psychologist, so you must not belittle or discredit things which she finds helpful . . . There is one last thing to say, which is on the subject of loyalties . . . my loyalty must be with my Jane, who is my life now, rather than with my family. That you must see is right and natural.[19]

By the end of 1944 the inhabitants of Clifton Hill had dispersed, and Jane and Peter decided to find another house. In March 1945 they bought Number 8 Edwardes Square, in Kensington. It was a pretty terraced house with some ugly additions, but since these were bathrooms they were left alone. There was an airy sitting room on the first floor which Jane painted white, with crimson and white striped curtains which she made herself. She bought a large oval gilt mirror for thirty shillings in the Portobello Road, and Harold Craxton found her a piano. The main bedroom was hung with William Morris tiger-lily paper, while Nicola had a day nursery and a night nursery on the top floor, where she slept with Nanny.

Jane thought that once the war was over and Peter was a painter again, everything would be better because they would be together as a family; but although Peter was very keen that their marriage should survive, he still hoped to be sent to the Far East with his own ship – which would mean him being away for months at a time. In early 1945 the Admiralty gave him command of a frigate, HMS *Cardigan Bay*. A frigate is smaller than a destroyer, and this one was still being built; but the *Cardigan Bay* was going to be fitted with all the latest equipment, and he was delighted.

The end of the war in Europe came on 8 May 1945, although it was still far from over in the Far East. Jane spent the day having her tonsils out in University College Hospital, and stayed on at the hospital to recuperate – during which time she had a surprise visit from Myfanwy, the woman whose baby she had looked after in Holyhead. She and her husband had come to thank her for saving their baby that night, and brought her a bunch of daffodils.

She needed a holiday after the operation; and with a friend called Marie Paneth, she set off on a two-week writing holiday on St

Martin's in the Isles of Scilly. Marie Paneth was writing a book about a children's project in Paddington; while Jane was still working on what had grown out of the story she had begun in Holyhead, based on her experience with Seth Holt. So many layers of writing and new ideas had overlaid it that she could no longer think of it as a short story, and it had nothing to do with Seth any more: it was growing into a novel. Jane was writing at such a rate that she could hardly keep up with herself, and in the evenings she and Marie read to each other from their separate works.

One evening their landlady told Jane she had a telephone call. There was only one telephone box in the village, and since no one would call unless it was an emergency, Jane thought something terrible had happened to Nicola and ran all the way. It was Peter: Nicola was fine, but he wanted to ask her advice. The Conservative Party had suddenly asked him to stand for Parliament, for the newly created constituency of Wembley North – despite the fact that the election was only a few weeks away, and that he had never thought much about politics in his life. He was tempted, but if he became an MP he would never take command of his frigate. What should he do?

Jane thought he should stand for Parliament: 'I felt that was what he wanted me to say.'[20] It was certainly the right answer, but it meant she would have to cut short her holiday – the beautiful wife of the gallant naval commander was very much part of the package with which the Conservatives planned to woo the electorate: 'Britain's greatness has been built on character and daring, not on docility to a State machine,' ran one line of Churchill's 1945 Conservative manifesto, and that was what Peter had to represent.

The next few weeks were a fearful ordeal:

> Then, as a politician's wife, I was expected to speak to between 50 and 100 women . . . two or three times a day – sometimes five times a day. These occasions were always preceded by huge teas, where every imaginable farinaceous delicacy was pressed upon or even down one . . . by the time I was through the third or sometimes the fifth tea, I felt like one of those fortresses that have been waiting for weeks, accumulating cannon balls and boiling oil, but with no enemy in sight.[21]

Among the people Jane knew and met – friends, family, fellow party members – everyone expected Peter to win by a comfortable margin; but the Conservatives had seriously underestimated the nation's desire for social reform. Labour won by a landslide; and Charles Hobson for Labour won 43.62 per cent of the votes in Wembley North, compared to Peter's 38.15 per cent. Peter was more disappointed by his failure than the loss of a Parliamentary seat, although it had been a valuable experience. For Jane, there was nothing but relief.

That spring her parents, in a state of great agitation, had come to Edwardes Square with a letter from her brother Robin. He had spent much of the war in Arizona, training to be a Spitfire pilot; and the letter announced that he had married an American girl called Hope, without his commanding officer's consent. Reading between the lines, it was plain that he did not think his family were going to approve of his choice. His parents had already turned the news into a family catastrophe, but to their daughter it sounded more like an exciting romance, and Hope might turn out to be very nice. Jane was flattered to be treated as an adult, whose opinion was worth listening to. Yet when they had left, she recalled a sense of unease between her parents that seemed unconnected to what they had just told her.

Its cause was rapidly coming to a head. Kit had spent most of the war in Sussex with Monkey, and with the perfect excuse of his work at Hendon Aerodrome, David had for some time been seeing a married woman called Ursula Beddard. She had three sons, a voluptuous figure, and she indulged David in ways that his austere and sex-averse wife never could.

David very much wanted Jane to meet her; and since she always sided with lovers, she agreed. At her father's request, her first visit to Ursula's Hampshire cottage was undertaken alone: David thought they would get on more easily without him. Sure enough, Jane found Ursula very warm and kind – and to her surprise, she found herself pouring out her heart to her father's mistress. Ursula listened with great sympathy, and told Jane that her own marriage too was deeply unhappy.

Jane was then invited to lunch by her father, who had made up his mind to leave Kit and wanted Jane's advice on how best to do it. Should he tell her while she was still living in Sussex, or buy a house in London for her and Monkey before breaking the news? Jane thought the latter option was the better.

So her mother started looking for a new house, still unaware that her husband was going to leave her as soon as she had moved in. She found one in Clifton Hill, down the road from where Jane had lived during the war. Jane thought it rather dark, but her mother was happy with it. Kit was still worrying about Robin's over-hasty marriage, but she had not seen him for over two years and was looking forward eagerly to his return.

There was no 'good moment' for David to tell Kit that he was leaving. Whenever he did it and whatever words he chose were going to plunge her into years of misery. In a late unfinished novel that explores her mother's life, and in her fictionalized version of the split in the Cazalet Chronicle (see Part II, *Casting Off*) Jane has her father break the news at the end of a home-coming party for a long-absent son, in Clifton Hill. Whether it was then or on another day makes little difference. Kit had known for a long time that he was seeing other women but she never imagined that he would abandon her, and leave her shattered by shock, rage and humiliation.

Kit was also estranged from her beloved Robin, whose new wife fell far below her exacting standards. She was appalled by Hope's lack of deference, her brash sexiness and her free and easy American ways. Robin had always been the confident, brilliant one – but in marrying Hope he dashed all his mother's expectations. She made her disappointment very clear, and not unnaturally he and Hope avoided her.

In the long term it was Monkey, aged eleven at the time, who bore the long penance of her bitterness. He remembered her coming to collect him from his prep school, Summerfields, at the end of the summer term and seeming unusually subdued. They had reached London when, to make conversation, Monkey said, 'Will Dad be home when we get back?' His mother pulled the car in to the side, put on the handbrake and burst into racking sobs over the steering wheel. Dad wouldn't be at home. He was never coming back.[22] From then on Kit made sure David had as little contact with his younger son as possible. Monkey only ever saw his father in clubs or restaurants, over awkward lunches where neither of them had much to say to the other.

7

Making the Break

ABANDONING HIS POLITICAL ambitions, Peter thought that he
might take command of HMS *Cardigan Bay* and sail to the Far
East after all. Then, in the first half of August, the United States
dropped two atomic bombs on Hiroshima and Nagasaki; and with
the surrender of Japan a few days later, the Second World War – and
Peter's naval career – came to an end. The time had come to pick up
the threads of his pre-war life, and he returned to his birds and his
painting with relish.

Peter Scott was the first to admit that he was not a great artist. What
he had was an enviable facility for painting the things he knew and
loved best: wildfowl, in their natural habitats. He could turn out
pictures at a rate of one a day, more if they were on small canvases, and
people flocked to buy them. His first post-war show, at Ackermann's
Gallery in November 1945, sold forty paintings; a success that inspired
the Harlow Gallery in New York to offer him an exhibition the following April. He and Jane would go together, and Peter began painting the
canvases for New York with his usual single-minded energy.

At the same time, he needed a new home for his collection of
wildfowl. He had been obliged to sell his lighthouse on the Wash,
since the land around it had been reclaimed for agriculture and was
thus no longer a refuge for wild birds. In early 1946 he leased twenty-
three acres on the Severn Estuary near Slimbridge in Gloucestershire,
that would eventually become the home of the Severn Wildfowl
Trust.

Jane did her best to remain busy too, working on her novel, seeing
friends, arranging dinner parties, and thinking about New York; it
would be her first time abroad. She was also being pulled into the
orbit of a strange man called Robert Aickman, whom she had known
for some years. His wife Ray had been secretary to Ronnie Jeans

when they were collaborating on Jane's play, *Triple Harness*, and Aickman had invited himself to tea one day when she was living at Clifton Hill. They did not come to dinner at Edwardes Square, because Robert hated parties; but she often went to Robert and Ray's flat in Gower Street. Peter too became a friend of Robert's when, in early 1946, Aickman and a narrow-boat enthusiast called Tom Rolt founded the Inland Waterways Association, to call attention to the plight of Britain's long-neglected canals and the declining world of the people who still scraped a living on them. A few years later Peter became vice-president of the association, and bought a narrow-boat to ease the lack of accommodation at Slimbridge.

Robert Aickman had married Edith Ray Gregorson, always known as Ray, in 1941. They had both suffered miserably difficult child-hoods, and had no intention of having children, whom they saw as an obstacle to civilized life. Jane found this view wonderfully refreshing, but she also noticed how Ray's world revolved around Robert's needs and comforts.

Aickman told Jane he was passionately in love with her. Yes, he had told Ray; and no, she didn't mind because theirs was 'a marriage of convenience', although that meant his convenience rather than hers. As for Jane, 'I was flattered to be so important to such an unusual and intriguing man.'[1] He was not particularly good-looking, with dark hair, thick glasses and a pale complexion. The small literary agency that the Aickmans ran from their flat in Gower Street, plus the occasional article by Robert, did not make much money; but they also had a modest annuity inherited from his father, plus whatever secretarial work Ray could find.

Jane admired Aickman's high-minded intensity. He deplored the advance of mechanization and technology while idolizing a rosy version of the past and, like many who pride themselves on their impeccable taste, he had very firm opinions about music, art, drama and literature. She was eager to learn and he became her mentor. He advised her on the progress of her novel, took her to operas and art galleries, and compiled reading lists to fill the lamentable gaps in her education.

Best of all, he said he needed her. Need was inseparable from love for Jane, and she often confused the two. She used to say that Peter didn't really love her whereas he did, very much; but he was always bound up in his work, whether that was painting or building boats or observing waterfowl, and being busy and emotionally self-contained, he did not *need* Jane the way she felt he should. So she was charmed by Robert Aickman, who wrote her long, anguished letters about how he couldn't live without her.

At some point she and Robert became lovers. This bitterly hurt Ray but she did not dare object – she was too afraid that Robert might leave her for this dazzling young beauty who hung on his every word. Jane said that she became friends with Ray, and saw almost as much of her as she did Robert. This was not the only time she softened the impact of her presence in a marriage by claiming that the wife 'didn't mind' and that they were friends. In reality, Robert made sure his wife was out of the way as much as possible when he and Jane were together.

As for her own marriage, Jane hoped that psychotherapy might clear her mind and give her the courage to end it. She seemed to live in a state of drift, with periods of calm alternating with spells of depression, sleeplessness and irrational fears.

Her friend Marie Paneth suggested she consult a psychotherapist, Dr Oswald Schwartz who lived near Leinster Corner. Jane described him as a Freudian, and although he had age and experience on his side (he had treated Rosamond Lehmann after her affair with Goronwy Rees), Jane seems to have knocked all the professionalism out of him. The sessions went well enough at first. Jane found herself confiding in him with increasing openness, longing for his good opinion. Their last meeting took place just before Jane was leaving for New York, and she saw that he had laid out some cakes and a small bottle of wine on a table. She was totally unprepared when he pushed back his chair, fell to his knees, declared his undying love and tried to kiss her. Appalled, she threw him back with both hands and fled, without even picking up her bag and coat. Someone delivered them to Edwardes Square the following day, and she never saw Dr Schwartz again.

When Robert Aickman heard that Jane was going to New York with Peter, he erupted into a magnificent tantrum. How could she be so callous as to leave him? He sulked that she should be going to America, the country he wanted to see above all others. He could not bear the thought that she would be gone for several weeks, and doubted whether he would survive such a long separation. There were endless scenes about it. One might suspect Jane of exaggeration, but Aickman had wound himself up to such a pitch that she was obliged to spend her last night with him before leaving for New York. 'I don't know how I swung this with Pete,' she wrote. 'I suppose he knew what was going on, and chose not to talk about it.'² Perhaps he felt it hardly mattered any more, since Jane was no longer sleeping with him. Peter went ahead to Southampton with the paintings and the luggage, and her father drove her down to join him early the following morning.

They sailed to New York in early April 1946 on the *Aquitania*, with hundreds of GI brides. Peter had been commissioned to illustrate Paul Gallico's *The Snow Goose: A Story of Dunkirk*. Of the two main characters in the story, one is the artist Philip Rhayader, a disabled artist who is loosely based on Peter in so far as he lives in a lighthouse and paints birds. The other is a girl called Fritha, who brings him a wounded snow goose. Rhayader looks after the goose and as it recovers, Fritha falls in love with him; but he dies while attempting to evacuate soldiers from Dunkirk. The frontispiece was to be a picture of Fritha, and Peter scoured the ship trying to find a suitable model from among the GI brides. None of them sparked his imagination, so in the end it was Jane who posed for the picture: 'I stood for hours holding a pillow, which he turned into the wounded snow goose.'³ Peter painted the moment when Fritha has just knocked on Rhayader's door. She looks cold and watchful, cradling the heavy bird in her arms.

Jane was dazzled by New York – a blazing city compared to London, which seemed very dank and threadbare. 'It was like meeting a person dressed entirely in sequins.'⁴ The city's department stores, filled with an abundance of luxuries that had not been available in London for years, were irresistible; but there is a kind of shopping that turns into an addiction, dulling the mind and drugging the senses. She bought Havana cigars for her father, a crate of Tabasco sauce for her grandfather, skirts and coats for several of her friends and relations (who had provided her with their sizes), two years' worth of frocks for Nicola, as well as ties and shirts for Peter and masses of clothes for herself. In retrospect, she felt that spending all that money had been a way of stifling her misery; and perhaps Peter knew it too, for he never questioned the quantities of stuff she returned with, nor how much she was spending. He rarely thought about money. To him it was easily made and easily spent, and with the exchange rate at around four dollars to the pound it seemed silly not to.

Jane gorged on the abundance of eggs, butter, ice cream and huge steaks and martinis, and eagerly devoured things she had never tried before such as aubergines and cherry-stone clams – all of which left her feeling rather liverish, until she learned to curb her appetite.

At a grand dinner given by the Pulitzers she met Robert K. Haas, then vice-president of Random House, and his wife Merle who had the distinction of translating Jean de Brunhoff's Babar books into English. Robert and Merle Haas took Jane under their wing, and he arranged a meeting for her with his chief editor, Robert Linscott. Bob Linscott was a very attractive man in his fifties who took her to lunch, and told her he would be very keen to see her novel when it was finished. She had brought a red notebook containing about sixty pages of the work-in-progress to show to publishers; but at some point it was lost – most probably forgotten in the back of a taxi. This was an appalling blow at the time, as if her whole identity had suddenly been stripped from her. Strenuous efforts were made to retrace the notebook but it never came back, and Jane resigned herself to the fact that it would all have to be written again.

Bob Linscott was bowled over by this beautiful, unpredictable Englishwoman; and the light-hearted, teasing note in his admiration was far healthier for Jane than the gloomy obsessiveness of Robert Aickman. Aickman was sending her tear-stained letters every day, making her feel disloyal and guilty for enjoying herself without him. Jane and Bob Linscott remained friends for years; and in one of the first letters he wrote after her return to England, he gives a little sketch of Jane at twenty-three:

> I still see you with infinite pleasure walking along Park Avenue in your marvellous Elizabethan gown, or floating down a flight of steps as effort-lessly as in a dream, or sitting on a sofa in my hotel room with your lovely long legs tucked up under you, or leaping from bed to chair to bureau with the grace of a swan and the agility of a marmoset. In short I miss you and regret only that we did not reach earlier in our friendship the degree of intimacy at which we arrived on our last evening together. Please write to me. Your letters have the wild and casual quality of unpre-meditated art; quite improbable yet wholly convincing. Always yours, B.[5]

Peter's exhibition at the Harlow Gallery was less successful than the one at Ackerman's. He was not that well known in New York, there was no particular interest in wildfowl, and – as his biographer astutely pointed out – his mother's stage-management was missing. Their voyage back to England was complicated by a vast number of crates containing toads, snakes, tortoises and alligators that Peter's friend Jean Delacour, the head of the Bronx Zoo, had asked him to take to London.

The crates all had to go into the Scotts' cabin, which was very big and had its own bathroom, and the menagerie was fed on whole lettuces and plates of raw mince brought by the stewards under discreet silver domes. Snakes and alligators were let out (separately) to play in the bath, and one day a garter snake escaped down the plug-hole. Peter wondered gloomily whether it would emerge in the bath-room of Lord and Lady Halifax, who were on one side of them, or that of the Canadian prime minister on the other – but Jane found it a couple of days later, coiled around a tap. She had also collected a number of terrapins with painted shells, which were then sold on the street corners of New York. Knowing that they would suffocate if the paint were left on she carefully cleaned it off with nail-polish remover, washed them and put them in the bath.

The fun of looking after a cabin full of reptiles brought them together as perhaps nothing else could. Had there been more animals in their short marriage, and fewer guns and boats, perhaps it would have lasted longer, but its eventual collapse was by then inevitable. Jane's infatuation with Robert Aickman and her ambition to become a writer were pulling her away from any form of domesticity; as she put it, 'Peter wanted me to settle down to marriage and a family, so that he could pursue matters that [interested] him.'[6]

That was true, but he wasn't trying to stifle her creativity, nor was he expecting her to cook, clean and look after babies all day. What he wanted was for her to become more like his mother: a competent woman who could manage children, nanny, cook and cleaner as well as pay the bills and give dinner parties, while pursuing her own work too. Jane would become just such a woman, but not for a few years yet.

What with the crates of reptiles and trunk after trunk of Jane's purchases, it took a long time to get through customs when they docked at Southampton. When at last they were done, Kathleen took Peter back to London in her chauffeur-driven car. The rest of the welcoming party, which included Nicola, her nanny and Jane's friend Marie Paneth, were told to find their way back by train with Jane. Marie was indignant, but Jane was glad because it gave her the opportunity to telephone Robert Aickman and tell him she was back.

From then on, she and Peter lived almost separate lives in Edwardes Square. Peter was setting up the Severn Wildfowl Trust and spending weekends at Slimbridge, while Jane spent as much time as possible with the Aickmans. Sometimes the lovers spent the weekend by themselves in the cold, dusty little house in Stanmore that had been left to Robert by his father. Ray packed food for them, but remained behind; and Jane was too much in love with Robert to wonder what emotional turmoil she was going through. 'To be with someone so tender, so admiring, so knowledgeable was more than I felt I could ever have hoped for,' she wrote.[7] She also felt that she might be able to ease his black moods, perhaps even change him.

'My God, baby, you are in a mess,' wrote Bob Linscott from New York. 'I wish I knew Robert so I could diagnose the situation more accurately . . . because I have a hunch that he may be a luxury you can't afford. If a person you love can be saved, you must save him but first you must calculate the chances . . . But you are one who will always toss caution and cool advice to the winds and dance on the brink.'[8]

That winter Kathleen became ill and early in 1947 she developed leukaemia. Jane sometimes read to her as she lay frail and helpless in a hospital bed; and thought about her courage in the face of death, her anguish at leaving her sons, and how she herself had let her down in every possible way. She died in July 1947; and the following month Jane walked out of the house in Edwardes Square for the last time.

So ended Jane's marriage to Peter Scott, a man who hadn't paid her much attention when she needed it, and with whom she had little in common. But he was kind and generous, and he cared for her still – even though he knew she would never come back. As late as July 1946, he wrote: 'I'm afraid it will not please you at all if I tell you how much I love you. *Embarras de richesse* – everyone loves you and why wouldn't they – poor things.'[9]

Jane cannot be blamed for her youth and ambitions, nor for the fact that she had been pressured into motherhood before she was ready. Yet it is sad that, having left someone who still cared for her and was willing to forgive her everything, she was to spend many years searching for a man who could love her with an equal commitment.

The worst part of shutting the door on Edwardes Square was that she was leaving Nicola behind, and for the rest of her life Jane accused herself of 'abandoning' her daughter. Yet Nicola says she did not feel abandoned (not in the way that Jane had as a child, when her mother left the house for a mere few hours). Nicola was a serious and self-contained little girl of four and a half, and the centre of her world was not Jane but Nanny Buss. 'My mother was very elegant and didn't really figure in my life – she was doing her own thing.'[10] Nicola loved animals and yearned for a dog. A year or so after Jane left, her father gave her a cheerful white Pekinese called Bushy, although sadly she was not allowed to keep him for long.

There was always a distance between Nicola and her mother. Jane said it was her fault, and so it was. But Nicola took after her father, and was by nature reserved. Even as a baby, Jane recalled that she tended to stiffen when being hugged or kissed, which her mother, so physically responsive, found baffling.

Jane had refused to take a penny from Peter, something his lawyers found very hard to believe. But she was the one who had left the family home and all her responsibilities: for her own self-respect, she wanted to make her way alone. Robert Aickman had provided much of the support and encouragement that she needed to make the break. He had also helped her look for a place to live, and before Kathleen's death she had taken a lease on a maisonette in Blandford Street, above a grocery and poultry shop. It had two rooms on each of its two floors and the rent was £150 a year, but it was in terrible condition with damp, bulging walls and rotting floorboards. Jane's father had given her some shares in Howard Brothers when she married, and these brought in about £120 a year.

She knew that she needed a lodger to help pay the bills, but that no one would join her until the place was done up. Jane says that it was Peter's new assistant, Elizabeth Adams, who lent her £300 to set up on her own. Elizabeth had met the Scotts through Wayland, whom she would marry the following year. She described her job as 'full-time dogsbody [at Edwardes Square], part-running the house (put-upon cook, hysterical nanny), part being with Jane – who was on and off the boil about going; and as best I could running Peter'.[11] She had been working for the Scotts for some months when Jane departed, and as she recalled, Peter had not been too upset: 'She was so besotted with Robert Aickman, that when she left it was something of a relief.'[12] Yet she had no recollection of lending Jane £300, which was a colossal sum in those days – the equivalent of about £10,000 now. 'Thirty pounds, perhaps – but three hundred? I couldn't have done, I didn't have any money then.'[13] One possible explanation is that Peter produced the money; but knowing that Jane would not want to accept it from him, he could have asked Elizabeth to pretend it came from her.

Blandford Street was still undergoing repairs when she left and she asked her father if she might have a room in the house he now shared with Ursula in Ranulf Road, West Hampstead. Her father agreed, and while he was around Ursula was perfectly amiable – yet she left Jane in no doubt that she did not want her there. During the day this was easy enough, as she was painting Blandford Street in fiercely brilliant reds and yellows. Evenings, however, were a strain and Jane moved into Blandford Street before it was really habitable.

She could not stay with her mother, for at this stage they were barely on speaking terms. At one of the tense meetings her parents held to discuss their divorce, David let slip that he had consulted Jane on whether to buy her mother a house before or after dropping his bombshell. Kit could not forgive this collusion for a long time. And when Jane told her she was leaving Peter to become a novelist, Kit turned on her and said, 'What on earth makes you think that anyone would ever publish anything that *you* wrote?'[14] Jane brooded miserably on those words for weeks.

Kit never celebrated her daughter's success, nor her books, which seemed to her to be obsessed with sex. She resented the fact that Jane had managed to make a career for herself, and become a person in her own right. At one point Monkey told their mother that Jane, through her writing, was the only member of their family who had made a name for herself. To which Kit retorted, 'Well it's a pity she hasn't got anything better to write about.'[15]

8

The Beautiful Visit

THE ODOURS OF damp and decay in Blandford Street had been stifled by coats of paint and coconut matting, but living above a poulterer was not for the squeamish. The North brothers who owned the shop would pluck, singe and draw the birds in their basement, and the resulting faint but perceptible stench of blood, guts and burned feathers rose upwards and clung to everything. Jane asked Jill Balcon whether she would like to share the house, but Jill declined; her first lodger was a painter, called Joanna Dowling.

Work on the novel was progressing, and from New York Bob Linscott was encouraging: 'I love your description of the novel – treacle and plum pudding, rich but indigestible. Do send it . . . and if it isn't finished send what is.'[1] But she also had to find work, and her first job was to be the part-time secretary of the Inland Waterways Association or IWA, of which Aickman was chairman. She shared the work with the long-suffering Ray, typing up the hundreds of letters and reports that Aickman dictated to local councils, landowners and the hostile officialdom of British Waterways (they had been nationalized in 1947).

Tom Rolt, an engineer whose book *Narrow Boat* (1944) had originally sparked Aickman's interest in the canals, was every bit as committed to the cause. However, he felt that the limited resources of the association should be concentrated on saving one branch of the system at a time, which led to bitter disputes with Aickman, who held that the IWA should fight on all fronts at once. In the long run this policy was justified; and in 1951 Rolt was elbowed out of the association he had helped to found. There was no doubt that Aickman was obsessive, demanding and utterly ruthless in getting what he wanted – but these qualities made him a brilliant campaigner. He knew he was right and never took no for an answer, and anyone who has ever steered a narrow-boat down a quiet English canal owes him, and Tom Rolt, a huge debt of gratitude.

In the two years after she left Peter, Jane travelled across the canal network with the Rolts and the Aickmans, and her friends James and Anthea Sutherland. In one letter to Anthea, written in the summer of 1948 shortly after the Sutherlands had left the boat, she described what was happening on the Huddersfield Narrow Canal:

> We have had a very tiring day. One lock gate was completely rotten, and when the lock was filled, it quietly caved in. Wilf mended it up with planks, and we got through in two hours. We have done 22 locks and three miles but the locks were if anything worse than the ones we did together. Tomorrow we tackle the environs of Huddersfield . . . Everything else is pretty rocky and very tiring (at least to me) but as the cabin is rather full, I cannot say very much more. I spent a really awful day cleaning the boat . . . I will write again if possible, but it is not easy. I seem to do far more work than when you were here, and wish, for many reasons, that you were both back.[2]

The main reason for wishing them back was that Robert was being impossible, and expected everything to be done for him. 'The only thing he wanted to do in a boat was to steer it and, in the beginning at least, he was very bad at it. This made him cross, he quarrelled with me, and argued with Tom.' She often found herself wondering, '*Why* does he have to spoil something so exciting and enjoyable with black moods and scenes?'[3]

The IWA took up a great deal of her time. Originally it had brought in £2.10 a week, but the work grew as the months went on. Jane also modelled occasionally for *Vogue*, which paid well, and wrote a couple of unsigned pieces for Siriol Hugh-Jones, the features editor. She wished she had more time to devote to her novel, the ending of which was proving very tricky. This could have been because it had been written without any structure, with each section developing out of the one before; but by early 1949, she had managed to bring it to a rather improbable conclusion.

Jane was at last beginning to come out of her infatuation for Aickman, and chafe at his desire to control every aspect of her life. He liked to see her severely dressed in dark skirts with white shirts and black ties, and hated her to have friends outside his circle. He also never let her forget that he was very depressed and in danger of going mad, which kept everyone around him in a state of protective anxiety. 'One of the most exhausting aspects of all this,' wrote Jane, 'was that life was chronically *serious*. We weren't supposed to be either light-hearted or happy about anything much.'[4]

She saw Nicola when Nanny had the day off. Nicola recalled that her special job at Blandford Street was to clean the dusty leaves of the rubber plant with milk, and as they were always thick with dust when she came again she assumed she was not in her mother's house very often. She has no recollection of Jane reading to her, nor did her mother – always an enthusiastic cook – ever make her a birthday cake. When they walked together in the street, Jane walked very fast so Nicola had to trot to keep up. Her mother was always pulling away from her, and she felt like an encumbrance.

A friend of Jane's had once remarked, 'You do all the dull things that mothers have to do for their children, but you never have any fun with her.'[5] Jane knew she *ought* to feel more for her child, *ought* to rejoice in her company; and her feelings of guilt translated into resentment rather than a resolve to do better. In her memoir, Jane wistfully noted Nicola's love of dancing and the way she instinctively reached out to any living creature she came across. But as her daughter was growing up, Jane shared very few of her joys or sorrows – even though she was scrupulous about taking her to the doctor or the dentist.

Robert could hardly object to Jane seeing her daughter; but she was also spending less and less time at Gower Street. She no longer idolized Robert as a lover but he was still an emotional responsibility, and she enjoyed being needed. Their relationship carried on long after it had gone stale, at least for her, while he was not told about the new man in her life for many months.

On the last day of 1948 Jane was invited to a New Year's Eve party by Dosia and Barry Craig. Although the party was given in Barry's spacious studio, everyone was in full evening dress: Jane wore a beautiful grey evening gown that Peter had given her, and an opal and diamond necklace with earrings to match. A dark and attractive man asked her to dance, and they both found they weren't very good at it.

Late the following morning, she was shaken awake by her lodger Joanna Dowling. There was a man at the door with a big black poodle, who said he had come to find out whether Jane was as beautiful by day as she was by night. Puffy and hung over, Jane wisely decided to stay under the bedclothes. But the man left his card, and invited her to dinner that evening. His name was Michael Behrens. From Dosia she learned that he was a merchant banker married to a woman called Felicity, and they had three sons.

When she arrived at his house in Hanover Terrace, the door was ajar and Mozart was playing somewhere upstairs. She walked up to a large and dimly lit drawing room. Michael Behrens (there was no sign of his wife) rose from a sofa, mixed her a martini, and announced that they were going out to dinner. 'As he held out the glass to me,' she wrote, 'I realised with a shock that I was physically attracted to him. It made me extremely shy and breathless.'[6] By the end of dinner, at the Étoile in Charlotte Street, he was captivated – and Jane was in love.

Behrens was a financier who was fascinated by making money, and he loved spending it too. He collected contemporary art and sculpture, and at one time or another he had pieces by Marino Marini, Elizabeth Frink and Frank Dobson, among others. He enjoyed surrounding himself with artists and architects, and the role of patron suited him: not just as a collector, but as a finder of other potential buyers for his protégés. Among his friends were the architects Hugh Casson and Denys Lasdun, and the illustrator Edward Ardizzone.

In the year he met Jane, Michael Behrens bought Culham Court near Henley-on-Thames: a magnificent estate with a large farm, and a commodious house whose gardens went down to the river. Michael had no particular interest in his children, who were kept well away from adult life downstairs: the boys ate all their meals in the nursery till they were about ten. To their youngest boy, Jeremy, it seemed that his parents' marriage was unusually controlled and unemotional, more of a partnership. They never seemed to have rows, and were together only on holiday or at weekends. Michael lived in London during the week, while Felicity's energies were devoted to the farm and gardens of Culham Court.

The perks of being the mistress of such a man were considerable: Michael bought her expensive presents. He indulged her taste for antique jewellery and took her not only to smart restaurants but for weekends in Paris, too. Sometimes he took a room for them at Claridge's if he wanted to see her between business trips. Jane admired the way he took control of everything, and knew exactly what he wanted. The downside was that while he found her beautiful and fascinating, she had been assigned to a particular compartment of his life and there she was expected to stay. A mutual friend of theirs said that 'He thought of Jane as a wonderful possession – he was a great collector.'[7]

A few years later, Jane described his particular combination of brilliance and ruthlessness in the character of Conrad Fleming, whose marriage to Antonia is the subject of *The Long View*:

> His incessant curiosity enabled him to amass a quantity of knowledge which his ingenuity and judgement combined to disseminate, or withhold, to the end of power over ideas and people. He made money out of both without people clearly recognizing it, since they were usually so dazzled by his attention that their own ends were blinded. He had a heart when he cared to use it; but on the whole, he did not care in the least about other people and neither expected nor desired them to care about him.[8]

He admired Jane and paid her compliments, but there was little sentimentality about their relationship. In an early letter of May 1949 he wrote, on office stationery: 'Jane, I am at last organized. I return to London at about 5pm and will proceed to Mr Claridge on arrival: I will then ring you. The rest of the day is yours – M. 5pm of course on Saturday but it's Air France so we may be late.'[9]

That they were having an affair was supposed to be a great secret: he wanted to keep it from his wife, while Jane wanted to keep it from Robert – not so much for his sake as for the long-suffering Ray's. At the same time, Michael very much wanted her for himself, and she was under pressure to cut free of this tail-end of her past at the earliest opportunity. Jane tried to explain what a difficult situation it was.

'I owe [Ray], at least, a good deal,' she wrote to Michael. 'I did inadvertently make her very unhappy for a long time and I cannot now simply leave her to cope with the debris I should leave behind. *Then* I didn't know (as I never saw her and was told a great many lies about their relationship) what I was doing, but now I do know.'

The Aickman problem was not something that could be solved in a moment. She admitted that he was a 'reminder that most of my troubles are due to impulses which seem too strong to admit of [sic] consideration at the time . . . I warned you that I was too much trouble. I do wish I wasn't . . . If you don't want to see me again, could you let me know, however briefly?'[10] But Michael did want to see her again, and was willing to put up with her complicated past.

In the spring of 1949, Robert – who acted as her literary agent – sent the manuscript of her novel to the publisher Jonathan Cape. It was called *The Beautiful Visit* and a few weeks later, to everyone's astonishment, it was accepted. Jane was asked to go and have lunch with Jonathan Cape himself, in his flat near the Cape offices in Bedford Square.

Jonathan Cape, with his partner G. Wren Howard, had founded the publishing company in 1921. They employed brilliant readers, including David Garnett and Rupert Hart-Davis; and over the course of his long career, Jonathan Cape published T.E. Lawrence, James Joyce, Christopher Isherwood and Ian Fleming, as well as American writers who included Ernest Hemingway and Eugene O'Neill. He was tall, craggy and supremely self-confident. As Jane came into his sitting room he said, 'I've just made rather a strong martini, very good for ladies who are menstruating.'[11] It was not a promising start but Jane chose to ignore it; after all, he had accepted her novel. As they had lunch, he said it would benefit from some cutting, but Jane was adamant that she did not want it cut at all. 'Well, I will publish it as it stands,' he said, 'and you will learn that way.' As soon as lunch was over he made a pass at her, and she found herself being chased round the dining-room table. Being far more nimble, she evaded him. Cape admitted defeat with a good grace, and gave her £50 advance against royalties.

Although Jane did not want the novel cut, she was willing to revise certain passages and the revisions were completed and delivered that summer before she went on holiday. In fact it was supposed to be something of a rest-cure, since Jane was wrung out from finishing the book, and very depressed by the dead-end of her relationship with Michael.

The emotional strain had resulted in her being unable to eat: for days or sometimes weeks on end, she could barely force herself to swallow anything. She says very little about this illness. She told me she thought she had suffered from a kind of mild anorexia, and perhaps she had. But in a later novel (*Getting It Right*, 1982) she gives such a harrowing description of both the mental and physical pain of binge eating, that it is hard to believe she wasn't writing from experience. I asked her if she had ever been a binge eater. She dismissed the idea with a casual shrug, but I still wonder.

Michael was forced to accept the continued presence of Robert Aickman in her life, but he had made it very clear that she was never going to be first in his. When she was driven by her own feelings to plead for more than he wanted to give, his anger was swift and, one imagines, pretty cutting. 'My darling Jenny, I never mean to hurt you – I only want you to be happy – much happier anyhow than you are. But when you are very tired your emotional requirements of course increase and my capacity to give – low at any time – decreases . . . So I write – a rare occurrence – to tell you you are loved and cherished, desired, longed for and in two weeks about to be very much missed.'[12]

This letter is undated, but it is likely that it was written just before Jane went on holiday to the south of France, in the late summer of 1949. Her hosts were René and Doreen Zunz, who were friends of her new stepmother: Ursula and David had married some months before. As the Zunzes were very hard-up, her father had suggested that she go as a paying guest, and he would bear the cost. She got a lift with Wayland and Elizabeth Young, who had married in 1948 and were motoring down to Italy. Jane enjoyed the journey, although unlike the Youngs, she preferred wandering round local markets to visiting churches. They dropped her off at the Zunzes' house in Mazargues, a suburb to the south-east of Marseille.

Doreen Zunz was English, her husband Jewish. He did not talk about the difficulties he had had during the war; but the couple – particularly Doreen – had never got over the death of their daughter Betty, who had succumbed to meningitis aged twenty. Doreen could talk of little else but her loss, which had brought on her chronic ill health; however her husband René thought that she might get better if she were only willing to make the effort.

Rich and elaborate meals were served by someone who came in to cook but Jane couldn't eat them. 'I'd sit before an immense juicy steak and delicious salad, trying to swallow the first pieces of meat, my stomach heaving, and wanting to cry from embarrassment.'[13] However she saw that the Zunzes were enjoying this unusual abundance, and she was happy to see them making the most of it. They were longing to take her swimming and sightseeing, but Jane was a very apathetic guest. All she wanted to do was to sit in their little garden, and write long letters to Michael. His letters were brief and to the point: 'It is too long till you come back lots of little emptinesses caused by your absence. Enjoy yourself – Do nothing and go to bed early. Eat a lot and drink a lot, lie in the sun and don't work: above all don't work. When you return we will do something memorable.'[14]

Towards the end of her stay with the Zunzes, she became aware of a tension between René and Doreen. René told her that he had fallen in love with her, and Doreen knew it. Jane was uncomfortably aware that she had been flirting with him; but she told René that he only thought himself in love with her because the Zunzes did not see enough people, and because Doreen would not pull herself together. She forced a confrontation between the three of them, and when Doreen said that she had ruined their lives, Jane threatened to leave there and then – at which their tone suddenly changed and they begged her not to go. This is a story that appears more than once in Jane's fiction, where a couple who have been getting along well enough are thrown into turmoil when a younger, more innocent (and usually more beautiful) third party comes into their lives.

Whether or not Jane felt better for her sojourn in the south of France, she had much to look forward to in the new year of 1950, which was going to see the publication of her first novel. Robert Aickman found it hard to rejoice, despite being her literary agent. The fact she was going to be a published author ahead of him was bad enough, but even more galling was that Bob Linscott had accepted *The Beautiful Visit* for publication by Random House in America. So far, Aickman's only published work was a few critical essays for the magazine *Nineteenth Century*. Linscott, on the other hand, was delighted. He wrote from New York to tell Jane that 'I can't tell you how happy your novel has made me. It's a lovely book, better than I dared hope . . . Don't expect too much in the way of sales, but it should at least have a very good press.'[15] Seven months later he was able to tell her that they had sold 2,500 copies.[16]

Shortly afterwards she sent him some publicity photographs, which gave Linscott a jolt – for Jane had cut off her abundant, dark blonde hair that had required so much styling and curling. Now it was severely short, and her off-centre widow's peak was hidden by a fringe. She hoped it would make her look more serious.

The book's English edition came out in the early spring, just before her twenty-seventh birthday. Her father wrote her a warm letter of congratulation, saying he would buy at least six copies – although he wasn't sure he would be able to read the whole book. Her mother read it, and told Monkey that it was full of nothing but sex. Michael took her to Paris for the weekend so she wouldn't have to see the first reviews; but as it turned out, the book's reception was very encouraging.

In the *New Statesman and Nation*, Antonia White wrote that 'Miss Howard is interesting and original. She has true imagination and a kind of sensuous power . . . Hers seems to me to be a remarkable talent, still in the awkward age, full of angles and scowls and posturings before the looking-glass but potentially far more exciting than that of many neater and better mannered first-novelists.'[17] The *Times Literary Supplement* was equally gratifying: 'Such a story of growing up is difficult to present convincingly, but Miss Howard has succeeded in tracing her heroine's steps and writing of her, without falsity or sentimentality, at each stage, not from the outside, but as she was then.'[18]

Yet the most perceptive and useful criticism came from Cecil Day-Lewis, in a letter written a few months after publication. Overall, he did not think she had a tight enough grasp of the 'direction a book is, or ought to be, going in; the meaning of the lives it is concerned with. I don't think, in your novel, the direction or the meaning are compelling enough.' However, he did admire 'your power to convey "the feel" of different kinds of happiness, and particularly the happiness special to a group of people: this power is *not* common . . . and you are charitable to your characters without the sense of strain one often gets when a novelist tries to be fair.'[19]

★

The Beautiful Visit grew out of the unhappiness of Jane's first marriage, and it asks the questions that were preoccupying her then. How do women find a place in the world if they are brought up unprepared and uneducated for anything but marriage? Does coupledom really bring fulfilment? Is it possible to find an identity outside it?

The unnamed narrator, daughter of an unsuccessful composer and a kind but timid mother, is sixteen when the book opens just before the First World War. The girl feels trapped in the threadbare tedium of their life in Kensington, and there seems no hope of breaking out of it.

A new world is revealed when she spends Christmas with distant cousins, the Lancings, and she is swept into a country-house life of pleasure and parties. She admires the independence of one cousin of about her own age called Elspeth; but she is particularly fascinated by Deborah Lancing, who enchants everyone with her flawless beauty. A young man called Rupert Laing joins her on a walk, and pokes fun at her naive faith in love and marriage. Her ignorance and inexperience make it easy for him to twist her words and make her blush. The scenes between Rupert and the girl reflect something of the encounters between Jane and Seth Holt, although Rupert is a more attractive and less dangerous character. He gives her a chaste kiss on the lips at the end of the walk, and tells her she may visit him. Rupert knows she is taking his casual attentions far too seriously, which is why he ignores her and flirts with the beautiful Deborah at the dance a day later. There is nothing like a dance to get a young girl's hopes up, so they have that much further to fall.

The heroine runs away from home to find Rupert with whom she thinks she is in love, only to find him living with a Spanish mistress whom he treats like a servant. 'Does she work for you?' asks the narrator. 'No,' he laughs. 'She just lives with me. I suppose it comes to much the same thing . . . I don't pay her, you see. She loves me.' 'As though you were married?'[20] she asks – good question. Once the romance has worn off, both marriage and cohabitation seem to mean little more than servitude for the female half of the couple. The following day Rupert leaves to join up, and the narrator has no choice but to go home.

Seeking escape again, she becomes a paid companion to an old lady called Mrs Border, living in seclusion in Sussex with her parrot. There is something very unnerving about the oppressive, overheated house and the maniacal laughter that occasionally peals out in the middle of the night, and she returns once more to London.

The war scarcely impinges until she falls in love with an officer called Ian Graham. He is kind and sensitive, the very opposite of Rupert. Over the few days of his leave they fall in love, but it's too good to last: almost immediately after his return to the front, Graham is killed in action. Rupert, however, returns at the end of the war and asks her to come and spend another Christmas with the Lancings. Gerald, the son of the house, is dead, while the beautiful Deborah is married with two children.

Far from being happy, Deborah takes no interest in her family and seems trapped in a kind of restless despair. Her husband Aubrey is one of those people who can't put a foot wrong. Arriving late for tea in the nursery,

> he begged not to interrupt; managed to be introduced to Rupert and me; to salute his elder child; to inquire respectfully of Nanny after his younger; to meet Deb's eye with affectionate admiration; and to seat himself at the table next to her with the kind of appetite Nanny would expect of him.[21]

In other words, he is Peter Scott; and Deborah – selfish, petulant and miserable – is Jane. The narrator overhears them arguing. Deborah says, 'I thought marriage meant more freedom, not less. I didn't know it meant years of plans, and having children, and sitting by myself all day.' She finds plans and arrangements stifling because they mean 'that I know what I shall be doing in five, ten, twenty years' time'.[22]

Thinking about what she has overheard, the narrator says that

> It was easier to feel sorry for Aubrey, but, without knowing precisely why, I felt more sorry for Deb ... At least Aubrey knew what he wanted, even if he was not getting it; while she, like I, was consumed with an aimless desire for something just beyond her imagination.[23]

It is because she can see this in herself that, when Rupert asks the narrator to marry him, she has no hesitation in turning him down.

The ending of the book is not very convincing and required a new beginning – in which the narrator wakes up on board a boat and neither she, nor the reader, have any idea where they are. Yet despite this awkward top and tailing, the novel has an impressive range. Quite apart from its big theme of a woman's identity both inside and outside marriage, it also touches on the hidden sensitivities of class; on how friendships are made and destroyed; on the profound significance of clothes; and how, if resentment and discontent do not find a release, they can build up like toxins and drive people to the brink of madness.

Jane also introduces her readers to a set of character templates that she will re-fashion again and again in her books. Rupert Laing and Ian Graham are at opposing ends of a masculine emotional range. Rupert is of the type one might call a seductive manipulator. He is expert at the sort of teasing that can harden into bullying, and seduces with a commanding confidence; but although this has its attractions, the instability it hides is eventually revealed. Ian, on the other hand, is the wise devotee. He is the protector of innocence, and combines the tenderness of a lover with the guiding wisdom of a mentor.

On the emotional range of female characters, there is a still point in the middle which is occupied by the ingénue – almost always a self-portrait. She is innocent but perceptive; and if she is swept off her feet by the seductive controller, she takes comfort from the wise devotee. She does most of the learning in the novel, but she often startles people because her innocence gives her the ability to see things as they are. If the ingénue is at the mid-point on the scale, at one end there is the strong and independent woman, in this case Elspeth, who is clear-sighted and speaks her mind without hesitation. At the other end is the spoilt beauty, in this case Deborah. She is as dazzled by her looks as everyone else, and feels they entitle her to all the world has to offer – so she is always doomed to disappointment.

Jonathan Cape invited Jane to an authors' party at 30 Bedford Square that spring, an occasion that marked her first introduction into literary London. She had dressed with great care, in a shirt of duck-egg blue satin with a high neck that buttoned up with rows of tiny pea-sized buttons, and she entered the room trembling with fear and excitement. Jonathan Cape introduced her to several people including Cyril Connolly, who was standing in a group with Rosamond Lehmann and Cecil Day-Lewis. Connolly was fascinated by her shirt: 'Do all those buttons actually *do up*?' he asked.

Jane was so overawed to be among so many well-known literati that she scarcely spoke a word – although she did recall that Rosamond

Lehmann glared at her, as well she might. Lehmann was then in a state of raging despair, for her nine-year affair with Cecil Day-Lewis was over. She had come to assume that Day-Lewis would eventually leave his first wife, Mary, for her; but in the new year, Cecil had told Rosamond that he had fallen in love with Jane's friend, Jill Balcon. He was going to marry Jill, a woman twenty-four years younger than her – and Rosamond could not bring herself to believe it, because to face the truth was to admit defeat. Instead she told herself that Cecil was in the grip of some transient madness, and insisted that he and Jill should neither see nor communicate with each other for three months.

At this stage Jane was a very close friend and confidante of Jill's, and they talked a great deal as the drama unfolded. 'I knew that the whole idea of the separation was wrong,' Jane told Day-Lewis's biographer Peter Stanford. 'It was like throwing fire on the oil [sic] . . . She was bowled over by him. Especially with her intense reverence for poetry, his attention was overwhelming for her. And he had clearly fallen very much in love with Jill and felt he had to make this move.'[24]

During the lovers' enforced separation, Jill asked Jane to have lunch with Cecil. The lunch took place at Antoine's in Charlotte Street. Jane had met Day-Lewis at the Cape party, but she had not taken in how attractive he was. 'I remember thinking that he really did look like everyone's idea of a poet,' she wrote. 'He combined good looks with urbanity and romanticism, plus a beautiful voice with a beguiling Anglo-Irish accent.' She also discovered that he was a brilliant storyteller, and that when he laughed – which was very often – 'his beautiful craggy face would break into volcanic fissures of amusement.'[25] He talked about Jill and how much he loved her, and how she was under huge pressure from her parents to end their relationship. Her father, Michael Balcon, was scandalized that his daughter should be living with an impecunious poet who had abandoned his wife, two sons and a mistress to be with her. Balcon wanted nothing more to do with his errant daughter until she had come to her senses, and he forbade his wife to see her either.

After their lunch, Cecil wrote Jane a letter to say how much he appreciated her efforts on their behalf. 'I must say it's a great comfort to me, now I have met you properly, to know that Jill has you to support her. If you feel at any time that this parent-trouble is getting too much for her, please let me know, and I would come to her at once: her peace of mind is much more important to me than any three-month guarantee.'[26]

It was around this time, at a party given by Jill in her flat in Pimlico, that Jane met a designer called Audrey Dunlop who had been living in Paris and now needed a room in London. They got on well; and since Jane's previous lodger Joanna was leaving, Audrey took her place. Jane loved giving dinner parties, for which Michael often provided the wine; and among her circle were Wayland and Elizabeth Young, the painters Bateson Mason and Michael Ayrton, Elisabeth Balchin whom Ayrton later married, James and Anthea Sutherland, the Aickmans and Jill Balcon. Michael Behrens brought a young cousin called Jeremy Harris, who started going out with Audrey and they eventually married in 1954.

The most vivid memories of the house in Blandford Street come from Audrey's friend Joy Law, who had a job with the publishing firm of Longmans. Joy was living with her parents; but because of tensions at home, she spent most of her evenings and weekends with Jane and Audrey. Joy described herself at the time as rather prickly and anti-social, 'but Jane's unfailing kindness . . . did much to put me at my ease'. She remembered Jane as a very dramatic presence, both in her looks and her seriousness. 'She had an idea of how she ought to be, and was terribly earnest about everything.'[27]

Audrey's main source of income was the *Daily Mail*. She was very good at designing simple, eye-catching clothes, and had a weekly craft and dressmaking column. Jane was doing whatever typing and editing jobs she could find, as well as making time for her own writing. Joy recalled that Jane would read the day's work to them in the evenings, and it rarely came to more than a paragraph or two: 'She wrote very slowly, and cared about every word.'[28]

Jane and Audrey lived on toast and herrings which were kept on the window sill, for they had no fridge. They would get up late, and 'drink coffee in our identical grey silk pyjamas and earnestly discuss our feelings for Michael and Jeremy and theirs for us . . . We spent hours every evening getting ready for our dates, washing our hair, doing our faces, choosing and discarding clothes. Audrey, after her *séjour* in Paris, took clothes very seriously, and taught me that one couldn't take too much trouble.'[29]

★

Nicola was still living at Edwardes Square with Nanny Buss; but Peter was seldom there, and Jane wanted to find her daughter a home in which she would feel part of a real family. The answer came through Michael Behrens, whose cousin Josie Baird was also his next-door neighbour in Hanover Terrace. She and her husband (another Michael) had two children, and were about to have a third. Their house was large and on several floors; and while Josie was young, she tired easily and had a persistent cough. She felt she really needed a nanny, although she was not sure they could afford one – but she could if she were to share the costs with Jane. It was the perfect solution: Nicola and Nanny Buss would go and live in Hanover Terrace. The arrangement was a success, and Nicola lived with the Bairds for two or three years.

Like almost everyone, Josie was struck by Jane's looks; but she also found her very irritating and unreliable. Jane was supposed to come and lend her a hand on Nanny's day off, but she was usually late or had to leave early. And when Josie asked her to give the children their tea or put them to bed, she would come down an hour later to find that no tea had been made or eaten, and no one was in bed. At that stage Josie had no idea that Michael and Jane were having an affair. There was a terrible moment when she had a dinner party to which she invited Jane, Michael and his wife Felicity, and one or two others; and she could not understand why the company was so ill at ease till the penny dropped.

Three years later, however, Josie was to be profoundly grateful for Jane's friendship. The persistent cough turned out to be undiagnosed tuberculosis, and so serious was Josie's condition that she was going to have to have a lung removed – under local anaesthetic, because they feared her heart might not be strong enough for a general one. Jane had no idea how bad things were when she came to see Josie at the University Hospital in Gower Street: but she saw immediately that Josie was terrified of the operation, and feeling very lonely. 'I'll come back every day,' said Jane. I bet you won't, thought Josie, but she did. Jane also asked the consultant if she might keep Josie company for the operation – could she not scrub up and don surgical clothes, and hold her hand through the ordeal? This was forbidden but Josie was very touched that she had offered.

Josie was weeks in hospital, and none of her children was allowed to visit – nor in the nursing home in Midhurst where she went afterwards to convalesce. Jane took huge trouble: she got Adrian to write stories for his mother, and taught Josie how to do patchwork and embroidery. Josie never forgot Jane's kindness. They stayed friends ever after, and every year Josie sent her a case of wine for Christmas.[30]

In August 1950 the Inland Waterways Association staged a Rally of Boats at Market Harborough, to which was attached (at Robert Aickman's insistence) an arts festival. It was a great success, although Jane was furious with Aickman for denying her the opportunity to see her work performed by real actors. A play was to be performed in the Assembly Rooms, and Robert – who headed the arts festival side – chose a sexy little farce called *Springtime for Henry* by Benn Levy. (One of the actors was Peter Scott, who to Jane's surprise turned out to be rather good.) But because the play was not very long, it was decided that there would be time for a curtain-raiser too. Jane had written a two-hander called *Illusion*. She showed it to the principal actors, Nicolette Bernard and Barry Morse – both professionals who, according to Jane, wanted to do it. But Robert, still smarting with jealousy that Cape had accepted her novel, couldn't bear the idea that a play of hers should be performed and insisted they perform something else.

A month later, she wrote to Anthea Sutherland asking if she could come and stay because 'the R[obert] business is so straining and painful that I would like to be out of London'.[31] And yet she still hadn't broken with him entirely: he clung to his role as an emotional responsibility.

In fact it was thanks to Jane that Robert finally made his debut between hard covers. He was beginning to develop the 'strange stories' that were to make his name in the sixties and seventies, although so far he had been unable to find a publisher; but Cape agreed to take a collection of six stories, three by Robert and three by Jane who, inspired by him, was also rather taken with the genre and its chilling effects. It is possible that the section concerning Mrs Border in *The Beautiful Visit* might have begun as a story in this genre, before being reshaped into the novel. It has a different feel from the rest of the book, and the narrator's night terrors are built up just as they would be in a ghost story.

A collection of sinister stories might not have been a very tempting prospect for a publisher the year before, when they were both unknown; but *The Beautiful Visit* had sold well, and in the spring of 1951 it won the John Llewellyn Rhys Memorial Prize. This prize was one of only three literary awards that existed at the time, the other two being the Hawthornden and the James Tait Black, both founded in 1919.

Jonathan Cape had entered *The Beautiful Visit*, and the announcement was made in a dusky little sitting room of a house in Maida Avenue. The shortlist consisted of Jane and two others. She was naturally overwhelmed at having won, although she was taken aback when Jonathan Cape said that, as her publisher, he was entitled to take 10 per cent. Luckily this was overheard by the ladies of the judging committee, who were scandalized by his predatory behaviour. Cape backed off, pretending it had been a joke. Then, a few days later, Robert Aickman sent her a letter to say that as her literary agent, he was expecting 10 per cent too. Jane wrote an angry letter back. He was not going to lay hands on a penny of her prize money, and she did not want him to be her agent any longer.

With Jane's consent Peter was filing for a divorce, on the grounds that she had deserted him without cause three years previously. His petition passed smoothly through the courts and the decree absolute was granted on 12 July. He and Philippa Talbot-Ponsonby, the woman who was about to become his second wife, were in Iceland on the trail of the pink-footed goose at the time. They probably had no idea that he was now free to marry, and neither did Jane until she emerged from the Tube to see the newspaper headline: 'Peter Scott Divorces Actress Wife'.

The collection of six stories, entitled *We Are for the Dark*, came out that autumn, and who wrote which was left a mystery. The book did not arouse much interest at the time, although it was to become much sought after by collectors and it included one of the best stories Jane ever wrote.

This was called 'Three Miles Up'. Two friends, Clifford and John, are taking a canal holiday and so far it has not gone well: neither of them is very experienced at handling locks and narrow-boats, and they are becoming very tense and quarrelsome. Then

Clifford comes across a girl, dressed in a black shirt and slacks, sleeping under a tree. She is called Sharon and she joins them on the boat. Sharon restores domestic order and soothes their nerves, although she never reveals much about herself. It is only when they come to a junction, and take a branch of the canal that does not seem to appear on the map, that things begin to go quietly and horribly wrong.

'Perfect Love' is much longer, a novella set at the turn of the century. At the heart of the story is what binds an impoverished young Italian girl with a beautiful voice to a sinister Man in Black who lures her into his carriage where some Faustian pact is made. Given the best singing tuition available, the girl becomes Mielli, the greatest soprano of her generation. But she is always afraid, dreading the day when the Man in Black will appear again. He does, and from then on she is haunted by the ghost of a child. No one can see it but her and like a real child it grows, becoming ever more diabolical and destructive.

This work is, at least in part, an exercise in different voices: for Mielli's tale is told through a series of different narrators, none of whom is in possession of the whole story. Yet Mielli's horror of real children, the way she viscerally rejects the ghost that is both part of her and not part of her, are perhaps echoes of Jane's sense of having been hijacked into having a child before she was ready.

The last story of Jane's in the collection was 'Left Luggage', which is the most conventional of the three: about a woman abandoned long ago, whose cloying spirit is locked in a dressing case that refuses to be left behind. In an introduction to a later edition of Jane's uncanny tales, Glen Cavaliero observes that all her stories 'play upon the peculiar anxiety dependant on departures, the clutch of fear at the prospect of abandoning ground base, of leaving home'.[32]

Jane hoped that Bob Linscott would publish the stories, but he found their elliptical and enigmatic elements irritating and thought an American audience would too. In 'Perfect Love', for example, 'there was evidence of an actual child . . . but what is its relevance and relation to Mielli? . . . I am only trying to discover the laws of verity and causality.'[33] And to avoid any ambiguity, he also insisted that the heroine of *The Beautiful Visit* have a name – so in the American edition she was called Lavinia.

He understood how difficult it was for a novelist to please readers on both sides of the Atlantic, but if she wanted American readers she would have to accommodate them.

There's a real difference in the fictional techniques of our two nations. We tend to over-accentuate structure and the story line; you, tone and level of intelligence. At worst American novelists become . . . all matter, no manner; you, all manner, no matter. The best of both countries combine the best of both traditions. But it makes it very perplexing when a novelist of either country is judged by the editor of another.[34]

That autumn, Jane made the final break with Robert Aickman. She discussed it with Ray, and felt bad that Robert would probably take out his rage at being abandoned on his wife. Ray said it couldn't be helped, and did not blame Jane in the least: in fact she was not sure how much more of him she could take herself.

Robert was as furious as Jane had feared, but she did notice that there seemed to be more anger than grief in his reaction. He felt utterly betrayed, he said – and she was relieved to find that she did not try to justify herself, or soften the blow. After the publication of *We Are for the Dark*, she owed him nothing more. Her defection meant that she could no longer work for the Inland Waterways Association, but that was as nothing compared to her feeling of liberation.

After the publication of *We Are for the Dark,* Jane was approached by the literary agent A.D. Peters who said he wanted to represent her. There were not many literary agencies around then, and even fewer with such a good reputation. A.D. Peters (the initials stood to Augustus Dudley but he never used either name) already represented Hilaire Belloc, J.B. Priestley, Evelyn Waugh and Cecil Day-Lewis. Their first lunch together was awkward and marked by long pauses, for both he and Jane were painfully shy. Did she have another idea for a novel? Yes, she did. It was a love story, but told backwards: moving from the moment when the couple are about to separate, to the moment when they first meet. He seemed dubious about this, but said, 'You must do what you want.'

He was not the only one who thought that telling a story back-wards flew in the face of storytelling: how could you build up any dramatic tension or capture the reader's curiosity if all was revealed from page one? But Jane, so unsure of herself on so many levels, was not to be budged.

If she did have her doubts, perhaps she remembered the letter that Cecil Day-Lewis had written to her that summer, when he said that he thought her next novel 'might be really good. It all depends, I'm sure, on luck – whether you find a subject which can possess you: when one does, I imagine that technical problems more or less solve themselves.'[35]

9

Between Courage and Despair

As far back as 1950, Bob Linscott had written to warn Jane of how difficult it would be to write the story backwards: not in order to dissuade her, but to point out that if she felt it wasn't working she should not be too proud to turn back.[1]

The warnings from both Linscott and A.D. Peters would have been easier to handle had she not found it so difficult to apply herself to the task. Largely educated at home by the indulgent Miss Cobham, she had never had to develop the self-discipline that trains schoolchildren to deliver essays on time or sit exams. Sometimes she felt she was not giving her novel enough time and energy, while at others, it hardly seemed worth the effort.

Jane's main preoccupation was Michael Behrens, from whom she wanted both more and less than he was prepared to give. He never spent a full night in Blandford Street, and did not appreciate its bohemian squalor. He wanted her to move to a more comfortable flat, and suggested that he help her out with the rent. Jane refused. She enjoyed the fine restaurants and presents, but did not want to be treated as a *poule de luxe*.

She brooded a lot about love, and how men and women seemed to have such different expectations of it. Jane loved Michael: her brother Monkey thought that perhaps he was the most important love of her life. What she wanted from him was that passionate, all-absorbing affection that always eluded her. Just as he was the centre of her world, she wanted to be the centre of his.

Michael, although very fond of her, was never going to let that happen. Absorbed as he was by his interests and his work, the idea of living closely with Jane and her turbulent feelings was the last thing he wanted. As far as he was concerned their relationship was just as it should be. She was there whenever he asked, looking not only

98

beautiful but perfectly dressed and groomed. He wished she was as comfortable in their relationship as he was himself. He wished she wouldn't take things so seriously, although her emotional neediness was easily subdued when it got out of hand and she could usually be coaxed into a more cheerful frame of mind.

However he could not stop her feeling increasingly restless and miserable as August approached, when he and Felicity took their annual holiday in the south of France. Michael refused to give in to her moods or feel sorry for her, rather the opposite: he would take Jane shopping, to help him choose presents for Felicity and their guests. This scene appears in *All Change*, when Louise is taken shopping by her lover Joseph Waring and is left 'confounded by his indifference to her feelings';[2] but Michael knew that Jane was quite capable of believing whatever she wanted to believe, unless obliged to face reality. She was left abandoned in the sticky heat of an August in London, dreaming of the villa and the pool to which she would never be invited.

At some point (it may not have been during the time she was dancing attendance on Michael), Jane was so bruised by male indifference to her feelings that she tried having an affair with a woman, because she felt that women were generally warmer and more supportive: 'I felt that women were kinder than men, and that was what I wanted more than anything else. It didn't work, at all . . . neither she nor I could summon up any real physical feeling for each other.'[3] This was perhaps the same incident she described in *Slipstream*, when she went to bed with the *Daily Express* columnist and broadcaster Nancy Spain who became a friend of hers in the Blandford Street days. Nancy Spain worked on a magazine, probably *She* (her lifelong partner was the editor, Joan Werner Laurie), and asked Jane to write reviews for it from time to time. She took a great shine to Jane, and used to invite her out to lavish champagne lunches at Wheeler's. After one of these lunches, they both went back to Blandford Street and Nancy suggested going to bed.

Jane did not think she'd be any good at it, but was anxious not to hurt Nancy's feelings. ' "Oh come on, darling. Just pop into bed with me and let's see how we feel." So I did. "Well?" the brown bird's eye was fixed on me. Eventually she said, "Well, it doesn't seem to be any good. Never mind." We got out of bed and put on our clothes . . .

She continued to employ me, and ask me to lunch, and never referred to the incident again.'[4]

Jane did not see much of Nicola during the holidays, because she no longer lived with the Bairds; she had left when Josie became ill, and now had a home with her father and stepmother. Peter and Philippa had married a month after his divorce, and they settled at Slimbridge. Their daughter Dafila was born in 1951, and their son Falcon in 1954 – yet Philippa remained very fond of Nicola, and never neglected her in favour of her own children. 'She tried so hard with me, she really made an effort,'[5] recalled Nicola; and when she went to boarding school, it was Philippa who wrote every week, with news of the ducks and Nicola's pony.

The novel progressed with agonizing slowness; but by March 1953 it was, she thought, almost finished. She sent it to Bob Linscott in New York, and his reaction must have filled her with both relief and utter dismay.

> I love it for its style, its wisdom, its truth, and its understanding. It is better than I expected and all that I dared hope. But, there must be another chapter at the end, bringing the story back to the present time and tying up the loose ends . . . Do please write me about this, and tell me what the final chapter will cover and when it will be finished . . . Incidentally, if we are to publish this autumn, we should have the final manuscript within a month. Will you have it completed by that time . . .? Darling, I cannot tell you what pleasure these 289 pages have given me.[6]

Bob Linscott had obliged her to name the unnamed heroine of *The Beautiful Visit*; he had turned down her ghost stories for being too unexplained; and here he was again, asking her to dot every 'i', cross every 't' of *The Long View*. Yet what he was asking for now would completely alter the shape of the novel and its purpose.

As Jane described it: 'I was . . . curious to see whether one could not better understand people and their situations by slowly stripping them of their experiences.'[7] So Jane began with a dinner party in 1950 which reveals that Mrs Fleming's marriage is only held together by a veneer of dinner-party conventions. She then moves back in time in a series of scenes, gradually stripping away her husband's domineering impatience and her refusal to be infantilized, until they stand before each other completely unknown at their first meeting in 1926. A last chapter to tidy everything up would therefore undercut the power of those final lines, which hold all the couple's hopes and potential for happiness. Perhaps Jonathan Cape had reservations too; for Jane's second novel was not to be published in England or America until 1956.

In the spring of 1953 Jane turned thirty; and having seen very little of each other for many years, she and her brother Robin decided to go on a motoring holiday through France and northern Italy that summer. Robin had to get back to work in two weeks, but Michael suggested that Jane stay on for a further fortnight to cheer up a friend of his, Paul Bowman, who worked in Michael's firm of Behrens, Trusted & Co. Paul's marriage was breaking up, and he was going to be alone and miserable in Saint-Tropez. Jane had met Paul with Michael, and liked the idea of a whole four weeks in the south of France. She agreed at once.

This was not the first time that Michael had sent her on a cheering-up mission. Some time before he had asked her to go to Monaco with another colleague called Roy, who was very upset after having split up with his girlfriend. Roy was involved in the negotiations then in progress between Aristotle Onassis and Prince Rainier III of Monaco, over the controlling stake that Onassis wanted in the Société des Bains de Mer, which ran the Casino and other engines of the Monégasque economy.

Jane and Roy were booked into the Hôtel de Paris, and were given adjoining rooms with a communicating door which was locked. The manager insisted on unlocking it, despite strong protests from his English guests. For the next few days Jane had dinner with the love-lorn Roy every night, but the communicating door between them remained firmly shut.

Although they had been close as children, Jane had seen very little of her brother Robin since they had grown up. He had been in America for much of the war and in 1946, to their parents' dismay, he had brought his American bride Hope back from Arizona. Despite Jane's pleas that Kit and David keep an open mind, they never approved of Hope. Robin was given a job in the family firm and the couple had a daughter, Claire, but the marriage was not happy. Hope had abandoned Robin earlier in the year, and their three-year-old daughter was given a home and raised by his mother: for beneath her critical and rather forbidding exterior, there was a great deal of kindness in Kit Howard.

Jane was very happy at the prospect of being with Robin again, particularly since he was running in an exciting new car – a Lotus Mark VI, an open-top silver two-seater and one of the very first Lotus cars to be built. It turned heads wherever it went, especially in Italy where people came up to stroke it tenderly and marvel at its beauty.

They drove through France and had reached Milan before it was time to head back, ending up in Saint-Tropez, where, quite by chance, Jane came across someone she knew slightly in London, Ruth de Lichtenburg. Ruth had two daughters, one of whom was called Nadia who was a ballet dancer. Robin fell for her instantly, and courted her until they were married in 1955. He went back to London the following morning, leaving Jane at the hotel where she was due to meet Michael's friend.

Paul Bowman turned out to be more attractive than she had remembered, and more courteous and considerate than she was used to. Perhaps they talked about his wife who was an actress, and his daughter who was at school; but Paul's family difficulties faded into the background. 'At night we showered and dressed and went out to dine in the warm velvet air. To be asked what I wanted to do, to choose equally with Paul where we'd go and what we'd do, was also a new and delightful experience.'[8]

They went back to their separate rooms. She lay in bed thinking not of Michael, but of Paul – and wondering why Michael had pushed them together. Was he trying to test her, perhaps even pass her on to someone else? Before long there was a knock at the door, and there was Paul. She let him in, they made love, and as usual Jane swept herself into an all-embracing, life-changing romance.

In the years following her divorce from Peter, Kit often asked Jane why she couldn't find another husband. The words were accompanied by a look implying that despite her beauty, she was getting something of a reputation for being 'fast'. Yet even if she were, the fact was that most of the men she knew were married; and they were not about to ditch their wives and children for a glamorous divorcee who took things rather too seriously.

She describes herself as having been 'frigid' throughout her first marriage and says that she only went to bed with men because she wanted affection, not sex[9] – and yet there was rather more to it than that. Jane was an intensely sensual person who did want sex as much as she wanted love, but she had never found fulfilment with anyone so far, and this tormented her like a physical ache. She was also a woman of her time, and a very romantic one at that. In the early 1950s even independent, bohemian women were expected to 'give themselves' to their lovers rather than overtly display their own desires. It was only permissible to respond to sexual stimulation after an act of enraptured surrender, and Jane was almost frightened of the intensity with which she surrendered and responded.

Paul saw the danger and, at least at first, was keen to keep her feet on the ground. 'Dearest Jane,' he wrote on 10 August, 'the weekend was delicious . . . I don't think either of us are under any misapprehension, and we will be terribly sensible and grown-up and not rush into an affair which would soon cease to be light-hearted and would most assuredly end in tears.'[10]

But he was not strong enough to stand up to Jane's emotional tidal wave, nor her beauty. It must have felt like being ravished by the Queen of Sheba. They spent the next ten days together in a cottage in the olive groves below Cabris. To Jane's delight Paul fell in love with her as madly as she had fallen for him, and he was also affectionate and intimate in a way that Michael would never be. By the end of it he asked her to marry him, and she accepted. Jane wrote that she told Michael about their affair as soon as she got home. He was furiously angry, and swore he would do everything to stop them getting married.

Yet the letters Paul wrote to Jane reveal that the affair endured a slower and messier disintegration. Back in London in September he did leave his wife and carry on his affair with Jane, in a louche flat in a mews off Park Lane that belonged to a 'friend' who was evidently an expensive prostitute. They had to be very discreet; and although she hoped eventually to marry Paul, she was also still seeing Michael, presumably still pretending to be the perfect mistress with him.

That December, to her astonishment, Michael invited Paul to join them for a weekend in Paris. 'I suppose Mike has talked to you about

Paris this weekend,' Paul wrote hastily to Jane. He wanted to warn her that if she came to Paris with Michael, she would see him too. 'The thing was sprung on me at lunch . . . I am frustrated and angry that it should have happened, but have no choice about going. '[11]

It is hardly surprising that Jane was beginning to wonder whether Michael knew that they had continued their affair; but from a subsequent letter of Paul's referring to 'the blow-up in January'[12] it is possible that he didn't find out until then. Michael's reactions were more complex than one might have expected. All his fury was directed at Paul, not at Jane: 'Paul has behaved despicably,' he wrote, 'but as I have always told you – and indeed others – you were perfectly free to act as you thought fit and as far as our relationship is concerned I think you behaved properly.'

This suggests that since Michael would not marry her, he could hardly complain if she took another lover; but it also indicates that Jane minimized the time she and Paul had been sleeping together, restricting it to the holiday in the south of France – or else Michael would hardly have credited her with 'behaving properly'. Yet he was shocked by Jane's suspicions that he had pushed the two lovers together in the first place. 'I was extremely hurt,' he wrote, 'that you should have imputed to me so many of the meannesses of spirit that you believed me to be guilty of.'[13]

Michael fired Paul from Behrens, Trusted & Co., and Paul had great difficulty finding another job. He had very little money, and was worried that he might not be able to keep his daughter at her school for much longer. Jane sold her jewellery, and her piano, to keep him in funds. They seemed no closer to getting married, and then Jane discovered she was pregnant. She had hoped that she and Paul would some day have children together; but with things so uncertain, she opted for an abortion instead. She became depressed and ill with a flu that never seemed to go away and her eating disorder, anorexic or bulimic, returned. Michael took her to expensive restaurants and watched while she barely ate anything at all.

Although now in her thirties, she seemed no closer to finding a solid and lasting relationship, while all around her were happy couples. Jill Balcon and Cecil Day-Lewis had married in April 1951, and now they were together with the turmoil behind them, their happiness was palpable. They touched and kissed at every opportunity, and laughed with unfeigned delight at each other's jokes. It was hard not to feel left out.

At the same time they were very fond of Jane, and not blind to her difficulties. She was a frequent visitor to their studio flat in Bedford Gardens, and on one occasion, when Jill was attending the tenth anniversary of the Old Vic Theatre in Bristol, Cecil took Jane out for the day. They drove to Dedham Vale on the River Stour in Essex, which is for ever associated with the name of the painter John Constable; and afterwards Cecil wrote a poem which he dedicated to her, called 'Dedham Vale: Easter 1954'.

Although Jane was excellent company, she was not one to hide her anxieties; and as well as being familiar with her loneliness, which they did much to relieve, the Day-Lewises were also aware she was living hand to mouth from one small typing or editing job to the next. One day in May, Cecil suggested that Jane come and work as an editor at Chatto & Windus. The letter Jane wrote to Jill to thank them for their help was written with a very full heart, and gives an idea of just how desperate she was at the time.

> I didn't at all expect it you see, and it makes the whole difference between courage and despair. I can't tell you this, because I should burst into tears which would be simply boring – but I do notice it all the time. The job has really saved my life. The least I can do is to try . . . to get back to some kind of balance of reality, and to work. But I shall *never* forget the feeling of being loved and cared about by both of you – I had got so sure that people didn't – and I am so glad to be wrong.[14]

Cecil had been a member of the firm since 1946, when he had been taken on as Chatto's principal reader. But he told them he would only work alternate weeks, since he wanted plenty of time to devote to writing poetry and he was frequently called on to give broadcasts and lectures. Jane could work with him at first, until she knew the ropes; and when she had familiarized herself with what had to be done, she could work the weeks he spent at home.

The offices of Chatto & Windus were housed in a dusty, soot-grimed building in William IV Street. Cecil's office, reached by an ancient lift, was at the very top on the sunny side, so it was baking hot in summer. At first Jane and Cecil worked side by side, reading the manuscripts that arrived on their desks in a steady stream. As well as manuscripts by established authors that had to be edited for publication, there were also submissions from new authors, which had to be read and passed on to the partners with a report. The partners, Norah Smallwood and Ian Parsons, would then take the decision on whether or not to publish.

The work brought in £6 a week, and although it wasn't much Jane was very glad to have a steady income with which to meet the bills – especially since Audrey would soon be leaving Blandford Street to get married to Jeremy Harris. Jane knew she ought to look for another lodger, but couldn't face it.

This was not a happy time for her, although she did enjoy working with Cecil. He was every bit as funny at work as he was at home, and the formidable Norah Smallwood had a very soft spot for him. He and Jane ate buns and pastries as they worked, and shared them with the pigeons on the parapet outside the window. Mrs Smallwood did not approve. ' "Eating *again*!" she would say accusingly, looking at the greasy paper bags held down by doughnuts like paperweights. "It's all the frightful books you make us read," Cecil would reply, in his weariest, most polite voice.'[15] The first book Jane edited on her own was Laurens van der Post's *The Dark Eye in Africa*: an appreciation of African culture so larded with high-minded generalizations and quasi-Jungian argument that it is as unreadable now as it was then. When Cecil asked whether she was enjoying it, Jane replied that it was 'like being trapped in a train with someone who told you every single thing that had happened to them for the last six months'. He advised her to plough on, because van der Post was under contract and Norah Smallwood was quite keen on him.[16]

By May 1954, both Paul Bowman and Jane were exhausted by the disappointment of an affair that seemed to be doomed. 'If you look back to the state of mind in which we both started our holiday [in France] – what happened there was quite inevitable,' he wrote. 'I think we both needed each other – I certainly needed you, and that was still true when we came back.' Yet the thrust of the letter was that it was over. Their love, he said, was built on bad foundations through no fault of their own. 'Dear heart, I will give this horrid dry and hopeless letter to you myself. I love you but I fear I am no good to you – P.'[17]

Jane admitted that had she taken the interlude with Paul as a holiday fling, she would not have been so miserable; but 'I was unwilling to accept that I was the sort of woman who had light-hearted affairs: it didn't fit with my grandiose and romantic view of myself. And so, I lied to myself.'[18]

About a week later Michael rang, and revealed a kindness and tact that Jane had never seen before. 'At one point he said, very quietly, "I know you've had a rotten time," and I realised he knew about the abortion, which I couldn't bear to talk about.' He had also bought back most of the jewellery she had sold. She was deeply touched by the trouble he had gone to on her behalf and soon they were back together again, but it was not the same. Jane saw that it was the promise of total commitment that had made Paul so irresistible. She had deluded herself there, just as she had with Michael. Now she understood that she had continued her relationship with Michael in the vain hope that it would, somehow, improve – although he seldom told her he loved her, and never suggested that they might one day be married.

Just where she stood in Michael's life was thrown into relief when Audrey announced, quite coldly, that Jane would not be invited to her wedding. Michael may well have asked Audrey to ensure Jane's absence, since he and his wife Felicity would be attending and it would be awkward if she were there too; Michael liked his life kept in separate compartments. Yet it is also possible that Audrey suspected Jane of having had a fling with her fiancé: Jane made no secret of the fact that she found him very attractive. In *Slipstream*, Jane wrote that she was bitterly hurt, because she and Audrey were supposed to be best friends. Yet it wasn't quite as bad as it sounded, for she was asked to the reception afterwards.

Jane had for some time been sick of Blandford Street, and the idea of living there on her own became unbearable. Quite apart from the fact that it was horribly run-down and still smelled of singed poultry it lacked the one thing she now pined for, a garden. Jane found her garden in Little Venice: a weed-infested plot the size of a tennis court, attached to a maisonette on two floors of Number 6 Blomfield Road (now Number 16), which looked over the Regent's Canal. On the ground floor was a sitting room, a dining room and a tiny kitchen, while upstairs were two bedrooms and a bathroom. The rent was £200 a year, which she could afford with a lodger, and Michael had the garden ploughed in as a housewarming present. Jane made a wide border on the sunny side and a narrower one in the shade, separated by a rectangular strip of lawn in the middle. Quite when she moved in is unclear, but it seems to have been in the autumn of 1954.

That summer, however, she was still at a very low ebb. Paul had gone back to his wife, and she was stuck in the same orbit on the outer fringes of Michael's life. Did he love her? In July he hoped that she was 'happy, relaxed, comfortable and secure – secure anyway that within my limitations I love you as much as I can ever love anyone.'[19] But when he asked her to book a room for them both at Claridge's a few days later, she was to confirm by sending him 'a cable . . . saying ARRIVING STOKE 7.30 PLEASE MEET (signed) BAKER. All very secret service but loving, M.'[20] Such 'secret service' games might have been fun in the beginning, but after five years they had become humiliating.

So when a new friend of hers called Lorna Mackintosh invited her to spend a fortnight at her family house in Connecticut, Jane accepted with gratitude. The daughter of an American heiress, who had left Lorna's father to marry a French duke, Lorna was a friend of Michael's and the lover of Roger St Aubyn, a surgeon. (They would marry in 1957 and have two children, one of whom became the novelist Edward St Aubyn.)

Jane was not sure that Chatto would give her the time off; but Norah Smallwood not only agreed, she also asked Jane to look out some American authors who might be worth publishing. The firm even paid her airfare. Jane and Lorna only spent a few days in Connecticut, since they were both longing to get to New York – although Jane would have nowhere to stay when she arrived, since Lorna had made other plans.

The last time Jane had been in New York, she had been petted and spoilt as Peter's young bride. Now she was alone, with very little money – and the only real friend she had was Bob Linscott. She asked if she could stay with him, and he agreed. She wrote later that he asked her to sleep on the sofa, but she did not stay there very long. A few months later Bob wrote: 'Why shouldn't people try to go to bed with you? I see you in all my dreams striding across the bedchamber, naked as a fish and lovely as a hawk.'[21]

Jane hoped that he would be equally bowled over by her still-unfinished novel, but whatever changes she had made to *The Long View* since Bob had last seen it the previous spring did not impress him. He showed the novel to Robert Haas, the vice-president of Random House whose family had been very kind to Jane when she was in New York in 1946. Haas still had a soft spot for her, and he took her out to lunch in order to break the bad news. Random House could not publish her novel – telling the story backwards just didn't work. Could she not tell it again, the right way round? No, said Jane, she could not; and the rejection was a bitter blow. Haas saw her disappointment: from his wallet he produced $100, and told her to buy herself a nice dress. 'I left lunch in a trance of gloom, bought myself a black velveteen coat for exactly a hundred dollars, and wrote to thank him.'[22]

Her mission for Chatto was not a great success either. She called on most of the publishing houses of New York, hoping to bring back some great author; but it was not long before she realized that the scripts she was given were the ones they had given up on, scrapings from the bottom of the publishing barrel.

She was home by the end of September, in a new house with a garden: which was in itself a sign of growing up and settling down. She was tired of being a mistress, tired of being not quite respectable; and some time that autumn, she told Michael their affair was over. 'I know that he was sad – "*Oh!* I shall miss you, Jenny" – but I don't know whether he was as sad as I was. Come to that, I didn't know how unhappy this separation was going to make me.' That winter dragged on in a cold fog of hopelessness and self-pity. 'I thought I was cut out just to be a kind of extra for people. There would never be anyone who would take me seriously or put me first in his life.'[23]

Michael, too, was far more unhappy than he had expected to be. 'There must be some way to deaden this pain,' he wrote in mid-December (the letter included a cheque, with which he suggested she buy herself a painting).

I think I must be in love for the first time in my life and I HATE it. I think of nothing but you – telling myself as I do it that I must stop and pull myself together and of course I don't: I return to thinking of you. All our friends believe that to see each other again would be madness – perhaps they are right – it is easy to be right in comfort. I am not in comfort and I don't know if they are right. I only know how much I miss you.[24]

Jane missed him too, but she had made the right decision. Cecil Day-Lewis and Jill Balcon knew how hard it had been. Their friendship continued, as warmly as ever. Jane was made godmother to their first child, Tamasin, and they included her in at least one country-cottage holiday with the baby. Thanking Jill, Jane wrote that 'I am deeply touched at being your third person for your holiday, and for giving me such a lastingly nice time. I do feel much calmer and more integrated and not so frightened.'[25]

Interestingly, she signs herself 'Your most loving Jane. Lizbie'. Whether it was Jill or Cecil who said she reminded them of Lizbie Browne, a beautiful and impulsive woman who is the subject of a ballad by Thomas Hardy, Lizbie became Cecil's pet name for her.

She was still working at Chatto's, and that winter was given a new task. She had been asked to write a report on a book about Bettina von Arnim (1785–1859), a writer and artist who knew many of the key figures of the German Romantic period and is best known for her correspondence with Goethe, published in 1835, three years after his death. The book, by Arthur Helps, presented Bettina through her correspondence with friends and family. As far as Jane could tell, he was a good translator and Bettina's letters had retained their liveliness, curiosity and passion. Yet the accompanying text was a mess. 'His well-stocked mind,' she wrote, 'rambled over time and place with nomadic abandon, and the book was like an immense heap of sand'.[26]

Chatto were still keen on publishing the book, and asked Jane if she would collaborate with Arthur Helps on the text. She agreed, but he was not an easy man to work with. After Cambridge he had joined the Malayan Civil Service, and had come to German literature fairly late, when working with German prisoners after the war in Egypt. Since then he had retired to become a farmer in Ireland and was very seldom in London, so they communicated largely by letter.

Jane was surprised that the book contained no mention of Beethoven. Surely Bettina would have met him? Helps grudgingly admitted that she had. They met in Vienna in 1810, and had several encounters that Bettina described at length – and there were letters between them. Yet because Helps had no interest in music, Beethoven – one of the greatest figures of the age – had simply been dropped. Jane insisted on his inclusion, and fretted about who and what else he might have left out. Her novel lay untouched for months as she cut thousands of words, struggled with the chronology and generally pulled *Bettina* into a readable shape.

It was around this time that Jane forged the most stable and enduring relationship she was ever to have with a man. He was not a lover but her younger brother, and he became the most loyal friend of all.

Monkey had been in his early teens when their parents divorced. From then on his mother Kit had made sure that he barely saw his father – although it has to be said that David made no effort to see his younger son, and was not encouraged to do so by his second wife Ursula. 'I was robbed of my father,' he said, although he could never properly express the void this had left in his life. His mother's tight-lipped silences left him in no doubt that David was beneath contempt.

He was no happier at his public school, Radley; and since Robin and Jane were adults who saw relatively little of their prickly mother, he rarely saw his older siblings. In 1953 he went to Cambridge to read engineering only to find that electronics, the subject he was most keen to study, barely figured on the curriculum. He began to lose interest in the course, but Cambridge was fun. Monkey loved classical music and jazz. He went to concerts with his girlfriend – being tall and very good-looking, he had no shortage of girls to go out with. Yet he was also beset by uneasy apprehensions too alarming to think about; and at some point in his second year, when he fell violently in love with a male friend of his, Monkey realized he was gay. Had the object of his affections been gay too, Monkey's life might have taken a very different turn; but although he remained a lifelong friend, this man was heterosexual.

The emotional turmoil in which Monkey now found himself led to a nervous breakdown and two attempts at suicide.[27] The father of the friend he pined for was a Jungian psychoanalyst and Monkey consulted him, without letting on that he was in love with his son; 'although I expect he knew perfectly well,'[28] he added. He was directed to a London psychotherapist, and left university to devote himself to the therapy sessions which took place three times a week.

His mother didn't help by keeping him too close, both emotionally and financially: he lived at home on a tiny allowance, and if Kit took a holiday he was expected to accompany her. Monkey could not tell Kit about the crisis that had turned his life inside out, and she could not understand why he had given up Cambridge.

So he came to stay with Jane at Blomfield Road, and she was appalled to see how far he had withdrawn into misery and despair. He scarcely spoke and was often in tears. Jane became so worried by what harm he might inflict on himself when she was out at work, that at one point she rang his therapist; but the therapist, thinking that she was trying to pry into a matter that was strictly confidential, told her to mind her own business.

At this stage, Jane felt that Monkey's problems went back to the fact that he was tethered to one parent and cut off from the other. She did not know about the struggles he was having with his sexuality, nor the hopes he had pinned on his psychotherapist. In the mid-1950s it was believed that people could be 'cured' of their homosexuality; and as far as Monkey was concerned, 'all I wanted was to be cured'.[29]

If Jane had known she would have been very sympathetic. Love seemed to her so precious, so rare, that she never thought less of anyone for finding it with their own sex. In time he did confide in her, and in later years he wanted to tell his mother too but she always deflected him as he approached the subject. Perhaps it was just as well: from things she said, he realized that 'she had a completely red-top attitude to homosexuality: prurience combined with disapproval'.[30]

Gradually Monkey made his way back into a more balanced frame of mind. He carried on dating girls, still hoping for a 'cure' – but he also learned to accept himself, and began his business of making customized stereo systems. Jane loved having him in the house, and the arrangement suited them both. From time to time he would move out and share a flat with a friend, but she never had another long-term lodger at Blomfield Road, and Monkey's room was usually ready for him to move back into whenever he liked.

IO

Literary Lovers

IN HER MEMOIR Jane says she has very little recollection of 1955: a turbulent year in which she had affairs with Arthur Koestler, Laurie Lee and Romain Gary, and began her unhappy entanglement with Cecil Day-Lewis. On some primordial level she felt that, having made the painful break from Michael, she deserved to find real love – and there seemed no reason why she shouldn't. She had looks, class and style of the kind that men like to be seen with, while for anyone looking for more wifely talents she was also an enthusiastic cook, a promising gardener and loved entertaining. What she hadn't taken into account was her own nature: a combination of insecurity and shyness, a tendency to romanticize both situations and herself, and an overpowering need for attention and affection.

In a party setting, many people have to brace themselves to enter a room full of people on their own. Jane was now used to Chatto parties, where she knew many people and was part of the furniture; but in a less familiar setting, she tended to freeze; she did not smile easily, and found it hard to respond to a cheery opening line. As far as men were concerned this attitude discouraged the hesitant, and left the field open to those with more confidence. The one thing that all her many men had in common was that they enjoyed the challenge of seduction.

Jane's resistance, although expected of all women at the time, thawed easily; and the attention and admiration of a socially confident man made her feel so elated, so complete, that it triggered the second position: a submissive eagerness to please which meant that she fell in with whatever her new partner suggested.

In January 1955 she went to a party given by James Sutherland's sister Moira Verschoyle, who lived in a smart little house on the north side of Knightsbridge. She knew no one but her hostess, and stood for a while nursing a drink and wondering when she could slip away. Then a stocky man with a thick Mitteleuropa accent, whom she described as crackling with energy, noticed her empty glass, fetched her another drink and asked for her name. 'I told him my name,' she wrote in *Slipstream*, 'and waited.'[1] (*Waited*? For him to tell her his name, presumably. Why didn't she say, 'And you are . . .?' It's a tiny indication of her party manner: reluctant to respond to the most basic social question.)

Her companion could not believe that she *didn't* know who he was. Everyone else in the room knew that this was the great Arthur Koestler: ex-Communist, anti-fascist agitator and international trouble-maker, indefatigable writer and commentator, and the author of *Darkness at Noon*: a novel of great courage, which opened people's eyes to the deceptions at the heart of Soviet Communism. The book was published in England in 1941, and soon after, Koestler – who had been interned as an enemy alien – was given British citizenship.

He took her out to dinner, in the course of which she found out that they shared an agent in A.D. Peters, and that Koestler's last wife Mamaine Paget had died the previous year. They went back to his house in Montpelier Square. He took it for granted that she would stay the night (she did) and he drove her home before nine the following morning because he was anxious not to scandalize his cleaning lady.

Jane never thought she was in love with Arturo, as she called him (he called her Janie), but she had never met anyone like him either. She was mesmerized by his raw energy and intellectual reach, the violence of his moods and emotions, the power he had to galvanize a room and put everyone on their mettle, his playfulness and his love of comfort. At the same time, she told his biographer Michael Scammell that she was 'staggered by his contradictions. He was full of idealism one moment and heartlessly cynical the next, arrogantly self-confident one day and extravagantly humble on the morrow.'[2] She found his force of character very alluring, despite its destructive edge; and there was something very flattering about being on the arm of one of the most celebrated intellectuals of the day. As for Koestler, there is only one brief note about Jane in his diary: on 31 January 1955 he wrote that his latest book was nearly finished and that Jane was 'shaping [up] well, touch wood'.

Koestler was about to turn fifty. Since separating from his wife Mamaine in 1951, he had had affairs with at least fifteen different women although he admitted to his diary that 'my harem is wearing me out'.[3] On one level, he yearned for a quiet life with a wife who would combine the roles of decoratively submissive odalisque and professional cook-housekeeper. Yet domestic peace would always elude him because he had to be in control – which led to fury and frustration for both parties. 'I can neither live alone nor with somebody,' he wrote, while noting that the women to whom he was attracted were often 'beautiful Cinderellas, infantile and inhibited, prone to be subdued by bullying'[4] – an uncomfortably accurate description of Jane at the time.

With his habitual impulsiveness he proposed to her on St Valentine's Day, and for once Jane was sensible. She would not marry him straight away, but agreed to come and live in Montpelier Square for three months to see how they got on.

Routine was what grounded Koestler's volcanic temperament. His mornings were devoted exclusively to writing. At that time he was working on a book about the seventeenth-century German astronomer Johannes Kepler. The project grew into *The Sleepwalkers*: a history of early astronomy that also examined how it affected the way people thought about their place in the universe.

After a lunch of cheese, coffee and salami, he spent the afternoon planning lectures and conferences, writing letters, accepting invitations (he loved parties), making dates with his friends and receiving callers. Many of these were ex-prisoners and dissidents: he listened to their stories with sympathy and encouragement, and often gave them money. Jane asked how he knew they were genuine and Koestler replied that it was easy to tell. All ex-prisoners, he explained, whether talking in German, French, Hungarian or Spanish, addressed each other informally in the singular: they never used the more respectful, plural forms.

He loved what he called 'being cosy', whether that was a pub lunch with the novelist Henry Green and his wife, or having an evening at home. ' "Janie! *Zis* is what I really like. So cosy – domestic bliss. *Vy* don't we have it every day?" '[5] But Jane knew he was too difficult a character to want the same thing every day. 'He embraced the ordinary as some do a bank holiday,' she wrote. 'Real life was a moody, tempestuous business hardly to be borne.'[6] He kept a portrait of his dead wife on his study wall. Jane resented the way she was made to feel that she could never match up to Mamaine – although Mamaine, too, had been tormented for not being perfect.

When they entertained, Jane was expected (often after a day's work) to produce a three-course meal, look demurely beautiful, and talk as little as possible; and if the slightest thing fell short of Koestler's obsessive standards of perfection, he would turn on her in a fury in front of their guests. Yet Jane was not always meek: she could shout back too, and was once so angry that she threw a carafe of water at his head. It missed him but she could see that he respected the gesture.

It was not only the dead with whom she had to compete. Koestler was as priapic as ever, and she knew that when she was not there he was quite capable of picking up a girl at a party. One of his younger and more reluctant dates was Marigold Hunt, later Marigold Johnson, who was very flattered to have been invited out by the great intellectual. She had expected dinner in a restaurant, but he cooked her a steak in the kitchen at Montpelier Square. Throughout the evening, Koestler was having to answer repeated telephone calls from Jane demanding to know whether he was alone. 'Yes, yes! Of course I am alone!' he hissed into the receiver. The last of these calls came when he had inveigled Marigold into his room and forced her down on his bed; but as he shifted his weight to reach the telephone, she was able to wriggle free and bolt out of the house. Marigold later became a friend of Jane's and reviewed several of her books, but she never told Jane of her close escape from Koestler.

Early that spring Koestler bought a blue canoe, which could be packed into canvas bags and loaded into the car at weekends. He and Jane would then reassemble it at some spot on the River Wey in Surrey or Sussex, for a day's paddling on the water. For Jane these jaunts were more of an ordeal than a pleasure, for whatever she did threw Koestler into a fury, and he raged at her clumsiness and stupidity. There were moments (usually during their picnic lunches) when he subsided into a gentler and more cheerful frame of mind; but by the end of the day he had usually reduced her to a tearful, cringing jelly. As Koestler's biographer Michael Scammell observed: 'Only much later did she realize that Koestler had a fatal urge to smash things up, like a small boy smashing his toys. His demand for perfection was a way of ensuring failure in advance.'[7]

After dinner and several drinks in a comfortable hotel, both of them felt better and Koestler, now charming and playful again, would apologize. In bed afterwards, all was forgiven; but on one such evening Jane demurred, having not brought any contraceptives – and Koestler lost his temper all over again. She always thought she knew best, but he was quite sure it was a safe time of the month and, to avoid any more rows that evening, she gave in.

But however much he ground her down, Koestler did do Jane one very great service. In the alternate weeks she was not working at Chatto's, he would lock her into the freezing sitting room while he worked upstairs; and one time when he came to unlock the door, she complained that she seemed incapable of finishing her novel – it was still *The Long View*, which she had been writing and rewriting for the best part of five years. Koestler said he would read it. When he had done so, he told her that she already had the ending, fifty pages back. This implies that she was still under pressure to write an epilogue, possibly from the American publisher Raynal who took the book on when Random House let it go. Koestler's verdict came as a huge relief and gave her the courage to stick to her original vision of the book. Yet much as she wanted to, she could not quite believe his pronouncement that her writing style was somewhere between Nancy Mitford and Evelyn Waugh.

In April Jane found she was pregnant. She felt a rush of love for Koestler and told him she wanted to keep the baby, but Koestler was horrified. He had always been determined not to have children, but that very month his French lover Janine Graetz had given birth to a daughter who was unquestionably his – and now Jane was threatening to do the same. He immediately set about arranging for an abortion. Jane refused to cooperate, but her tearful entreaties only strengthened his resolve that she should get rid of the child.

In a long letter to Koestler after it was all over she wrote: 'The weeks after that I have spent desperately and unsuccessfully trying to control the conflict about the child and my feelings about you which has included wanting you physically – what a word for it – and feeling very sick.' In the end, Jane felt she had no choice but to stop the pregnancy, although she was determined to arrange things herself. Unfortunately, the arrangements unravelled. There were delays and misunderstandings, and by the time she booked herself into a nursing home, Jane must have been more than three months pregnant.[8]

Abortion was strictly illegal; and because a recognizable foetus some three inches long would undoubtedly emerge from the procedure, the doctor made sure that neither matron nor any of her regular staff were on hand for this particular 'dilation and curetage' – an intervention not always associated with unwanted pregnancy. Matron was told that nothing much had been removed, and she assumed that Jane was ready to go home: but Jane was far weaker than the staff suspected. The only person who did suspect was Kit. She telephoned and asked a lot of awkward questions, although she never offered to come round.

Shaky and in pain, Jane went home to Blomfield Road at the end of July, at the start of the bank holiday weekend. Koestler visited, evidently keen to leave as soon as he could; he said he was going to Hampshire with his friends Arthur and Celia Goodman (Mamaine's sister), and it was clear that he did not want to see her again. So Wayland and Liz Young looked after Jane for the next few days, and then brought her back to her empty house.

Jane resumed the routine of one week at Chatto's, one week off to write; but the days when she was supposed to be writing were spent in numbness and apathy. Another love affair had ended in tears; but had she ever been really in love with Koestler? 'For you, I've been no extraordinary experience,' she wrote, 'probably getting into a category with about a dozen other women. It hasn't been like that for me. I haven't wanted many people, and I've never wanted anyone who hasn't wanted me. More important than that – I've never loved anyone before whom I've objectively thought was "good" for want of a better word.'[9]

Given his behaviour over the last page or so it's astonishing that Jane should still see him as 'good'. But she was drawn to him as a champion of truth and justice on the world stage, regardless of how he had behaved to her; and then she tried to invest in him the same weight of emotional capital as she had in Michael Behrens and Paul Bowman.

Whoever was to blame, the fact remained that Jane was alone again with no one at the centre of her life; and while that most vital part of her being was unfulfilled, she could not find the creative energy for writing. 'Repetitive experience can be brutalizing,' she wrote. 'The less I understood my experiences, the more I repeated them, each time becoming less aware of what I was doing.'[10]

Her beauty confused things. She spent time and money on her hair and clothes, and enjoyed turning heads. She carried herself with grace, but like many tall women she felt too big to share in the fragile, fairy-tale sort of beauty of romantic heroines. Some women knew how to sparkle and flirt, but Jane didn't have to. Huge eyes, beautiful bones, and her deep, husky voice with its hint of a childish lisp were enough to attract considerable attention, despite her shyness. One of her psychotherapists remarked that Jane's life had, to some extent, been blighted by her looks. 'She never knew whether the things people did for her, or wanted her to do, were prompted by her as a person or by her blinding beauty. You don't know who or what to trust. It made her a very bad judge of men – and as she felt (thanks to her mother's preference for her brothers) that men were better and cleverer, she always valued them and their company and their wishes too high.'[11]

The summer wore on although there was some good news. *The Long View* had been accepted by Jonathan Cape, and would be published in early 1956, while her agent, A.D. Peters, wrote her a generous letter admitting he'd been wrong about its structure. A French fan called Danièle Clément had translated *The Beautiful Visit*, and on the strength of it having won the John Llewellyn Rhys Prize it was taken on by the publishers Gallimard, who also took *The Long View*, which became *Le Long Regard*.

She had not seen Koestler for weeks; but he sent her the money to cover the cost of the abortion, and a letter that read:

Darling Jane, all this is terribly sad, and there is no point in my making counter-excuses or counter-self-accusations. We have both tried, each according to his one's [sic] own lights and capacities, and the equation did not work. Inquests have a point only when one expects to discover some unknown factor; but in this case all the relevant factors are known to both of us – I hope you will go away for a holiday; I think you should; I too shall probably tear myself away from Keppler and Copernic later in August. I also feel that there should be a pause in seeing each other, since at present it would only be mutually distressing; and meet again when we are both back in September, sunburnt, aired and revived. Love and bless you, AK.[12]

Jane's much needed holiday materialized after a dinner she had given for Laurie and Kathy Lee; Monkey had suggested she invite them, because they always cheered her up. Laurie Lee, who had been born in rural Gloucestershire and had walked through Spain playing the violin, was another man of moods and violent responses; but this was a side that most of his many friends would not have recognized. To them he showed a sunny, playful temperament which was gloriously engaging in company, and people loved to be around him. He was a great friend of Cecil Day-Lewis and Rosamond Lehmann, who had been very supportive when Laurie had been tortured by the infidelity of his first great love, Lorna Wishart.

Jane had first come across him at Chatto, when she had read *A Rose for Winter: Travels in Andalusia*. Cecil Day-Lewis thought it was good, although a bit overblown in parts; but Jane was enthralled by his descriptions of people who, though desperately poor, lived in a brilliantly coloured world in which every sensation was felt with a raw purity.

Laurie Lee was then in his early forties, while his wife Kathy, whom he had married in 1950, was half his age. Born with a guileless, golden beauty, Kathy was quite without vanity; yet she proved strong enough to stand up to his determination to keep her as an idealized child-bride, who was utterly dependent on him. Her name had originally been Kathy, but Laurie had decided that Cathy looked and sounded softer, so Cathy she remained, and when he died she reverted to the original spelling. 'And that,' she told Lee's biographer Valerie Grove, 'tells you everything you need to know about our marriage.'[13] At parties Laurie would sing and play his guitar, while Kathy – a passionate dancer – danced flamenco and sardanas with a conviction that few English people could pull off. Jane saw them as often as she could, although Laurie was often ill: he suffered from epilepsy, and had frequent chest infections.

Laurie saw at once that Jane was miserable and asked what she was doing that summer. She had nothing planned. He and Kathy were going to stay with their friends Anthony and Nicolette Devas in Guernsey in September, but the Devases could not accommodate Jane too; so he asked her whether she might like to come to Spain with him for two weeks – just the two of them. Kathy would not be coming. Would she mind? 'Of course she won't,' said Laurie.

And perhaps, up to a point, he was right. Kathy had lived all her life in bohemian circles, and accepted that her husband was a free spirit. No one had the right to own someone else, she wrote to an outraged friend who had just found out that Laurie had had an affair with her daughter. 'I'm lucky,' she went on, 'that I have so much love in me that I find it easy to forgive.'[14] Besides, Kathy may well have welcomed the odd short sabbatical from her marriage, that gave her a respite from Laurie's demands and expectations; and he did reassure her that he was taking Jane purely as a friend who needed a break.

Emotionally susceptible, Jane was more likely to get hurt; but she had never been to Spain, and it would be an adventure to travel with someone who knew the country so well. They set off on 4 September, travelling third class over two days from Paris – neither of them had much money. Jane had never travelled in such discomfort. 'You sit on a hard bench,' she remembered, 'up to five a side, and as night falls all the men take off their shoes and put their feet on the bench opposite. The windows are shut and their socks make you feel as though you are sitting on a vast crater entirely filled with erupting Stilton cheese.'[15]

They arrived at Gerona at noon the following day, to find a gaggle of English friends at the station who had been on a painting course with the artist Rodrigo Moynihan. He was the only one Jane knew, but it meant that there might well be whispers about their holiday when they got home.

Laurie and Jane trudged off with their bags, the sun beating down; and when Jane felt she was about to faint with heat, they stopped at a hotel. At this point, they had separate rooms. Jane was desperately thirsty and there was no water, but it did not stop her falling on to the bed and sleeping till dusk.

They went to bars where Laurie introduced Jane as Isabel, since he said 'Jane' was unpronounceable in Spanish. She obediently adapted to this new name, yet it acted as a release. Lonely, careworn Jane began to fade, replaced by the radiant, carefree Isabel. They went to the fishing village of l'Estartit, where they danced sardanas on the beach to the songs of the peasant girls who followed them around. Jane noticed the great white scar across his chest, from where he had had a lung removed three years before. After a few days they went back to Gerona where he took a single room this time, with no window, in a warren-like tenement hotel. They sat down on the bed, and he produced a bottle of brandy.

Over the last few days Jane had lived in a haze of lightness and joy; but now, when it was obvious what was going to happen next, she suddenly felt tense and awkward. She didn't want to go through the charade of love-making yet again, which invariably ended in misery, tattered excuses and disappointment; but as she tried to tell him he murmured, 'Don't say any of that. I'll find you.'[16]

What followed was, she claimed, a sexual awakening – she had never had such a skilful and considerate lover. And in later years when journalists asked her which of her many men she had been happiest with, the answer was often (but not always) Laurie Lee.

Yet her pleasure in this particular evening faded as she was overcome by an urgent need for the loo. Laurie said that there was a place in the courtyard, but it was better for women to use it in the morning. Could she not hold on till then? His tone implied that there was something rather feeble in her desperate need for a pee.

Surely I didn't want a *lavatory*. Cross and nervous, I decided to look for one. There were a number of doors on the dimly-lit landing; none of them had any labels on them. Desperate, I tried a door which revealed a middle-aged and completely bald man dressed only in a pair of black boots. He was angry, and then nothing like angry enough. I fled downstairs to the ground floor where there was the dining room or restaurant. I was wearing a night dress and a cardigan, I remember, and had reached the point when it was essential to find somebody who would instruct me about my simple but urgent need. The dining room was huge, brightly lit and absolutely full of men eating enormous hot dinners. Silence began to fall and increased to a breathless hush as I seized the nearest waiter by his sleeve and whispered '*toiletta?*' at him. He smiled, embarrassed, but eventually he got the point and indicated a sort of kiosk nearly in the centre of the room. It was small, vaguely round, and its walls stopped short a good foot from the floor. You could have heard a grain of rice drop as I made my way towards this goal, which was indeed a lavatory, of a kind.[17]

The following day they went to a bullfight. Jane could see the courage and skill involved, but she found the despatch of a beautiful creature goaded into defending itself no less brutal and cruel for that. They went to a guitar shop: Laurie had been feeling unwell and he went into an epileptic fit; it only lasted a few seconds and he recovered swiftly, but Jane found it terrifying. He bought himself a new guitar, and tried to commission one for his friend Julian Bream. They played dominoes. Jane won and Laurie was furious, sulking for hours afterwards. They headed for the coast again and one day, as they were lying in the sun, Laurie said that nobody as beautiful as she was could be any good at writing. For this absurd statement Jane pushed him into the sea. More days flew by until suddenly, almost without warning, it was time to leave.

Rosamond Lehmann had once told Laurie that 'I think you are, without . . . meaning to be, rather dangerous for women! You seem to expand with such warmth and freedom towards them, it goes to their heads – it's such a rare pleasure for them to find so much subtle understanding, sensibility and attentiveness in the male sex . . . Then suddenly they discover they've come to a walled enclosure with a sign: Keep Off. Keep Out . . . No One at Home. And they get upset.'[18]

Jane was desolate, although she knew all along that they would part as soon as they were back in London. 'I'd had two weeks of unalloyed happiness,' she wrote, 'so why should I cry?'[19] Laurie, on the other hand, was looking forward to seeing Kathy and his friends again, and resuming his life in the pubs and book-lined rooms of literary London.

Laurie remained very fond of her and, in a letter written seventeen years later, he recalled their time in Gerona.

It is always with me, but I have never even talked about it, let alone try to write it. Yet the most vivid impressions remain. Your lovely exhausted exquisite shape face down sleeping in your stifling room after the two days' train ride from London. The admiring secret-police jokers in the bar. Your face half-lit over the table on the beach, with the dark sea behind you; and the unexpected euphoria around us. The game of love that kept on refusing to behave as if it was a game. Panic, protection, but most of all freedom, happiness, and always your extraordinary beauty.[20]

This letter was a gift, written to please her and unlock shared memories; but one can't help wondering why the game of love was more serious than it should have been, and what 'panic and protection' signify: perhaps his epileptic fit, and her care of him afterwards. Whatever the words meant, Isabel seems to have shone an unexpected light in his life too.

She was alone again, in much the same place as when she had left Michael Behrens the year before; yet despite being a year older, her morale was more buoyant. The beneficial effects of the holiday, plus anticipation of *The Long View* finally coming into print in March, pulled her out of the creative doldrums. In the autumn of 1955, during the weeks she was not working at Chatto, she began her third novel. It was going to address the question of 'what people could change about themselves and what was immutable . . . I'd begun to discover that if an idea lay in the back of my mind little by little some flesh began to cover its bones.'[21]

Another literary admirer appeared on the scene. The novelist Romain Gary was an immigrant from Lithuania, who had been a pilot with the Free French during the war. He had fought with such distinction that he was made a Compagnon de la Libération, the highest possible honour among the ranks of the Free French. He became a career diplomat after the war, and married a British journalist called Lesley Blanch. Both were notoriously unfaithful, but Gary had come to depend on Blanch to organize his life.

Then in 1954 Lesley Blanch published the book for which she is best remembered, *The Wilder Shores of Love*. The book's success turned her away from her husband to develop her own career. He had spent much of early 1955 in a profound depression. His diplomatic career had all but stalled, and what he called his 'elephant novel' was giving him a lot of trouble. He wrote the final part that summer, and it was published the following year as *Les Racines du Ciel* – the book that won him his first Goncourt Prize (Romain Gary is the only author to have won it twice).

He got in touch with Jane in late November, and told her, quite formally, that he had been in love with her from the moment they had met at a dinner with her and Arthur Koestler. At the time, she had noticed the way he refused to look her in the eye. In a thank-you letter to Koestler, he wrote: 'Please convey my very decidedly warm feelings to Jane, and apologies for not looking at her when talking: she always makes me think of something else – bad in a discussion!'[22]

Gary told her that he had just been appointed Consul-General in Los Angeles; and since his wife refused to accompany him there, he suggested that Jane might like to join him as his *maîtresse en titre*. He urged her to think about it seriously, and telephone him that evening at his hotel with her decision. Jane did not go into the practicalities of this transaction, but one assumes that he would give her board and lodging – plus an allowance, perhaps? – in return for sex and social hostess duties. She found him attractive, was grateful that he hadn't pounced on her, and she didn't seem to mind that he was treating her like a high-class geisha. In fact that particular aspect of it, which some women might have found insulting, does not seem to have crossed her mind at all. She still hoped that one day someone would come along and sweep her off her feet; and how could she tell if Romain Gary was the love of her life unless she gave herself the opportunity to find out?

Jane rang Gary, and told him she would come and spend a week in Paris with him. Gary introduced her to many of his friends (to get their reactions to her later, she thought); he showed her round the Gallimard offices and introduced her to Albert Camus, whom she found 'a very beautiful man, one of the few I have ever met'.[23] Yet the week was not a success, and Romain Gary left for Los Angeles in January on his own.

As autumn gave way to winter, Jane began to see more of Cecil Day-Lewis than was wise. He had been attracted to her for many months, and now stepped up his campaign to seduce her. She remembered that 'we spent a couple of afternoons on Hampstead Heath – looking back he was awfully good at finding very private places there . . . I wonder if he'd done it before.'[24] She thought Cecil one of the most handsome men she had ever met, and loved the way he could purr continuously like a cat.

On 11 December he wrote:

> I've hardly stopped thinking of you for a moment . . . Yesterday after-noon I walked to the bus stop where we kissed each other, to make sure it was really true. It *is*. You haven't felt you said anything absurd or to be regretted at dinner? You didn't — everything you said was beautiful and true. And I'd drunk very little myself: I got drunk on you and I'm glad glad glad we told each other what we did . . . I shall write a poem, if I can, about our fox, to give you for Christmas . . . And of course I'm afraid — not of you, but of everything that would follow — those terrible conflicting tides.

This was a reference to his much earlier vacillation between his wife Mary and his lover Rosamond Lehmann — a dilemma that left him so churned up and muddied and disgusted with himself that the only solution was to escape into the arms of Jill: a woman for whom he was still a hero, not a dithering coward.

> You won't be impatient with me, will you, for not hurrying myself into that sea again straight away, though I want you so badly and have for ages . . . Well you know now that I do, and that I'm passionately in love with you, my Lizbie. You're so beautiful to me, and we do warm each other's hearts, don't we? I think mine will blow up when we meet tomorrow. C.[25]

They saw each other on the 12th which was Monday, and on the Tuesday he wrote to her again.

> It fills me with pride to be seen with you, especially in your fur hat . . . I know now what Anna Karenina looked like . . . How well our minds go together. And I know our bodies would go well together — but of this I try not to think too much, in fact . . . Whatever decision we make, whatever happens to us, you know you are loved and can always come to me for love, understanding, sympathy, bad jokes — whatever you need. My Lizbie, you need never feel unloved, unsure again. Cecil.[26]

This letter, of 13 December, makes it clear that they are not yet lovers: that was a line which, once crossed, would plunge them both into horribly familiar dangers. Cecil's next letter is undated, and delivered by hand so there is no postmark but it is still before Christmas. As he saw it, they had three options. The first was that they should withdraw, meet in public, and ensure never to be alone again. The second, to go on as now – with kisses and caresses, and be happy on those terms. The third was to become lovers. He cannot bear option one, and option two would probably lead to three in the end.

How Jill might feel about them having an affair does not seem to have entered his calculations at all. She would not know, and therefore could not be affected. Jane did feel bad about Jill, one of her most stalwart friends. At the same time, she felt that being in love always gave her an excuse for pleading diminished responsibility. Her conscience could not be expected to stand up against a tide of overwhelming emotion. 'I wasn't able, then, to recognize that such things need not happen if they are resisted in the first place; I thought they simply struck one – like lightning – and that one had no choice.'[27]

At the same time, both she and Cecil were aware that if they had an affair, she was the one who would be hurt, not him. Sometimes he wondered whether the risk was worth it – but never for very long. 'You see,' he wrote to Jane:

> I have already made a mess of two women's lives. I cannot afford, morally or emotionally, to have any more messes of this kind. Supposing I involved you again in the sort of three-cornered situation you were in with Michael – I saw how it made you suffer. But as you know it's not the suffering one minds: it's the poisoning, eroding process: I dread that happening to our love . . . To give each other up now would be the way of least pain all round . . . You've just rung up, left me shaking and breathless with my love for you.[28]

The long wait was nearly over, as he predicted in the poem about 'our fox' which he gave her for Christmas.

Delight and danger, that scene foretold.
Now the right hour to say
'I love you' is here, two breathing worlds
Are fused, as when that thing from the wild
Comes out in the light of day. [29]

This is the last verse of the poem – omitted by Jill, when she came to edit the *Collected Poems* after Cecil's death: by then, she knew it had been written for Jane, but in the winter of 1955 she didn't know of the poem's existence.

The 'danger and delight' heralded by the fox's appearance happened in the new year. Jane told Cecil's biographer that 'He made a huge pass at me and I didn't have the strength to resist him. I was surprised and shocked. It had never crossed my mind as a possibility.'[30] Yet in view of the fact that he had written her any number of letters and two poems before she succumbed, it seems unlikely that his pass came as that much of a surprise.

11

The Long View

JANE'S AFFAIR WITH Cecil Day-Lewis was at its most intense during the winter of 1955 and spring of 1956. They both had sensual natures, and every sense heightened the pleasure they took in each other; while at the same time they were on the same wavelength of laughter, conversation, jokes and gossip. Yet every time they made love (Jane said there were only three) ended with him going back to Jill, while she was left with the desolate empty bed. Her own marriage had happened too soon in her life, and now it was too late for every other man who might have loved her. Jane seemed to be cursed by bad timing.

Day-Lewis had put considerable effort into seducing her, but she took the implications of the affair far more seriously than he did. She was betraying one of her oldest friends; but he did not seem very disturbed by the idea of being unfaithful to his wife, and in an attempt to reassure Jane, he wrote a letter explaining his relationship with Jill. Passion had subsided into affection, but he still loved and respected her and didn't like telling her lies. He felt responsibility for her because she is 'unconfident, low-moraled, oversensitive and touchy, impulsive and often generous'. His feelings for her were still positive; he was not, he assured Jane, at the stage where 'pity and guilt have to substitute for love',[1] a state he was very familiar with.

Yet despite his admission the month before that he had wrecked the lives of two women and could no longer afford 'messes of that kind', he was now ready to juggle wife and mistress again. Looking back on their relationship, Jane also felt it was something to do with being a poet. 'He wrote best when feeling a terrible sense of emotional conflict. I think he needed it. I think he contrived it – not deliberately and intellectually, he just needed to have it emotionally to make him tick.'[2]

In the same letter quoted above, he declared that Jane inspired in him 'a love more passionate and affectionate than any I've ever felt before.' He always knew he was capable of loving two women at once; but because Jane was so amenable and understanding (unlike Rosamond), he found himself loving both her and Jill with 'no sense of conflict or guilt . . . You have so much of me – you know that – and yet you are never possessive.'[3]

Jane always said that it was her feelings for Jill that made her so uncomfortable about the affair with Cecil, yet equally strong was the terror of finding herself trapped in the same emotional dead-end that had made her so miserable with Michael Behrens. Day-Lewis wrote to her several times over the course of the summer, trying to argue that he was very different from Michael ('I'm a less complicated chap in many ways') and that the pattern would not repeat itself; although he did admit that 'I should be satisfied . . . by having you as my mistress: you would not be satisfied by this relationship, and I don't blame you.'[4]

Yet however disappointing her personal life, the reception of *The Long View* – which came out in February 1956 – made up for all the difficulties she had had in writing it. Jane said it took her an unconscionable four years to complete but in fact it was more like five. And yet, however small her daily output of words (300 on a good day: she once described the process as like trying to get condensed milk out of a tin with two holes in it), her voice on the page sounds remarkably assured: each sentence follows the next with the authority of someone who knows exactly what they are doing, and where they are going.

John Davenport reviewed it for the *Observer*. 'Miss Howard's *The Long View* is by no means a short book,' he wrote, 'but one would not wish it reduced by a single paragraph . . . There is nothing oversimplified or banal about this richly rewarding novel, which combines wit and sensibility in a most unusual degree.'[5]

In the *Times Literary Supplement*, Marigold Johnson said that the success of her backwards method was surprising,

for such changes occur gradually, not in the series of pin-pointed crises and gaps which her long view involves. Two talents contribute to this: she makes her characters spectacular – the over-intelligent, sensation-exploiting husband is as carefully drawn as Antonia – and thereby fixes them consistently in her readers' minds. Also she has a talent for compressing detail into phrases which repay close reading – 'Her voice had become less steady. She shook it out with a little laugh.'[6]

Much of the book is in dialogue: power struggles and tests of strength between Conrad and Antonia, which often sound as declamatory as if the novel were a play. Jane's early training in the theatre is never far below the surface of her novels. The scene is always set, giving the reader a clear idea of where her characters are in a room – and sometimes even when they are up or down stage. Yet despite this theatrical quality, she also follows the currents of their inner reactions with an uncanny precision.

She was right to hold on to the backwards structure, in the face of all the advice from her elders and betters. We know from the first chapter that Antonia and Conrad's marriage is in ruins. Yet their characters are so vividly drawn that what pulls the reader along is the desire to know *why* they ever married, and what they were like before the passing years distorted the love they had for each other.

The crux of the novel is the 1937 section, where Conrad falls in love with a young woman called Imogen, and Antonia has a casual fling in Marseille with a friend of Conrad's called Thompson. (Just as she was not sure whether Michael Behrens had set up her encounter with Paul Bowman, so Antonia wonders why Conrad – whom she has driven to Marseilles so he can catch a flight to Paris – insists on taking a luxurious double room for her that night, and then introducing her to his friend.) Conrad and Antonia flinch from thinking about each other's infidelities, and fret over their own; but in both cases, their scruples seem to be about pride as much as the ambivalent feelings they have for one another.

Conrad admits that he married her because 'You have beauty now, but the most exciting thing to me is that you are clearly going to become steadily more beautiful – for years and years, and I am going to see you do it.'[7] In fact the burden of beauty, as borne by Antonia, is one of the more subtle themes of the novel. When she marries Conrad, she's too young to recognize it. He gives her that consciousness and at first it is a gift, a sensuous pleasure, as are the simple but expensive clothes he loved to see her wearing. Conrad teaches her how best to display herself: he becomes her Pygmalion, just as she becomes a reflection of his taste and discernment: 'She washed her long thick hair free from salt every day; her skin was becoming an even gold which darkened smoothly, enabling her to wear paler and paler colours, until at any moment she would be able to reach the final contrast of white. That was the kind of decorative timing which he had taught her.'[8] Yet for the older Antonia, beauty is as hollow as her marriage: a thing of bone structure and exacting standards, which she maintains out of habit.

Just as Michael Behrens was the main ingredient for the character of Conrad Fleming, so Antonia is a version of Jane. Youth and inexperience are what prompt her to accept Conrad's proposal. Over the years she accommodates herself to him because she acknowledges that he has saved her from an impossible situation, and because she needs to maintain her dignity in the world. The result is that she allows herself to drift through the years without ever insisting on her right to be an equal partner. She might have succeeded, but every time he defeated her – or she defeated herself:

> 'What's the matter, Antonia? Has something happened while I was out?'
>
> 'Nothing at all.'
>
> 'You have not had a letter, or anything of the kind?'
>
> She put down her paper, whose pages were beginning to tremble. 'No. But supposing I had: I can manage my own letters, surely?'
>
> He sat down. 'Of course you can. Why not?'
>
> There was a silence between them. Then, because he showed no sign of giving her an opening, she cried: 'You don't take me seriously.'
>
> She said it too sharply, and brought tears to her eyes.[9]

The book's dedication reads, 'For E.M.' – at a guess this was Michael Behrens, whose first name was Edward. Whether she made this gesture as a tribute to her old lover, or a tease, or just to see whether he would notice is impossible to tell.

And there is another conundrum. How could this novelist who wrote with such insight about men and women and what they do to each other, take herself through these bouts of emotional turmoil that invariably ended in disaster? She knew that the engine that drove her was emotional need and the insatiable desire for love and affection, and knowing it did not make the urge any less imperative. Yet while she tried so hard to adapt herself to her lovers, the very earnestness of her efforts turns inwards – she was watching herself through their eyes, not looking at them. In the same way, it's interesting to note that in all Jane's sex scenes it is female arousal that she describes, not the man who has aroused those sensations.

Jane's future stepson Martin Amis observed: 'She's got a lot of imaginative sympathy, and a penetrating sanity on the page . . . In fact I've always thought that was one of the mysteries about Jane: the penetrating sanity on the page, but when she's off the page, she's actually not that clever with people.'[10]

It was as if she had to turn her experiences into fiction before she could make sense of them. She was happily carried away by the rituals of conversation and food and drink and cigarettes, the flattery and the seduction; and on some other level, another part of her was taking a series of very detailed impressions and locking them away for future use.

In early May 1956 Jane went to a dinner given by Stephen and Natasha Spender for Charlie Chaplin, who was then in his mid-sixties. Born in London, Chaplin had spent most of his professional life in Hollywood. But as anti-Communist frenzy in America gathered strength, Chaplin began to lose his popularity. In 1955 he was more or less hounded out of the United States by a combination of toxic publicity, much of it whipped up by the FBI, and accusations of having Communist sympathies. He and his wife Oona had settled in Switzerland; but they were now in London to film Chaplin's new movie, his eightieth, called *A King in New York*.

The other guests at dinner included Clarissa Eden, whose husband Anthony was then prime minister, as well as the writer and diplomat Harold Nicolson and the biographer James Pope-Hennessy. In his diary, Spender noted that Chaplin 'seemed distinctly damped down as long as Clarissa was there. When the ladies left the room he brightened up considerably and chatted away a great deal about the film he was making.'[11] At the end of the evening, Jane invited the Chaplins to dinner at Blomfield Road, and much to her surprise they accepted.

The Chaplins were in no way 'damped down' by dinner with Jane and her brother Monkey; in fact they were so happy and relaxed that Jane asked whether she could come and watch the filming. Chaplin not only agreed, but suggested that she write a profile on him too. He was not allowing any other journalists on the set, so this would be a world scoop. Terence Kilmartin, who was then literary editor of the *Observer*, agreed to take the piece, although Chaplin asked for it to be held over until the film was released.

Jane was fascinated by Chaplin's charm and agility, the way he worked, the way he controlled every aspect of the filming and every expression on the faces of his actors. She saw how he could be mobbed by fans and autograph hunters, and began to understand the sometimes intolerable pressures of celebrity. At one point she also stayed with the family in Switzerland, at their house in Corsier-sur-Vevey. But when she delivered the piece to Terence Kilmartin, he was disappointed because 'I hadn't written about Charlie's political opinions. I hadn't because I thought that was the dullest part of him.'[12]

Considering the circles in which she moved and the times she was living through, this was an obstinate display of political parochialism. The whole point of *A King in New York* was that it expressed Chaplin's outrage at America's anti-Communist witch-hunters, and the effect their paranoia was having on people. Kilmartin found it incredible that Jane could be so uninterested in the principles of free speech that Chaplin felt were being blatantly violated, or the nature of his political feelings. He urged her to give the piece more political context but she refused. In the row that followed, Kilmartin vowed she would never write for the *Observer* again, and she never did.

Instead he gave the job to Chaplin's friend Ella Winter. She and her husband, the scriptwriter Donald Ogden Stewart, had also been up against the House Un-American Activities Committee, and Winter wrote a piece that captures Charlie Chaplin's voice, his energy and his opinions. 'As for politics, I'm an anarchist,' he told her. 'I hate governments and rules and fetters . . . Can't stand caged animals . . . People must be free.'[13]

Jane had a greater success with a piece she sent to Stephen Spender at *Encounter* magazine, about her two grandfathers: Sir Arthur Somervell and Alexander 'the Brig' Howard.[14] Some of the Howards objected to her recollections of the Brig terrifying little Jane by pretending to be a lion; but Spender himself was very complimentary. 'I think your grandfathers are marvellous and this is one of the best pieces we have ever had sent to us. It is amusing, beautifully written and very sad – which is how it should be.'[15]

Perhaps encouraged by the success of her book, Jane finally broke off her affair with Cecil Day-Lewis in the early summer of 1956: the joy of being with him was not enough to obliterate the guilt of betraying Jill, and the hopeless misery of knowing that Cecil would never leave her. She also stopped working at Chatto, and found a job as a deputy fiction editor at Weidenfeld & Nicolson working under Barley Alison.

The Long View was still selling steadily, and in June it was given a further edition by the Reprint Society. 'I am delighted,' wrote her agent A.D. Peters, '. . . apart from anything else, this ensures you plenty of time to write the new novel without doing any other work'.[16] The idea of not having any steady salary was understandably terrifying, and Jane did not want to give it up; but at the same time, after a day's work at Weidenfeld's she was too tired to do any serious writing in the evenings.

The stable relationship she yearned for seemed equally elusive. 'It's no good telling me anything about love,' she wrote to Bob Linscott in May. 'A number of extremely unsuitable gentlemen have suggested marriage to me during the last few weeks but, either they are married already, or they are drinking themselves to death, or they are the world's best destroyers of themselves and anybody else they come into contact with . . . So I remain with a small single heart, all the contemporary equipment for the sad life.'[17]

One of her admirers was the editor and critic Cyril Connolly, who immortalized his own failure to become a great writer in his book *Enemies of Promise.* His magazine *Horizon* had aspired to discover all that was best on the contemporary scene, but it did not survive into the new decade. Connolly was in his early fifties when he knew Jane, and chief reviewer for the *Sunday Times.* That March his second wife, Barbara Skelton, had fallen for the publisher George Weidenfeld; but instead of making a clean break she spent the following months lurching between the two men, unable to decide which of them she really loved. This left Cyril utterly demoralized, in an emotional limbo that made writing almost impossible (a state Jane knew all too well).

He was good if gloomy company, and she was deeply envious of Kiko, his ring-tailed lemur, whom he brought to lunch one day. 'It sat on the lawn and lunched lightly off some white lilac, half an apple, and some very thin bread and butter. It was an animal possessed of the most lightening charm and I want one very badly.'[18] Reading *A Ring of Bright Water* by her friend Gavin Maxwell four years later, Jane must have been glad she did not achieve her desire. When Connolly could no longer cope with Kiko's occasional bouts of savage fury he passed her on to Maxwell, still grieving over the senseless death of his first beloved otter, Mijbil. But after Kiko's third attempt to murder him, which left Maxwell with a severed artery, he was obliged to give her to a zoo.

That summer, Jane enjoyed what one might call a short service commission with the writer and theatre critic Kenneth Tynan. She had been asked to a party at the Tynans' flat in Mount Street, and not long after that Ken invited her to the theatre. He told her that his wife Elaine Dundy had left for a three-month stay in America, and wondered whether Jane would be his 'evening companion' while she was away – on condition that the moment Elaine returned, Jane would vanish into the shadows.

This was the second time that Jane had been offered something in exchange for her company and sexual services, as if those were things to be traded. Yet she didn't seem to mind, and it was fun being with Tynan. He was then reviewing for the *Observer* and they went to the theatre every night, which was always followed by dinner in a restaurant, and a party or a nightclub after that. Jane described him as 'a creature of self-constructed layers': he loved glamour and panache and exotic food and clothes, yet although he seemed so effortlessly cool, Jane felt that he was 'an unconfident, uncontrollable romantic who was constantly warding off disappointment lest it should turn to despair'. She might have said the same of herself, and they also shared a need to be noticed and admired. In the warm weather Jane often wore a white dress – she claimed it was the only decent dress she had but Tynan said, 'You *would* wear white,' and added that she was only doing it to attract attention to themselves as a star couple.[19]

The only place they didn't have much fun was in bed, for they were sexually incompatible. Jane is evasively discreet about this in *Slipstream*, saying that both of them were shy and that she had no idea

- Miss Jane Forestier :-

Jane's mother, Kit Somervell.
With the Ballets Russes,
she danced as Jane Forestier.

Kit and David Howard,
Jane's parents, on one of
their regular skiing holidays.

In Jane's memoir, the caption to this photo reads, 'My mother with Colin'. In fact the baby is Jane herself.

'I spent the mornings up apple trees reading Captain Marryat and R.M. Ballantyne – I had a great wish to be shipwrecked.'

Jane, her mother and her brother Robin, c.1933. Jane was in no doubt that Robin was her mother's favourite.

Jane and her father. 'He always seemed pleased to see me, to spend time with me, to laugh at my jokes.'

Jane, as Juliet, aged fourteen.

Fifteen-year-old Jane with Colin, in Holland. Colin, aged four, is wearing Dutch costume.

Mr and Mrs Peter Scott, 28 April 1942. Jane's dress is made of lace,
which was not subject to rationing.

Peter Scott with his mother,
the sculptor Kathleen Kennet:
'She loved him too much to let
anyone else love him,' wrote Jane.

Peter's portrait of Jane as Fritha, in Paul Gallico's *The Snow Goose*. 'I stood for hours, holding a pillow which he later turned into the wounded snow goose.' The portrait was painted on board the *Aquitania* on which Jane and Peter travelled to New York in the spring of 1946.

This photograph of Jane was taken around the time she stood for the portrait.

Nicola was christened on board HMS *Discovery*, spring 1943.

Nicola at work at her father's easel.

Peter's half-brother,
Wayland Young (later 2nd
Baron Kennet), in 1942.

Michael Behrens:
financier and collector
of beautiful people
and objects.

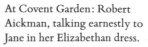

At Covent Garden: Robert Aickman, talking earnestly to Jane in her Elizabethan dress.

Aickman's muse: 'He wanted me to wear straight black skirts and shirts with ties.'

Jane's brother Colin, known as Monkey since prep school, with one of his mother's tortoises.

what he wanted. In fact she was left in no doubt, because Tynan's sexual tastes ran to the sadomasochistic. 'I didn't like all that spanking,' she said.[20] She preferred to remember him dancing around the room stark naked, singing 'The Rain in Spain' from *My Fair Lady*, a musical Tynan had seen on Broadway. Jane had no trouble making a graceful exit when Elaine Dundy returned to London.

Cyril Connolly was still seeing Jane from time to time, still fantasizing about the deep peace of the marriage bed, and still tormented by his ex-wife's emotional indecision. Barbara Skelton and George Weidenfeld were married in late August, and spent their honeymoon on the island of Ischia. Cyril, poised to rescue Barbara from a new marriage she already feared was doomed, took up a position on the other end of the island and continued to weigh his options.

He told Jane that he was astonished by her suggestion, relayed by Natasha Spender, that 'I live with you "platonically" for three months . . . and helped you with your writing! Of course I want to live with you, but not platonically (I think that should be left open) – my only goal is marriage and I only want to live with someone with that in view. I don't want to be a private tutor!' At the same time, he had not stopped pining for Barbara. She had telephoned him every day since she had married George, he told Jane, and added gleefully, 'What will [George] say when he gets his telephone bill?'[21]

Jane wrote back, saying she had never made 'such a naive and embarrassing suggestion . . . I do want to be married – we've talked about that – but I don't want to do it either clutching or being clutched at as a straw.'[22]

They never did have an affair. Cyril's puggish looks did not appeal, and his emotional neediness was too close to her own. Her fling with Ken Tynan was enjoyable while it lasted, and left her emotionally untouched. Yet the separation from Cecil Day-Lewis was still hurting, and they were still acutely aware of one another's presence when in the same room, at parties or book launches.

She kept her distance, while Cecil wrote her warm and affectionate letters urging her to change her mind. He loved her still, whether they were lovers or not. He did not want to put pressure on her, he said, but they should not deny themselves the pleasures of the flesh; that what Jill didn't know couldn't possibly hurt her; and that by removing herself from him, Jane was cutting the very essence of love out of her life. In other words, he exerted a great deal of pressure. As the year wore on she and Cecil still met for lunch from time to time, and he missed her terribly. 'If, just occasionally,' he wrote to her in September, 'we can be alone together, it would make the public meetings so much easier.'[23]

Jane had been surprised to find how little money she had made from her novels; yet her agent A.D. Peters felt that the time had come for her to quit the day job, for she had reached a critical moment in her career. The success of *The Long View* had loaded expectation on to her next novel, and he wanted to make sure that it had all the attention it deserved. At his urging she left Weidenfeld's to write full time, and in September he gave her £300 on which to live while she finished the book; but being without a steady salary was very unsettling, and so she continued to take on small editing jobs as they arose.

At first, writing in the mornings had an energizing effect. She began to live in the story as she was writing it, and various knotty problems unravelled of their own accord. Yet as the year wore on, the initial burst of speed began to falter as her confidence ebbed. She told herself that the two novels she had published had been beginner's luck – she couldn't imagine how she had written them.

It was around this time that she met the dress designer Victor Stiebel, through the actress Judy Campbell whom she had met with Peter. Stiebel was one of the most celebrated fashion designers of the time, whose beautifully constructed dresses were well beyond Jane's reach. But they became great friends, and when she heard that he was looking for a high-quality audio system (his partner for many years was the composer Richard Addinsell) she suggested that her brother Monkey would be just the man to make it.

Monkey duly made the system, and when it was finished he asked Stiebel to give Jane a dress in lieu of payment. Jane was delighted by the prospect, and dreamed of the perfect little black dress that would do for every occasion; but Monkey had far grander ideas.

Those were the days when a designer's important clients had their own fashion show; and as Jane and Monkey sat on little gold chairs and watched the models swishing by, one of them appeared in a magnificent ballgown of Wedgwood blue silk. Monkey immediately decided that that was the dress he wanted to see her in; and as Jane put it, 'I realised I couldn't disappoint him. I was going to have to take a dress I'd probably never get a chance to wear.'[24] Luckily, Victor understood Jane's sartorial needs far better than Monkey and suggested that she try on some black cocktail frocks too. She found one in corded silk with a plain round neck and a bell skirt, and Victor said she should have them both.

She only wore the ballgown once, at a dinner in the Guildhall for the Arts and Sciences. 'The first person I met before dinner was Rosamond Lehmann. She looked at me with cool distaste then pointed out that I had a shoulder strap showing.'[25]

That October, *The Long View* was chosen by the Book of the Month Club – an accolade always guaranteed to boost sales and much respected in the publishing world. It coincided with the Cheltenham Festival, to which Jane had been invited as one of a group of young writers (the others were Elizabeth Jennings, Charles Whiting and Gillian Freeman). She took part in two Brains Trust sessions, and on the Friday afternoon she and Cecil, who had also been invited, were to head a Schools Debate. The proposition was 'That it is better to have taken Quebec than written Gray's *Elegy*' – a rather contorted way of saying that life is better spent in action than in contemplation. Day-Lewis would take the side of action with Jane opposing him.

Since he rarely missed an opportunity of seeing her alone, Cecil wrote to ask whether she would come and join him at the Ellenborough Park Hotel just north of Cheltenham. 'I shall arrive there about 1 pm on Friday, so why not if it's a fine day meet me there laden with buns and we will drive out for a picnic, or if it's wet have lunch with me at the hotel? I'd be a nice change for you from the culture-vultures. I'll drive you back to London on Saturday. Hope the bracing intellectual climate of Cheltenham is suiting you, my love. C.'[26]

Jane did come and see him at the hotel. He noted that she 'looked so beautiful when we had lunch, but rather pale and hollow-cheeked'. Then they spent two hours in his room, going over all the arguments: he trying to persuade her to come back to him, and she determined not to. Remembering that afternoon a few weeks later he wrote: 'I did feel resentment, my Lizbie, and had a longish struggle to dowse it . . . Certainly I'd have gone on going to the limit of risk, as your lover, because your mind and body have given me more joy than any other woman's: but not if I'd felt it was disintegrating my relationship with Jill.'[27]

Whatever her problems with Cecil, Jane had been very intrigued by the possibilities of the Cheltenham Literary Festival. In a letter to the chairman John Moore she wrote: 'Do you want ideas for next or future years? All festivals fascinate me and naturally a festival concentrating on literature is the most interesting of all.'[28]

She spent Christmas in Cornwall, with Roger St Aubyn and Lorna Mackintosh. Jane was very fond of Lorna, although she found Roger terrifying. She described his treatment of Lorna to Cecil, who wrote: '*Why* doesn't Lorna leave him? Surely they have reached the stage when he's got beyond her help and will become ever more exasperated by her presence and her ineffectuality to do anything for him.'[29]

It is always easy to see what ought to be done from the outside; but as Jane knew well, women are adept at finding reasons to be with someone they love – however much they may get hurt. Cecil had sent her a poem for Christmas, a sad poem of love and acceptance, yet it is not altogether without hope, and in the new year of 1957 his persistence paid off: 'My Lizbie, all mine now . . . feeling you turn to fire and melt in my arms – you are so wonderful to make love to and be loved by . . . Are you as glad as I am? . . . I adore your body, the touch and taste of it; and to feel the power mine had over it, and the way our bodies recognized each other at once and were at home together in all the strangeness and excitement.'[30]

Cecil's triumph was short-lived. Jane insisted that it had been a momentary lapse, never to be repeated – it just wasn't worth the emotional fallout. They continued to see each other and in March he wrote: 'I am deep deep *in love* with you still, dear heart – time doesn't seem to make it any easier, and our unsexed relationship (quiet chats about books and patchwork) goes right against the grain for me, try as I will to accept it.'[31]

He comforted her when she heard the news that Paul Bowman, whom she had almost married three years before, had committed suicide; and at the end of 1957, when she sent Cecil an early draft of *The Sea Change*, he proved a constructive and generous critic. 'I see why you felt Em's childhood had to be done this way, but you seem to have lost grip here – to be a bit showy and flustered, as if you'd lost confidence . . . Do look at this bit again and see if I am not right. Otherwise it's a splendid book and I can't wait to read the rest. You're getting better and better – sinking deeper into people.'[32]

Jane's relationship with Cecil Day-Lewis was one of the most important in her life, and certainly few men understood or appreciated her as he did. Yet in later years Jane told herself that her final refusal had provoked a backlash of bitterness and resentment, and that he had called her a whore.[33] In fact, this was Jane's far too personal interpretation of his sonnet sequence called 'Moods of Love'. He had sent her the ecstatic middle sonnets (IV and V) in manuscript, dedicated 'For Lizbie'.[34] And when it was about to appear in *Encounter*, in early 1957, he sent the whole sequence in proof. Jane claimed that the penultimate sonnet, No. VIII, was a poisoned dart aimed directly at her:

> Better the brutal twitching of the reins
> And off, than this devouring pious whore
> Who in soft regret will twine you fast
> Where thigh-bones mope along the tainted shore
> And crazed beachcombers pick over their past.

Yet the proof was dedicated 'For Loved Lizbie': if he really thought of her as a *pious whore*, would he have sent the sonnets with an affectionate dedication? It is far more likely that he was thinking of Rosamond Lehmann, although 'Moods of Love' is deliberately enigmatic. It describes a love affair which is part odyssey, part creation myth: from its innocent beginnings, through the mystery of flesh and spirit made one to its sad dissolution. The arc is inevitable; yet love can and does continue after the ecstasy and the bitterness are over, as the last lines of the poem indicate:

> But chance and fretting time and your love change her
> Subtly from year to year, from known to new:
> So, she will always be the elusive stranger,
> If you can hold her present self in view.
>
> Find here, in constant change, faithful perceiving
> The paradox and mode of all true loving.[35]

Another possible but by no means overt dig at Jane has been noticed by some in Cecil's novel, *End of Chapter* (1957). This is one of the detective novels he wrote under the pseudonym of Nicholas Blake, in which the murder victim is Millicent Miles: a bestselling novelist who has taken over an attic room in the publishing house of Wenham & Geraldine, where she is busy writing her memoirs when sudden death overtakes her. In her imperious manners, Millicent Miles displays more of Rosamond Lehmann than she does of Elizabeth Jane Howard; but Jane might well have seen the book as further evidence of a grudge against herself.

For much of 1957 Jane was absorbed by *The Sea Change*, a story of four people. Each of them has a voice, distinct and individual, and the story emerges as they live it, scene by scene – in London, New York and the Greek island of Hydra.

Emmanuel Joyce was born in London, to a tormented Jewish mother and a violent drunken Irish father. He had escaped his impoverished background and, through luck and hard work, had become a brilliant playwright (we are never told what sort of plays, but perhaps like those of S.N. Behrman in the 1920s and 1930s, which include *Biography*, *End of Summer* and *No Time for Comedy*). When the story opens he is in his early sixties with a string of box-office hits behind him, but he is emotionally drained, and fears he will never be able to write another play again.

One of the reasons he is so tired is because his wife's mental and physical health are a constant source of worry. Em feels emotionally responsible for Lillian, a beautiful, restless woman who has never got over the death of their only child, Sara, who died of meningitis at the age of two. She clings to this tragedy which prevents her from doing or enjoying anything, and she carries her daughter's photographs everywhere; along with her innumerable trunks of expensive clothes, and the battery of pills and drugs she needs to calm her weak heart, help her sleep and ease her depressions.

The Joyces have no settled home. They are constantly moving between luxury flats and hotels all over the world, wherever Em's latest play takes them – and all the arrangements for their complicated lives are made by Jimmy Sullivan. He has to make travel reservations, book rooms, hire cars, navigate Lillian's luggage through customs, and take her to lunch when Em has better things to do. And as Em's Man Friday, he also negotiates contracts and supervises auditions.

Into this mix comes nineteen-year-old Alberta Young, the daughter of a clergyman, hired by the Joyces as a secretary. But as a classic example of the Elizabeth Jane Howard ingénue – bookish, unworldly, innocent and with a childlike directness which comes like a breath of fresh air – she is the catalyst that will change their lives for ever.

In the spring of 1957, Jane met a man full of energy, intelligence and humour called Leigh Goodman. He was married, in a loosely uncoupled way, to a Swiss woman called Suzanne who worked for a company that published art books – work that often took her abroad, leaving Leigh alone in a beautiful flat in Onslow Square. It was not long before Jane was keeping him company, although his life was more complicated than he had at first made out. His fervently Jewish family ran a prosperous company in the East End of London, making uniforms. They had no idea about Suzanne, and would have been horrified to hear that he had married a non-Jew; although he had only married her, he said, because she wanted British nationality.

That summer, Jane and some friends took a house in Saint-Tropez. The party consisted of Arthur and Celia Goodman who had remained friends with Jane after her break-up with Arthur Koestler; and the architect Martyn Beckett and his wife Priscilla. Jane invited Leigh, who got on with everyone and was a great success. They spent their mornings on the broad sandy beach of Pampelonne with a picnic lunch, and watched Brigitte Bardot 'covered only partly by her tawny mane and more efficiently by a bronzed young man'.[36] After a long siesta they would have dinner at their villa, and then wander down to drink at one of the bars in the old port. Leigh was funny and entertaining, a warm and loving presence; but sometimes when they were alone she would look at him and see nothing but despair.

Back in London it became clear that his marriage was not quite the casual contract he had thought: Suzanne began to need more of him, and he felt responsible for her. His moods began to swing alarmingly from manic gaiety to utter dejection, and Jane put him in touch with Dr David Stafford-Clark, a psychiatrist and bestselling author of *Psychiatry Today* (1951), with whom she had been on a TV panel. He took Leigh Goodman on as a patient, and from then on Jane and

Leigh saw less of each other although she tried to keep in touch. Whenever she rang to ask how he was, he was always upbeat and non-committal; but a few months later, he committed suicide – and was found holding a note from Jane in his hand. David Stafford-Clark assured her it wasn't her fault; but Jane took it very hard nonetheless – particularly after Paul Bowman's suicide earlier in the year.

She hated living alone, hated being single, and the fear of not finding someone who would complete her life ate away at her from inside. There were outside pressures too. At a time when most women married in their early twenties, to be unattached at thirty-five was seen as a failure, and she had been divorced for seven years – at a time when divorce still carried a perceptible stain. 'I succumbed to almost any distraction that involved being with people. Evenings, in particular, weren't for writing, but parties or concerts, theatres or cinemas – or simply going out to dinner with men who asked me.'[37]

One hot summer evening, on one of Nicola's rare visits to Blomfield Road (she was then about fifteen, and at boarding school), the telephone rang. It was Ingaret van der Post. Would they like to come round for a drink? The van der Post house was in Chelsea, two bus rides away, and it was so hot that Jane almost thought she wouldn't bother. Once there she was glad she had made the effort, for the only other guest was a man who instantly caught her attention.

James Douglas-Henry was tall, with dark hair and a big laugh. A friend once described him as 'an incredibly charming rapscallion, with no social background that you could measure, no school, no university, just the stories of hitchhiking across Africa and smuggling cigarettes from Tangier to Marseille'.[38] Another, not so much of a friend, said that 'if he were in a room full of people and you were asked to pick out the rogue, you'd pick him'.

And so, for very different reasons, did Jane.

12

A Matrimonial Mistake

JAMES DOUGLAS-HENRY WAS the son of an Australian army officer, Major P.J. Douglas-Henry DSO, and his English wife Norma Mitchell-Innes. Born in Salonika in 1928 and brought up in England, Portugal and Australia, he had left school at sixteen and made his way to Sydney. There he did odd jobs, working in the theatre, and learned enough about sailing to be taken on as a crewman. He left Australia in about 1948 and came to Britain, where he stayed with his mother's family. Then he sailed to Tangier and started a cigarette-running business, which was also used as a cover to help people escape from Franco's Spain.

In England he had worked as a stockbroker, and briefly had a job with George Weidenfeld working on coffee-table books. He read omnivorously, and a literary friend described him as 'exceptionally shrewd and perceptive about books and writers'.[1] He was also a keen member of the Ouspensky Society, which sought to awaken true self-awareness. This was perhaps why, despite being normally sharp and funny, his conversation sometimes took off in esoteric abstractions that left his listeners mystified. Although five years younger than Jane, she loved the fact that he was taller, almost by a head; most of her lovers had been on the short side. She wrote an ecstatic letter about Jim to Bob Linscott, who suggested she hold on to him tight.

She did. Their affair had started soon after they met in 1957, and in the summer of 1958 she and Jim spent four or five weeks on the jagged Greek island of Hydra. The village climbed steeply above the little harbour, in a series of haphazard whitewashed terraces linked by stairways: Jane described it 'as though someone had spilled a packet of lump sugar from the top of the mountain and most of it had rolled to the bottom'.[2] She loved it all: the people in their sun-faded clothes, joking and haggling in Greek; the blue shutters; the leathery octopus hung out to dry; the rough straw chairs and battered oil lamps; the donkeys who formed the only transport; and the half-starved cats for whom she put out food. While she was there, she was writing the New York sections of *The Sea Change*; but Hydra, with its burning rocks and dazzling blue sea, became the setting for the second half of the novel.

There was a disagreeable moment when, as she was changing out of her wet bathing costume after a swim (there was only one place to bathe in Hydra), Cecil Day-Lewis suddenly appeared, having arrived with a party of people on a cruise. 'He looked aghast and I was rather shaken. "I'm just having a quick bathe and then back to the ship," he said in brisk, business-like tones.'[3]

When she and Jim had left for Greece, her father had not been well; and by the time they returned he was dying of cancer. Jane visited him when he was near death, and held his hand for some time. She could think of nothing to say, and felt that her speechlessness had really let him down. 'I knew that he passionately didn't want to die: that he'd endured months of pain and illness and fear of death in silence. He was certainly too ill to talk to me by then, but he might have *heard* me, and I'd said nothing.'[4] David Howard died in September, and was buried in Hawkhurst, Kent, where he and Ursula had settled.

Jane was one of those people in whom self-doubt rises too fast and stays too long. She learned in childhood that she would never fulfil her mother's expectations; and this sense of moral failure was reinforced by her broken marriage, her infidelities, her inability to bond with her daughter, her remorse about Jill and the other women she had betrayed, about Leigh Goodman and Paul Bowman whom she had failed to save, and now her father whom she had been unable to comfort. She did not see these episodes as 'sins', for apart from a sudden burst of enthusiasm for God when she was at the cookery school in Beaconsfield she was not religious. But she had made mistakes, and these seem to have created fractures in her mind that oozed with sighs and groans, clouded her judgement and stopped her being whole.

This was why she was so drawn to the character of the ingénue in her novels. This childlike figure is the self she was so desperate to reclaim, the person she felt she had been before her mistakes had turned her into a glamorous, discontented femme fatale. If she could find the right man and marry him, she knew the healing process would start at once.

In a later novel, *After Julius*, she dramatizes the tension between the innocence she longed for and the experience in which she was trapped through the characters of two sisters: Emma and Cressy. Very early in the book Emma (the innocent one) asks Cressy if she would like to get married and Cressy replies, ' "It's the one thing I really want in the world. If I could find the right person, I'd do anything to keep things good and make them better. I feel wrong all by myself: you don't; I suppose that's why I have affairs and you don't?" '[5]

And now, with Jim, she had the chance to regain her innocence, and become a better and a wiser person. With his encouragement, she joined the Ouspensky Society.

The early twentieth century had witnessed a great surge of interest in a broad spectrum of spiritual teachers, gurus and healers, of whom one of the most successful was a Greek–Armenian mystic called George Gurdjieff. One of Gurdjieff's many followers, the Russian mathematician and philosopher Piotr Demianovich Ouspensky, used his teachings to form the basis of what he called 'The Fourth Way'.

Ouspensky taught that ordinary consciousness is incomplete. In order to achieve true self-awareness, the student must develop their intellectual, emotional and physical faculties to their fullest. This was achieved through study, group seminars, mental exercises and 'the Movements': sacred dances that Gurdjieff had learned during his travels in Asia, accompanied by music. When Ouspensky died in 1947, his work was continued in London by Dr Francis Roles, who gave up his medical career to set up the Study Society (informally, still the Ouspensky group) based at Colet House in Baron's Court, west London.

Although conscious that she was still at the larval stage of self-development, Jane was not as inspired by the society as she had hoped. The people around Dr Roles seemed very pleased with their higher initiations and their arcane knowledge, and she found the secrecy of it rather silly and self-regarding. But she hoped things would get better, and she was still besotted with Jim. 'The fact that he had no visible means of support did not present itself as any kind of warning. He said he loved me? Then of course he did.'[6]

Jane later said that she married Jim because she was fed up with people wanting to go to bed with her after half an hour's acquaintance; but she had always found it hard to resist the advances of a confident and attentive man, and seldom did. At the same time, she longed for stability and was desperate to wed again, if only to stop Kit's constant reminders of her state as a single divorcee who couldn't find anyone to marry her. She also felt that she was now ready to have more children. Jim also wanted children but felt that Jane was happier with the idea of them than the reality. After all, since she often forgot to feed the cats, how would she cope with a child?[7] It was just as well they remained childless because the marriage would prove to be unhappy for them both; but to distance herself from it still further, Jane claimed there were external pressures too. Dr Roles, she would say, had declared that he didn't want his followers living in sin. But a fellow member of the society thought this highly unlikely, since several people within the group were cohabiting and she had never heard Dr Roles express any disapproval of them.

In the spring of 1959, shortly before her second marriage, Jane took on the job of book reviewer for *Queen* magazine. In the late 1950s *Queen* – which came out twice a month – was under the editorship of Beatrix Miller. She had a style sheet entitled 'Caroline' that was given to all contributors, which described the magazine's targeted reader. 'Caroline' was young, educated, fashion-conscious, socially ambitious – and she wanted to know about the sort of books, plays and cultural celebrities that were the subjects of conversation at London dinner parties.

Jane was given the job thanks to a friend she had met through the Spenders – Francis Wyndham, who was then working as theatre critic on the magazine. Wyndham had worked in publishing for Derek Verschoyle and André Deutsch, and promoted the careers of Jean Rhys, Vidia Naipaul and Bruce Chatwin among others. He and Beatrix Miller decided that Jane had just the right profile to advise 'Caroline' on her reading. Miller asked her to review about four books (fiction and non-fiction) in 1,200 words every fortnight.

Jane sought the advice of A.D. Peters, who said she ought to be writing her novel not taking on jobs. 'Don't do it for less than a thousand a year,' he said.[8] It seemed like a fortune but *Queen* were willing to pay, and they commissioned Tony Armstrong-Jones to photograph her. The photo they chose is very odd. It shows Jane in profile outside a window, while in the foreground (presumably on a window ledge) are a full ashtray, a bottle of ink and another bottle that might contain either whisky or lighter-fuel. Beside this was a headline that read: 'Our new book critic, Elizabeth Jane Howard, whose novel *The Long View* was a bestseller in 1956, sums up her personal approach to reading and reviewing.'

Jane took her new job very seriously, and every word of every book was read with care. She gave her readers much more than a brief synopsis. It was as if she could handle the work, feel its weight and see its colour; and she managed to convey all this with enviable brevity. Most of her fiction reviews begin with short thumbnail sketches of the main characters in their setting, often with a vivid description that captures the essence of the whole work.

Take *Sammy Going South* by W.H. Canaway,[9] which is about a ten-year-old boy who lost his parents during the Suez crisis in Egypt and, having no one to turn to, sets out to walk to his aunt's in Durban, South Africa. He is utterly vulnerable, and yet resilient in a way that Jane found very moving: 'Like a small animal thrown out of his element into water,' she wrote, '[Sammy] thrashes and swims or drifts with the currents because it never occurs to him that he might drown.' Being a novelist herself, she can also give intriguing insights into the writer's mind. Of Muriel Spark's *The Bachelors*, she wrote: 'Her dispassionate amusement is infectious, but her indifference is alarming'; and on another occasion, described her writing as 'always a little yeasty with the macabre'.[10]

Her own tastes are never in doubt. She enjoyed Anthony Powell's fifth volume of *A Dance to the Music of Time*,[11] while admitting that she had not read the preceding four. She admired his measured skill, and the way he aims 'just off the bull's eye of his target in order to make sure you've noticed exactly where it was'; yet she was left 'with a hunger for some more passionate nature than I found in Mr Powell's ecology'.

At the same time, she never fails to notice how a work is put together. In *The Old Men at the Zoo* she took great pleasure in the way that Angus Wilson produced 'a structure that exactly contains another structure with no space wasted, this process continuing as far as the mind cares to pursue it'.[12]

On the whole she is a generous reviewer, always delighted when a book exceeds her expectations or she finds a new voice (David

Storey and Susan Hill, for example). However, it is interesting that one of the books about which she was unusually scathing was by her future husband, Kingsley Amis, whose fourth novel was *Take a Girl Like You*. 'Mr Amis,' she wrote, 'is at his best with inanimate objects; he can be very funny about boilers and food and cars and bars; but except when he finds his people absurd – when they are also funny – they are simply dull, and they are dull an awful lot of the time.'[13]

The books she reviewed between the spring of 1959 and the autumn of 1961 form a snapshot of English literary life at the time. At the more intellectual end of fiction she reviewed Graham Greene and Anthony Powell and Iris Murdoch, with Alistair Maclean, Agatha Christie and Ian Fleming at the other; and in between she considered Muriel Spark, Robert Shaw, John Wyndham, Rumer Godden, Angus Wilson, Pierre Boulle, Penelope Mortimer, V.S. Pritchett and Isobel English among others. She also had a good working knowledge of the current literary landscape: books she mentions in passing include A.J.A. Symonds's *The Quest for Corvo*, Sybille Bedford's *A Legacy*, J.D. Salinger's *Catcher in the Rye* and Cecil Woodham-Smith's *The Reason Why*.

In non-fiction, she reviewed Peter Fleming's *The Siege at Peking* and Sybille Bedford's *A Visit to Don Otavio* with great enthusiasm, and described Laurie Lee's *Cider with Rosie* as the book she had most enjoyed since joining the magazine.[14] It is obvious that she liked being a regular reviewer, and she was certainly good at it; but as A.D. Peters had warned, it took up a great deal more time and energy than she had thought it would.

Neither Jim nor Jane had any money for a honeymoon; but thanks to Jack and Margaret Huntingdon, whom Jane had met with A.D. Peters, an opportunity arose for a short break in France. Jack Huntingdon, known as 'the Red Earl' for his Communist sympathies, was a painter who had studied and been assistant to the Mexican artist Diego Rivera; while his wife, Margaret Lane, had been a successful author and journalist who had interviewed Al Capone. A few weeks before the wedding, Jack and Margaret invited Jane and Jim to visit them in Hampshire; and during the course of lunch, they suggested that they might like to take their yacht, the *Sharavogue*, down through the rivers and canals of France to Marseille. Jim and Jane were delighted by the idea, and it was arranged that they should go with an experienced skipper called Glen, and a young man called Stephen Asquith, more commonly known as Kipper or Kip, who was a cousin of Jack's.

Selina Hastings, the Huntingdons' daughter, was about fourteen at the time and charmed by Jim, who treated her like a grown-up. She also remembers her father talking about his plans to go treasure-hunting in Mozambique. Jim became very excited, and dropped a hint that he would leap at any chance to join the expedition. Her father mumbled something non-committal; but after Jane and Jim had left, Jack Huntingdon declared that 'I wouldn't go to the bottom of the garden with that man, let alone East Africa.'[15]

Jane and Jim were married on 2 April 1959, at Kensington Registry Office with two others in the Ouspensky group. They were Gillian Grant and the sculptor David Wynne, known to Londoners for his sculpture *Boy with a Dolphin* on the Chelsea Embankment. After the wedding the two couples had a long and bibulous lunch together in a pub.

Soon after, they sailed the Huntingdons' yacht across the Channel. The *Sharavogue* was built for Atlantic racing so although it was a choppy crossing, even Jane enjoyed the way she sliced effortlessly through the water. But while the yacht's six-foot draught gave her stability at sea, it created problems as soon as they reached the first canal. In Lyon, they were told that the Rhône was so dry that if the *Sharavogue* was ever to reach Marseille, she would have to be hoisted on to a *péniche*: a broad, flat-bottomed workhorse of a boat, used to ferry goods up and down the French waterways.

A *péniche* was duly hired; but at that point it emerged that Glen, the skipper, had no idea how to set about heaving the yacht aloft with chains and then chocking her up in the hold. Luckily Jim knew exactly what to do, manned the chains and the chocks and saw the *Sharavogue* safely stowed. Jane was impressed at how he seemed far more willing to face a problem and get his hands dirty than Glen. When the job was done, the captain of the *péniche* invited Jane and Jim into his cabin for a drink. Everything was spotlessly clean, and she was intrigued to see that the interior was decorated in exactly the same gypsy-wagon style, complete with coarse white lace and orna-mental plates, as the English narrow-boats.

The honeymoon was not yet over when Jane found herself in a situ-ation she had never imagined: Jim made it clear that he did not love her. She was left utterly bewildered and humiliated, and – as someone used to having men call her irresistible – Jim's resistance eroded her confidence as nothing else could. A friend remembered 'Jane's phys-icality towards him, the way she would want to kiss and touch, be puppyish and flirty'.[16] He deflected her with a laugh or a joke, and she was left following him round the room with her eyes.

He knew that she needed warmth and an intense physical inti-macy; and in suddenly going cold, he had plunged her into an anxious limbo of sexual tension. There were other strains too. Jane wrote that they had been married about six weeks when Jim presented her with a bill for some fabulously expensive hand-made shirts from Jermyn Street, for which she was expected to pay.[17] But according to Jim, it was she who had told him to smarten up his wardrobe with some decent shirts, and he had asked the shop to send her the bill as a joke.[18]

The Sea Change was almost ready for the printers when Dr Roles, who led the Ouspensky group, demanded a copy of the typescript so he could check that the novel disclosed none of the organization's secrets. Jane thought it a ridiculous request but complied, and the typescript came back with some prissy and irrelevant cuts.

In the week before publication, the *Sunday Times* ran an 'Atticus' piece about high-achieving women in the public eye. Among them were Mrs Thatcher, the newly appointed MP for Finchley; the slogan writer Nona Johnston; Nancy Thomas, assistant producer of the BBC's arts programme *Monitor*; Siriol Hugh-Jones, whom Jane had known from her early days with *Vogue*; and Jane, whom 'Atticus' described as, 'for my money, the most beautiful woman novelist living in London'.[19] She wished she could just be a novelist; but being known as a 'woman novelist' seemed inescapable – particularly since her main preoccupations were with love and relationships.

Her first and most encouraging review, from John Davenport in the *Observer*, appeared on 15 November. '*The Sea Change* is a string quartet, beautifully shaped and interrelated,' he wrote. It's 'not quite Mozart but well into the [Gabriel] Fauré class'. The triumph of the book, he claimed, was the young and innocent Alberta: 'You just try portraying somebody young, pretty, clever and good, without sentimentality. There is nothing soppy or priggish about Alberta, who has the spring of a Turgenev heroine.' He ended his review with the wonderfully emancipating words: 'this is not "a woman's book": it belongs to all of us. Happy us.'

In the *Times Literary Supplement* she was again reviewed by Marigold Johnson, who said that 'Miss Howard has already won a high reputation with her two earlier novels, and *The Sea Change* confirms her place among the important women novelists now writing.'[20]

In the *Sunday Times*, however, J.D. Scott was not so impressed. He described the novel as 'cleverly managed and smoothly entertaining, but neither makes any pretences nor takes any steps to be anything more . . . This is eminently a woman's novel and a library novel, but . . . above average in both classes.'[21]

Nevertheless she had the satisfaction of being listed as one of the *Sunday Times*'s Outstanding Books for November. On the fiction side, *The Sea Change* took its place beside John Braine's *The Vodi*, *The War Lover* by John Hersey and Vladimir Nabokov's *Lolita*, which had just been published in London. She was also very pleased to note that among the non-fiction books listed that month was Laurie Lee's *Cider with Rosie*.[22]

Cider with Rosie was a huge bestseller, which marked the height of Laurie Lee's career. *The Sea Change* was a more modest success; but she and Laurie appeared on ABC Television's book programme, *Book Man*, that November: Jack Lambert interviewed her about *The Sea Change*, and Lee about his early life in Gloucestershire.

That winter, Dr Francis Roles heard that an Indian guru had come to Britain from America, where he had made a considerable impact. His name was Maharishi Mahesh Yogi, and he was a small, smiling man in his early forties with flowing hair and a beard, dressed in white robes and sandals. The Maharishi gave his first lecture in London at Caxton Hall, in Westminster, on 18 December 1959.[23] Dr Roles was deeply impressed, and decided that he had found the missing piece that Ouspensky had told him to look for. This was the exercise with which the Maharishi hoped to transform the world: Transcendental Meditation.

In the spring of 1960 the Maharishi settled into a flat in Chelsea, where Dr Roles encouraged everyone in the Ouspensky group to visit him to be inducted into the principles of meditation. They found the Maharishi sitting on a raised platform surrounded by flowers, while his visitors sat on the floor in front. Before beginning, the · Maharishi would ask each of his visitors in turn: 'What do you desire the most?' Jane replied that she wanted to be 'a better person'.

She took up meditation in earnest, as did Jim; but while the practice did bring her some clarity, it could not change the fact that she was married to a man who made her miserable. Many of those who came to lunch or dinner at Blomfield Road would have been surprised to hear how unhappy she was. The house was filled with plants and flowers, while books, seed catalogues and magazines lay on every available surface. It was also home to three cats, whose desire to claw the cushions and rugs – in patchwork or petit-point that Jane had worked herself – required constant vigilance. (One of these cats, a black female called Katsika, had been smuggled into England from Hydra.) The conversation buzzed, wine flowed, and Jim gave every impression of being an affectionate and attentive husband.

Nicola too was prepared to like Jim, at least at first: 'He was a rather piratical figure, and full of good stories.'[24] Monkey still came and went in the house, and he and Jim got on extremely well. 'He had a great sense of fun,' said Monkey. 'We used to play tennis together on the courts in Hall Road, and he taught me how to play poker. Soon I was playing a good deal better than him.'[25] There were frequent all-night poker sessions, although Jane never joined in: she retired early to read and write, sew and brood.

As well as reviewing for *Queen*, in the spring of 1960 Jane began to make regular appearances on the BBC's television programme *Something to Read*. She had been on television before in the early 1950s, on panel programmes (such as the one with David Stafford-Clark) and *Table Talk*, a light-hearted political commentary that was aired after the *Six O'Clock News* (Jane was asked to participate because they needed a Tory-voting woman). She had also done the odd reading on the radio, thanks to her friendship with Jill Balcon. *Something to Read* was more ambitious. This afternoon show aimed to give an overview of the month's books, and – in the words of its producer, Olive Shapley – 'to give viewers the chance to take a long, uninterrupted look at the authors who were in the news'.[26]

The programme's main presenter was Brian Redhead, who had been a journalist on the *Guardian*. Shapley's bosses were worried that his Geordie accent might not appeal to the middle-class and largely female audience they were aiming for, but he was a brilliant communicator and very popular. The other presenters were Nancy Spain, broadcaster and columnist on the *Daily Express* who switched, that year, to the *News of the World*; and Jane. All three reviewed books and interviewed guests, on a set designed to look like a comfortably gracious sitting room.

The show was broadcast from the Dickinson Road Studios in Manchester; and from April 1960 to May the following year, Jane took the train there once a month to make the programme. She interviewed Isabel Colegate, David Storey, Penelope Mortimer, Elizabeth David, Susan Hill, Monica Dickens, John Braine and Katharine Whitehorn, among others; but the most nerve-racking interview she had was with the novelist Elizabeth Taylor, who had just published her eighth novel, *In a Summer Season*. Jane was a huge admirer of her work, and had put together a long list of questions; so, for once, Jane looked forward to conducting an interview with interest and confidence. In the event, Miss Taylor was so painfully shy that she answered each question with a yes or a no, and would not be drawn out; as a result Jane was left floundering with no more questions to ask, and several minutes of airtime still to run.

In 1960 Nicola was seventeen. She had been taken out of her boarding school at Westonbirt the year before, because – according to her stepmother Philippa – Jane wanted her to learn how to sew and cook. This was true, but Nicola concedes that another reason for her leaving Westonbirt might have been because her father could no longer afford the fees – Peter Scott's finances were perpetually overstretched. Whatever the reasons, Nicola was bitterly disappointed. She had been preparing to take an A-level in combined science, but instead found herself attending Mrs Benson's School of Pattern-Making and Mrs Pomeroy's Cooking School.

After a few months of sewing and cooking, Nicola decided that she wanted to become a stage manager; and that September she began a course in stage management at LAMDA, the London Academy for Music and Dramatic Art. She moved in to the spare room in Blomfield Road. Sometimes she shared it with Monkey, and later, with a young woman in her early twenties called Kristin Linklater. What she did not know was that Kristin and Jim had been having an affair for over a year, and it was still going on.

Kristin Linklater was a voice coach at LAMDA, but since she worked with student actors and Nicola was learning stage management, their paths had barely crossed. Kristin also gave lessons in voice development to the Ouspensky group, at Colet House, and that was where she had met Jim Douglas-Henry. She had not been teaching the group long when he approached her, asking whether she would be willing to give him private lessons. He had a vast collection of folk songs from all over the world, he told her, but sadly he couldn't sing any of them because he was tone-deaf. Kristin started giving him lessons in a basement room in LAMDA, and found herself very attracted to him. She cannot remember exactly when their affair started, but it was soon after Jim and Jane were married.

Jim and Kristin would meet at her bedsit in Lupus Street, Pimlico; but after a few months, he suggested that she move into Blomfield Road and share the spare room with Nicola. Jane, he assured her, would be very happy with the arrangement. In other words, Jim was suggesting that Kristin move into his wife's house, and share a room with his stepdaughter. Jim was pretty sure that Jane, with her craving for love and attention, was already seeking solace with other men; and moving Kristin into Blomfield Road was a demonstration that two could play at that game.

As for Kristin, she admitted that 'I was completely besotted [with Jim], brain-dead . . . But it was a fun house to be in. Jane entertained a lot, she was a fantastic cook, and Jim would be the most charming host at these little dinner parties, and Monkey was there too – I don't know how long it lasted. We'd all have breakfast together on her huge bed.'

At first, all was amicable and discreet. 'We were, let's say, resourceful,' said Kristin, 'one would find places and times . . . I once invited them to stay a few days with my parents in Easter Ross. My father [the novelist Eric Linklater] thought Jane was the most delicious and fabulous woman, and Jim and I went for long walks.' Jane later confessed to strong feelings of jealousy, but Kristin was not so sure. 'She had this very patrician, very cool mask and you didn't know what was going on behind it.'[27]

One cannot blame Jane for maintaining a rigid sangfroid. The years she had spent as a serial mistress to a succession of married men had left her feeling that she was somehow doomed to play second fiddle, but now she was married to Jim, her situation was infinitely worse. All her expectations of loving coupledom had been destroyed, and her husband had installed his young lover in her house.

By the spring of 1961, a split was developing within the Ouspensky group. Dr Roles saw the Maharishi and his message as the last piece in the great pattern of the Ouspensky System. But as Jane put it, the Maharishi packed 'a far greater spiritual punch'[28] than Dr Roles. Compared to the simplicity of Transcendental Meditation, which was available to everyone and could be explained in a few sentences, the secret knowledge and graded initiations of the 'System' looked distinctly out of date. Soon most of the younger members of the Ouspensky group had left Dr Roles to follow the Maharishi, with Jim and Jane among them.

On 13 March 1961 the Maharishi addressed a crowd of 5,000 people in the Albert Hall, to launch the First World Assembly of the Spiritual Regeneration Movement; and soon after that, he convened a three-day retreat in the country. Since the Maharishi was very much in the news, Jim decided to write an article about the retreat which probably took place towards the end of March. He wanted Kristin to come too, to take notes; and Kristin felt she ought to tell Jane what they were planning.

Kristin summoned up her courage when she and Jane were putting fresh sheets on the enormous marital bed. She said that Jim had asked her to accompany him on the retreat, to help him gather material for his article – would Jane mind if she went along? Kristin looked across the bed, 'and I saw that her face had gone absolutely dead cold; and she said "Well, you must do what you want." '

They set off in Jim's Karmann Ghia on Friday afternoon, and were due to stay until Monday morning; but at lunchtime on Sunday, Jim announced that they had to get back to London immediately. He raced the car home, and the moment they arrived he bounded into the house shouting, 'Hello, we're back!' Kristin had only reached the hall when she understood, from noises upstairs, what Jim was up to. He had guessed or been tipped off that Jane would have someone staying that weekend, and he had hurried back early to catch them in bed together – which is exactly what happened.

Jane, who saw herself as the tragic heroine of her marriage, was furious at being caught in the act like the naughty wife in a bedroom farce. A terrible row ensued, and Kristin was thrown out of the house; 'which I certainly deserved,' she added, 'no question about that.'[29]

From then on Jane knew she had to get free of her second husband. She saw less of him when he found a job with Television Wales and the West. One of the programmes he was involved with was called *Discs a Go-Go*, a pop music programme that required good dancers. Nicola would sometimes take part, for which she was paid her expenses and twenty-one shillings. From mid-1961 Jim was often in Bristol; but he liked having Blomfield Road as a pied-à-terre, and had no intention of relinquishing his right to be there. He would come back unannounced, and stay for a few days or a few hours, without explanation. Jane was afraid of him finding her with another man and throwing a scene, just to embarrass her, but even when she wasn't with someone else, she was afraid of his mockery.

Jane's last appearance on *Something to Read* was in May 1961, and the show was not given another series. She still had her reviewing at *Queen*, but in late 1961 that too was terminated with terrible abruptness. Jane says that it was because Penelope Gilliatt, who had taken over as theatre critic from Francis Wyndham, had found out that Jane was being paid more than her – the implication being that Gilliatt somehow engineered her dismissal. Yet magazines are always renewing and reshaping themselves, and *Queen* was no exception. Jane managed to get three months' paid notice, but she needed to find another job fast.

It was at this point that the film director Cyril Frankel came to the rescue, suggesting that she write the screenplay for a film he had been commissioned to make. Jane had met Frankel during his brief flirtation with the Ouspensky group, and he was also a friend of her doctor John Allison and his wife Susie.

The project had been set up by Raymond Stross, an American producer who had recently married the English actress Anne Heywood. He was determined to make his wife a star, and had seen an article about a young woman being stalked – a storyline he thought would make an excellent showcase for her talents. The screenplay had to be ready in six weeks, for which Jane would receive £600. She had never written a screenplay before, and had no idea about technical issues such as where the camera ought to be for a certain scene. Cyril told her not to worry. All she had to do was create characters and write the story, and he would do the rest.

Jane wrote a story about a housewife called Tracy (Anne Heywood insisted on her character having that name), whose husband is an architect, played by Richard Todd. Their cosy world is upset when Mullen, a young man obsessed by Tracy, breaks into their house and attacks her. From then on the terrified Tracy is stalked by Mullen, played by the young Jeremy Brett, who later became famous as Sherlock Holmes in a long-running series for Granada TV. Jane completed the script on time, and found that she enjoyed writing scenes for people to act: her training as an actress meant that she had a very clear visual sense of where people are in a scene and what they are doing, and sometimes it felt as if she were simply watching the action unfold. Once the script was done she thought her part was over – till Frankel summoned her to Dublin, where the film was being shot, for two frantic days on set to rewrite the final chase.

A year later she accompanied Frankel to the press showing of the film, now entitled *The Very Edge*; and the sickly smiles of the critics (some of them dubbed it *The Very End*) told her all too clearly that it was a flop. Jeremy Brett put in a creditable performance, but the main problem was Anne Heywood. Frankel had tried to improve her acting with lessons from Iris Warren, a voice coach whom Frankel had found invaluable 'when working with non-actors and children';[30] but even she could not add any depth to Heywood's performance.

Jane continued working for Cyril Frankel, whose warmth and kindness she very much appreciated. Raymond Stross promised her £6,000 for the next script. However, he didn't like her handling of the story (in which Anne Heywood was to play an angelic prostitute who ends up in jail, and escapes with another female inmate) and refused to pay her. Jane was forced to go to court for the money, at which point Stross turned out to be bankrupt. It was a heavy blow, to both bank balance and morale; but in the early stages of 1962 Jane's fortunes began to change.

She had recently spent a few days near Glenelg, in the West Highlands of Scotland, in the crofter's cottage that Gavin Maxwell shared with his otters Edal and Teko. One morning she went for a walk, accompanied by Teko. This African otter was a large and companionable animal, with a glossy coat of chocolate-coloured fur; and as he rambled and rootled about he picked some dandelions. These he carried until they reached the seashore, where they were discarded because he needed both hands to tear limpets off the rocks. After a while, Teko noticed that Jane was not joining in. 'He looked at me in a pitying way, and then – quite suddenly – handed me a limpet.'[31] It was an extraordinarily human gesture from a creature half wild, half tame; and for Jane, a moment of pure joy.

On 1 February 1962 Jane saw Maxwell again, this time in London and without his otters. Jane was having lunch with someone in a restaurant in Kensington Church Street, and at a nearby table she spotted Gavin and the woman he had married that morning, Lavinia Renton. 'After my host left, they asked me to come and sit with them. I remember that half hour particularly, because we were all three so exhilarated: we were all – if only temporarily – in love with our lives.'[32] If Jane was 'in love with her life' at this time, it was because she was about to be offered an extraordinary opportunity. The Cheltenham Literary Festival were looking for an artistic director, and she had been told that they were going to ask her.

The Cheltenham Arts Festivals (which at this stage meant Music, Literature and Art) had been going for almost ten years, and had relied on the energy and vision of two men: the nature writer and conservationist John Moore, and the writer and broadcaster Robert Henriques. A limited company had been formed to manage and conduct the events, but the town's corporation maintained control. Festival staff were drawn from its employees, and members of the borough council made up the majority of its board of directors. Moore and Henriques often found themselves at loggerheads with the supervising committee, and on a knife-edge with the Arts Council, which had agreed to underwrite any losses that the festival might make. At the same time it required strenuous efforts to secure the sort of writers people would want to hear, and to create a programme that, while maintaining popular elements like the Brains Trust, would look fresh and intriguing.

Henriques resigned in 1956 and John Moore the following year, although the latter always remained involved and ready to help. By the end of the 1950s, the Festival of Literature was floundering in financial difficulties. Despite a huge effort to revive its fortunes, attendances in 1960 were down and in 1961 the festival had to be cancelled altogether. This could have spelled the end, but a hard core of supporters were determined to keep it alive – among them Tom and Sonia Rolt, whom Jane had known when she worked with Robert Aickman for the Inland Waterways.

Jane was formally offered the job at a meeting of the Arts Council in February. Her main supporters were the Rolts and John Moore, who had perhaps remembered the letter she wrote to him after appearing at the festival in 1956 – and she was indeed bursting with ideas.

'Festival' was the key word: there would be no whiff of sober penny-pinching about her programme. Great authors from around the world would be asked to put their questions to the Brains Trust. There would be playwrights as well as historians, novelists and biographers, an exhibition of contemporary writers in the art gallery, and an auction of donated manuscripts. Perhaps London Zoo might lend her some animals to make a little literary zoo, which might include a Peter Rabbit and a Tigger. British Rail might be persuaded to offer cheap tickets to Cheltenham; and instead of having the usual publishers' displays or a 'Books of the Year' exhibition organized by the National Book League, why not actually *sell* books after the events? On the last night she wanted a party in the Pump Room with champagne and prizes, and the festival would come to an end with a magnificent firework display.

Staggered by the breadth of her vision, the borough council fell back on the usual excuse that it would all be far too expensive. Nicola

Bennett, who wrote a history of the festival, captures the energy of Jane's response.

> She was sure she could raise the money. Perhaps the newly-launched *Sunday Telegraph* might be interested in sponsoring a day? Could they not find someone with in-house publications who could produce the handbook for them? Perhaps another auction of manuscripts could be held on the last night. She could probably persuade quite a lot of her friends to come down for free. As long as they had a marvellous time. There was one thing though: she could not afford to do it without being paid and she would need secretarial help.[33]

It was agreed that she should be paid a flat fee of £300; and at first, her secretarial help was an ex-girlfriend of Monkey's. Later she found another secretary, who was far more efficient. Jackie Gomme was in her late twenties, and she came recommended by John Moore. She was also a driver, an invaluable skill since Jane could not yet drive. Jackie was used to writers and academics, but Jane's household was a revelation: 'They seemed like magical people, so exotic and sophisticated.' When she spent the night at Blomfield Road, the only place where there was room to put a camp bed was under the stairs; but rather than sleep, Jackie found it much more fun to join the late-night poker sessions with Jim and Monkey. These didn't end till the early hours of the morning, usually with a breakfast of bacon and eggs and mugs of Ovaltine. Then she went up to the tiny boxroom over the porch where Jane had her desk, and began work. At first, Jackie had had doubts about having a female boss but Jane was very professional. 'She knew exactly what she wanted and explained things clearly; and if it wasn't exactly right, or something couldn't be done in time, she worked round the situation rather than fret about it.'[34]

Jane had composed hundreds of letters: to writers asking them to come; to people who owned paintings or drawings or pieces of sculpture, for the exhibition of contemporary writers; to advertisers to take space in the programme; to yet more writers for manuscripts they felt they could donate; and to schools offering events. Her letter-writing impressed Eric Linklater, Kristin's father. 'Should you choose to abandon the upper levels of literary practice,' he wrote, 'you will easily earn a living writing begging letters.'[35]

She also wrote to the Publishers Association, trying to secure agreement about the festival's bookshop – something they were very reluctant to do. It would antagonize all the local booksellers, and they would not sell any books anyway. But she would not let the matter drop, and in the end they agreed to give it a try, although the 'Book Market', as it was called, was only open at odd hours in the Festival Club.

London Zoo refused to lend a Peter Rabbit let alone a Tigger, and British Rail were unwilling to lower their fares to Cheltenham; but Jane did manage to get the Schweppes drinks company to sponsor the programme, and the *Sunday Telegraph* agreed to sponsor one evening for £1,500 – a decision no doubt helped by some judicious lobbying from Jane's cousin Peregrine Worsthorne, who was assistant editor on the paper.

The *Sunday Telegraph* told Jane they wanted a symposium on Sex in Literature, to be chaired by their editor, Donald McLachlan. Jane had persuaded the American writers Joseph Heller and Carson McCullers to speak at the festival, and put them on the panel along with Romain Gary, who had agreed to come over from Paris. This seemed to her a pretty good line-up, even if there was only one woman (Mrs McCullers); and she thought the matter was settled – until Anthony Curtis, the *Sunday Telegraph*'s literary editor, announced that he had also invited Kingsley Amis.

By 1962 Amis had written four novels, although he was still principally known for the first, *Lucky Jim*. He had turned forty that year; but along with the playwright John Osborne, he was still branded as one of those Angry Young Men from the lower middle classes, whose work revelled in pouring scorn on the establishment and conventional society.

Furiously indignant, Jane immediately telephoned Peregrine Worsthorne. It was outrageous of the *Sunday Telegraph* to invite Amis without consulting her: four speakers plus a chairman was too many for that kind of discussion, and although she had met Amis once or twice, having an Angry Young Man in the mix would throw everything off balance. (She may also have mentioned that she had given Amis the thumbs down for his last novel in *Queen*, which was potentially embarrassing.) Could Perry not get the invitation revoked? He could not. Kingsley Amis was coming to the festival and that was that.

Jane made the best of it. As the Sex in Literature symposium was an evening event, she wrote to ask whether Amis and his wife would like to stay the night in the house she had taken in George Street, Cheltenham, for the use of herself and participating speakers. She had no answer, and wrote again. This time she received a very nice letter, enclosing a copy of his earlier reply that had gone astray. He and Hilly would be happy to accept.

By August everything seemed to be in place, and Jane decided it was time to recharge her batteries. She was still doing Transcendental Meditation, and had heard that the Maharishi was spending the summer teaching in the Austrian Alps. He and his followers had taken over a hotel in the delightfully named Hochgurgl, near Zwieselstein. Jane decided to go and took her mother, who had also taken up meditation. It was the only time they ever went abroad together.

Jane always held a great respect and admiration for the Maharishi. While at Hochgurgl she helped him with his enormous task of translating the *Bhagavad Gita*, and in *Slipstream* she described two instances of the supernatural powers that, without fuss or comment, he could deploy at will. Yet the Maharishi's way was not for her. He taught that no one could make any spiritual progress without cultivating non-attachment to the things of this world, and that was the last thing Jane wanted to do. She wanted to be in the middle of ordinary life, trying to make the best of it.

Back in Cheltenham, there was the usual rash of last-minute problems. About a week before the festival was due to begin, Jane received a cable from New York to say Carson McCullers was going to need a fully qualified nurse around the clock. She had undergone a long and painful operation on the tendons of her left hand, and had a tumour in her breast removed at the same time. Jackie came to the rescue – her sister Jo was a fully qualified nurse, and willing to take on the job. They were put up at Claridge's by the *Sunday Telegraph* for two or three days before the festival, during the course of which Jane did a long interview with Carson McCullers, whose work addressed matters that preoccupied her too: at one point in the interview Jane reflected that 'It seems to me you are writing about this agony of loving without being loved . . . the other person doesn't even know how you feel and can't respond even if they want to, they can't.' McCullers replied, 'Yes, I think that's it, Jane.'[36]

Jane had been lucky there; but she had to hang the exhibition of portraits herself, because the gallery owner said he wanted nothing to do with it; and she was appalled by how little effort Cheltenham's borough council had put into promoting the festival. Unfortunately she mentioned this last concern to a journalist, who put it about that Jane was about to resign – which caused a flurry of panic and ruffled feathers.

On Saturday, 29 September, Peter Scott opened the exhibition of contemporary writers at the art gallery. He and Jane had remained on good terms, and like many of her friends, he had drummed up help and support. The festival opened on Monday, 1 October. Ignazio Silone, Compton Mackenzie, François Mauriac, William Gerhardie and Robert Frost were among the great lights who posted their questions to the Brains Trust, who included Edna O'Brien, Frank Tuohy, David Caute, Lynne Reid Banks and Andrew Sinclair. Laurie Lee joined the footballer Danny Blanchflower, Elspeth Huxley and Alec Waugh to discuss the pleasures and problems of autobiography; Margaret Lane did a schools event on how to make your own library, and Laurens van der Post talked about the Lost World of Africa. Peter Shaffer, John Mortimer and Gwyn Thomas discussed whether or not the living theatre was still alive, Joy Adamson recalled her days with Elsa the lioness, and Cecil Woodham-Smith took a look at some of the more light-hearted moments of her career as a historian.

The famous symposium on Sex in Literature took place on Thursday, 4 October. Monkey had already driven Carson McCullers down with her nurse Jo Gomme, and Joseph Heller was chauffeured by his publisher Tom Maschler. *Catch 22* was the first book the young Maschler bought for Jonathan Cape. Yet despite the sex symposium's intriguing title and a capacity audience, it never sparked into life. Ill and in pain, Carson McCullers's gentle Southern drawl was almost inaudible; while Donald McLachlan had no experience of chairing an event. He kept trying to get the discussion back to *Lady Chatterley's Lover* – a book so talked about since the famous trial of 1960 that there was little more to say about it.

The symposium was due to be followed by a late dinner at the Ellenborough Hotel, with the Curtises, Worsthornes, Amises, Donald

McLachlan and Jane among others. The evening ended well after midnight. Jane and the Amises were driven back to her house in George Street, and Hilly Amis immediately retired, exhausted. Kingsley hated going to bed, and said he would have a nightcap. Jane kept him company; being a good hostess, she thought it would be unfriendly to leave him drinking alone. They had talked a great deal over dinner, and she had had a long day. He might have felt a mild disappointment if she had said goodnight and slipped away, but no more.

The truth was that neither of them wanted the evening to end. 'We talked and talked until 4 a.m.,' she wrote, 'about our work, our lives, our marriages and each other . . . When he kissed me, I felt as though I could fly.'[37] Amis did not remember it as quite so rapturous, but he was talking long after his marriage to Jane was over. 'I sort of threw a pass at Jane,' he told Eric Jacobs, 'which was sort of accepted.'[38]

13

Lucky Jane

A QUIET WEEK WITH Cyril Frankel and his partner in France provided the ideal place to enjoy that slow unwinding of body and mind, that comes when a long bout of hard work has been brought to a satisfactory conclusion. The festival had been a great success, even turning a small profit – the first time it had ever done so. The board and management both hoped that Jane would be artistic director next year. But the job had involved eight months of solid work with very little pay and barely a moment to write, so she was not tempted to do it again.

She thought a lot about Kingsley Amis, and what a grave mistake it would be to fall in love with him. He was married, with two teenage sons and a daughter, and they were about to move to Spain: if she fell for him, she would be back in the mistress role she had endured with Michael, Paul, Laurie, Cecil – and she had learned enough to know that this state of mind not only made her miserable, it also made writing impossible. But soon after her return to London, he rang up; and whatever resolve she had mustered evaporated instantly.

They met in a bar one evening near Leicester Square. 'Before we even have a drink,' he said, 'I have to tell you something.' He had booked a room for the night in a nearby hotel. He knew he was pushing his luck and quite understood if she didn't want to sleep with him, but if that was the case, it was only right to cancel the room immediately.

Some might have seen this move as presumptuous and manipulative. Others might have concluded that he had put down a deposit on the room, refundable on cancellation. But such suspicions never crossed Jane's mind – the point was that he wanted her urgently: a male reaction that made her feel so alive, so complete, that she could never resist it. She marvelled again at his open honesty, his fairness, which she had so admired that night in Cheltenham.

Jane was violently attracted to Kingsley; but because she thought she was not going to see much of him, she did not want to disappoint him. When they were in bed she cheated, and pretended that sex with him was the best she'd ever had;[1] yet he was undoubtedly one of the funniest men she had ever met, who could make her cry with laughter and delight. As for Amis, he was bowled over by Jane's beauty and elegance, her intelligence, her sexual responsiveness, her delight in everything he did or said. There was also a thoroughbred quality to her that was new to him; she was posh, no doubt about it, despite her assurances that she wasn't as posh as he thought. They just came from opposite ends of the middle-class spectrum. Kingsley was the only son of a clerk who worked all his life for the mustard-makers J. & J. Colman, and he had grown up in the suffocatingly respectable suburb of Norbury in south-west London. Jane fascinated him and he certainly wanted to know her better, in every possible way: it was going to be a glorious affair.

At that time, Amis had been married for fourteen years. He had met his wife Hilary Bardwell in 1946, while finishing his English degree at Oxford, which had been interrupted by three years' national service in the Royal Signals: his preferred posting since he had the maths for the job, and there was less likelihood of being killed. He was twenty-three, and she a seventeen-year-old art student. He called her Hilly, and she was a pretty, unpretentious, funny girl with a rebellious streak. Described in one report as 'unteachable', Hilly had run away from every school she ever attended.[2] Her sister Margaret thought she might have been dyslexic. For someone like Kingsley, with his violent emotions and prejudices, his phobias and his insistence on living every minute at full throttle, Hilly's relaxed cheerfulness was very soothing. She was not afraid of his brilliance and cleverness, although she loved his jokes and his extraordinary talent for mimicry. She laughed easily, and was perfectly happy not to speak at all unless she had something to say.

When they married in January 1948, Hilly was already pregnant. Their first child, Philip, was born that August, and by the end of the year she was pregnant again. With a growing family Kingsley hoped that a postgraduate B.Litt. would help him secure a job in one of the new universities. For the moment, his ambitions to be a poet and a novelist had to take second place. But his undisguised admiration for thrillers and science fiction, combined with a vociferous disdain for certain authors in the classical canon (Chaucer, Spenser, Keats and Browning, to name but a handful) contributed to his failure to achieve a postgraduate degree. Despite this setback he secured a job at the University of Swansea in Wales, shortly after the birth of their second son, Martin, in August 1949.

Although Hilly never doubted Kingsley's fondness for her, she was wounded by his unquenchable desire for other women; and because he barely attempted to hide his affairs, her pain and resentment never had a chance to heal. She tried not to mind, and to believe him when he said his affairs meant nothing; but as she told Amis's biographer Zachary Leader, 'I wasn't old enough or sensible enough or wise enough to handle them better.'[3] There were frequent rows on the subject, but Kingsley made no effort to change his ways.

Who can blame Hilly for feeling that, if Kingsley was going to behave like that, she was going to have some fun too. In their raffish, bawdy circle of young dons and journalists and postgraduates she drank and smoked and flirted, although her son Martin feels she was 'a reluctant swinger, a swinger by default: her heart wasn't in it'.[4] Kingsley was pretty sure that Sally, born in January 1954, was not his child; but given his own behaviour there was little he could say, and he always loved and accepted her as his daughter.

Everything changed in 1954, with the publication of *Lucky Jim*. From then on Kingsley had a lot more money and fame, as well as work. His second novel, *That Uncertain Feeling*, was published the following year. As well as his teaching at Swansea he began reviewing fiction and started his next novel. There were more trips to London, supposedly to see friends and editors but also for parties and affairs. Hilly and the children remained the bedrock of his life, but in 1956 he nearly lost them. Hilly fell in love with an irresponsible charmer who was quite prepared to wreck his own marriage and hers, but Kingsley saw him off with a blistering letter.

Amis published his third novel, *I Like It Here*, in 1958: and that year he was offered a job at the University of Princeton, teaching what he called 'Creadive Wriding'. The whole family, including his recently widowed father William, who was known as Daddy A., moved to

New Jersey. Daddy A. often found himself left in charge of his grand-children, while his son and daughter-in-law were swept into a non-stop round of hard-drinking friends whose relentless partying led to the wildest period of their marriage. When the year was over they went back briefly to Swansea, but it seemed rather lacklustre after Princeton. *Take a Girl Like You* (the one reviewed by Jane in *Queen*) appeared in 1960, and in 1961 Kingsley was offered, and accepted, a college lectureship in English at Peterhouse, Cambridge.

A few months later, the family moved into an eight-bedroomed house at 9 Madingley Road, with a large garden, a greenhouse and a shed that housed their donkey, Debbie. 'The house in Madingley Road,' wrote Martin Amis, 'differed from every other don's house in the city. Students could be found in it, regularly. They stayed the night. They drove the car. They read or dozed in the garden. They made some of my meals.' The students were all young men; but there were lots of women around too, and a friend told Martin that the house 'was the locus of considerable sexual activity . . . Certainly the atmosphere was lawlessly, innocently convivial. It was no big thing (for example) to watch my mother and our family friend, Theo Richmond, both of them exhausted by laughter, riding through one of the sitting rooms on Debbie . . . who, every morning, would stick her head through the kitchen window and neigh along with Radio Caroline.'[5]

Martin, the middle child then thirteen, describes himself as the easiest of the Amis brood. Philip, aged fourteen, was often away at boarding school: he was a more sensitive, uneasy presence, while Sally, aged eight, was a waif-like child who flitted around in fancy dress and wanted to be a ballerina. Hilly wanted her children to grow up with as few constraints as possible. She set no rules, and had a refreshing disregard for health and safety. 'We spent all-day and all-night car journeys on the roof rack of the Morris 1000, the three of us, in all weathers, slithering in and out while my mother frowned into the windscreen.'[6] And there was the famous occasion when Martin and Phil, with a nod from their mother, attempted to paddle a canoe across the treacherous waters between Swansea Bay and Pembroke Bay. Despite Phil's best efforts the boys failed to get into danger, but there was a great hue and cry and scrambling of lifeboats nonetheless. A rackety household, then; but Martin Amis was in no doubt that he and his siblings were much loved, and that his parents' marriage was rock solid.

In the summer of 1962 Amis was commissioned to write a profile of the poet Robert Graves, whose work he had always admired, for an American magazine. Graves lived in the village of Deya on the island of Majorca, which was where Kingsley would have to interview him; and since the fee offered was a generous $800, Kingsley decided to take his family on holiday at the same time.

Graves and his wife Beryl loved their life in Deya, and that August all their four children were there too. The two families got on well. Kingsley was particularly impressed by the huge body of work Graves had managed to produce by living in bucolic seclusion. His books filled an eight-foot shelf above his desk.

Admittedly Graves was sixty-seven, with most of his working life behind him; but Kingsley was forty, and all he could point to were four novels and a few published poems. Since his appointment to Peterhouse, teaching and reviewing had taken up almost all of his working life. His social life consumed every bit as much energy, his affairs required strenuous juggling, and not surprisingly there was very little time for his own writing. He had started his next novel, *One Fat Englishman*, but it had not advanced very far. He felt it could be different if they lived in Majorca, in a sunny climate with few distractions. Perhaps the time had come for him to give up teaching and write full time.

By the end of that summer, a plan had evolved. Kingsley would resign his post at Peterhouse, and they would move to Majorca for a year: not to Deya, but to the town of Soller. Hilly was all for it. A quieter life with fewer temptations might begin to repair the cracks in their marriage. (In later years Jane reported that Kingsley had told her that Hilly had become pregnant again, and knowing the child wasn't his, he insisted on an abortion. This turned out not to be true: Hilly had suffered a miscarriage.)

Then came Cheltenham. Hilly had a feeling that something had happened between Kingsley and Jane, and that Jane was 'tossing her hair at him', as she put it.[7] He had always made regular visits to London, but as he shuttled back and forth on the train during the winter of 1962 he seemed to be looking better, both energized and abstracted. She had a pretty good idea that Jane had something to do with it, but the affair would soon blow over. They all did sooner or later, and then the family would move to Soller.

Yet something was happening between Kingsley and Jane that marked this relationship as something much more momentous. Each was not just a lover but a rescuer, making the other feel better, brighter and stronger than they had for a long time. He was rescuing her from the pit of despondency into which she had fallen after three years of marriage to Jim Douglas-Henry; while she was offering him a vision of a new life in which, with her guidance, his anxieties would be soothed, he would drink less, write more and be infinitely happier.

'If I were living with you,' she wrote on 6 February 1963, 'we would stop drinking brandy and not drink spirits much at all, and we would try and design life around you writing more. I think that would charge you up about your sense of identity. If one has some feeling from time to time of what one is *for*, one doesn't need to question who one is.' This long letter ends: 'Sorry I kissed you *so much* in the restaurant . . . I love you more than I have loved anyone else. Had to wait to be sure it was true. It is.'[8]

'I was so moved by your letter,' he replied. 'I was in a low state of morale when I got hold of you, as you know. Now greatly restored. I told you [that] you make me feel like a man – not that I feel particularly feminine most of the time but I don't usually feel *confident*, non-harassable etc.'[9]

Although Amis is always admiring ('I love all of you, not just your beauty and brightness and tenderness and funniness. You made me laugh like an idiot about the Amis scent'),[10] Jane could not stop worrying that she might bore or somehow displease him; and at the same time, Jim was suddenly becoming more attentive.

Am still ashamed of wanting to touch you: I would get better about that – will, rather, with more time. Jim was in bed and said he was ill and tried to ask a lot of teasing questions about you, and also tried to provoke my affections (this was the worst because I don't feel them and can't pretend and suspect he knows both these facts). He kept trying to touch me because he knows I would dislike it – not at all because he wants to . . . My whole body feels different: breasts so sharp with feeling it hurts to put on a brassière. Perhaps people in love shouldn't wear clothes?[11]

'You mustn't be ashamed of wanting to touch me,' he wrote back. ' "getting better" about that would be touching me more, not less . . . Bill [Rukeyser, an old friend of Kingsley's] . . . heartily approves of you, both as a person and as a beauty. He's the only person I can talk to about you, and I want to do that all the time.'[12]

Jane hoped she was not being too feminine, or unintelligent, or over-tactile, but she was such a mass of new sensations that 'I'm not known to *myself* any more, so have nothing much to rely on in that respect.'[13]

Kingsley had already begged her not to go on apologizing. 'I repeat that you didn't come within two miles of boring or annoying me . . . But I don't want you to feel you *need* to. *Everything you do* is better than all right with me.'[14] And again: 'You mustn't be less effeminate. It's one of your glories – being that as well as tough (I've always said you're that) and capable and intelligent. Being effeminate isn't the opposite of being intelligent – with you they set each other off.'[15]

Towards the end of March, they managed to escape for a few days together. Kingsley wrote: 'Those three days were the most wonderful time I've ever had . . . I can't describe how wonderful I found you – beaming-plus-awed by it all. More than anything else I was moved by you as a young bride – this is where love and sex meet: I mean I was sexually excited by it in all possible ways but also felt so full of love I would have cried, if crying were possible while making love.'[16]

'You as a young bride' can only mean a sexual role that Jane had played out, a role that she found particularly satisfying: the role of trust and innocence, that childlike part of herself that made her feel whole. Yet it is interesting that Kingsley sees her very much as an adult. His letter goes on: 'You are a splendid, loveable, wise, alto-gether decent woman and I'd feel this if I were 9 or 90 . . . *Waking Beauty* will be in *The Spectator* next week.'

Kingsley wrote the poem 'Waking Beauty' at the height of his love for her, and here again she is fully grown, fully experienced. The poem reworks the fairy tale it echoes: his anxieties are the thorny briers he hacks through to reach her but they fall apart 'like cut yarn', and she wakes instantly, responding to his kiss. Then a new anxiety arises: has he become responsible for her? Does he have to hack his way through even thornier brambles, 'Dry, aching, encumbered / By a still drowsy girl?' Luckily she is not an infantilized princess but a woman, and his equal:

> Your eyes cleared and steadied.
> Side by side we advanced
> On those glossy giants
> And their lattice of barbs:
> But they had all withered.[17]

That sense of healing and moving forward together is expressed in every one of their letters. Zachary Leader, Amis's biographer, writes that Kingsley's letters to Jane 'are unlike any other letters of his I have seen . . . What is clear is that he fell madly for Jane, almost as madly as she fell for him. The emotional openness of the letters is striking, as is their happiness, optimism, gentleness, willingness to try new things and confidence.'[18]

On 24 April Kingsley wrote:

> Darling, take no notice of this if it makes you feel shy, but I thought it would be very lovely if when you let me in you were wearing less than you usually are. In fact as little as possible. In fact – well nobody can see you as you open the door, and I'll ring 4 times as usual, and since I've asked you it won't look 'forward' on your part . . . I reproach myself rather for my insensitivity in not realising much sooner that you liked making love better when it was all gentle: you'd have got to know me better sooner and we'd have got to our present absolutely paradisal state that much earlier . . . I want you to know how supreme it is for me to make love to you and how utterly your pleasure transports me. Your joy is literally my joy. I always thought that was just a figure of speech – 'it's great fun when you realise she's having a good time.' But it's a solid fact. I've never been so close to anyone's body before. You haven't a square inch of coarse skin anywhere on you.[19]

Kingsley had taken to signing himself off as 'Hunter' – often with an eye-catching title like Admiral of the Fleet, Grand Vizier or Lord Warden of the Cinque Ports. This was hardly a very effective disguise, although Jane tried to keep their relationship secret, particularly at home, where Jim would still appear from time to time. She and Kingsley spent stolen weekends at the house of their mutual friend, the publisher Tom Maschler. He was very discreet, but they could not avoid running into friends and acquaintances in restaurants or on the street.

Yet however much he was in love with Jane, Kingsley still had no intention of leaving Hilly and the children. Jane even remembers him telling her, 'If this comes out, I will blacken you – I want you to know that.'[20] She interpreted this chilling threat to mean 'that "if he wanted to keep his family together, he would have to side with them. I could see that this was very nasty for me, but again he was being honest about it . . ." A part of her also thought: "it's quite difficult to blacken me. I'm pretty black already." '[21]

Plans for the family's move to Majorca gathered pace. Kingsley gave notice to Peterhouse in December 1962, telling them he would leave at the end of the academic year. During the spring vacation he and Hilly went house-hunting in Soller, and in early April they had found a house three miles from the sea and surrounded by orange trees. They returned to find that Kingsley's father was very ill. Hilly had found a nursing home near Cambridge and they moved him in, but he died of cancer on 18 April.

A few days after that, Hilly found a letter from Jane in Kingsley's pocket, and now the rows became louder and more hurtful. Hilly's fury was kept at fever-pitch by her friend Pat Gale, a fearlessly over-dramatic, hard-drinking woman who had a powerful influence on her at the time. Pat's husband, the journalist and editor George Gale, was a close crony of Kingsley's and Pat referred to them both as 'drunken louts'.[22] Hilly also confided in Jim, who was as keen as she was to stop the affair. Kingsley told Hilly that he would not give up Jane, and announced that he was going to take her on a three-week holiday in Spain. At the same time he made it clear that he still intended to move to Majorca with Hilly and the children, from where he would make occasional forays to London.

In the middle of these dramas, preparations were under way for the wedding of Jane's daughter Nicola to Kip Asquith, the young cousin of the Huntingdons, who had accompanied Jane and Jim on the voyage of the *Sharavogue* through the rivers and canals of France. Nicola and Kip had met soon after, and had been seeing each other ever since. Jane was worried by how young they were: Nicola was only nineteen, the age Jane had been when she married Peter. But the Asquiths were a celebrated family, and it was certainly seen as a good match by both Scotts and Howards. Nicola and Kip had known each other for four years, and they both loved country life. Kip had inherited a farm in Gloucestershire where they would live, and he was planning to go to agricultural college. There seemed no good reason to keep them apart.

The couple were to be married from Stanway, one of the most beautiful Jacobean houses in England, on 12 May. In *Slipstream*, Jane says that the wedding was 'occluded by sadness' because she felt that Nicola was closer to her stepmother than she was to her.[23] Since Jane had been absent for much of Nicola's life and utterly absorbed with Kingsley since October, this was hardly surprising. Yet she did have one intimate moment with her daughter, which she described in a letter to Kingsley a week later:

> I went, the night before the wedding, to talk to Nic while she had a bath. She said something about being Mrs Asquith next day, and then said 'Of course for you, Mama, with all your names you wouldn't even notice. Isn't it about time you changed?' I said why. Then she said, looking touchingly worldly and mature, 'Well I suppose Jim would be quite a good friend for some people – but one couldn't *marry* him. Aren't you in love with *anyone*?' I felt awful lying to her, but there didn't seem to be an alternative at that point. 'Well do *try*, Mama,' she said.[24]

Nicola was surprised to read this letter, because she has no recollection of any such conversation with her mother. It was certainly high time that Jane shook herself free of Jim, although he was not so easily shaken off. He turned up at the wedding with his mother Norma, and Jane had to stand beside him in the receiving line as convention demanded. 'The last three days have been the most socially/emotionally exhausting of my life,' she continued in her letter to Kingsley.

Jim arrived in the middle of it and did a tremendous act of being devoted and understanding and kept getting me into corners and trying to kiss me and saying were you there, and didn't I *want* him to stay the night? I can't, in those circumstances, bring myself to say yes . . . because although I'd been given a bedroom and dressing room at Stanway, I knew he wouldn't sleep in the dressing room without a scene lasting most of the night. I missed you all the time, but I expect you would have hated it. The mixture of Peter who got very sentimental about him and me, and Jim, and not feeling all right with anybody, and standing for hours shaking hands with about 400 people . . . was too much and went on too long . . . I feel I am on the brink of a major scene with Jim which is like someone putting icy feet at the back of one's neck. He's going on and on about why don't I come to Greece.[25]

Jane's anxieties spilled into her sleep, and her nightmares seeped into daylight hours; yet it was not Jim she worried about, it was Kingsley. 'It isn't just a dream,' she told him, 'it's a recurring thing when I'm awake . . . I was so afraid that once I was away somewhere with you you'd change, that I couldn't feel anything except the enormous going-on fright, and this made you angry and then I couldn't stop being frightened . . . But the *more* I love you, and feel about you, the more I feel that all my disadvantages would annoy you, and the more difficult they are to manage.'[26]

These terrors were driven by her lack of faith in herself, the feeling that she had made a mess of everything. She had already expressed them in letters to Kingsley. As an anxious person himself he was sympathetic, and had done all he could to reassure her of his love and admiration. Yet at the heart of Jane's apprehension is also an uncanny degree of prescience. When she wrote this letter Kingsley was completely infatuated with her; she could do no wrong. Yet within a few years he would be gritting his teeth every time she came into the room, and part of her seemed to foresee it already.

Kingsley and Hilly had been invited to the Festival of Science Fiction Film in Trieste in July, although in the days leading up to their departure Hilly was so distraught that she didn't know whether she would be able to face coming with him. In the end, she did; and it was after one drunken lunch that Hilly got out her lipstick, and on the sleeping Kingsley's back she wrote 'I FAT ENGLISHMAN. I FUCK ANYTHING'.

Later that month – Hilly remembered it as her birthday, 21 July, but it was in fact a day or so earlier – Kingsley left the house in Madingley Road to embark on his holiday with Jane. He had told Hilly that this would be a working holiday, since he had promised to deliver *One Fat Englishman* to his publishers, Gollancz, by mid-August. Did he really think the situation would be any better when he returned? Or was it simply a gesture of defiance – a grand final fling that he felt he deserved, before settling down to a quiet and industrious writing life in Majorca with his family?

After a few days in London, Jane and Kingsley travelled to Sitges, south-west of Barcelona. They moved into a little flat with one big room in which they worked and slept, a balcony, a bathroom and a galley-kitchen. Jane bought brilliantly coloured vegetables and tried to tempt Kingsley with ratatouilles and piperades, without much success; while he lined up a gruesome regiment of liqueurs like Crème de Bananes and Parfait d'Amour (Hilly's favourite, which tasted of violets). They worked for most of the morning and then went to the beach where Jane swam and Kingsley had a token dip. Then they ate lunch at a little restaurant nearby.

Kingsley did not like foreign food, but since the Mediterranean coast of Spain was already seething with English tourists, menus were geared to the gastronomically unadventurous. They went back to the flat for leisurely sex, a siesta and a bit more work, and then as the light faded, they strolled down to the waterfront for drinks and dinner. Sometimes they would finish off the evening with a round or two of floodlit mini-golf, which they found surprisingly enjoyable. Jane's nightmares receded, and were soon almost forgotten.

The fact that they could both work together cemented what was beginning to look like a perfect partnership – although, as Jane pointed out, 'people in early love are generally hell-bent on finding the best in each other'.[27] Jane was working on *After Julius*, a novel she had started before accepting the directorship of the Cheltenham Literary Festival; while Kingsley was into the home stretch of *One Fat Englishman*. Yet he did make time to read *The Sea Change*, the first novel of Jane's that he had ever opened. Over the two days he was reading it he said nothing about the book at all, leaving her in an agony of apprehension. At last he said, 'That's a very good novel indeed. I'm so relieved. I was afraid you wouldn't be any good.'[28]

They formed a habit of reading aloud what they had written at the end of the day over a drink, each commenting on the other's work. Jane described it as the most enjoyable and enduring part of their relationship. One day, they had the idea of writing a passage in the other's work in progress. They both read the work so far, and then each had to write a scene; as it turned out, both scenes were set during an extended party.

'Our very different writing behaviours were reversed. Normally I'd sit groaning and biting my nails, staring into space, and Kingsley would think for a moment, and then, suddenly charged up, would tap away at a steady rate, sometimes laughing aloud at his characters. So now while I was laughing and typing away, he was groaning and staring into space.' The two passages have never been removed or altered, although Kingsley's in *After Julius* is perhaps the more recognizable.[29]

So determined was Victor Gollancz to have the typescript of *One Fat Englishman* – he wanted it in the bookshops by Christmas – that he sent one of his employees out to Spain to collect it. Kingsley handed it over on 14 August at the BEA office in Barcelona, and the messenger took the next flight home. Kingsley went back to Sitges, where he and Jane had now been for almost a month. Their holiday was coming to an end, but Kingsley knew he faced some hard decisions. He preferred not to think about them. Jane didn't ask about what was happening to his marriage, and he was grateful for her tact.

A few days after delivering the manuscript, they were still in bed when the doorbell rang. Jane went to answer it in Kingsley's dressing gown. At the door was a man from the *Daily Express*. 'We got dressed,' wrote Kingsley, 'without having admitted him to our flat, and gave him an interview in the porch downstairs. It consisted of me telling him a lot about my book and saying "no comment" and "that's my business" to everything else. "Are you in love?" he kept unavailingly asking. J[ane] was a curious olive-yellow colour, made up of tan and pallor, and I worked away at preventing my head from trembling.'[30]

They found another flat in Sitges, where they stayed for a further two weeks before returning to London on 8 September; and two days later, Kingsley went back to Cambridge and the house in Madingley

Road. It was locked and empty. Hilly had walked out of the house and out of her marriage, without even leaving a note.

The boys already knew that their father had a 'fancy woman' in London, thanks to their housekeeper, Eva Garcia; and soon after Kingsley's departure Hilly told them that she and their father were going to separate. The house was packed up and they moved to Soller, into the house with the orange orchard where she and Kingsley had planned a new life.

Hilly admitted to being 'in a terrible state', and the part of her that wasn't furiously angry and bitter hoped that Kingsley would follow them too. It was not so unrealistic, for when she moved he was still with Jane in Sitges, a ferry-ride away across the Balearic Sea. Had she been a bit more calculating Hilly might have made a more serious bid to reclaim him at this point, but calculation was completely alien to her.

Once Kingsley was back in England Jane held a far more powerful hand, for he was incapable of travelling long distances alone. As Martin Amis put it, to accomplish the journey from London to Majorca he would have needed 'someone to make all the bookings, someone to get him to Southampton, someone to share his cabin on the boat, and someone to lead him from Palma to Soller and right up to our front door. The only possible candidate for the task was Elizabeth Jane Howard.'[31]

The empty house in Madingley Road left Kingsley feeling shaken and desolate, but it also made the decision for him. Hilly had put herself out of reach. If that's what she wanted, fine. He took the next train back to London and Jane.

They could not stay at Jane's for long. Jim had a flat in Bristol but he might turn up at Blomfield Road at any time – and had he found them there, he would have stirred up as much trouble as possible. To avoid him they took a furnished flat in Basil Mansions in Knightsbridge, and considered what to do next. The shock of Hilly's departure had given way to a 'see if I care' attitude in Kingsley, although both Jane and Monkey noted that he never said a word against her.

Monkey stayed at Blomfield Road, and if Jim turned up he was to say that he had no idea of his sister's whereabouts. He remained fond of Jim, with whom he still played poker; but he was aware that Jim had made his sister miserable, so he was delighted to see how happy she was with her new man. 'I adore Monkey and find him terribly funny, also kind,' wrote Kingsley to Jane,[32] and Monkey felt equally warm towards him. They relished each other's verbal acrobatics, word games and impressions, and they shared tastes in music – both classical and jazz.

Soon after getting back from Spain, Kingsley introduced Jane to Geoff and Mavis Nicholson, who had known the Amises since Swansea days. Mavis had had an affair with Kingsley in the early 1950s but it hadn't stopped her remaining friends with Hilly, who recalled that 'somehow she was never a threat, we were all in love with Mavis'.[33] Because he was so happy with Jane and so determined to turn over a new leaf, Kingsley had cut down on his alcohol consumption. Mavis was glad to see it, yet she warned Jane that this relative sobriety was unlikely to continue indefinitely. Kingsley was a defiantly heavy drinker and always would be.

Mavis also noticed how Jane had mannerisms that Kingsley would have scoffed at in any other woman. That night she was wearing a long silk skirt and shirt, with her hair piled up in a bun; and after dinner she sank down to the floor next to the fireplace, and very slowly started to take the pins out of her hair so it tumbled around her. This was obviously done for Kingsley's benefit yet far from being mesmerized, he carried on talking and rolled his eyes towards Mavis as if to say, 'What a show-off!'[34] Yet Jane's occasional moments of theatricality did not prevent her from keeping calm in a crisis.

14

After Julius

THE HOUSE IN Soller was dank with unhappiness. Hilly was so depressed that on some days she never got out of bed at all. 'I couldn't believe what had happened,' she told Zachary Leader. 'I thought, how have I managed to get into this situation?'[1] The boys missed their father so much that every morning they would go and sit on the wall by the road and wait for the postman, hoping for a postcard from Kingsley. Their lives began to improve when a new term began at the International School in Palma, and after Hilly (out of guilt) bought them both motorbikes. Philip was fifteen and Martin only fourteen, but in Spain this was not considered unduly young.

One morning in mid-November Philip and Martin were told that they were going to see their father for a few days, and Hilly put them on a plane to London. They were overjoyed, and very excited to be flying on their own; but it was a long journey, the plane was delayed and it was past midnight when they finally rang the bell of the flat in Basil Mansions. Hilly said she had sent Kingsley a telegram to announce the boys' arrival, but it never materialized (or she had forgotten to send it) and their appearance on the doorstep came as a total shock.

'I can see Kingsley now,' wrote Martin, 'in his striped pyjamas, rearing back from us in histrionic consternation . . . It wasn't just that he was surprised to see us. He was horrified to see us. We had busted him in *flagrante delicto*.' The boys too were stunned; for instead of finding him on his own, there was 'the fancy woman' with her long gold hair, wearing a white towelling bathrobe. Without any fuss she started cooking bacon and eggs, and finding fresh sheets and blankets for the twin beds in the spare room.

Martin immediately noticed not just Jane's beauty, but her experience. 'It isn't just a matter of sexual experience,' he wrote. 'The older woman' (she was five years older than his mother) 'brings with her the glamour and mystery of life lived – people met, places seen, experiences experienced. Jane had been around, and at a high level – higher than my father's. I acknowledged the appeal of that with simple resignation and I did not feel disloyal to my mother.'[2]

There followed a week of extravagant treats, punctuated by long and often tearful sessions spent by the boys alone with Kingsley. Jane saw how they pulled and pleaded in different directions. The boys wanted Kingsley to desert her and come home with them, whereas Kingsley wanted them to love and forgive him, and perhaps even one day, they might come to love Jane.

Only a few weeks before, Jane had been braced for Kingsley to follow his original plan and leave her when the Sitges holiday was over. Now, under pressure from his two fair-haired sons barely out of their childhood, he might feel that he really ought to get back to his family. Kingsley assured her that that wouldn't happen, and the boys too saw that he was trying to explain his position, not change it. The weeks in Sitges had not only been idyllic, they had been extremely productive, and enjoyably so: he had finished *One Fat Englishman*, and made a good start on his next novel, *The Anti-Death League*. Jane was not only beautiful and sexually satisfying: she was a writer who understood the demands of writing, and was as ambitious for him as he was himself. She was also well organized, well connected, and keen to create a life for them both that was focused on his needs. With her help he could realize his literary potential.

The boys returned to Majorca towards the end of the month, but not before hearing the most dramatic news of the year. The *Daily Express* journalist George Gale had come to dinner – without his wife Pat, who remained steadfastly loyal to Hilly. He had not been there long when there was a telephone call. Kingsley took it, and Martin heard him shout '*NO!*' into the mouthpiece. George struggled into his coat to get back to Fleet Street as fast as possible. It was 22 November, and they had just heard that President Kennedy had been shot.

Kingsley's nine-year-old daughter Sally also paid a visit, and Jane found her unnerving. At least on the surface, she seemed unaffected by her parents' split. She was determined to have as many treats as the boys, and enjoyed prancing about in Jane's clothes and make-up – daring Jane to remonstrate and so prove herself a kill-joy.[3]

Early in the new year of 1964 Jane had a call from her agent A.D. Peters, asking her whether she would be willing to interview Evelyn Waugh on television. His first interview had been in 1960, when he did the *Face to Face* programme with John Freeman. Waugh was extremely nervous and tetchy throughout, and visibly annoyed by Freeman's probing questions. He had refused all subsequent requests for TV interviews. But in 1964, as he was approaching sixty, he had agreed to do one more. This was largely because he was offered a fee of £300, and the interview would be aired on the BBC's most respected cultural programme, *Monitor*. Waugh had two conditions, the first being that he would set the questions. The second was that the interviewer should be either his old friend Christopher Sykes, or a pretty woman who was familiar with his novels. The BBC decided that they would prefer the latter.

Jane accepted the challenge, and met Waugh over lunch at Brown's Hotel with the producer Christopher Burstall. She and Burstall were on their best behaviour, and Waugh decided to tease their evident nervousness. 'Ah, Miss Howard,' he said. 'And have you had anything to do with literature?'[4] He then explained to Christopher Burstall that the knives and forks on the table were to be used from the outside in. They all relaxed as the wine flowed, and Waugh produced his list of questions, which Jane thought very mundane.

The filming began the following afternoon, with Waugh in a far more genial mood than he had been with John Freeman. Jane slipped in the odd question of her own when she knew the reel was coming to an end: at one point she asked:

'Do you look at your own books and read them again?'
  'Constantly.'
  'And shriek with laughter?'
  'Yes, I must admit—'
  'And rediscover things you've forgotten?'
  'I remember them all pretty well, but I must say it causes me continual pleasure. Except for those awful moments when I come across the bad bits; the bad bits about the same number as the good, you know.'[5]

Waugh was evidently enjoying himself. As the reel ran out and the camera was being reloaded he asked, 'When is Miss Howard going to take off all her clothes?' The most alarming moment for Jane came on the second afternoon, when she was told to 'amuse' Mr Waugh while the camera filmed his reactions to her conversation. 'In the end I told him in some detail about my lack of education which he seemed to enjoy, or at any rate he remained benign throughout.'

The two interviews show the polar opposites of Waugh's character. In *Face to Face*, the Waugh on display is paranoid, reactionary and irascible. But Freeman keeps him on his toes, and the interview crackles with a dangerous energy. In his interview with Jane, which was broadcast on 16 February, he is far more at ease and in control but this was no battle of wills or wits. 'A dreary exhibition I made of myself on the television,' he admitted to his friend Ann Fleming.[6]

Nicola's first child, Daniel, was born on 9 March; and soon after the birth Jane suggested that she and Kingsley come for a visit, so Jane could be with Nicola and help with the cooking. Nicola could not think of any reason to put her off, although the house that she and Kipper were living in was extremely small and Kingsley and Jane had to sleep in a room under the eaves. Jane had had a monthly nurse in Nicola's infancy, so she had never experienced how totally absorbed a first-time mother can be in looking after a newborn – nor imagined how little time and energy Nicola would have for her own mother. Mother and baby were in a downstairs room, while Jane complained that she was left alone in the kitchen. Kingsley spent most of his time at the pub in Sapperton.

Hilly had decided to leave Soller that spring to come back to England, so Kingsley would have to find a place for her and the children to live. Jane's house in Blomfield Road was too small to accommodate her, Kingsley and Monkey, so she decided to sell the house and find somewhere bigger, and that spring, she and Monkey began house-hunting – for Monkey was going to live with them too. Kingsley hated being alone, welcomed Monkey's company and was anyway used to big households. Having Monkey with them would bring in some much needed extra cash in rent, and his invaluable electrical skills would come in useful. Kingsley took no part and showed no interest in house-hunting. As long as he had a room to work in and a drinks tray, he was utterly indifferent to his surround-ings – unlike Jane, for whom her house was an active extension and reflection of herself.

Jane's divorce from Jim Douglas-Henry came through in May 1964. In later years, whenever the subject of her second marriage arose, it seemed to touch a place so raw that she could hardly bear to recall it. She never had a kind word to say about Jim, in her memoirs or in interviews; yet although he was hurt, he never publicly criticized her. Perhaps the reason she was so vitriolic was that not only had he humiliated her, he had also forced her to confront that craving for love which gave rise to all her self-deceptions and her romantic illusions. For that, she would never forgive him.

Hilly and the children returned to England that spring; and in June she moved into a dilapidated house, Number 128 Fulham Road, opposite the Queen's Elm pub. The rent was £12 a week. Martin and Sally were enrolled in London day schools, while Philip became a weekly boarder at his old school in Saffron Walden. Somehow Hilly made all the arrangements, despite being profoundly depressed. She was already drinking heavily, and now began taking amphetamines to give her a lift and barbiturates to make her sleep.

One night, during a very drunken dinner with Sybil Burton (whose husband Richard had abandoned her for Elizabeth Taylor), Hilly took an overdose of sleeping pills. Mavis Nicholson had phoned earlier, and was alarmed by the slur in Hilly's voice; and when she called again she was answered by a terrified Sally, who could not get Hilly to wake up. The girl's terror was very real, for she knew what it was like to be left alone with a corpse. In March 1957 Kingsley's mother Peggy had agreed to look after the three-year-old Sally; but at some point she had suffered a massive heart attack, and died before she hit the floor. Sally had been left alone with her grandmother's body until William Amis came back from work that night.

Mavis rang Kingsley at Blomfield Road. Jane was out that evening and Kingsley and Monkey had taken advantage of her absence to get pretty drunk, but Mavis told Kingsley he had to go to the Fulham Road house immediately. Kingsley was reluctant to go, but luckily Monkey realized the urgency of the situation. The comatose Hilly was taken to hospital, and in a few hours she was out of danger, saying her overdose had been 'accidental'. She went home, and a couple of days later Jane had a telephone call. It was Hilly, saying, 'Well, I'm off now, it's all up to you.'[7] She had taken Sally and gone to stay with the Gales at Wivenhoe in Essex, leaving Martin and Philip to fend for themselves.

Jane went round to Fulham Road to take charge. 'I can't describe the state of the house,' she wrote to Jill Balcon. 'Three months' dirty laundry – nothing clean; every single object filthy. The children hadn't had a decent meal for weeks.' Jane found Martin in bed, fully dressed and with a high fever. She wanted to give him a cup of tea and an egg and make his bed, but there was no tea, no egg and not a single piece of clean linen. Jane insisted that she and Kingsley move in to restore order and look after the boys, but Kingsley preferred to spend his days writing at Blomfield Road as usual, and it was she and Monkey who spent six weeks cleaning and painting and making the house habitable again.

'One thing all this did,' she told Jill. 'It made them decide to divorce. K was really shocked at all that came to light.' Kingsley was used to Hilly's slap-dash housekeeping; but he was aghast that she had taken the overdose in front of Sally.

Jane too had hardly been the perfect mother; but at least she could tell herself that Nicky had lived a well-regulated life with twice-yearly visits to the dentist, even if love was lacking. Hilly was the opposite: however hopeless a housekeeper, she was a warm and loving presence in her children's lives – at least until her own life fell apart. Jane did not see that the state of the house in Fulham Road reflected Hilly's pain and desolation: all she saw was negligence, incompetence and carelessness. 'I know I sound harsh about her,' she told Jill, 'but the last three months have left me with not an atom of respect for her . . . Oh well. It's awful to feel like that about anybody and I often longed to ring you up and get some of it off my chest, but I was never reliably alone.'[8]

It is hard to explain her lack of sympathy. Jane had certainly had her share of heartache, but more often than not it was she who had walked out – on Peter Scott, Robert Aickman, Michael Behrens and Jim Douglas-Henry. She had never been married for as long as Hilly, nor abandoned so publicly for another woman. One cannot help feeling that she should have felt a few pangs of compassion and remorse for Hilly, for whose misery she was, at least in part, responsible. Jane chose to look at it from another angle. The break-up of the Amis marriage was well under way before they met in Cheltenham, and Kingsley's wife had been holding him back. Hilly was not up to the task of looking after him, nor her own children come to that. Jane was right to have rescued Kingsley, and that cancelled out any guilt she may have felt.

Since there were still a few weeks to run on the house that Kingsley had taken for the year in Soller, they went out to Majorca that August. Blomfield Road had been sold, and Jane recalled the joy of her last night there, 'lit up by warmth and excitement. At last, I thought, life was everything I could have hoped for . . . I lay awake that night for a long time, thinking how miserable I'd been in this place and think-ing how wonderful it was to be starting again.'⁹

By then she had bought a new property in Maida Vale, which she described to Jill Balcon:

> I got £5,500 [for Blomfield Road] which was cheering because H. had spent all K.'s money (out of £4,000 he'd earned since Jan she'd had £3,800 of it). We found a delicious mouth-watering house called Adelaide Villa in Edgware Road. Only a 13 year lease, but so cheap that it's worth it. 150 ft garden, enormous conservatory, 5 beds, 4 recep., enormous kitchen in which we can eat, and dining room. A study for K, one for me, and a workroom for Monkey.¹⁰

Kingsley's old friend the historian Robert Conquest, accompanied by his wife Caroleen, came out to Majorca in September. Here the two men wrote *The Egyptologists*, a comic novel about a spurious society that exists as an excuse for husbands to get away from their wives. In October the lease on the house in Soller ran out. Kingsley and Jane moved briefly to a hotel in Pollensa, where Jane put on a burst of writing speed and completed 14,000 words of *After Julius*. This was the only time that she admitted to rewriting part of a novel. Kingsley thought her first version of Julius's trip to France wasn't quite right, so she rewrote it.

They were back in London in early November, but the house in Maida Vale was still not ready so they took a small flat in Keats Grove, Hampstead. Kingsley had to bring the coal up five flights of stairs to keep them warm; while Jane cooked, and watched the squirrels whom she had lured to the window with saucers of nuts or biscuits. It was here that she finished *After Julius*,

> On a dark grey evening in November. The feeling after completing a novel is for me like no other. It's as though with that last sentence, I have released a great weight that falls away, leaving me so empty and light that I can float out of myself and look down at the pattern of the work I've made.

After this moment of ecstasy came the sadder thoughts: 'Parting with people one has been living with for so long and know so intimately is poignant. They remain crystallized exactly where you left them.'[11]

Kingsley's possessions consisted of books, clothes, a typewriter and some bottles. Jane had a little furniture and a few pictures, but nothing like the amount she needed to furnish the house in Maida Vale. Junkshops were cheap and plentiful, and she spent happy hours rummaging about in the dustiest recesses of Church Street and the Portobello Road. Her brother Robin had taken over the family timber business, and in the course of his travels to buy hardwoods he had made some useful contacts in Rangoon, so Jane had access to inexpensive silks and printed cottons with which to make curtains. One day she and Monkey saw some builders in Primrose Hill throwing slabs of black and white marble into a skip. The builders had no objection to them taking the marble, which two art students turned into a beautiful floor for the conservatory. All this she paid for herself, since the bulk of Kingsley's income was going to Hilly and the children.

By February 1965 they were in the new house, and Jane had delivered her typescript to Tom Maschler at Cape. He sent her a telegram that read: 'IT'S YOUR MOST SERIOUS YOUR MOST MOVING AND YOUR MOST ENJOYABLE IN FACT YOUR BEST BOOK CONGRATULATIONS LOVE TOM.'

Jane and Kingsley were married on 29 June 1965 at Marylebone Town Hall. 'Mr Amis, 43, and Miss Howard, who is 42 and a grandmother, arrived together at the register office,' wrote the *Daily Mail*. 'His shimmering turquoise bow-tie matched the colour of her patterned silk dress.' The ceremony was briefly held up to wait for a very pregnant

Nicola, who had come up from Sapperton with Dan, then just over a year old. 'After they were married,' continued the *Daily Mail*, 'the new Mrs Amis proudly flashed around her new wedding ring – a gigantic wide affair covered with gold spiky lumps. "Specially designed for us by a wonderful English jeweller called John Donald," said Miss Howard proudly.' The reporter was disappointed to note that they left the town hall to return to Maida Vale in a grey Ford Cortina.[12]

That evening there was a party given by Tom Maschler. In almost every newspaper photograph taken that day, Jane gazes adoringly at Kingsley, as he flashes his Lucky Jim smile at the camera. They had a two-day honeymoon in Brighton, where their presence and walks on the beach attracted more press attention (again, organized by Tom). They had suddenly become a power couple: not perhaps on the same scale as Richard Burton and Elizabeth Taylor, or Arthur Miller and Marilyn Monroe, but intriguing and glamorous nonetheless; perhaps more like Ted Hughes and Sylvia Plath, with a less harrowing story.

This moment of great happiness for Jane coincided with a crisis in Jill's marriage to Cecil Day-Lewis. On holiday in Ireland that year, she had discovered a letter in his jacket pocket from the writer A.S. Byatt. Jill had so far tried to turn a blind eye to his affairs, but at this point her patience snapped. She walked out on the family for two days (she did not make a scene, because that's what Rosamond Lehmann would have done), wondering whether she would ever go back to him. Perhaps it was the first time that she had realized just how much his infidelities hurt her. Cecil was shaken by her fury and very contrite. They made it up, and when Jill was back in London she had lunch with Jane in the Charing Cross Hotel. She told Jane what had happened, and how she had found the letter from Antonia Byatt; Jane took this as a cue to discuss her own affair with Cecil, express her remorse, and make it clear that it was she who had ended the relationship. It wasn't the best moment to do so. Jill had a pretty good idea that something had happened between Jane and Cecil, but this was a double betrayal and she didn't want to hear any more details. She never felt the same about Jane again.[13]

That September Jane and Kingsley took a holiday in Greece with Kingsley's old friends Mike and Mary Keeley. Mike, known professionally as Professor Edmund Keeley, is an American scholar and translator of modern Greek literature and an expert on the poems of Constantine Cavafy and George Seferis. He and his Greek wife, Mary, had met Kingsley and Hilly when they came to Princeton in 1958. They had liked Hilly and were sorry that the marriage had split up; and despite Jane being rather queenly at first, as she often was when she was shy, once she relaxed they became very fond of her.

Kingsley and Jane had travelled overland as far as Venice. Having left Kingsley safely parked in a bar, Jane spent several hours walking beside canals and over little bridges until it was time to take the boat to Piraeus, where they were met by Mike and Mary and driven to Athens. Kingsley, who had already written a potboiler called *The James Bond Dossier*, was far more interested in Greece as the setting for his own Bond novel than for its cultural treasures; but they visited several islands by ferry and then boarded the *Altair*, a comfortable caique belonging to Aleko Papadogonas, a friend of Mike and Mary's. Since Kingsley wanted to include at least one underwater scene in the book, this was all grist to the mill – particularly since their host had been a submarine commander and was an expert diver.

Mike Keeley noted that with Hilly he had 'a slightly comic relationship, we flirted – but I never flirted with Jane'. But he liked the way Jane talked so freely about herself and her life, 'and she was fond of my wife Mary, too, called her the Dormouse.'[14] Mary and Jane had one big subject in common: their longing for children. At one point they even lit candles in a church to advance the possibility of conception, although it never happened for either of them.

After Julius was published that autumn, alongside a list that was particularly strong in woman novelists: Margaret Lane's *A Smell of Burning*, Muriel Spark's *The Mandelbaum Gate*, Iris Murdoch's *The Red and the Green*, Edna O'Brien's *August is a Wicked Month*, Doris Lessing's *Landlocked* and the last volume of Olivia Manning's Balkan Trilogy, *Friends and Heroes*.

The action of *After Julius* takes place over a single weekend, and as in *The Sea Change*, the five main characters speak and observe each other in their own voices. Jane wrote most of the novel in a state of happiness, a promontory from which she could look back at her emotional life; and it is through the character of Cressy that she describes what it was like to live with the restless neediness that drove them both.

Julius Grace, who was forty-nine in 1940, felt he must contribute to the war effort even though he was too old to fight. In late May, without telling his wife, he bought a little boat and sailed to Dunkirk to rescue as many men as he could. He managed to rescue three, but died when the boat was attacked on its return by enemy aircraft. Julius's self-sacrifice was the fulfilment of his public duty; but in performing it, he ignored the private obligations he owed to his wife and family. This is a variation on the misery of her first marriage when Peter Scott, by immersing himself in the war, had neglected her when she needed him most. Yet Julius's wife Esme cannot see herself as wronged, since at the time of Julius's death she was having an affair with a young medical student called Felix King. Julius's death affects Felix as profoundly as it does the lives of Esme and her children.

The novel opens twenty years later, when Esme has invited Felix – now Dr King – to spend the weekend at her house in Sussex. They have not met since 1940: she is almost sixty, he in his mid-forties. Also in the house that weekend are Esme's two daughters, Cressy and Emma, who share a flat in London and have already been mentioned as prime examples of experience and innocence in Jane's fiction. Cressy has had many lovers, but little happiness. She was seventeen when she last saw Felix, and his reappearance awakens painful memories.

Emma is a simpler, happier soul who was her father's favourite, although she was only seven when he died. She works in the family publishing firm of Speedwell & Grace where she meets Daniel Brick, a working-class poet who turned up in her office demanding a cheque. Having secured £50 for him from Accounts she takes him out to lunch, and then invites him down to her mother's for the weekend.

Over the course of Saturday Cressy vents her rage against Felix whom she knew was having an affair with her mother, while Emma delights in the plain-speaking, rough-cast manliness of Dan. Everything comes to a head at the dinner party on Saturday night, when Cressy is faced with her latest lover and his jealous wife. The disintegration of the dinner party into tears and recriminations, despite Esme's gallant efforts to maintain decorum, includes the section written by Kingsley.

The two-dimensional Dan is loosely modelled on Laurie Lee. His romance with Emma, who is a virgin although Dan assumes she is not, ends with him forcing himself on her. It shocked John Betjeman when he read the book: 'oh poor girl, that trying to rape her and him smiling, so nasty',[15] he wrote. Yet the scene ends with Dan making a rapturous declaration of love, to which the tearful Emma responds with joy. Did Jane expect the reader to condone it as an example of Dan's natural and uncorrupted ways, and rejoice with them? Rape is taken more seriously now than it was in 1965: Kay Dick, who reviewed the book for the *Sunday Times*, described Dan as a character 'whose frankness and spontaneity make him a sparkling hero'.[16]

It is only at breakfast on Sunday morning that Esme comes to the crushing realization that her erstwhile love, Felix, has fallen for her daughter Cressy. It's a terrible humiliation, but the rules of the game oblige Esme to hide her pain under a bright and cheerful façade. Whatever happens to her daughters, Esme is condemned to a life of loneliness.

Felix and Cressy go back to London, although Cressy's failures in love have reduced her to such a state of numb despondency that she has lost all hope. She lets him take her to a hotel, where she expects the sad, sordid cycle of an affair to begin again; and in a long passage describing her experience of love so far, one can hear Jane's voice with unmistakable clarity:

> Anything to get away from these precarious, nerve-racking experiments. People always thought you did these things because you got paid, or loved sex or being flattered: they never seemed to think that you might just do them because you knew that they were the ropes and you wanted to get into the ring, or go on the voyage or whatever the ropes were supposed to be about . . . That was when she realised how much of her life she'd strung along with people; as they seemed to know what they wanted, things had generally gone their way. That her natural responses had gradually withered under their collective indifference had not struck her at all till now. But oh God, it did now.[17]

The strange thing about this internal soliloquy is that Cressy never says exactly *why* she is disappointed. She refers to 'the ropes' and 'the voyage', but these are evasions. What they point to is that in the sexual theatre of her time there was no role for a woman's desires: no room in the script for her to say, 'This is what gives me pleasure', and above all, 'You may have finished but I'm not there yet.' (Kingsley

Amis, at that time a very considerate lover, reveals how hard she found it to express her sexual desires in his letter quoted on p.174.)

Jane described Cressy's soliloquy as 'the song of a virgin – she's not a virgin technically, but she's never had proper sex or love . . . bed for her didn't have any significance – like being sexually psychotic, she doesn't respond. Her responses have been driven under.'[18] Felix understands why she seems so frozen: 'How many times,' he asks, 'have you let yourself be raped in return for a little affection?' It's as if Jane is asking us to compare the 'rapes' endured by Cressy, submitting to what is expected of her as an experienced woman, and Dan's rape of the innocent Emma, which – for all its violence – is an act of love.

Most reviewers were enthusiastic, and commented on the novel's masterly structure. In the *Guardian*, Fiona MacCarthy called it 'a fastidious and moving book', while Kay Dick in the *Sunday Times* compared Jane's reputation to that of Elizabeth Bowen in the thirties, only Jane was much funnier. One dissenting voice was Marigold Johnson's in the *Times Literary Supplement*. She felt the novel was made up of too many disparate elements, and it was a disappointment 'from a writer with so deservedly high a reputation as hers'.[19]

Laurie Lee wrote to congratulate her: '*After Julius* is superb – compact, super-charged, so well-written, and also very funny. There is no one like you – I find no dead patches, every page is crowded with value . . . Of course I have a family interest in the ghost of Dan, but I really go for the girls . . . I think this is one of your best.[20]

Cecil Day-Lewis wrote to say that:

Cressy is my pin-up – rings true wherever one taps her: you have put so much of yourself and experience into her . . . The Julius-rescuing operation moved me very much indeed . . . I thought Emma came a bit off the top of the head . . . I felt some of the scenes between her and Dan were rather the Teddybears' Picnic. This is partly because I could not believe much in Dan . . . I cannot imagine what kind of poetry he writes – or indeed his writing poetry at all.[21]

John Betjeman's letter, already quoted above, was also perceptive.

Cressy would have, of course, got me on the hop, Emma is sweet but I don't know what she looks like only how she thinks . . . Esme is infinitely sad and a masterpiece ... I think your boldest thing is the final acknowledgement of the truth in their last confrontation of Esme and Felix. It *is* a good book and so well constructed.

Yet the passage in his letter that Jane enjoyed most was not about her book at all, but about the devotion of her new husband. 'Old Kingsley was wonderful when he came over to Feeble's [his long-term companion, Elizabeth Cavendish] and you were laid low. He spoke so movingly of your excellence as a writer as well as a person that you would have shivered with pleasure.'[22]

15

Stepmother

JANE WAS PROFOUNDLY relieved that she had not had a child with Jim Douglas-Henry; but now with Kingsley, the desire for children was reignited. The house was certainly big enough to accommodate babies, 'which I hope we shall have as soon as we can get married,' she told Jill Balcon. Yet it seems strange that Jane, who had not much enjoyed the experience of raising her first child, should want to try again. Had she not walked out on her first husband and daughter in order to write, and now that she was a published author, did she really want to revert to a life dominated by domestic chores, the school run and nanny's day off? By the time they moved to Maida Vale, she and Kingsley had been living together for at least eighteen months. She must have known that if she did have a child, the task would fall to her alone. She could expect no help from him.

Kingsley had grown up with parents who did everything for him. His clothes fell to the floor as he took them off, because his mother had always picked them up. She had also force-fed him with a spoon so eating was never a pleasure, more a bodily invasion. And although he had spent three years in the army, he was still congenitally untidy. His father had dealt with his bills and looked after his bank account until he married. Jane wrote that she had never met a man so indifferent to his surroundings, and Hilly's scattiness and good humour had been a welcome relief after all these people trying to organize him. And now, since all his energies were devoted to the task of writing good, entertaining novels, any further effort – beyond mixing the drinks – was out of the question.

Jane knew all this, but as so often, cautious reflection was overridden by more highly coloured impulses. Jane wanted to prove to herself that although she had failed as a mother the first time, she could get it right: she could give a child unconditional love –

something her mother had failed to give her, and she had been too immature and confused to give Nicola. She also wanted to show Kingsley how children ought to be raised, and prove that she could be a better mother than Hilly.

Her doctor assured her that there was no reason why she should not conceive but when she asked Kingsley to attend a fertility clinic, he refused. Whatever the cause, she never became pregnant again and claimed it was a source of great regret; but once she had embarked on the task of being a stepmother, some part of her was surely thankful that she didn't have a baby to deal with as well as two teenage boys.

Soon after Hilly had recovered from her breakdown, Jane suggested that Philip and Martin should come and live at Maida Vale. The Fulham Road house was as chaotic as ever. Hilly now had three young lodgers to help pay the bills, so people were always drifting in and out amid a succession of impromptu parties. She also took on a number of part-time jobs, of which the most enjoyable was being a keeper at Battersea Zoo. She had never made any attempt to control her sons, who were now smoking dope and hanging out in the Picasso coffee bar on the King's Road, where they would try to pick up girls. They bunked off school regularly, and Jane felt that they would never complete their education or pass any public exams unless she and Kingsley stepped in. It was a generous offer. She knew it would not be easy, and did it only because she felt it was the right thing to do.

Yet why did Hilly let this happen? Why did she leave her sons in the care of the woman who had usurped her place? One can only assume that as they grew older and more overtly male, they became more Kingsley's sons than hers, and as young sexual predators they modelled themselves on him. So she presumably thought: fine, he can have them.

All Jane's early efforts on behalf of her new stepsons would be practical, focusing on regular meals and regular schooling. She knew she could not expect to win their affection, at least not yet. Her big mistake was to assume that she would have Kingsley's moral support – a miscalculation that was to have far-reaching effects on their marriage.

Philip and Martin, now aged sixteen and fifteen, moved into Maida Vale in the spring of 1965, a month or two before Jane and Kingsley's wedding. The plan was that they would spend their weekdays at Maida Vale and their weekends with their mother, although she would not be in London for much longer. Hilly gave up the Fulham Road house in July 1965, and moved to Wivenhoe in Essex with Sally to be near her friends the Gales.

Jane had expected a certain amount of surliness, hostility and lack of cooperation from her stepsons (although it must be said that they brought the happy couple breakfast in bed on their wedding day, as a peace offering). What she had not foreseen was the depths of Kingsley's inertia. He did not seem to mind that their education had stalled; as one of his biographers pointed out, he 'had made an art out of not noticing'.[1] Either from indolence or guilt he invariably sided with the boys, leaving Jane to dig herself ever deeper into the role of nagging scold.

She gives the example of the second-hand bar-billiards table bought for the conservatory, which required the insertion of a shilling in the slot before playing a game. There was general agreement that the money collected should go to charity; but the boys found a way to break into the box of shillings, so it was always empty. As far as Jane was concerned, it wasn't the money that mattered, but the principle – they were effectively stealing. 'When I approached Kingsley about it, he simply said, "Well, it isn't very much money," as though the amount was the point. This was in front of the boys, so they *knew* I was a prig, and their father was a good sort.'[2]

The situation would have become unbearable for everyone had it not been for Monkey. He understood the bitterness and emotional turmoil that Philip and Martin were going through, because he had been through it himself when his parents separated. 'I could see Jane was having an impossible job because I would have been totally unwilling to make any concessions to my father's second choice and I couldn't see why they should,' he told Zachary Leader. 'I think she had the most appalling battle over that and I'm sorry for everybody.'[3] He could reason with Jane because she never doubted his loyalty, and with Kingsley, who was grateful for his company and the way he could defuse the tension.

The boys enjoyed the daily communal breakfast on the broad expanse of Jane and Kingsley's bed, where everyone gathered to drink coffee, smoke cigarettes and read aloud the latest political idiocies in the papers. They had access to food, alcohol, television and cigarettes;

they could bring friends back, and go out whenever they liked – but Jane and her standards were never far away.

She enrolled Philip and Martin at Davies Laing & Dick tutorial college in Holland Park which specialized in steering pupils through O- and A-level exams, but they seldom attended. She made them a den off the kitchen where they could lounge about and play their hi-fi. That Christmas she gave them gold watches with engraved initials as well as bulging stockings, and they had money from their father. Jane's Christmases were always lavish, and this time she surpassed herself. The trouble she had taken with the festive food and decorations begged for wonder and admiration, but the boys were unwilling to oblige. 'All we want are the presents,'[4] said Philip – a sentence which, as intended, reduced her to tears. On that occasion Kingsley did tell the boys to apologize, but Philip was never going to tolerate the woman who had taken his mother's place.

In January 1966 Jane and Kingsley were treated to an all-expenses-paid holiday in Jamaica, with Bobby and Dolly Burns. Bobby Burns was a retired surgeon and Dolly, then in her seventies, was the only daughter of the art dealer Lord Duveen. She collected people and spent much of her considerable fortune entertaining, with house parties, lunches and dinners for never fewer than twenty guests in London, the Côte d'Azur or Montego Bay. At this stage, Kingsley – newly married to Jane, and venturing higher up the social ladder – was intrigued by the luxurious world of the very rich.

While they enjoyed the voyage out on a well-appointed banana boat (Jane was delighted to see her first flying-fish), the holiday was not a success. The routine of their days at the Burns residence, Fairlea, was stifling. Every morning they swam at Doctor's Cove, the smart place to swim. Then back to the house for lunch and a siesta, and every evening there was a full black-tie dinner. Whether given by Dolly or someone else, the same bland and well-fed guests turned up every time. Kingsley was struck by the disparity between the 'rather horrible rich white people' who came for holidays, and the 'rather miserable resentful black people' who lived on the island all year round in poverty. 'My old left-wing, or just humanitarian, feelings came back with a rush,' he remarked later.[5] He had no interest in sightseeing, but Jane managed to make two excursions into the interior: one to see a woman who attracted swarms of humming-birds to her house, lured by the dozens of sugar-feeders she put out for them; and one to get a glimpse of the Look-back Lands, a densely wooded area that was home to a people who had cut themselves off from the rest of the island. She saw nothing but lots of little tracks winding through the vegetation, but it was worth it just to get away from Fairlea.

One afternoon Kingsley stormed into their room to announce that he wasn't going to stay a minute longer. He had asked Dolly whether they could have some Foreign Guinness (his favourite beer) at lunch, instead of Jamaican Red Stripe; and Dolly said no, because the Guinness cost a few cents more per can. Kingsley flew into a rage, accused her of trying to control everything, and said he could not believe such penny-pinching stinginess from so rich a woman: he and Jane would be leaving at once.

Jane remarked that since Kingsley would not take a plane, they were in no position to make a dramatic exit. Then Dolly arrived in tears accompanied by her husband, and begged them to stay. They did; but Kingsley vowed he would never be a house-guest of the Burnses again, and once they were back in London, he repaid Dolly the cost of their passage to and from Jamaica.

They were back in time for the publication of Kingsley's novel *The Anti-Death League*. It was reviewed in the *Sunday Times* by Frederic Raphael, who observed that 'Mr Amis has discovered love. His whole book is transformed (on reflection it seems full of a curious sunlight) by the new standard by which men and motives come to be judged.'[6]

Flashes and fragments of Jane appear in Kingsley's fiction over the course of their marriage, and when it was over, he wrote a nightmarish distortion of her in *Stanley and the Women*; but in this novel, the reader sees the Jane he fell in love with. Kingsley told one interviewer that the novel was partly about 'a girl who had always been treated badly by men and how difficult it is for her to agree to being treated nicely by a man'.[7] Kingsley asked Jane to choose a name for the woman who would be modelled on her, and she chose Catherine Casement. Like Jane, Catherine had married too young and had many lovers; and with Kingsley's uncanny ear for voices, she talks just like her – the Jane who is also Cressy in *After Julius*.

In a conversation with her lover, James Churchill, about her sexual experience Catherine says, 'So I wasn't getting a great deal out of it at that stage, early on. I thought that perhaps the people who said they got a lot out of it were natural exaggerators, or else that I was somebody it didn't happen to appeal to an awful lot. I thought that getting married and being with someone all the time would make it better. So you see I was to blame too for things going wrong.'[8]

Yet the vulnerable Jane as portrayed in *The Anti-Death League* was already out of date. The arrival of two teenage boys in the Amis household marked the end of the honeymoon stage, and Jane was now a married woman and a stepmother who took her responsibilities seriously. Drugs might be tolerated at 128 Fulham Road, but they were not in Maida Vale; and in March 1966, the month in which *The Anti-Death League* was published, Jane found a stash of drugs in Philip's room.

'It was no great feat of detection,' wrote Martin, 'because they were kept in a box with PHIL'S DRUGS written on it in eyecatching multi-coloured capitals.'[9] The seventeen-year-old Philip was summoned for a serious dressing-down in front of his father and stepmother, but he was already beyond their authority. Furiously defiant, he left the house that night; and although he did return from time to time, it was as an autonomous adult. He was no longer a child of the house. 'He was so angry,' wrote Zachary Leader, 'she couldn't have got it right, nothing could have made it better.' Philip agreed. 'I don't think anyone could have coped with me at that time, I was just nuts.'[10]

Martin accepted his brother's leap to freedom with admiration and a lurch of dismay; but once Philip had gone the atmosphere in the house lightened, and Martin gradually became more tractable. Jane found him lounging about doing nothing one day, and asked him what he wanted to do when he was older. He said he wanted to be a writer.

'You – a *writer*?' she scoffed. 'But you never read anything. If you're so interested in writing, why don't you read?' Martin shrugged and asked her to give him a book. She gave him *Pride and Prejudice* and left him to it. There are two versions of what happened next. According to Jane in *Slipstream*, he came to her study and begged her to tell him how the story ended.

' "Of course I won't. You find out for yourself." He argued with persuasive charm, but I felt on firm ground. He was obviously enjoying it.'[11] Martin says that he was indeed anxious to know whether Jane Bennet would marry Mr Bingley, and Elizabeth would marry Mr Darcy. 'So I knocked on her study door and put the question; and she turned round with smiling, dewy eyes and breathed a tremulous "Yes!" '[12] Whichever version was correct, the combination of Jane and *Pride and Prejudice* set Martin on the path to educational and literary success. Over the coming months he made forays into the works of Dickens, Evelyn Waugh and P.G. Wodehouse, and read *Middlemarch* in three days.

Kingsley and Jane spent much of July and August in Greece, once more with the Keeleys. The weather was uncomfortably hot, and Mike remembered how Kingsley described the cottage as having belonged 'to a family of malevolent midgets, since you couldn't move from one room to another without cracking your head on some picturesque antique lintel or beam'. He also remembered Jane, cracking her skull in the same place for the second time that day, whimpering, 'I will just squat here and cry and never move again.'[13]

Jane described these Greek holidays with the Keeleys as times of particular happiness. Kingsley enjoyed the company of Mike and Mary, and, later, the historian Paul Fussell and his wife Betty. They were also, more importantly, times when they could be alone together. Looking back on her years with Kingsley, Jane felt that their relationship might have lasted longer had they had more time on their own in the early stages; but given their love of entertaining and the fact that they both felt more comfortable in large households, being alone together was something that did not happen very often.

They came back from Greece to find that the boys had done even worse than expected in their exams. Jane decreed that if Martin did not manage to do better in the January retakes, he would be sent off to crammer. As for Philip, he had no intention of submitting to Jane's authority again and declared that school was a waste of time. He had always been interested in art and design, so with the support of Monkey's friend, the painter Sargy Mann, he applied to the Camberwell School of Art. Sargy himself had been trained at Camberwell, and was later to become one of the school's star teachers: so he was in a good position to prepare Philip for art school, and advise him on his first portfolio.

Sargy was a frequent visitor at Number 108 Maida Vale, which he had helped Monkey to rewire when they first moved in. He was driven by intellectual curiosity, and a desire to push the boundaries of visual perception as far as they would go. At the same time, he had the enviable ability to make whoever he was talking to feel like the most interesting person in the room. It was through their mutual love of jazz that Sargy Mann first came into Monkey's life, and increasingly into Jane's too. She had first met him at Blomfield Road when she was married to Jim, and the twenty-two-year-old Sargy often came to supper and stayed on for the poker game. 'She was lovely, sophisticated but not a bit patronizing,' he said, 'and she became like a second mother to me.'[14] When he completed his training at the Camberwell School of Art and went to live in a tiny bedsit in the Tottenham Court Road, Jane bought him a cooking pot and taught him how to make stew.

Jane felt that Martin's work would improve if he were away from the temptations of the King's Road and the Picasso, so the following year she enrolled him at Sussex Tutors in Brighton. This required some doing. He was seventeen, had passed only three O-levels, and had spent years avoiding school whenever possible. But she was able to persuade Mr Ardagh, the senior tutor in English, that Martin was highly intelligent and had potential. During the year he spent in Brighton, Martin sat more O-levels as well as A-levels, discovered poetry, and learned how to write and talk and think about books. For all this, he paid generous tribute to Jane: 'She was generous, affectionate and resourceful; she salvaged my schooling, and I owe her an unknowable debt for that.' He also began to feel something more for her. 'It is very difficult, it is perhaps impossible, for someone who loves his mother to love the woman your father left her for . . . However this may be, I got very close to loving Jane.'[15]

Philip never came even remotely close. He would leave obscene drawings of Jane and Kingsley lying around, and mimic her voice and her mannerisms. He was also resentful of the way Kingsley showed no interest in his choice of a career. Sargy remembered that 'Sometime after Philip had enrolled at Camberwell, Kingsley asked him what he was *doing* . . . Anyway Phil told him and he grimaced and said, "But painting, visual arts . . . it's all very second-rate, isn't it?" Maybe he was joking, it was difficult to tell with Kingsley, but I thought it one of the most hurtful, poisonous things I'd heard him say . . . He could make fun of people without being vitriolic but this upset Phil greatly.'[16]

★

An image of Jane at this time has been preserved on film, when she agreed to be interviewed by Alan Whicker. *Whicker's World* cast a spotlight on exotic places across the globe, from Papa Doc Duvalier's Haiti to the Far East; but it also examined social and political issues. This particular programme was called 'The Stresses of Divorce', and its opening sequence shows Jane walking down Maida Vale resplendent in a pale coat with a rolled collar, her hair arranged in her trademark chignon. In the conservatory, over a trembling cigarette and a very full ashtray, she tells Whicker the familiar tale of how she married Peter Scott too young and how the war had pulled them apart; how he had only wanted to talk about Oerlikon guns and boats, about which she knew nothing. The viewer is struck by her beauty and her husky voice; yet it's interesting to note an almost childish earnestness, and the little-girl touch to her 'r's: 'I was *fwightfully* young and stupid in those days.' Also interviewed was Peter Scott and his wife Philippa, at home in Slimbridge. When Peter was asked what went wrong with his marriage to Jane, he said simply, 'Whenever we were together, we made each other miserable.'[17]

In October 1966 Kingsley and Jane were invited on a six-day visit to Prague. They would be the guests of the Czech government, which was just beginning to show signs of opening up to the West – although Kingsley was surprised, since by 1966 (and in sharp contrast to the days of his youth) he had become very right-wing and vehemently anti-Communist. Their invitation was due to the fact that Communist bureaucracy, being decades behind the times, still had Amis pigeonholed as an ardent socialist and an Angry Young Man.

In fact, Kingsley had been moving to the right ever since the Russian invasion of Hungary in 1956. In a *Sunday Telegraph* article entitled 'Why Lucky Jim Turned Right' he declared that what he objected to was the left's fuzzy liberalism, its reluctance to see straight and think clearly.[18] This, in his view, is what had already undermined the rigour of the educational system and created a generation that romanticized the left because it felt good to do so, while blaming all society's ills on 'the establishment'. These views had been honed at what became known as the 'fascist lunches', when Kingsley and the historian Robert Conquest (often dubbed Kingers and Conquers) met up at Bertorelli's in Charlotte Street, where there they were joined by other right-wing journalists, academics and historians, including the Hungarian Tibor Szamuely, who had had first-hand experience of Communism.

Jane, who had scant interest in politics, played little part in Kingsley's political volte-face. Monkey, who held more extreme right-wing views and discussed them with passion, may have had more to do with it. Yet Kingsley's realignment probably felt easier and more natural since, for the first time in his life, he was living with people who had never voted Labour.

At the suggestion of the British Council, Jane and Kingsley both filed confidential reports on their visit to Prague; and Jane's shows that she'd had very little idea of the miseries of life behind the Iron Curtain.

'Everybody was extremely kind, hospitable and charming to us, but the visit was, nonetheless, the most shattering, impersonal shock I have ever experienced,' she wrote. 'Of all the Czechs we met, only one attempted to tell us how good everything was: the rest were pessimistic, despairing, many of them frightened in some degree or other.' It was taken for granted that every room was bugged: any unguarded talk had to happen in the open air. 'One very intelligent writer we met – also a qualified doctor – said that he would not have any children, because he could not face the lies he would have to tell them. "Children are not children" was another remark.' The only time the Czechs felt better about things was when they went to Russia, where things were evidently far worse. Even their interpreter (aged twenty-eight) said his wife couldn't face having children: 'she works nine hours a day in an office six days a week, and they both have to work to afford a flat ten by ten metres.'[19]

Their next move into unfamiliar territory took them to Nashville, Tennessee, in October 1967. About a year before, Kingsley had been contacted by an old Princeton friend, Russell Fraser, who was now heading the English Department of Vanderbilt University in Nashville. He invited Kingsley to teach at Vanderbilt for a semester – in other words, from August 1967 to March 1968. Despite the fact that they could speak the language, it felt every bit as foreign as Prague; and just as in Prague, they were perceived as exotic, outlandish creatures.

Although he had been offered similar teaching opportunities at other more celebrated American universities, Kingsley decided to accept. His fondness for Russell Fraser was one reason, and another was the unlikelihood of coming across any ghastly expat Brits in that part of the world. Yet a third was identified by his biographer, which was 'to irritate the Lefties: first-hand observation was bound to refute knee-jerk reactions about the South'.[20]

Martin was safely at Sussex Tutors, and Monkey would be left in charge of the house with Jane's cousin Perry Worsthorne. Perry had joined the household that summer, while going through a marital crisis; but just before Jane and Kingsley were due to leave, he felt he had to go back to his wife, who was not well. At this point Jane suggested that Sargy come and keep Monkey company, and Sargy was delighted to oblige. Maida Vale was considerably more comfortable than his little bedsit, and it came with a garden and a cleaning lady. He and Monkey were left with money for the house and food, and Sargy was charged only a peppercorn rent – in return for which he would help in the garden, feed the cats and cook the occasional fish finger. Martin came for holidays and weekends, and Philip looked in from time to time.

Kingsley and Jane boarded the *Queen Mary* on 30 August, bound for New York; and after a few days with the Keeleys at Princeton, they took a train to Nashville. The house they had been allocated, 3627 Valley Vista Road, was a low-slung bungalow and Jane's heart sank when she saw it. It was 'a drab and tasteless little place', she remembered, and although Kingsley was impressed by all the gadgets (the ice-maker in the fridge, the remote-control for the television), within a week almost everything had broken down.

'The owner was there to hand over,' wrote Jane, 'and so was the black lady who cleaned the house. "You'll have to give her something at Christmas", she said as the maid was standing by. "Just something cheap and gaudy – anything will do." Deeply ashamed, I glanced at the maid. Her expression was impassive, and she didn't meet my eye.'[21]

Since Kingsley couldn't drive, Jane had to hire a car and drive him the two miles to the Vanderbilt campus, twice a day. The car was useful at the supermarket too, although this was a way of shopping she did not get used to. She missed not having any local shops, and the fact that one couldn't walk anywhere – it attracted police attention, and the risk of being arrested for soliciting. She was hoping to teach at Fisk University, one of the first black universities to be established in the US. For someone who had come in contact with very few black people, 'it was a revelation to see countless young, beautifully-groomed black students' on the Fisk campus.[22] The head of staff was keen to have her and she very much wanted to teach there, but it proved impossible to work out a schedule round her primary task of ferrying Kingsley to and from Vanderbilt. Jane resented this more and more, and hankered after her lost opportunity to teach at Fisk.

This sense of claustrophobia and powerlessness was made worse by the fact that in Nashville she was no longer a figure in her own right, she was just Mrs Amis; and while the people they came across knew she had written books, no one had read them. She felt confined and very far from home, in an ugly house in which she could not be herself; and much of this feeling spills into the novel she was writing, called *Something in Disguise*. No wonder she regretted not teaching at Fisk: she would have learned much and acquired some standing, at least in her own eyes. (One can only assume that the work she was offered was unpaid; for had she been earning, she would have happily spent it all on a driver for Kingsley.) As it was, her role was reduced to that of chauffeur and cook, fitting in her writing around his hours of teaching.

Things were certainly easier for Kingsley. The faculty was very hospitable, and there were countless dinners and parties in his honour. His students were more earnest and polite than any he'd come across in England and Wales, and they found his willingness to engage with them as equals very refreshing. In a world where most people relied on black servants, he and Jane had weekly dinners with the only other two 'self-catering' couples on campus – Russell Fraser and his wife Phil, and Richard Porter, a young Russian scholar who was married to a lively German called Birgitte. Desperate for some exercise, Jane joined a gym. Birgitte said she'd like to join too. When Jane asked at the gym if this would be possible, 'the secretary asked me whether this person was – well – *coloured*? Because, if so . . . I wanted to say "No, she's possibly the daughter of an SS general, but she's not black" but of course I didn't.'[23]

Both Kingsley and Jane were deeply shocked by the casual racism they encountered. According to their friend Richard Porter, many people at Vanderbilt were upset by the articles they wrote when they got back home, particularly since they claimed the Amises had never objected to racist comments at the time, and their descriptions of what they had heard were exaggerated. The instances Jane cited are chilling nonetheless. She wrote that 'White women, whether they know it or not, have been conditioned to fear and dislike the Negro male.' Jane met a student of Kingsley's who said, 'I expect you've noticed that most of the trouble with Negroes is in the North: *we* know how to keep them in their place.'[24]

At the same time, the Amises themselves caused quite a stir. Kingsley sported tweeds with brightly coloured shirts and ties, as well as dazzling socks hand-knitted by Jane; while she wore mini-skirts that would not have raised an eyebrow in London, but scandalized Nashville. They both drank prodigiously and said 'fuck' and 'shit' a lot, which drew gasps of horror. Sometimes Kingsley would become 'aggressively rude, which was mortifying – I didn't know what to do'.[25] And while being argumentative was tolerated in a man, it was not expected from Jane. She felt bored and fractious because while Kingsley was lionized, she often found herself left to one side with the women. 'Jane was brilliant and urbane; many of the women were neither,' commented Porter.[26]

The most enjoyable and relaxing evenings were those the Amises spent alone with the Porters and Frasers. Several times Richard and Birgitte arrived when Jane and Kingsley were reading the day's work to each other, a habit they had formed in Sitges and maintained ever since. Then, as Dick Porter recalled, they seemed 'enormously fond of each other, wonderfully compatible'.[27] Yet things were not as rosy as they seemed. For Jane, the semester at Vanderbilt had been a series of missed opportunities: she had not been able to teach, she had not written enough, and she had not taken the opportunity to hear Kingsley lecture: which gives one some idea of how much she resented her driving duties.

That winter was bitterly cold, with heavy snow. Jane hated the house in Nashville more and more. The heating didn't work, and their sex life had broken down – largely because the bed was so narrow and uncomfortable that Jane had taken to sleeping on a divan in the same room.[28] They felt depressed and homesick. 'We lived on letters from Monkey and Mart,' wrote Jane.[29] There was no mention of letters from her daughter, or news of her grandchildren: Monkey and Mart were her immediate family now.

Soon after Christmas, they heard that Martin had won an exhibition to Exeter College, Oxford – and Martin was well aware of who had helped him most. 'VERY *seriously* though, thank you, O Jane, for quite literally getting me into Oxford,' he wrote. 'Had you not favoured my education with your interest and sagacity, I would now be a 6-O-levelled wretch with little to commend me. I have a huge debt to you which I shall work off by being an ever-dutiful stepson.'[30]

The other good bit of news was that Hilly had remarried. Her new husband was David Roy Shackleton Bailey, Fellow in Classics, an expert in Tibetan, and Bursar of Gonville and Caius College, Cambridge. He was very shy and had a reputation for stinginess, but he was also as unlike Kingsley as it was possible to be. Perhaps that was the secret of his attraction to Hilly. They married in Wivenhoe that November.

When the semester at Vanderbilt came to an end in mid-January, Jane and Kingsley went to Mexico for a two-week holiday with Mike and Mary Keeley. Jane and Kingsley both felt in need of rest and warmth; and if they found some quiet and congenial retreat, they planned to stay on in Mexico and finish their respective novels. Jane was working on *Something in Disguise*, and Kingsley on *I Want it Now*.

They met the Keeleys in Mexico City, where Mike hired a car and they drove north, their destination being the seventeenth-century town of San Miguel de Allende, some 270 miles north-west of the capital. It was a very different sort of travelling. In Greece, the Keeleys spoke the language and they were largely in one place, surrounded by bars and restaurants. In Mexico, things were harder to control. Every morning at eleven thirty, Kingsley insisted they stop the car for a drink. He would get out the straw basket that contained his travelling cocktail cabinet and mix a demon cocktail, and Jane would usually join him. Mike, and especially Mary, did not really want a cocktail at that time in the morning; but since Kingsley did, that is what happened. They would drive on and by one o'clock, Jane wanted lunch, and expected it to materialize soon. If they were on an empty road with no restaurant likely to appear for miles, 'She would get very touchy, very difficult,' said Mike.[31] When they reached San Miguel, everyone's spirits rose. It was a beautiful town of cobbled streets and colonial architecture, and over the years it had attracted a small colony of artists and writers from America. The Keeleys took Jane and Kingsley to meet several of their friends. A few days later, on 4 February 1968, they had to leave, because Mike needed to return to Princeton.

Jane and Kingsley installed themselves in the Posada de las Monjas, a little hotel run by a Spanish grandee whose English was peppered with slang from the 1920s. The pleasurable working routine they had developed in Sitges was revived. They stayed six weeks, by the end of which Kingsley had finished his novel. Jane had not yet finished hers, but she was happier and more relaxed than she had been for a long time.

They were back in England by 20 March, to be welcomed home by Monkey and Sargy. After a large celebratory dinner, Sargy said that now they were back perhaps he ought to be leaving. Instantly Jane said, 'Don't go!', and since Kingsley and Monkey were equally keen for him to stay, he did – until he married eight years later.

For some time, Jane had been worried about the short lease on the house in Maida Vale. After four years, it had only another nine to run. Jane tried to extend it, but the Eyre Estate refused. Kingsley suggested that perhaps they should move to the country: he worked better when he was away from his London haunts. They looked at various houses, none of which appealed until Jane saw an advertisement in *Country Life* for a house called Gladsmuir in Monken Hadley, near Barnet in Hertfordshire. Monken Hadley had been the site of the Battle of Barnet, a crucial moment in the Wars of the Roses which brought victory to the Yorkists in 1471. Fifteen miles north of central London, this was where suburbia gave way to country living, but it was still linked to the Underground network. Gladsmuir was a short car journey from High Barnet in the west and Cockfosters in the east, final stops on the Northern and Piccadilly lines.

It was a late Georgian house of rich red brick, with white-painted sash windows. To the north side lay Hadley Common, while the south side looked on to the garden. Jane first saw the place in May. She saw terraced lawns going down in generous steps, set about with some of the most magnificent cedars she had ever seen. There was also a little wood of silver birches, a line of lime trees, and an abandoned rose garden.

This was the view from the sitting room, dramatically framed by three floor-to-ceiling windows in a curved bay. The kitchen-dining room, once the old coach house, was huge with a high roof and looked out on to a sunny courtyard the other side of which was a self-contained cottage. Across the hall, a graceful staircase swept up to a long corridor off which were eight bedrooms, and a more modest staircase at the end of the corridor led up to three attic rooms, each with its own fireplace. There were also a double garage, stables, a barn, a tool shed, a potting shed, two ranges of cold frames, and a conservatory equipped with five grape vines and a 'Gardener's W.C.'[32]

'Everybody was mad about it, including me, but I realised we couldn't afford more than token help, and it would take a great deal of work to run.' It would also require a great deal of money. Jane sold the rest of the lease on the Maida Vale house for £10,000, and she arranged a mortgage to buy the house in Monken Hadley.

Gladsmuir was to be sold at auction at the Red Lion Hotel in Barnet on 23 May. Jane (who naturally handled everything to do with the sale on her own) put in a bid of £48,000 and was overjoyed to hear that she was the highest bidder. The house was theirs: but when she rang the accountant, it turned out that he was on holiday and the mortgage had fallen through. It later emerged he was bankrupt. It was at that point that Tom Maschler suggested they go to Anton Felton, an accountant who specialized in literary clients. Anton Felton borrowed and called in money from wherever he could, and found them another mortgage. Kingsley even auctioned his early manuscripts at Sotheby's – *Lucky Jim* and several others fell under the hammer, but only raised £2,500.[33] The mortgage was not their only financial commitment: they later discovered that they had fallen into arrears with their tax bills as well.

About a month later, Hilly and Shackleton Bailey (inevitably known as Shack) set off for America, where he had secured an appointment as professor of Latin at the University of Michigan. Before they left, they had a meeting with Kingsley and Jane about Sally, with Mavis Nicholson in the role of umpire should one be needed. Jane had found Sally a boarding school, Moira House in Eastbourne, where she had settled in well; but since she wanted to accompany her mother to the US, Hilly proposed taking her out and finding her a school when they were settled in Michigan. Kingsley had no objection, but Jane thought it a bad idea. Sally's education had been considerably disrupted already. Would it not be more sensible to leave her at Moira House? Hilly disagreed; at which point Jane said, 'Take her away if you wish, but don't send her back to me in two years' time because I won't be able to cope.'[34]

Behind this blunt and hurtful remark was Jane's opinion that Sally was already very difficult and emotionally unstable, and that Hilly was not a good influence on her daughter. Jane blamed herself for not making any attempt to form any kind of relationship with Hilly. She felt that it should have been possible to rise above their mutual fear and hostility, if only for the sake of the children; but there had been too much resentment on either side for that to happen.

In mid-August, Martin helped Monkey and Sargy rewire the new house. Kingsley was very worried by the build-up of Warsaw Pact troops on the border of Czechoslovakia, where he had made many contacts when he had been there with Jane in 1966. The stream of Czechs who had come to visit him in England had been a family joke. 'There were bouncing Czechs,' wrote Martin, 'certified Czechs, and at least one honoured Czech, the novelist Josef Skvorecky. And then on the morning of 21 August my father appeared in the doorway to the courtyard, where the rewiring detail was taking a break, and called out in a defeated and wretched voice: "Russian tanks in Prague." '[35] Martin turned nineteen a few days later, and in September he went up to Oxford.

When they moved into Gladsmuir in November, one of the first things Jane did was to change the name which they all disliked. She had found an old map of the property, on which one of the sloping paddocks beyond the garden was marked as 'Mr Lemmon's Field'. Gladsmuir was relegated to history, and for as long as the Amises lived there the house would be called Lemmons. Kingsley installed himself with great satisfaction in his panelled study with its parquet floor.

Even before they had bought the house, Jane convened a meeting with Monkey, Sargy and Kingsley to warn them of the work a property that size would entail. She could not do it alone, she said. She would have to rely on their help, both inside and out. They all nodded seriously and promised to support her, and in the beginning, things did get done; but as time went on they lost interest. Sargy began teaching at Camberwell, Monkey had his hi-fi business; and at the weekends, which were the busiest time for Jane, hardly anybody lent a hand.

Gradually Jane put together a skeleton staff. After a series of useless cleaners Monkey put an advertisement in the local paper with the proviso, *Only Professionals Need Apply*. Mrs Lily Uniacke presented herself, and as Jane was out she was interviewed by Monkey. He had never interviewed anyone before and came straight to the point. 'Mrs Uniacke,' he said, 'I hope you're not an old slag, because we've had enough of them.'³⁶ Mrs Uniacke thought this very funny, took the job, and stayed with Jane until she retired almost twenty years later. Mr Mayhew came three hours a week to help in the garden, and that – with someone to do the ironing – was it.

Jane did all the shopping, cooking and washing up, most of the gardening, and all the administration: Kingsley expected her to deal with everything from the income tax to insuring the car, as well as attend meetings with accountants and literary agents. Since he could not drive, she was the one who drove Kingsley and their guests to and from the station. Anyone coming to dinner from London was invited to stay the night, so she and Mrs Uniacke prepared the rooms. The sheer size of the house and its many occupants made the simplest chores an effort: Jane once told Fay Maschler that it took her an hour to empty all the wastepaper baskets.

Martin and Philip came at weekends, bringing friends and girl-friends. Kingsley too liked entertaining, and at lunch on the weekends there were often a dozen or more sitting round the table.

To onlookers Jane seemed not only enviably competent, but generously welcoming too. One meal followed another with seamless regularity. The larders and cellars were well stocked, the garden well tended, there were fresh flowers in the rooms, logs by the fire, clean towels in the bathrooms. It all came at a cost: Jane felt perpetually tired and run down.

Money had been too tight to go on holiday to Greece with the Keeleys in 1968; but by 1969 their finances were a bit more stable, and the following year Jane felt she needed a dog. She had set her heart on a Cavalier King Charles spaniel, and found a breeder in north London who had a litter of red ones, known as rubies. Jane chose one, a bitch, 'and we drove home with her sitting, tiny and dignified, on Kingsley's knee'.³⁷ Jane called her Rosie Plush.

That summer she and Kingsley went on holiday with the Keeleys, who had installed themselves in a hotel on the island of Rhodes with another couple, the writer Paul Fussell and his wife Betty. Paul Fussell was still some years away from writing his most celebrated book, *The Great War and Modern Memory* (1975). He was then teaching at Rutgers University, where he was a scholar of eighteenth-century English literature. Kingsley was as wildly funny and amiable as in previous years, but he saw off a friend of the Keeleys who had tried to join their group, and he nearly had a row with Fussell about Teddy Kennedy and what happened at Chappaquiddick. Mary Keeley noticed that he was drinking even more than usual. He and Jane seemed to be getting on well, but at one point he confided to Mike Keeley that 'not a day goes by that I don't think about Hilly'.[38]

It was on Rhodes that Jane wrote the first chapter of her next novel, *Odd Girl Out*; and that November, *Something in Disguise* was published. This novel is one of the funniest of all her books, and most of the plot is driven by two over-controlling men.

One is Colonel Herbert Browne-Lacey: a pompous, self-centred stuffed-shirt with a veneer of old-fashioned gallantry. His third wife is May: a kind soul, and thanks to a windfall, rich. The colonel had persuaded her to buy Monk's Close, a monstrous Tudor-bethan house in Surrey. She finds it hideous, cold, oppressive and inconvenient, and on the colonel's insistence it is run with the minimum of heating and staff. May tries to remind herself that he's a good man, whatever his faults; but her judgement and confidence have been shaken by a charismatic teacher called Dr Sedum, a wonderfully comic figure based on Dr Francis Roles of the Ouspensky Society.

The novel opens with the wedding of the colonel's only daughter, Alice. Her mother died when she was young, and her father treats her – as he treats May – as an unpaid servant. Alice is too downtrodden and unattractive to think she will get two offers of marriage in a lifetime so she accepts the first, from a property developer called Leslie. He installs her in an ugly bungalow on the edge of the estate he is building. Jane makes the reader's heart ache for Alice: if she ever had any desires or responses they have been buried so deep that she has lost touch with them, and she can feel nothing for the baby she's carrying. She misses May, who was kind to her; and Claude, the enormous greedy cat who is the only other inhabitant of Monk's Close.

The other strand of the plot concerns Elizabeth and Oliver, May's grown-up children from her previous marriage, who live in Chelsea. Elizabeth does dinner parties for people. Her earnings support herself and her brother, who has done nothing but go to Oxford and be brilliant. Oliver abhors work and hopes to marry a rich woman. Yet it is Elizabeth who hits gold first, when she cooks dinner for John Cole and his alcoholic ex-wife. Too much vodka with the caviar causes the ex to pass out, with her face in her plate; and after John has taken her home, he has little trouble in getting Elizabeth into bed. It's love at first lay for both of them, and soon she is ensconced in his villa in the south of France. Yet Elizabeth is worried by the efforts he goes to keep his ex-wife and their daughter Jennifer, who is twenty (the same age as Elizabeth) apart. Her alcoholic mother is not a good influence, he says, but surely Jennifer should be treated as an adult?

The book never stops being an entertaining comedy of manners; but towards the end, the plot becomes considerably darker. John Cole dies, as he goes to collect his daughter off a flight she was never on; while the death of Claude the cat reveals the colonel to be a psychopath who preys on women, and slowly poisons them for their money.

The critics, whether they enjoyed the book or not, tended to pigeonhole Jane's work by gender and *Something in Disguise* was no exception. Julian Symons, writing in the *Sunday Times*, was underwhelmed. The characters the author dislikes, like the colonel and Alice's husband Leslie, are caricatures. The ones for whom she has sympathy are little better, and the book operates 'on the plane of women's magazine fiction throughout'.[39] William Trevor, who reviewed it for the *Guardian*, was much more impressed. '*Something in Disguise* has all Elizabeth Jane Howard's particularly feminine perception and is distinguished by neat prose yet what lingers in the mind is its delicious funniness: this is a comic novel that more than once recalled for me my first encounters with Waugh and Nancy Mitford.'[40] She also had a very nice letter from Olivia Manning, whom she had met with Ivy Compton-Burnett.

'I felt I must write and congratulate you on *Something in Disguise*. The characters are beautifully done – embossed – they rise from the page. I brought it here to the clinic where I'm to have a horrid eye operation . . . and it has been a great comfort to me, except for poor

Claude's terrible fate. I could not bear it. Claude is one of the great cats in fiction.'[41]

None of the critics, however, seems to have noticed how well Jane portrayed the characteristics of a psychopath in Colonel Browne-Lacey. With uncanny accuracy, Jane had endowed him with traits common to almost all psychopaths: he has no friends, and no empathy for anyone beyond himself. Yet when a real psychopath appeared in her life twenty-six years later, she failed to recognize the tell-tale signs.

16

Lemmons

JANE HAD BEEN right about Sally. She turned up with no warning and wearing no coat in January 1970, having taken a plane from Chicago. Hilly's marriage to Shackleton Bailey was not going well, and she could no longer handle her daughter. Neither could Jane, as things turned out.

Sally's early traumas must be taken into account. When she was almost three she had fallen off a garden table and fractured her skull, an accident that had led to vomiting and convulsions and a spell in hospital. She had recovered, but not long after that she had spent hours alone with her grandmother's dead body. Now sixteen, she smoked marijuana, took LSD, shoplifted occasionally and was wildly promiscuous. Martin felt that she was a victim of the sexual revolution, which gave her complete freedom but no framework. 'She really had the mental age of twelve or thirteen and I think she was terrified. I think what she was doing was seeking protection from men but it went the other way, she was often beaten up, abused.'[1]

She enjoyed making trouble for Jane, and keeping her on her toes. Empty vodka bottles appeared in her room. At one point Jane was knitting a scarf for her friend, the novelist Elizabeth Taylor. The scarf vanished, and was later found scrunched up at the bottom of Sally's cupboard. School was no longer an option, Sally refused to go – yet she had been happy at boarding school and had enjoyed communal life. It was thought that she might do well in the Wrens, but that idea lasted less than a week. There were various briefly held jobs in London shops but sooner or later, Sally came in stoned or walked out, and Jane was the one who had to pick up the pieces.

Although he never lifted a finger around the house, Kingsley was working very hard. During the eight years they lived at Lemmons he wrote six full-length novels, poetry, short stories, TV plays and five works of non-fiction – as well as countless articles and reviews. There were also lectures, interviews and television appearances. Jane described him as one of the most disciplined workers she had ever come across. No matter how bad his hangover, he would stump down to breakfast in his dressing gown to cook himself a fry-up with well-charred sausages. As he ate, he would read the papers: it was important for a writer to keep up with the news, he said, and it also provided conversational fodder. Then, after washing and dressing, he had to steel himself to face the piece of paper he had left in the typewriter the day before. It needed courage: writing was hard labour that did not come easily, and was beset with moments of black despondency. He would work until eleven thirty, and then brewed up a jug of Bloody Marys so strong that they were known as Fucking Marys. After a lunch of cheese and pickles washed down with beer, he had a nap before settling down to work again. The afternoon dragged, even when punctuated by a cup of tea. He tried to leave the day's work at a point where he could easily pick it up again, but at five thirty precisely the working day was done, and he could begin drinking in earnest. Now, whether he entertained his friends or argued with his sons or read or watched television, his glass was never far away; and by the time he went up to bed, he had drunk the best part of a bottle of whisky.

Jane had a study too, in one of the bedrooms; but the administration and logistics of running such a large household left very little time for writing. She also began to feel sidelined. In 1964 Kingsley had left his former publishers, Gollancz, for Jane's publisher Tom Maschler at Jonathan Cape, who had been a good friend to both of them. Kingsley's agents were then Curtis Brown; but he lost patience with them and, in 1965, was taken on by Jane's agent A.D. Peters. Peters had a young South African protégée, Pat Kavanagh, who handled both Jane and Kingsley's journalism. On one level, it was very cosy to have the same agent and publisher, but since Kingsley produced a greater volume of work and sold many more books, they spent more time and energy on him. Although this may have been perfectly logical, Jane could not help resenting it.

A constant stream of people still flowed through the house. Tom Maschler came with a succession of girlfriends until he married Fay Coventry in 1970. Pat Kavanagh was a very frequent visitor too with her then partner, an Australian psychiatrist called Jim Durham. Other guests included Robert and Caroleen Conquest, Tibor Szamuely, Iris Murdoch and John Bayley, Anthony and Violet Powell, Ann and Anthony Thwaite, Paul and Marigold Johnson, the journalists Colin Welch and Bernard Levin, the Keeleys and Fussells when they visited England, John ('Oh, I *am* enjoying myself!') Betjeman, Cecil and Jill Day-Lewis with their children Tamasin and Daniel, and Huw and Jay Wheldon. The novelist Elizabeth Bowen came for one evening and stayed the night. Jane brought her breakfast in bed the next morning, and Miss Bowen immediately spotted that 'You've forgotten the marmalade spoon.' Jane rushed down to get it. She also entertained one of the novelists she most admired, Elizabeth Taylor, although by the time she visited Lemmons she was already ill with the cancer that killed her.

Jane never knew how many people she was going to have to feed, since Philip, Martin and Sally's roving bands of long-haired, short-skirted friends never bothered to tell her. Christopher Hitchens was already one of Martin's closest friends; while Martin's girlfriends included Tina Brown, Gully Wells and Tamasin Day-Lewis.

Gully Wells remembered two glorious weeks with Martin at Lemmons, 'holed up in unwedded bliss' in his room; and in her book *The House in France*, she describes that sense of generous abundance that people always felt at Lemmons. The walk-in larder looked like a corner of Harrods Food Hall with whole hams and Stiltons, and rows of chutneys, gherkins and pickled onions – which had to be present at every meal, because Kingsley ate them with almost everything. 'Jane was a truly gifted cook,' Gully wrote, 'but whatever she made – ethereal *blanquette de veau*, sublime risotto of wild mushrooms . . . Kingsley's plate was always piled high with his palate-annihilating pickles.'

One thing the house never ran short of was ice cream, which Monkey bought in catering-sized tubs from Marine Ices in Camden Town. With the ices came a rainbow assortment of sugar sprinkles, Flake bars and chopped nuts. The Amises' hospitality 'went way beyond the delicious profligacy of her cooking and his skills with the corkscrew; it was about sitting down at a huge round table and know-ing that whatever else happened, the next few hours were absolutely guaranteed to be *entertaining*.'[2] Kingsley kept the party gasping at the outrageousness of his opinions on everything from Vietnam to education to the Labour government. Heated exchanges developed frequently, but the jokes and impressions and party-pieces were never far below the surface and could erupt at any time. Martin recalled that Kingsley was 'the hub of all humour and high-spirits, like an engine of comedy'.[3]

Jane remembered how Kingsley and the journalist Colin Welch 'improvised a Somerset Maugham radio play about tea planters in Malaysia. Colin's quiet, lugubrious voice was the isolated tea planter's wife, while Kingsley supplied all the explosive jungle noises that punctuated her ruminations.' On another occasion, 'Kingsley suddenly enacted a whole B-feature wartime movie. It included a destroyer coming up the Thames directed by its Nazi captain, an air raid with anti-aircraft guns and bombs dropping, a refugee waiter letting off carrier pigeons from his window sill, and triumphant German newscasts of the event. It went on for about twenty minutes and was a masterpiece – we cried with laughter.'[4]

In the summer of 1970, Sally rejoined her mother and Shackleton Bailey, who were taking a tour round Europe. The marriage was at breaking point, and in a large flat in Ronda, in the Spanish province of Malaga, they played out the threadbare arguments and silences of the last act. When it was time for her husband to return to Michigan for the new semester, Hilly refused to accompany him. She and Sally stayed on in Ronda, perched over its dramatic gorge.

One day Sally came across a language school in the nearby Palacio de Mondragon. It was run by a charming Scottish aristocrat called Alistair Boyd, and very soon he and Hilly were in love. For several months she helped him run the school, which they tried to relaunch in Seville without success. They moved back to Ronda in 1971, and took in paying guests and ran art classes. Later they opened a bar together. Hilly was better at this enterprise, because she had established and run a fish-and-chip shop in Ann Arbor called Lucky Jim's. Sally stayed on too, for several months, until she got into trouble for seducing the local gypsy boys. She decided there was more fun to be had in London, and returned to Lemmons.

Another responsibility for Jane to shoulder was her mother Kit, now in her late sixties. She had been living in a little house in the grounds of Robin's home in Tunbridge Wells; but a lifetime of chain-smoking cheap cigarillos had taken such a toll on her health that she could no longer cope on her own, and Jane felt she ought to come and live with them. When she put this to Kingsley, he was not only very understanding: he even wrote Kit a letter to say how glad he was she was coming, which pleased her very much. At first, she was lodged in one of the upstairs bedrooms; but at some point during the early months of 1971 she broke her hip, and the stairs became impossible. One of the downstairs rooms was turned into a bedsitting room for her with an adjoining bathroom, and Tessa Craig – the daughter of Jane's old friend Dosia, who had become a nurse – was hired to look after her. Kit was grateful; but her nature was too austere to condone the noise, the laughter, the extravagance and lack of thrift, the drunken dinners and late breakfasts, and the swaggering non-chalance of Philip and Martin and Sally, who terrified her. Martin thought her 'a snob and a grouch', and felt that she had been 'a harsh mother, particularly to my sweet-natured step-uncle, Colin'.[5]

Jane's excessive burdens might have been easier to bear if she had enjoyed, if not Kingsley's practical support, then at least his affection and appreciation, but he was unmistakably pulling away from her. It had been years now since he had surprised her with a present or taken her to lunch at the Étoile in Charlotte Street, and she seemed to exist only to perform the tasks he was unable, or simply unwilling to do himself.

He had been working on a novel called *Girl, 20* which was published in 1971. This is a satire on the permissive radical-chic of the 1960s, reflected in the character of Sir Roy Vandervane, a successful composer well advanced in middle age, who wants to be trendy and is besotted by a sneering young beauty called Sylvia. To help save Roy from himself, his wife Kitty summons Douglas Yandell, a friend who is also the narrator. He visits Kitty at home, which is very obviously Lemmons. Kitty bears more than a passing resemblance to Jane, and has a ruby spaniel called the Furry Barrel.

Kitty talks in a tone of exaggerated feeling. When Yandell asks the age of her little son Ashley, 'She gazed at me with rather too rich a mixture of emotions, so that I hardly knew whether she regarded her only child with pride-plus-grateful-humility or with apologetic horror.'[6] When remembering her courtship with Roy, 'There were tears in her eyes, but then there so often were.' Kitty is far more sympathetic than the pouting Sylvia, but she doesn't see how her manner rubs people up the wrong way: 'She gave me a brave, jerky smile that irritated me and made me feel sorry for her. "Oh, you know," she said with an affectation of affected lightness. "One carries on. One has no alternative." '[7]

At this stage, Jane and Kingsley were still reading each other's work, and a draft of *Girl, 20* exists with her annotations. Jane was aware of her connection to Kitty, and it hurt; they both used autobiographical elements in their fiction. The point here was not the elements themselves, but how they worked in the novel. There is one passage in the book, as the Furry Barrel – with a badly injured leg – comes up to greet Yandell, when Kingsley's voice breaks through the text with chilling clarity: 'I stooped down and stroked the dog's silky head, feeling as if something dismal had happened right in the middle of my own life and concerns, something major, something irretrievable, as if I had taken a fatally wrong decision years before and only now seen how much I had lost by it.'[8]

This passage, and those concerning Kitty, are a sort of message in a bottle to Jane: not an apology, nor an accusation; more of a hopeless recognition that, all unwitting, he has made a terrible mistake.

Both Kingsley and Jane were delighted when Martin received a congratulatory first from Oxford in 1971. Soon after that he found a job as deputy literary editor on the *Times Literary Supplement*, and from then on he spent only weekends at Lemmons.

Unlike his character Roy Vandervane, Kingsley was no longer the philanderer he had been. Over the course of his second marriage he had one or two afternoon flings that barely counted as affairs, and he and Jane made love less and less. Jane, for whom a healthy sex life was the wellspring of a good relationship, found his lack of interest both humiliating and inexplicable: Martin recalled that 'even in 1975 [Jane] was telling me more about my father's growing remissness in that area than I really wanted to know'.[9]

Kingsley made it very clear that he had more fun drinking and talking with his male chums than being with his wife, who was always fretting about something – often Sally and Philip, about whom he felt more anguish than he cared to admit. There were countless rows about what she felt he ought to be doing for them, how he might curb the hostility and mischief-making they directed against her, and how wretchedly helpless and miserable they made her feel. Jane does not talk about them much in *Slipstream*; but elsewhere she wrote that her anguish about them 'dominated my life for the last twelve years'.[10]

She confided her troubles to Anton Felton, who lived close by, and her old friend the dress designer Victor Stiebel, now in a wheelchair with multiple sclerosis. His gaiety and curiosity about the world seemed untouched by the relentless progress of his illness, to which he never referred; and Jane relied more than she knew on his kindness and encouragement.

One person she did not confide in so much at this time was Monkey, who had demons of his own to grapple with. He had accepted his sexuality but was never really at ease with it, and never found a long-term partner. He suffered from severe depression, and although he worked obsessively on his individually crafted stereo systems, the business never took off in the way he had hoped. What did annoy her was how little practical help he offered, despite promising much when they moved to Lemmons. But like the rest of the household, Monkey found Jane's parade of her endless domestic chores hard to watch without irritation. On Sundays, while she was slaving over yet another lunch of several dishes, he was in the pub with Kingsley, Sargy, Martin, Philip and whoever else had come to join them.

The trouble was that Jane could not do things by halves. Instead of setting out a cold ham, a pile of baked potatoes and some cheese and salad (Kingsley would have been perfectly happy, as long as he had his pickles), it had to be the works: a joint of beef with proper gravy, roast potatoes and Yorkshire pudding, or a painstakingly prepared *boeuf en daube*, always with two veg and a home-made pudding and cream to follow.

One of the few to point out the extent to which she was making a martyr of herself was Victor Stiebel. 'You always want to do things in the most difficult way, don't you?' he said gently. 'It was the first time I looked at myself from the outside,' she wrote, 'and saw how much I colluded in, even encouraged these situations.'[11] Her doctor discovered her one Sunday morning weeping silently into the sink as she peeled a mountain of potatoes alone, while everyone else was in the pub. 'He prescribed Tryptosil and Valium in what today would be regarded as over-generous quantities,' she wrote.[12] The drugs sapped both her energy and the will to write consistently, but she had managed to complete one more novel before the anaesthetizing fog descended. It was called *Odd Girl Out*, and was published in March 1972.

Jane's sixth novel is about a sybaritic couple called Edmund and Anne Cornhill. Edmund is a prosperous estate agent, while Anne stays in Berkshire arranging flowers and cooking exquisite meals. They both relish their worldly perfection, and every detail of their comfortable and cultivated lives is lovingly described. Into this ménage drops a rich, emotionally neglected girl called Arabella who is a distant connection of Edmund's. First she seduces Edmund, who falls in love with her. He tries to persuade her to join him in Greece, where he has been sent to explore the holiday-let market; but Arabella prefers to stay with his wife Anne, whom she seduces too. Arabella doesn't love anyone, and she never lies: so the scene where Edmund and Anne are dismayed to learn that she has seduced them both is very funny. But their long discussions about love and truth are little more than that, since one can't take any of them that seriously. Jane tries to give the novel more depth by introducing a pitiful young actress called Janet, whose useless husband has abandoned her and her two children. Janet and her fate are very moving, but they feel as if they had fallen out of a novel by Mrs Gaskell.

The reviews were not very enthusiastic. The *Sunday Times* described *Odd Girl Out* as 'a rather synthetic book that wrings both comedy and sentiment from the woes of the upper class';[13] while the anonymous reviewer in the *Times Literary Supplement* felt it would have been reassuring if 'some of the comic touches, laboriously directed at elderly buffoons, dentists and daily helps, [had been] allowed to subvert the sentimental respect with which the Cornhill culture is offered.'[14]

It was probably this book that Jane took as a present, when she and Kingsley went to lunch with the bibliophile Anthony Hobson and his wife Tanya. The Hobsons lived at Whitsbury in Hampshire, and when they arrived Anthony had a pile of Kingsley's novels on a table waiting to be signed. Jane's novel was barely mentioned. Jane had often lived through similar scenes, and they did nothing to help her confidence.

At about the same time as her novel was published, she was commissioned to write a profile of Cecil Day-Lewis for *Queen* magazine. The interview took place at Cecil's house at Croom's Hill, Greenwich; and although Jane knew he was ill, she was not prepared for the change. 'I was appalled by his appearance,' she told his biographer Peter Stanford. 'He'd lost a lot of weight and was almost skeletal. His face was grey. He insisted on going through with the interview . . . Afterwards Jill didn't want to discuss how he was except in general terms. She didn't use the term cancer.'[15] He had been diagnosed with pancreatic cancer early the previous year, and Jill had been advised by the doctor not to let Cecil know that he only had about a year to live. 'There has to be hope,' he said; and perhaps underneath those words was the tacit admission that if nobody mentioned it, then death was easier to handle all round. This was the conventional wisdom of the time, and keeping the taboo in place suited Cecil. He was a man of immense courtesy, convinced that no one wanted to talk about his illness, and to bear it alone was a kind of damage limitation.

During this visit, Jill told Jane that she had a small part in a television mini-series called *The Strauss Family*, to be filmed at Elstree Studios in Hertfordshire. She was already exhausted by caring for Cecil and had not slept well for weeks, but since they had very little money she could not afford to turn down work. Since the journey to Elstree would take almost two hours each way, Cecil would have to go into hospital as there was nobody to look after him.

Jane immediately suggested they come to Lemmons while Jill was filming. She would move Kit back into her old room, for her hip was mended and she could once again manage the stairs. Jill would be fifteen minutes' drive from the studio, and Cecil would have a trained nurse (Tessa Craig) on hand if he needed her — as well as lots of friends to keep him company. Was it not the perfect solution?

Up to a point. The memory of Jane and Cecil's affair still rankled, and Jill did not want to be beholden to one of her husband's old mistresses. But she also felt that this was Jane's way of making amends. Her offer was a lifeline, as Cecil agreed. Kit moved upstairs with a good grace, and the Day-Lewises arrived on 6 April with Tamasin and Daniel. Daniel went back to Bedales, and was only at Lemmons occasionally during that time; but Tamasin, who was Jane's god-daughter, had applied to read English at Cambridge and was there more often. She was fond of Jane, whom she described as 'one of the first grown-ups to become a friend without being judgemental or parent-like'. Like Jane, Tamasin loved food and cooking. 'I became Jane's jobber and chopper, and I think she was quite pleased to finally have a female ally in a house that . . . relied entirely, domestically speaking, on her.'[16]

At first it was agreed that they would only stay a week. Jane looked out some books, Monkey installed a record player. 'Nobody was better at getting the most pleasure from the simplest things as Cecil,' Jane wrote in an article for the *Sunday Times* after his death; 'a toasted bun, a gramophone record, a piece of cherry cake, a new thriller'.[17] When the week was up, Jane asked Cecil if he would like to stay on until he was better; and he said he would like to stay for as long as possible, because 'I am very anxious to give Jill a proper rest.' In the second week he asked Jill to buy him a notebook; and in it he wrote his last poem, 'At Lemmons'.

Kingsley, who had barely known Cecil before his final illness, grew very fond of him. He would drop in on him with his record catalogue in the evenings so Cecil could select some music for the following day. 'Cecil would implore him not to do or tell more than one funny thing as Kingsley made him laugh so much he thought he'd have a heart attack.'[18] The kindness that Jane and Kingsley showed towards Cecil and Jill had a healing effect on their own relationship too: 'Jill remembered asking the new doctor: "How can I ever thank these people for what they are doing for us?" He replied, "it might be doing something for them" ',[19] and he was right.

Three birthdays were celebrated that April in Cecil's room: Kingsley's fiftieth on the 16th, Cecil's sixty-eighth on the 27th, and Daniel's fifteenth on the 29th. By now, Cecil must have known he was near the end. Kingsley felt that 'he came to draw his own conclusions from his physical decline and increasingly severe . . . bouts of pain, but, out of kindness and abnegation of self, chose not to discuss the matter'.[20] Tamasin, on the other hand, was tormented by the conspiracy of silence around her father, which made his dying fraught with anxiety and isolation. 'If there was to be no chink in my father's private armour against the pain,' she wrote, 'how could we show him that we could see what he wasn't prepared to show us?'[21]

On Friday, 19 May, at the start of the Whitsun weekend, Cecil's strength began to fail. Tessa the nurse, who had that weekend off, came back on Saturday; and Jane called Ursula Vaughan Williams, the widow of the composer, who was a great friend of Jill's. Cecil died in the early hours of Monday 22nd. A few hours later, in that numbness before grief descends, Tamasin and Jane suddenly felt very hungry. They drove into Barnet to the baker's, and 'bought a bag of dough-nuts which we somehow had to eat there and then and not bring into the house. We ate the whole bagful . . . all six of them gone in minutes as we sat staring sightlessly out of the front windscreen through the rain.'[22] Cecil was buried a few days later at Stinsford in Dorset, near the grave of Thomas Hardy.

Stephen and Natasha Spender had understood that Jill would be physically and emotionally drained after Cecil's death, and they had invited her and Jane to their house in France in mid-June. 'It was the first time I'd been away without Kingsley since we were married,'[23] she wrote; although she does not mention that Kingsley was outraged that she was going away, leaving him to be looked after by Monkey and Sargy for two weeks. As early as 14 May, Kingsley had written in his diary: 'I started big row last thing: break-up mentioned.'[24] Over successive days there were further rows and reconciliations, but Jane refused to give in to him.

The *Sunday Times* had commissioned her to write a piece about Cecil's last days in her house; and with Jill's agreement, she did. It was finished while they were in France, and published on 30 July. Most of the letters she received were complimentary – but not the one from Rosamond Lehmann.

> That was a very embarrassing piece you wrote about CDL in last week's *Sunday Times*. Naturally you won't consider me an impartial critic . . . but I am not alone in deploring it. You say some true things about him; but on the whole it is a chocolate box portrait. Apart from that, I simply cannot understand why you should wish to share the intimate account of his last hours with readers of the *Sunday Times* . . . I must be grateful to you, I suppose, for referring to me merely as an emotional involvement – we shared what I thought the deepest possi-ble commitments for 10 years . . . He broke our mutual vows, and laid

waste my life as well as his wife's. I am not able to be proud, as once I was, of being 'the great love of his life'; but I know what I know, and it is reflected in . . . the ruinous mask that fastened onto his once beautiful face . . . I do ask you to ask yourself whether it isn't better to keep silent rather than publish half-truths that can only cause added distress and bitterness to those whom Cecil wounded most.[25]

'Jill wrote and said you had had a very hysterical letter from Rosamond,' wrote Stephen Spender a day or two later. 'I hope you weren't too upset by this because it really has nothing to do with your article which was very good.'[26]

Jane was very glad to hear from him.

I felt awful, because although I have had abusive letters before from people I didn't know (offending them with my disgusting, sexual writing) I have never had a letter like that in my life from someone I *did* know, although not at all well. I think that was the worst thing, apart from anyone thinking that I was *trying* to hurt their feelings in public as it were. But I have had to date sixty letters . . . saying that they were glad I wrote the piece, and the *Sunday Times* has had many more . . . I truly loved Cecil with all my heart, and the thought that one was being vulgar at his expense is awful.[27]

While a few might have seen Jane's tribute to Cecil as 'vulgar', at least it did not leave her or Kingsley open to ridicule – unlike their endorsement of Sanderson Fabrics. Their tireless accountant Anton Felton kept up a constant pressure on Kingsley and Jane's agents, A.D. Peters, to find more money for them; and the agency suggested that funds could be raised by using Kingsley's name in advertisements – as long as the product was exactly right. Kingsley hoped that a reputable whisky or vodka manufacturer might step forward, but Sandersons were the first to make an offer. They would decorate one of the rooms in Lemmons, take a photograph of Kingsley and Jane in it, and display it with the slogan 'Very Kingsley Amis, Very Sanderson'. They were willing to pay a handsome fee, but Jane knew that their taste would be very unlike hers. She insisted that all the fabrics they chose for the photo be stretched on battens, so they could be instantly dismantled as soon as the shoot was over; and looking at the panels of what looks like flock wallpaper and silk-polyester dupion curtains, how right she was.

Jane agreed to join her old friend Geraint Jones as co-director of the first ever Salisbury Arts Festival, which took place in July 1973. Geraint Jones was responsible for coordinating over a dozen concerts, including a recital of her favourite composer, Scarlatti, in the double-cube room at Wilton. She organized lectures by Peter Scott and Angus Wilson, and Sargy Mann's first solo exhibition. Almost all the paintings were views of Lemmons: mostly outdoor ones painted in the garden and the field beyond, but several were done in one of the three bathrooms upstairs. Jane was a tremendous help to Sargy in these early days. Not only did she buy several of his paintings herself, but she encouraged others – John Betjeman and Iris Murdoch, to name but two – to start collecting them as well.

In February 1974 she began writing for *Brides and Setting Up Home*, then under the editorship of Drusilla Beyfus. Copies of the magazine provide a reminder of just how long ago the seventies were. Readers were warned of the dangers of living with a man – the principal one being the risk of losing all social status; while another article in the home section was entitled 'Call it a Continental Quilt – Duvets Explained'. Jane wrote about taking up needlework (she recommended patchwork as the place to start), gave some good advice on letter-writing and present-giving, and outlined the perils of going on holiday with a man who liked things authentic – this last being her account of trying to find a loo in a 'simple' hotel in Spain with Laurie Lee. She also proposes 'A Home Cooked Feast', which assumes that the reader has undertaken to prepare a wedding breakfast for seventy. She wrote four articles a year for *Brides* magazine, for three years: amusing, helpful pieces that read as if they had been written by an enviably competent woman without a care in her well-ordered life.

That spring, soon after the publication of his novel *Ending Up*, Kingsley decided he was ready to go abroad again. He had not set foot outside England since a summer holiday in Portugal in 1971, when he had been struck by the idea that anything he might like to do in Albufeira (i.e., read in a comfortable chair or have a drink) was more enjoyably done at home, with far less trouble and expense. Jane, on the other hand, needed to unwind in the sun every now and again to give herself a break from the responsibilities of Lemmons. So she would go abroad with friends and he would sulk.

The reason Kingsley was prepared to spend three weeks in Rome with Jane is that they would be there with Jim Durham, whom he described as 'the only sane and sensible psychiatrist I have ever met',[28] as well as being a hard drinker, good talker, loud laugher and all the other things Kingsley approved of in a man. In the company of Jim and his new wife Nita, Kingsley did more sightseeing than he had ever done in his life. This irritated Jane, who had never been able to make him look at anything, even in Venice. Her bad mood made her feel left out, and Kingsley made it obvious that he was happy with the Durhams and didn't much care how she felt. 'Jane I like,' said Jim Durham later, 'but she did get on Kingsley's nerves in a thousand little ways . . . He didn't pick quarrels with her . . . He showed her the conventional signs of his affection, but he wouldn't mask his irritation.'[29]

That summer, Jane was asked to be one of the judges on the Booker Prize for Fiction, which was to be chaired that year by Ion Trewin. 'I was astonished to be asked to chair the judges,' wrote Trewin, 'being only thirty-one and in my third year as literary editor of *The Times*. It was Tom Maschler, very much the founding father of the prize, who was responsible for the invitation.' As well as Jane and Ion Trewin, the only other judge that year was A.S. Byatt. 'Having only three judges rather than five was probably an experiment, but the prize was in its formative years,' Trewin added.

In his memoirs, Tom Maschler wrote that Jane bowed out of judging the Booker when she realized that Kingsley's *Ending Up* was one of the contenders.[30] Her fellow judges said that she did no such thing. 'We met to choose the winner in the old offices of the National Book League in Albemarle Street,' wrote Ion Trewin. 'Jane said there was only one winner in her view – *Ending Up*.'[31] According to Antonia Byatt,

> When we came to making the shortlist, Elizabeth Jane argued exclusively for Kingsley Amis. She dismissed my own favourite – Anthony Burgess – because 'he gets drunk and falls down stairs' . . . Anyway we got a shortlist and Amis was on it. By then both Ion and I were behind Nadine Gordimer. Elizabeth Jane would not have her as a winner. She

said, 'She fails Kingsley's readability criterion.' She asked if there was any rule about dividing the prize . . . I think she thought that if she allowed the unreadable Gordimer to have half the prize Kingsley could have the other half. But we did not want that and Ion introduced the idea of the wonderful Stanley Middleton whose work I had not previously known.

Thus the Booker Prize for 1974 was split between Gordimer and Middleton; but the final irony came at the award ceremony itself. 'We stood in some kind of receiving line,' wrote Byatt, 'as the authors came in. Nadine Gordimer swept past me and flung her arms round Elizabeth Jane. "The value of this prize to me," she said, "is that *you* have awarded it." '[32]

Whether it was her own unhappiness or the lukewarm reviews for *Odd Girl Out*, Jane did not feel that she could produce another novel for the time being. She sorely missed A.D. Peters. He had always been a stalwart supporter of her work, but ill-health had forced him to retire in 1972 and he had died soon after. Jane was still represented by the agency, and told them she wanted to do more film scripts. Although Anthony Jones, who handled those commissions, did not seem very interested in promoting her, Jane asked him to get in touch with London Weekend Television. They had a long-running series called *Upstairs Downstairs*. Could she not write an episode for them?

Her idea paid off. Jane was briefed at the London Weekend Television Centre, where Alfred Shaughnessy (who wrote a great many of the *Upstairs Downstairs* episodes) and his colleagues were outlining the next series. This sees the Bellamys and their faithful staff facing the First World War. 'I was given a play that was to take place during the First Battle of the Somme, and was told three or four things that had to happen in it. Their knowledge of all the characters was impressive. When I asked whether Mrs Bridges had ever had a marriage or an affair, they said no at once.'[33]

The episode was called 'The Glorious Dead'. In it the housemaid, Rose, hears of the death in action of her young man, an Australian sergeant. Mrs Bridges tries to convince Rose that the pain will pass, and tells her about the young groom she was in love with: he had joined his master to fight in the Sudan and died of a fever, 'alone among all those savages'. Meanwhile Major James Bellamy comes home on leave to his wife Hazel. He has been awarded the MC, but he is deeply depressed by the pointlessness of the war, and the thousands of lives it has claimed. However, when he goes to see Rose and express his condolences, he finds himself telling her that the man she loved died a hero's death.

Jane was asked to write another episode, although it wasn't used. But the job did lead to her writing one of a collection of six plays on love called *She*, also for London Weekend Television. The play, called *Sight Unseen*, is about an ageing model called Delilah, who meets Sam, a young painter who lives on a barge. Sam is losing his sight; and in this respect he is based on Sargy Mann, who had to undergo an operation for cataracts in 1972 in his mid-thirties.

Because Sam cannot see very well, Delilah pretends that she is a successful young actress, but the reality is very different. Her busty figure was all she had, and because of the way she looked she was either pounced on or humiliated by the men she came across. Now in her forties, even the modelling jobs have dried up. She comes to Sam's barge when she is thrown out of her lodgings, but Sam is in a nursing home following his operation. Delilah, with nowhere else to go, gets a job in the local pub and makes herself useful by cleaning up the barge. When Sam returns, he still can't see very well. Delilah confesses that she is not young, or pretty, or successful – but she infinitely prefers her life at the pub to the life of modelling. He says that it does not matter, because she is kind and good; and that he had already made up his mind to marry her. So two essentially innocent characters find true love and happiness: a comfortable and undemanding story, as her life so rarely was then.

Arthur Koestler: 'You mean you don't know who I am?'

Laurie Lee, who took Jane on holiday to Spain after her affair with Koestler.

Jane with Charlie Chaplin, on the set of *A King in New York* in 1956. He had been hounded out of the US for his supposedly Communist sympathies.

The christening of Tamasin
Day-Lewis, autumn 1954.
Jill Balcon holds Tamasin
with Cecil in the background;
Tamasin's godmother, Jane,
looks on.

Jane and Cecil
having a picnic,
possibly at Dedham
Vale in April 1954.

Jim Douglas-Henry and
Jane at Nicola's wedding to
Stephen Asquith, May 1963.
Jane was already in love with
Kingsley Amis.

Nicola with her father,
Peter Scott.

Edna O'Brien and Jane with John Moore in October 1962, when Jane was director of the Cheltenham Literary Festival.

Jane and Kingsley at their wedding reception, June 1965. In all the photos she is gazing at him, while he flashes his Lucky Jim smile at the camera.

Jane on holiday in Greece.

Jane and Kingsley in Prague as guests of the Polish government, 1966. Thinking that Kingsley was still Communist, their hosts had not realized how far he had swung to the right.

Jane was keen to tell everyone that this was not her idea. The wallpaper and curtains were put up on battens, and removed as soon as the shoot was over.

Very Kingsley Amis, very Sanderson.

Kingsley in his panelled study with an impressive collection of empty bottles, shortly before leaving Lemmons.

Sargy Mann, Monkey and Jane in the kitchen at Lemmons.

Martin Amis, Jane and Kingsley at Gardnor House in the late 1970s, not long before Jane walked out on Kingsley for good.

Jane in her Delancey Street garden with Darcy, her second Cavalier King Charles spaniel.

Monkey, in later life. It was he who had to tell Jane that her lover, Malcolm, was not what he seemed.

Sybille Bedford and Jane at a party to launch *Casting Off*, the fourth novel in the Cazalet Chronicle.

Jane in her garden in Bungay with Eddie, her rescued lurcher.

Jane in her ninetieth year, signing copies of her last book *All Change*, November 2013.

17

'An Agonising Decision'

MANY THINGS CHANGED in 1975. Sargy had fallen in love with one of his students at Camberwell, Frances Carey. She dared not say much on her visits to Lemmons at first, being rather alarmed by Kingsley; but her natural warmth and kindness shone through anyway, and she was a welcome addition to the weekend influx of guests. Meanwhile, Nicola's marriage to Kipper Asquith finally broke down. She moved into a near-derelict house in Condicote where there was room only for her and Dan, so her two daughters – Emily and Lucy-Kate – stayed with their father.

Jane's mother Kit had moved back into the downstairs room at Lemmons after Cecil's death. She had never eaten much, and as the months passed she became more and more frail. She seldom left her room, and her memory became 'wilfully selective'. She would tell Jane she had not seen her for days, when she had been in and out of the room for hours; and Robin was told that Jane never gave her lunch. 'Sometimes I used to feel unbearably sorry for her,' wrote Jane, 'and the next minute exasperated, repelled. Monkey bore his half of the brunt, and although she loved him, it was never enough.'[1]

She died on 5 April, the cause of death being given as emphysema and chronic bronchitis. Jane had been with her for much of the evening, after a visit from Kit's very unsympathetic doctor; but when she came back after dinner with a hot drink, Kit was dead. Jane blamed herself bitterly for not being there to hold her mother's hand, and felt she had failed her. But when she began clearing up Kit's papers, she discovered that while her mother had kept many letters from Robin and Monkey, she had not kept a single one of hers.

Jane makes much of her mother's death in *Slipstream*; but however much guilt and remorse she felt there must have been some element of relief as well. And it was not as distressing as the great shift into darkness that was taking place in her emotional landscape. 'I began to know that Kingsley no longer loved me, and curiously, I think this failure on his part was as painful for him as it was for me . . . Alone, he hadn't much to say to me, and his discomfort led to endless criticism. It was my fault that he no longer wanted to go to bed with me, my fault if we were late arriving somewhere.' On one terrifying evening, when Jane was driving them home after a party, Kingsley, by then very drunk, started shouting. He thought she was driving on the wrong side of the road, and tried to wrench the wheel out of her hands.[2]

That summer, after another trip to Rome with the Durhams, Jane published a volume of her short stories called *Mr Wrong* – the title of a ghost story in which a young girl buys a second-hand car, in which terrible things have happened. It was loosely based on an actual case known as the A6 Murder of 1961; and every aspect of the plot fits perfectly together, from its beginning to its horrible and inevitable end. Among the other stories in this collection are 'Pont du Gard', about a fractious couple on holiday and the husband's attraction to his daughter's school friend; and 'The Whiphand', about a child star getting her revenge on her over-controlling mother. Jane had always written short stories, and there are innumerable unfinished fragments and treatments for them among her papers. She might have written one or two on commission in her early days, but no cuttings from magazines survive to indicate where they were published.

The collection of stories had a better reception than her last novel. The *Guardian* noted that 'Miss Howard has a gift for tilting our sense of reality so gradually that we have slid into the realm of the strange and the mysterious even before we are aware.'[3]

A few weeks after that, the novelist Julian Barnes met her at a party in a London garden. 'She seemed to me formidable: tall, poised, coiffed and gowned, waiting to be diverted out of some grand boredom.' Barnes had just given *Mr Wrong* an enthusiastic review for the *Oxford Mail*, which he thought would be a good conversational opening. 'I mentioned this as unobsequiously as I could; she was neither diverted nor, as far as I could tell, remotely interested.' He followed this up by saying, 'in a book-nerdish way', that he had noticed that the front matter of *Mr Wrong* did not list where her stories had first appeared: why was that? She said she hadn't noticed.

Years later the story appeared in the *Guardian*, as an excerpt from an anthology called *Mortification: Writers' Stories of their Public Shame*.[4] Jane saw it and wrote Barnes a card, putting her side of things. Far from being haughtily dismissive she was utterly terrified by literary parties, and spent a lot of time crying in the ladies' loo. She only attended them because Kingsley didn't drive. It gives one an idea of just how unhappy she was at the time, that she couldn't find any pleasure in an attractive, intelligent young man paying her compliments on her writing.

Misery makes one poor company; and Julian Barnes was not the only person who remarked that at this time in her life she could seem aloof, indifferent and wrapped up in herself. This was partly what people read into her physical presence, her perfectly groomed beauty – but it was nothing more than an empty shell, hiding the shattered remains of her confidence.

Jane often complained that the effort required to maintain such a big house and garden, plus feeding an endless succession of guests, left her with almost no time to write; but on another level she had put down roots at Lemmons, and was proud of what she had created. Every cushion and hand-worked rug, every painting and table and comfortable chair, every flowering border and newly planted tree gave her a purpose and identity. But by the summer of 1975, Kingsley had had enough. He used to take the Tube into London, and one day found himself stuck in an empty Tube carriage outside High Barnet station. It wasn't for long and the train was above ground, but it left him feeling very anxious. The experience contributed to a growing conviction that it was time to move. 'I don't want to live here any more,' he told Jane, 'it's too bloody cut off. I want to go back to London.'[5] To Paul Johnson he said, 'I want to get away from that horrible garden.'[6] For Jane, the idea of leaving Lemmons felt like an amputation; but she was willing to make the move, if only to make Kingsley happier and give her marriage one more chance.

Kingsley had been worried for some time by the extent to which his travel phobia and fear of being alone had increased, while his interest in sex had all but disappeared. Until he met Jim Durham, he had regarded psychiatrists as figures of fun, peddling platitudes to those too feeble to face reality. But Jim had said that some sessions might help, and Kingsley was at such a low ebb that he was willing to give the idea a go. He could justify it on the grounds that even if the treatment didn't work, it might still make good copy for a novel.

He started going to a psychologist called Dr Patricia Gillan, who ran a sex clinic at the Maudsley Hospital where Jim was a consultant. Given the state of the Amis marriage, Kingsley's therapy included a certain amount of marriage guidance counselling too. After three or four sessions, Dr Gillan asked to see Jane on her own. 'She was an interesting mixture of shrewdness and naivety,' wrote Jane, 'and after a few minutes exclaimed, "From all I've heard about you, I thought you were going to be simply awful, and you're not, are you?" '7 There were two further sessions where Jane found out to her relief that she was not frigid, just out of practice. She even found she could bring herself to climax in front of someone else, and remembered how amused she was by 'the immense sweetness and funniness of Prof. Brindley saying in his gentle, pedantic, courteous voice, "I do hope that you had a satisfactory orgasm, Mrs Amis." '8

Yet Jane felt that she needed to give up cigarettes more than she needed sex therapy. She had a semi-permanent cough about which her doctor had given her serious warnings, and smoking had certainly hastened her mother's death. Dr Gillan felt that aversion therapy would be helpful, and put her in touch with a behavioural psychotherapist called Kate Hopkinson.

The first appointment with Kate Hopkinson took place in January 1976. Jane liked her immediately. She was about twenty years younger than Jane but very professional, and her voice had a steady, reliable quality. Mrs Hopkinson decided against aversion therapy, much to her patient's relief: the results could be dramatic, but didn't always last. She asked Jane to keep a smoking diary instead, and observe when she most wanted to smoke.

During the second session, Jane confided that she felt that she was increasingly dull and boring to others; and as she was talking, she was shocked to find herself weeping uncontrollably, as if a dam holding back a lake of sadness had suddenly burst. She must have cried for the best part of the hour, during which Mrs Hopkinson sat quietly and made no attempt to stop the flow. Jane was grateful for her calm understanding, and soon she wanted Kate's advice or reassurance on every aspect of her past and present life.

In early February, on the advice of Dr Gillan, Jane and Kingsley took a long weekend together in Oxfordshire. They stayed one night at Steeple Aston with Iris Murdoch and John Bayley, and the next at a hotel in Woodstock, from where they walked around Blenheim Park with Rosie Plush. 'That was my last truly happy time with Kingsley,' she wrote over twenty years later. 'He was relaxed, affectionate, funny, communicative ... It was like old times – not the breathless beginning but something that held the promise of endurance, of an honest and companionable future.'⁹ Yet her description of this winter break written a few months after it took place is not so happy. Although the rows were fewer, 'we were very out of practice in affectionate companionship; I felt (and I was right about it) that I bored him, and our sex life, which had begun to get off the ground before Christmas, was suffering a reverse.'¹⁰

They were in the dining room on the Sunday morning when Kingsley silently handed her the paper – in which she read that Victor Stiebel had died. 'I had always known what an enormous amount of love Victor had given me,' she wrote; 'his warmth, his wisdom, his sharpness of appreciation and understanding, the quality of his sense and his humour. At least I had really appreciated all these things at the time ... there was no feeling of waste or recrimination, just pure, horrible loss.'¹¹

The death of Victor Stiebel made Mrs Hopkinson an even more important factor in Jane's life, and she became utterly obsessed with her therapist. She described her feelings for this young woman as 'exactly like being in love without the sex'.¹² The phrase comes from the journal which Mrs Hopkinson had suggested she keep at the time, a fifty-page document written between 1976 and 1977. One might expect it to be overflowing with feelings of rage or guilt about Kingsley, or mulling over where it all went wrong – but the main subject is Jane's one-sided infatuation for Kate Hopkinson. The journal makes it clear that Kingsley is already in the past, her marriage beyond repair: this is Jane clinging to the emotional wreckage, and Kate has been cast as her rescuer.

Kate agrees, and points out that 'I set off all sorts of emotional reverberations which ante-dated Kingsley (for instance, Jane's mother and I were both Katherines, and both former ballet dancers). So a lot of early, impacted distress fused with her current frantic anxiety and confusion, and got focused on me.' Jane stored up her praise and re-assurances – 'bones', she called them, that could be dug up and gnawed for comfort. She wrote Kate long letters which they would then discuss, and gave her little hand-made gifts.

While Kate had to be vigilant in maintaining professional bound-aries with Jane, she felt that accepting the letters and the gifts was a concession worth making. 'Writing things down enables communi-cation of material which may not be easy to raise in the face-to-face context,' she observed, while the little presents 'provided [Jane] with a vehicle for expressing and relieving her feelings, as well as sharing her creativity with me. It has always seemed to me important to have some positivity "in the room", as well as the inevitable vast expanses of defeat and despair. Overall, these small concessions helped me to keep the main boundaries clean and focused, in the face of Jane's repeated attempts to change the relationship.'[13]

Jane often needed reminding that 'I'm not your friend, I'm your therapist.' Yet Jane was a very strong character, who had persuaded herself that unless Kate acknowledged her feelings she would collapse under their weight. Jane even felt she had deserved 'treats' – time with Kate outside the consulting room. These were gently but consistently denied, but it did not stop her from fantasising about showing Kate the garden at Lemmons, or taking her to a concert.

Then came a moment when Mrs Hopkinson said she was going to Holland, and Jane would not see her for eighteen days. 'I felt sick and shaky and I couldn't sleep and totally irrational fears accompanied this state. That she was really going for good: that she didn't care about me: that I was going mad: that if one's heart ached as much as that something actually broke.' Kate Hopkinson reassured her that these feelings would pass, and Jane accepted her reassurance. 'I think, in emotional extremis, one is more like an animal: it isn't what you say anything like so much as the tone of voice in which it is said.'[14] Jane also found that she was rediscovering the strategies that children instinctively revert to at times of great emotional stress. She had bought a cuddly sheep for one of her godchildren, and ended up keeping it for something to cuddle herself; and a cushion or pillow can be very useful if you need to scream.

In June the Amises were invited to stay with the philanthropist Drue Heinz in Berkshire. They were given a distant room in her very large house and when they finally reached it after dinner, Kingsley (by then very drunk) 'suddenly started screaming that he didn't know who he was again and again. It was very loud and very frightening. I did not know whether he had suddenly gone mad, or was it to do with drink.'¹⁵ Jane was terrified he would wake the whole house, but before he could she seized a pillow and gave it to Kingsley to scream into. When the fear at last subsided, he fell instantly asleep.

By now Lemmons had been put on the market, for £125,000. It attracted many sightseers as well as potential buyers, but Jane had to drop the price to £110,000 before it could be sold. With Monkey's help, she found a house that fulfilled Kingsley's only proviso, that it should be within five minutes' walk of Hampstead Tube station. It was a graceful eighteenth-century house in Flask Walk, built by a Mr Gardnor who had made his fortune managing the springs in Well Walk: waters that were then considered almost as health-giving as those of Tunbridge Wells or Bath.

Martin Amis recalled that Jane insisted on doing the whole move by herself – a decision that prolonged it into an ordeal lasting what felt like weeks. She said they could not afford professional movers, but Martin disagrees. 'There was no reason why they couldn't afford [them],' he said. 'They were selling one grand house and moving to another, equally prestigious, even if it didn't have the garden and outhouses, but no, she had to parade her loss, her overwork.'¹⁶ Jane refutes his charge that she was making herself a martyr: 'Actually my daughter Nicola, who knew how much I minded leaving, rallied round with the wife of a friend of Sargy's, Jane Raybould . . . I agreed because, apart from being touched by their offer, I really didn't care as I was so upset about leaving.'¹⁷ So Jane trudged about, sighing under loaded tea-chests; while Nicola's huge horse-box shuttled back and forth between Hadley Common and Hampstead, and the atmosphere in the house became 'close to excruciating'.¹⁸ Kingsley, of course, did very little except finish up the tail ends of various bottles of liqueurs.

'My feelings of despair and dread about leaving my garden [at Lemmons] and moving to London were becoming more and more intense,' she wrote – until Mrs Hopkinson advised her to make the most of the time she had left, rather than dread the leaving. 'After this, I used to go into my garden and be there, and feel it for good memory. This made me cry, but in a better way. I also screamed about it a bit.'[19]

They moved into Gardnor House in the summer of 1976. Set back from the road, it is the grandest house in Flask Walk, with big rooms and ample windows looking over the walled garden at the back. Jane's friend Kay Dick, who had lived there, warned her that the ghost of 'Lady Gardnor [sic] walked the first floor, and that she has a down on women.'[20] To appease her spirit, Jane stood in the middle of the drawing room and told Lady Gardnor she would do her best to look after the house.

As at Lemmons, Kingsley's study was on the ground floor while Jane used one of the bedrooms. There was a room for Monkey, and the top floor was made into a self-contained flat for Mrs Uniacke. Sargy had married Frances in January, and they had moved to Camberwell. Martin, who in 1974 had won the Somerset Maugham award for his first novel *The Rachel Papers*, was living in Bayswater and now worked as deputy literary editor of the *New Statesman*. Philip had a steady job as a graphic designer, and a steady girlfriend whom he married later that year. Even Sally's life was teetering on a narrow ledge of middle-class stability: aged twenty-two, she had married a man almost twice her age called Nigel Service, the owner of the wine-bar where she had a job.

Monkey was very unhappy. Perhaps it was to do with Martin's success, or Sargy's leap into happily married life, or his own disappointed expectations; but Jane couldn't help seeing how tense and overwrought he was, particularly since he so often turned his anger against her. With the zeal of a convert, Jane tried to persuade him to try psychotherapy again. But he was done with therapists, and like Kingsley he was irritated by Jane, who seemed to be walking around in a miasma of shaky vulnerability. She had hoped to start work on her new garden, but the summer of 1976 was one of prolonged drought with water-rationing in force.

A few weeks after the move, Jane went on holiday with her old lover Michael Behrens and his wife Felicity, who had a house inland from Sainte-Maxime on the French Riviera. She had an idea for a novel that she was hoping to develop, and Kingsley wrote her some very affectionate letters while she was away. 'I was thinking the other day,' he wrote, 'how much I enjoyed our winter holiday in Woodstock etc. I remember those two walks in the park with amazing (for me) vividness, and us snuggling in the hotel. Couldn't we go again this coming Feb?'[21] He was also kind and helpful about her writing: 'Don't worry too much about your novel,' he wrote. 'You have a very good idea there. Let it just roll around your head without actually contemplating sitting down and starting. Then when you get back I'll give you some good pep-talks wrapped up in treats and between us we'll get the thing off the mark.'[22]

The holiday was not a huge success. It was too cold to do much swimming, and Michael Behrens 'made me feel pretty bad', she wrote. 'Dull, unattractive and generally as if he wished he hadn't asked me. This situation was made funny – and therefore saved – by both of his sons flirting with me, which made him cross, saved some of my *amour propre* and made me laugh.'[23]

Back in London, Mrs Hopkinson suggested that Jane might benefit from group therapy; apart from anything else, they both felt that Jane must somehow break her emotional dependence. The thought of life without Mrs Hopkinson reduced Jane to a panic-stricken jelly; but she felt she had learned a lot from her therapy sessions, and eagerly looked forward to joining the group in November.

About two weeks before the group therapy was due to begin, Jane endured four days of abdominal pain, backache and nausea. Her doctor diagnosed a severely inflamed gall bladder, and an X-ray revealed that it contained nine separate stones. The condition had probably been developing for months.

Kingsley accompanied her to King Edward VII's Hospital on the evening of Sunday, 21 November and left her there. It was not his presence she missed, but Mrs Hopkinson's, whom she felt was the only person who had 'any real concern' for her. The operation lasted two hours, and a nine-inch drain was left in the wound which was extremely painful. That night, 'I wished my mother was alive . . . I remembered her smell – very sweet, like sweetbriar – and how she was if things were really bad, and I realised that I had nobody in the world to take her place: in a way, it was yet another thing I was laying on poor Mrs H.'[24] In fact Jane had relied on Mrs Hopkinson being within reach, and when she heard that Kate was going away for Christmas for three weeks she was nearly hysterical.

Dosia Verney, with whom Jane went to recuperate in Mortlake after the operation, managed to find Mrs Hopkinson's home number and made an emergency appointment. But when Jane arrived, it was obvious that Kate was very displeased.

'Do you know what is your favourite game?' she said in a voice I had never heard before. '*Ain't it awful.*' . . . She said I used up energy rehearsing internal monologues. That I used up energy protesting that I tried about things. That I must take responsibility for my own life . . . That most people in therapy only had one hour, did not keep ringing up and writing: that she really wondered whether these privileges weren't making things worse. I could be very difficult, she said. I knew that. My heart was hammering so hard and loudly that I thought she must hear it . . . I wanted to scream shut up I can't bear this – there is *nothing* in my life that I can stick at the moment, I love you very much: it is bitter enough that you don't love me without you making it clear how much you despise and dislike me.[25]

Jane dreaded her return to Flask Walk. She knew that neither Kingsley nor Monkey would make any effort to cheer her, soothe her or even sympathize with the pain she was in. The wound with its nine-inch drain was still very sore, and the drain was not removed till several days later. Gardnor House was full of stairs, it was hard to sleep and she was exhausted. 'Colin continued to be hostile, and I felt I had to be very careful with K[ingsley].' By that she meant that talking to him was like walking a tightrope: the slightest mistake and he would turn on her with venom. 'I *was* careful. I didn't want any more misery. A nice, rather intellectual woman from an agency came to cook for the three days of Christmas, which was the most un-Christmassy I have ever spent.'[26] She went over and over her last meeting with Kate Hopkinson, what had gone wrong, and why she had turned against her. When they saw each other again in January, Kate said that 'she had wanted me to get some armour on quickly with which to cope with the three weeks' of her absence.[27]

Despite good intentions on both sides, it was becoming evident that Jane and Kingsley's new life in Flask Walk was built, as Martin had observed, on 'a massive foundation of resentment'.[28] Jane spoke of her 'worsening relationship with Kingsley, who I now began to realise not only didn't love me but actually *disliked* me. In company he maintained neutrality; alone he was either surly or ceaselessly finding fault with me, until I became nervous of being alone with him.'[29] There was one fleeting moment of affection. 'I was standing by the window of our bedroom one morning . . . feeling very sad. He came to me, put his arms round me and gave me a long, gentle kiss, and said, "I used to be so much in love with you." Before I could say anything, he turned and walked out of the room.'[30]

In 1977 Jane had been asked to compile an anthology called *The Lover's Companion*, and working on it provided some solace from the barren desert of her life with Kingsley. It came out on Valentine's Day 1978, and Valerie Grove came to interview her the day before for the *Evening Standard*. Valerie described Gardnor House as 'the unhappiest place you can imagine – it was *bleak* with unhappiness. At one point Kingsley scuttled past with a tray, on which was a very basic lunch – an egg and half a tomato . . . There was *nothing* between them, not even recognition.' Jane told her that she hoped her latest book was 'for lovers to read aloud to each other in bed', but it was obvious that not much of that was going on at Gardnor House.[31]

Although Kingsley scoffed at Jane for seeing therapists, he had been doing exactly the same throughout 1977. According to his memoirs, they didn't do much good; and yet his biographer cites four different specialists whom he was consulting at one time or another between 1976 and 1980.

In April 1977 Kingsley began writing *Jake's Thing*, about a don at Comyns College in Oxford called Jake Richardson who is losing his libido. He and his wife Brenda attend a number of group therapy sessions. Kingsley had gone to some trouble to enlist the help of Dr Gillan, so he could get the details right. But when she read the book she felt very let down. The sex therapy in *Jake's Thing* is exactly what Amis went through – even down to the ring-like device called a plethysmograph, which he had to wear at night to measure penile tumescence; but in Kingsley's sardonic prose it all becomes a farce, sometimes even a con-trick. Jane too was hurt. In Jake Richardson's savage rejection of women in general, she read Kingsley's rejection of her in particular:

their concern with the surface of things, with objects and appearances, with their surroundings and how they looked and sounded in them, with seeming to be better and right while getting everything wrong, their automatic assumption of the role of the injured party in any clash of wills, their certainty that a view is the more credible and useful for the fact that they hold it, their use of misunderstanding and misrepresentation as weapons of debate . . .[32]

And so it goes on, for another nine relentless lines.

She also could not forgive the character of Geoffrey Mabbott: who, with his unconventional clothes, his exaggerated gestures and his wilfully eccentric opinions, was an unkind portrait of Monkey. Jane had noticed how Kingsley had changed towards her brother, 'endlessly sniping at him and putting him down and grumbling about him when he wasn't there'.[33]

Colin had lived with his sister, her husband and her stepchildren for over ten years, in four separate houses: Blomfield Road, Maida Vale, Lemmons and now Gardnor House. The time had come to leave, once and for all. Jane was very sad, although she knew it was the right decision for him. Monkey found a little terraced house in Tufnell Park, and moved out as soon as it was habitable.

For the first time, Kingsley and Jane were on their own together – and as far apart as two people could be. Jane dreaded the evenings they spent alone. She had long given up trying to curb his alcohol intake. They stopped sharing a bed because when she turned, he said she woke him up – so she moved into another room, and he was angry about that too. Kingsley's fear of being left in the house intensified. He would go to the Garrick Club for the better part of the day or an evening, but he wanted to know that Jane would be there when he got back. He bitterly resented the amount of time that she spent with her therapists. On one occasion, when Kingsley was complaining that Jane was going out yet again and that he would be left alone, Jane pointed out that Mrs Uniacke was in the house. Kingsley replied, very slowly and through gritted teeth, 'Mrs Uniacke doesn't count.'[34]

In the late spring of 1978 Kate Hopkinson advised Jane to join a women's group, run by an American therapist called Jenner Roth. Jane realized that this woman had a 'remarkable skill: she was the first person I had ever met who could say anything to the people with whom she worked without bruising their sensibility'. One of the first things that Jenner said to Jane was, 'You are a bottomless pit of neediness.'[35] The women's group brought Jane into a circle of women who all listened to and supported each other, and with their help she finally began to accept herself and grow up.

She was still seeing Kate Hopkinson for one-to-one sessions; but that September Kate's partner was involved in a fatal sailing accident. For one terrible week she did not know whether he was alive or dead; but when she heard that his body had been found, the news left her so shocked and emotionally drained that she had nothing left to give her patients. 'I still feel bad that I couldn't prepare Jane in a controlled way for the next stage,' she said. 'Instead it was like dropping her off a cliff.'[36] Jane's feelings for Kate subsided, as they were bound to do in time. They remained friends, but from now on, Jane relied on Jenner Roth and the women's group to keep her steady.

Sally was much on Jane's mind again. Her marriage to Nigel Service had lasted only a few months, after which she sank once more into drugs and alcohol and depression. By 1978 her life was a series of catastrophes, punctuated by spells in rehab. Kingsley never knew when the phone would ring, summoning him and Jane to deal with some emergency or other – and it left them both feeling anguished and helpless. 'It must be worse to lead her life than to have to be with her and cope with her,' he wrote to Bob Conquest, 'but that's not much consolation.'[37] In May 1978 she became involved with a violent Irishman. He was imprisoned for theft, and she found she was pregnant. She gave birth to a daughter, Heidi, in December 1978, but was persuaded to give her up for adoption when she was a few weeks old.

Although Jane's agents had found her some work writing film scripts, they had never really shown any enthusiasm. So towards the end of her time at Lemmons, her accountant Anton Felton had introduced her to a literary agent called Jonathan Clowes. He had set up his agency in 1960 with authors who were then drawn from his left-wing friends, one of whom was Len Deighton. Clowes held out for a good deal when he sold The Ipcress File to the film producer Harry Salzman, and he had a reputation for being fiercely loyal to his clients. Like Kingsley he had been a Communist in his youth, and had been imprisoned for refusing to do National Service when Britain was at war with Korea; but his exciting past was hidden by a calm and quiet manner, and he was very active in promoting Jane and securing commissions for television work. Jane wrote the screenplay for a three-part adaptation of *After Julius* for Yorkshire Television (which was broadcast in April–May 1979) and Thames Television commissioned a seven-part version of *Something in Disguise*.

In January 1979, Thames Television asked Jane to come down to the studios in Richmond when they began filming, so she went to bed early the night before. This annoyed Kingsley, who was already fretting that she was going to be gone for most of the next day, and he was always more irritable with most of a bottle of whisky inside him. Just as she was falling asleep there was an alarming crash. He had fallen downstairs. As Jane helped him up he complained that his shoulder hurt, but since he could still hold his arm out and clench his hand without pain she assumed nothing was broken.

The next morning, the pain in his shoulder was such that they both felt he should see their doctor, John Allison. Jane made the appointment and arranged for a taxi to collect Kingsley and bring him back, but she refused to go with him because she had to get to the studios. By the time she returned that evening, Kingsley had worked himself into a towering rage. He had broken his arm, high on the bone so that it could not be put in a splint, and she was so full of herself and her own concerns that she hadn't even bothered to accompany him to the doctor.

His arm healed, but the relentless onslaught of alcohol meant that the rest of his body was never given a chance to recover. He was not yet sixty; but as he told Philip Larkin that September,

On my self-pity themes, don't tempt me, son. They include year-round hay fever, high blood pressure so that I stream with sweat at the slightest exertion or upset, permanently itching places on my scalp (side-effect of anti-blood-p pills) . . . increasing phobias that stop me travelling almost anywhere (that one's not so bad) and make me hate and dread being alone, this along with a wife who puts herself first and the rest nowhere and constantly goes out to GROUPS and WORKSHOPS and crappy 'new friends', and total loss of sex-drive; I haven't had a fuck for over a year and a wank for over a month.[38]

Both he and Jane accused each other of being monstrously egocentric, which was perhaps a case of what one most dislikes in oneself being particularly annoying in someone else. Yet Jane cites concrete examples of Kingsley's behaviour, while all he can come up with is that she goes out to workshops and has new friends.

In the summer of 1980 Anthony and Violet Powell invited the Amises to join them on a two-week cruise down the Atlantic coast of France, Spain and Portugal; then through the Straits of Gibraltar and so round to Nice. Paul and Betty Fussell joined the party as well, at Kingsley's suggestion. It was to be the last trip he would ever make abroad, and the last time he and Jane travelled together.

The trip got off to a bad start because Jane misread the time of embarkation. After a frantic taxi ride around Southampton Docks, they reached the ship just as the gangway was being pulled up. They managed to get aboard, but Kingsley had been reduced to a jelly of nerves and was furious with Jane's incompetence. He enjoyed the holiday, even the sightseeing; although he still had little appreciation of gardens and tapestries, perhaps because they reminded him too much of her. 'Kingsley's irritation with me was like the atmosphere of an impending thunderstorm,' she wrote, 'and this dominated the cruise for me.'[39]

When the party split up in Nice, Kingsley and Jane had arranged to stay for ten days with Jane's old friend Joy Law, who had a house near Souillac. They travelled by train, a journey Kingsley had been dreading. So by the time Joy met them at the station, soon after midnight, he had been drinking for several hours and had almost passed out. The two women had great difficulty getting him into the car.

'The following week,' wrote Joy Law, 'settled into a fairly regular pattern. Breakfast all together, whereafter Kingsley would go up to his bedroom to write . . . and I would go off to the village shop for luncheon, more often than not accompanied by Jane . . . [She] would sit in the village square in tears, telling me how awful her life was.'[40] At mealtimes, Joy and her other guests could hardly believe the poisonous barbs that Jane and Kingsley hurled at each other with lightning speed. 'It really was like watching table-tennis,' said Joy, 'worrying because of the animosity but wonderful to listen to.'[41]

The piece Kingsley had been writing in France was an account of the cruise for the *Sunday Times*; and when they got back to England, he accused Jane of destroying it. 'This shocked me more than anything else that had happened between us,' she wrote. 'The idea that I would destroy anyone's writing, let alone his, made me realise how much and how thoroughly he disliked and despised me.' When she found the piece in a zipped pocket of his luggage 'he said simply, "Oh. You've found it, then." '[42]

But however difficult things were for Jane, she was terrified of walking out. It would be her third failure at marriage, she was fifty-six, and she knew she could not live off her novels. In any case Kingsley could not bear being alone, so she had to stay. And besides, where would she go? The answer to that last question came from Ursula Vaughan Williams, who said that Jane could stay with her in Gloucester Crescent.

The final straw came with their two-week visit to the Edinburgh Festival. They had been invited by Dickie and Patricia Temple-Muir, whom they had met at a party with George Gale. Dickie Temple-Muir then owned half of the Roxburghe Hotel in Edinburgh, and Kingsley was very gratified by the bottle of whisky he found waiting in their room on arrival. However, after one play which he did not enjoy he refused to go to any other event, all of which were dismissed as trendy or lefty or both. He did not want Jane to go either; and rather than go out to dinner, he insisted on sandwiches and drinks being brought to their room. Then a friend of the Temple-Muirs invited them to lunch to meet Claudio Abbado, who was conducting a series of concerts at the Festival. Kingsley drank far too much, and when Abbado made some comment about Mozart, Kingsley proceeded to tell the celebrated conductor that he didn't know what he was talking about.

When Jane later told him that he could have disagreed with Abbado 'more gracefully', she was instantly branded as being upper class by suggesting that people shouldn't say what they think. Kingsley had been irritated by her classiness for years: it meant that instead of being natural she was actressy, all airs and graces (although it is hard to be 'natural' in front of someone who dislikes you intensely and challenges everything you say or do). Her friends were stuck-up and boring, or trendy and boring. She always had to be right. Her cooking was too elaborate and didn't taste of anything unless it was smothered in HP sauce, and she masked her condescending attitude to 'the staff' with an exaggerated politeness. A perfect example of how this grated on Kingsley comes in *Stanley and the Women* (1984) when the daily, Mrs Shillibeer, walks out on Stanley and Susan Duke. Stanley asks her:

> 'Why don't you like working here? Not because of me, I hope?'
>
> 'Ooh no, not you, Stanley, you're a darling, you are. No, it's that stuck-up cat you married . . . Have you ever noticed the way she talks to me? . . . "Oh Mrs Shillibeer, would you very kindly, very sweetly chop up these shallots, not too fine, you know the way I like them, and tell me when you've done them." . . . Never once talks to me like a human being. It's not much to ask.'[43]

When Kingsley first fell in love with Jane, part of her splendour was that upper-class elegance, that unspoken assumption of entitlement and abundance. In the early days he had enjoyed the Earl Grey tea, the scented soap, the china and the paintings, although he could easily have done without them. But as he became disenchanted with her, so everything she had brought into his life became dry, fussy, useless and irritating.

When they returned to London, Jane announced that she would be going to a health farm in Suffolk, called Shrublands, for ten days in November. She did not tell Kingsley that she would never be coming back. She had been to Shrublands once or twice before, and this time she asked Patricia Temple-Muir to come with her. Jane warned her of her plan, and also Mrs Uniacke, Monkey, Anton Felton and her secretary, Helen Benckendorf. All were sworn to secrecy: Kingsley must know nothing yet. Helen Benckendorf was to take Rosie Plush, because Jane was afraid Kingsley might use her as a hostage. So whenever Kingsley was out of the house enjoying long lunches at the Garrick, she smuggled clothes, her typewriter and her quarter-written novel over to Ursula Vaughan Williams's house in Gloucester Crescent.

Jane set off for Shrublands on 1 November. When she said good-bye to Kingsley that morning he was reading the paper, and barely looked up to see her go. Marigold Johnson, who was at Shrublands at the same time, recalled that Jane was very much as normal and working on a huge piece of patchwork. Kingsley expected her back on the 10th, but that morning a letter arrived from her solicitors:

This is to tell you I'm leaving. You know that I have been – we've both been – unhappy for years. I've thought about things for a long time and have come to the conclusion that there isn't the slightest hope of things getting any better. They don't, they simply get quietly worse. You are not going to stop drinking and I cannot live with the consequences – I tried to tell you in Edinburgh that it was not the rows that were the worst thing – it was the awful sterile desert in between them that I can't take any more. I'd rather live alone than the way we've been living for the last few years. I've tried to talk to you about our parting amicably, but you simply accused me of blackmailing so the only thing to do is just go, before we make each other even more miserable.

This has been the most agonising decision and I've taken all the trouble I know to be sure that it is the right one, but I have made it, and it is final.[44]

In a letter to Philip Larkin of 5 December, Kingsley mulled over the reasons why she had left him:

She did it partly to punish me for stopping wanting to fuck her and partly because she realised I didn't like her much. Well, I liked her as much as you could like anyone totally wrapped up in themselves and unable to tolerate the slightest competition or anything a raving lunatic could see as opposition and having to have their own way in everything all the time. Well, I expect reading between the lines there you can sense that we hadn't been getting on too well of late. Yeah, but not having her around and trying to take in the fact that she will never be around is immeasurably more crappy than having her around. I've had a wife for 32 years.[45]

'Not a word from the old bitch yet,' Kingsley told Brian Aldiss, halfway through December. 'By God she was hard to live with but living without her seems altogether pointless. I had no idea she meant so much to me.'[46]

Meant so much to me: what exactly did he mean? Kingsley had long ceased to feel anything approaching warmth for Jane, yet he needed her more than anyone ever had. Yes, he had lost his chauffeur, cook and doer of chores too tedious to think about, but that was the least of it. In *Stanley and the Women*, Kingsley wrote that 'Stopping being married to someone is an incredibly violent thing to happen to you, not easy to take in completely, ever.'[47] She had become woven into the fabric of his life, and in ripping herself out of it she had left a torn and bleeding hole.

18

Introducing the Cazalets

IN THE FIRST weeks after leaving Kingsley, Jane stayed in Ursula Vaughan Williams's spare room surrounded by piles of clothes and books. She was in touch with Mrs Uniacke, who did her laundry. Jane would come with her washing in the car, and Mrs Uniacke would be outside on the street with the freshly ironed pile of the week before. It was from her that she heard how Kingsley's children were taking it in turns to be with him at night ('dad-sitting'), particularly Philip, who had just left his first wife.

When the composer who had been living in Ursula's basement flat left, Jane moved in. It had two rooms, and Ursula installed a little gas stove for her in what had been the coalhole. It felt like going back to Mon Débris, the flat she had shared with Dosia before her marriage to Peter Scott, but without the joy or the fun. Worst of all, she was once more living alone. This had always felt like an unnatural state for Jane, who had grown up in a big family and took little pleasure in solitude. She could not shake off the feeling that being alone represented failure – the failure to make a loving relationship work, no matter how often she tried. On 29 December Kingsley wrote her a letter.

> Dear Jane,
> Life with you wasn't much fun towards the end, but it was far better than life without you has been. I miss you dreadfully, much more than I could have expected. But I won't pile on the agony, just ask you if there are any terms on which you would come back. I have very little hope, but I think it would be wrong not to ask. An unadorned negative will suffice.[1]

Jane was willing to consider returning on one condition: that he give up alcohol – not just cut back, but renounce it altogether.

To balance his sacrifice, she would give up smoking. (Despite all Mrs Hopkinson's work, she was still addicted to nicotine.) Jane believed that it was the drink that brought out the demons in Kingsley, but it was not as simple as that. He drank to dull the edge of a hyper-acute perception and a terror of non-existence that could not bear isolation or emptiness. This sharpness of observation is a key element of his comedy; but it can also be almost oppressive in his novels, provoking a response similar to that when someone stands too close to you at a party: you want to step back, hold the book further away. He could not stand back. He had to live with it, and whisky helped. It was impossible for him to give it up, and Jane never really expected he would. A few more chilly notes went back and forth, and then stopped.

Kingsley never forgave Jane for walking out. In an interview with Michael Barber, 'he admitted that his professional self-confidence, so vital to an ageing writer, had taken a "helluva" knock when his marriage ended, not least because in losing his wife he also lost a valued critic and confidante'.[2] So shattered was he by her defection that, for the first time in his career, he had to abandon a novel of which he had already written 130 pages: its title, ironically enough, was *Difficulties with Girls*.

The only thing Jane could do was concentrate on work. She had begun a novel about a hairdresser called Gavin Lamb who was terrified of women. Although the character of Gavin was heterosexual, he was based on a couple of gay friends of Monkey's who used to come and paint the house and do odd jobs. 'They were funny, interesting, devoted to each other and wildly unfaithful: they got on, or off, with everybody.' One of them was surprisingly well informed; and Jane thought 'it would be interesting to write about someone who, on the face of it, had no cultural or educational advantages . . . but who'd acquired his interest – sometimes his passion – out of sheer curiosity and love of various subjects'.[3]

Yet it was very difficult to immerse herself in the world of Gavin Lamb when her financial future looked so uncertain, and her emotional isolation so unbearably bleak. Paul and Marigold Johnson kept up with Jane, but many of those whom she had entertained at Lemmons either sided with Kingsley, or behaved as if she no longer existed. She went to stay with Nicola, who was still living in Gloucestershire and had recently married a painter called Elliott Starks. In 1981 her agent Jonathan Clowes married Ann Evans. Together they ran his agency, and took Jane for weekends to their house in Penhurst, East Sussex. Anthony and Tanya Hobson had her to stay in Hampshire (she had become godmother to their daughter, Charlotte, in 1970). Jenner Roth, who ran the women's group, became a personal friend along with her husband, Terry Cooper, and also made Jane godmother to their son. Most stalwart of all was Ursula. Jane had already seen what comfort she had brought to Jill Balcon, as Cecil Day-Lewis was dying; and to Jane she was an unfailingly kind and steadying presence.

Ursula had met her second husband, the composer Ralph Vaughan Williams, when they were both still married. Ursula's husband was an army officer who died in 1942. She then became assistant to Vaughan Williams and carer to his wife Adeline, who was crippled with arthritis. They married after Adeline's death, but had only been together five years when Vaughan Williams, who was much older, died in 1958. She published several volumes of poetry in her lifetime, as well as her husband's biography, her own autobiography, four novels and libretti for various composers.

Jane had negotiated a loan of £5,000 (the advance on her next novel) from her bank, but she never had to use it. Ursula quietly supported her – and her dog Rosie – for eighteen months. It was a generous act, for Jane would have no capital until the sale of Gardnor House. In the meantime, Jane heard what was happening at Gardnor House from Mrs Uniacke. Lots of people came to support Kingsley, particularly Philip and Martin; and then, in the summer of 1981, there came a development that left Jane thunderstruck. Kingsley was going to be looked after by the woman Jane had replaced: Hilly, his ex-wife, now Lady Kilmarnock.

After their months in Seville, Hilly and Alistair Boyd returned to Ronda, and in 1972 she gave birth to a son, Jamie. Three years later, on the death of his father, Alistair became 7th Baron Kilmarnock and Chief of Clan Boyd. Jamie would never inherit the titles, for he was born while Hilly was still married to Shackleton Bailey, who had been very obstructive about granting her a divorce.

The Kilmarnocks lived in Spain for as long as they could; but Ali's title had come without land or money, and in 1975 he moved back to England and took his seat in the House of Lords. The idea was that Hilly and Jamie would join him once he had found a job and somewhere to live. After two very difficult years he was no closer to achieving either, and his only income was the stipend he received for his regular attendance in the House of Lords (he joined the newly created Social Democratic Party when it was founded in 1981). Hilly decided to come back anyway; and when Jane left Kingsley, she and Jamie were living in a cottage in Buckinghamshire left to Alistair by his old nanny, while he stayed with friends in London whenever the Lords were in session. It was hardly ideal; and money was so tight that at one point Hilly and a friend set up a hot-dog stand on the motorway to make a little extra. Everything changed when her eldest son Philip rang her in the summer of 1981, and suggested that she might be the perfect solution to the Kingsley problem.

To look after your ex-husband while living with your current one and your nine-year-old son sounds mad; but on every practical level it made perfect sense. Kingsley would have not only a companion and housekeeper, but a woman he was deeply attached to. As his dislike of Jane grew over the years, so the glow round Hilly had increased until she looked like a pearl of great price, thrown away in a moment of madness. As for Hilly, she was settled and happy and had no reason to regret leaving Kingsley; but she was fond of him, and his offer meant that she and her family would be together in London. Their living expenses would be taken care of, and Kingsley also agreed to pay Hilly £50 a week to keep house for him. At first Philip and Martin thought the arrangement would last six months, perhaps a year at most – and so did the Kilmarnocks. They held on to their house in Spain, and the cottage in Buckinghamshire.

Jane claimed that she was glad Kingsley was no longer alone, but it must have been hard to accept. Robert Conquest told Larkin that she was furious at the idea of Hilly living in her house, and mortified. Jane was the one who was left living on her own as a third-time divorcée; while Hilly, whom she had always thought of as a bad mother and worse housekeeper, was living at Gardnor House with the husband who had left her *and* the one she was married to.

In February 1981 Jane filed for divorce from Kingsley, on the grounds of 'unreasonable behaviour'. Gardnor House went on the market that spring, and the long and acrimonious division of the spoils began. Jane wanted half the proceeds from the sale of Gardnor House, plus the £14,000 she had spent on buying their first house in Maida Vale. Kingsley said she was asking for too much, and grumbled to his friends about her insistence on 'a Rolls-Royce divorce'.

She was still living with Ursula Vaughan Williams, for until Gardnor House was sold she could not even begin to look for a place of her own. The new novel was both hard work and an escape; yet much was riding on *Getting It Right*. Jane felt she had to reconnect with her writing and her readers, and this was her first book that would not be published by Cape: Jonathan Clowes had set her up with a new publisher, Christopher Sinclair-Stevenson of Hamish Hamilton. At the same time, she could not escape the rancour of her ongoing divorce. She felt that Kingsley had deliberately delayed putting the house on the market, and was doing all he could to make sure she got as little money as possible. Predictably enough, Kingsley and Hilly were appalled by the rapacity with which Jane came and stripped Gardnor House of all its best furniture, china and carpets – all of which Jane maintained she had bought herself. That year was not one that either she or Kingsley would want to revisit. Jane kept all her pocket engagement diaries, but 1981 is conspicuously absent. Yet by the end of that year Gardnor House was sold, and her novel *Getting It Right* was almost finished.

Kingsley and the Kilmarnocks moved into a small house in Leighton Road in Kentish Town in January 1982, and Jane began house-hunting in earnest. She eventually settled on 28 Delancey Street in Camden Town, and moved there in April. It was a narrow, four-storey house, with two rooms on each floor and one bathroom. Mrs Uniacke had always planned to come and join her, and Jane made a self-contained flat for her in the basement.

Monkey came to do the wiring and install a hi-fi system; and another person who worked on the house was Daniel Day-Lewis. He had finished his training at the Bristol Old Vic and was taking whatever acting jobs he could find; he had a bit-part in the film *Gandhi* which came out that year. He told Jane that she had rescued him from having to sign on while looking for acting work. From then on he decided that he would always take whatever job he could find, rather than go on the dole.[4]

Getting It Right was published in May 1982, soon after the move to Delancey Street. Gavin Lamb, her protagonist, is a thirty-one-year-old hairdresser who still lives at home in Barnet with his obsessively house-proud mother and his father, a builder-decorator. Gavin enjoys his job at a salon in London run by a tight-fisted martinet called Mr Adrian. He has a number of loyal customers, who are of course female; but apart from them, Gavin is terrified of women and parties. He prefers listening to classical music, reading, going to exhibitions and the occasional opera. One evening Gavin's gay friend Harry and his partner, the handsome and heartless Winthrop, drag him off to a party given by a very rich woman called Joan. She is in her fifties with brilliant orange hair, orange lips, huge tinted glasses and tight, spangled clothes. She is sensual, striking and not a bit shy; yet she seems to feel as out of place at her own party as Gavin does. She draws him into a quiet room, and there they play a truth game: inspired, perhaps, by the ice-breaking exercises that Jane would have done in the women's group. This is Jane looking at her older self: a fundamentally sad person who presents a glittering carapace to the world, but who is the victim of her own experience: she knows she is too restless and emotionally damaged to find love again.

That night he also meets a grubby, skinny girl who calls herself 'Lady' Minerva Munday. Not yet twenty, she comes from a rich, loveless family and is so desperate for human warmth, that if anyone is kind to her (Gavin makes this mistake) she latches on and won't let go. She insists on giving him a lift in her Mini to Whetstone, where he left his motorbike at Harry's house. It's well past midnight when he sets off for home, and, to his horror, she follows him all the way back to Barnet. Unable to face the drama his mother will make out of him sneaking a girl into the house, Gavin flatly refuses to let her come in; whereupon she sinks to her knees in the road and bursts into tears. She has nowhere else to go, or so she says – so of course Gavin relents. He puts her on a sofa in the lounge, and retires to his own room at the top of the house. Minerva, or Minnie (it's worth noting that Kingsley used the name as an endearment when he was in love with Jane), has no trouble charming Gavin's parents the following morning. They are so overawed by her being 'a Lady' that she can do no wrong, but Gavin never wants to see her again.

He would much rather see Joan, with whom he can talk about books and music. They meet at the opera, after which she deftly seduces Gavin and relieves him of his virginity; but when he tries to see her again, it transpires that she has gone to America with Harry's partner Winthrop, leaving Harry heartbroken. Gavin is shocked by her indifference – but that is the way of things: one person's joy is another's desolation.

All this time, Minerva has been trying to get Gavin to come and meet her parents. She knows he doesn't like her but her father is threatening to cut off her allowance, and if he could see that she had just one presentable friend he might change his mind. Gavin gives in eventually, and has a horrible Sunday lunch in Weybridge with her drunken mother and boorish father (who has a knighthood for services to industry, but no peerage). After coffee, the father summons Gavin into the study for a man-to-man chat, and accuses Gavin of debauching his daughter so as to get hold of her money. Feeling both indignant and mortified, Gavin escapes into the shrubbery and walks back to the station, without even saying goodbye to Minnie.

There is a junior at the hairdressing salon where Gavin works called Jenny. He has worked with her for three years and never thought much about her; but when she wishes there was more to her life, he begins to introduce her to books and music. Jenny lives with her mother and her illegitimate son Andrew. Here is the ready-made family into which Gavin will happily be drawn; but before that happens, he feels he must see Minerva again and apologize for his sudden disappearance after lunch at Weybridge.

With a heavy heart he turns up at her flat, which is in the basement of her father's town house. She lets him in to a scene of utter squalor. The bare room is littered with empty packets of food, and rank with the stench of vomit: Minerva is on a bulimic binge, being periodically sick into a brimming bucket by her unmade bed. 'I've got *such* a pain,' she tells him. 'It *never* – goes. It doesn't matter what I do.'

Gavin kneels beside her as she crams Jaffa Cakes into her mouth; her belly looks painfully distended. He tells her she needs help.

'Oh no I don't,' she replies with a look of hatred. 'You mean to pass the buck and have someone paid to treat me like a looney. Don't think I haven't been through all that . . . You just want someone *else* to help me. To get me off your back . . . I've given up on all that. Now I just put things on top of it. Have a binge . . . You just piss off.'[5]

The binge scene, raw and shocking as it is, takes the reader completely unawares. Most of the novel is written as social comedy: playful in its treatment of the shy self-educated Gavin, his turbo-charged mother, the exigent clients in the salon, the awful but opulent party. But Minerva's pain and the inner desolation she tries to fill with junk food feel horribly dark and real. It is an expression of Jane's own craving for love and reassurance, and the whole passage provokes both sympathy and revulsion. Minerva is also a reflection of Sally Amis, and Jane's despair at her own inability to do anything for a girl who was desperate for stability and affection, while remaining aggressively unlovable and unhelpable.

Joan and Minerva emerge from somewhere much sadder than Gavin's world, or indeed Jenny's. They are, once again, figures of experience and innocence; but while the experienced Joan is, for all her unhappiness, a survivor, Minerva's innocence has been so broken by indifference and lack of love that her self-destruction is inevitable.

Although Jane did not produce many novels during her years with Kingsley, he taught her a lot about how to be funny; yet the hardest part of novel-writing is the connective tissue, the bits that take you from one scene to the next. In the *Times Literary Supplement*, Anne Duchêne wrote that 'incident follows incident at the author's will, not by any natural progression'. She also felt that there was too much of 'back-combing and back-biting in the dreary salon', as well as of Gavin's rather vapid cultural musings.[6]

In a letter to Jane, Victoria Glendinning was far more enthusiastic.

I just wanted to tell you that I think *Getting it Right* is WONDERFUL, a winner – I read the first 20 pages and put it down, thinking, it *can't* go on being this good, and I'll feel so sad when it starts being not-so-good – but it didn't, it kept up all the way, and made me laugh and laugh – and almost cry, at the end. I wanted to tell you because some-times people don't *know* when they've done something marvellous. But I hope you do.[7]

Glendinning wanted to review it in the *Sunday Times*, but unfortunately the publication of *Getting It Right* did not fall into one of her weeks. Instead it was reviewed by Nicholas Shrimpton, who picked Jane up for thinking that *Match of the Day* was broadcast on Saturday afternoons and observed that she did not seem to know very much about what motivated autodidacts. 'A little more reading and a little less writhing and this would have been an impressive novel,' he concluded.[8]

More praise came from her friend Angus Wilson, a celebrated critic, but maddeningly this too was in a letter, not in print:

> What a marvellous novel – funny and moving and v. clever in the right sense. I read it each night when motoring in France and cut many cathedrals short to get in a longer reading . . . And as to the treatment of the gay world – thank you very much for the sympathy, good sense, and truth to life. But, of course, what matters is Gavin and marvellous he is. I'm just a bit doubtful about his range of taste – Moriarty, Mrs Jellaby, Jane Austen – I don't know. Music and painting I feel happy about. Many, many congratulations . . . Love, Angus.[9]

The book reached number three in the *Sunday Times* bestseller list at the end of May; and considering that numbers one and two were Frederick Forsyth (*No Comebacks*) and Wilbur Smith (*The Angels Weep*), her new publisher must have been delighted – even more so when the book was awarded the Yorkshire Post Literary Prize.

Despite its uneven reviews, *Getting It Right* had been a success and Christopher Sinclair-Stevenson was keen for her to start the next. Jane had two ideas, and could not decide which to embark on; so she invited her stepson Martin round for a drink to ask his advice. One idea was an updated version of *Sense and Sensibility*, on which she had already done some preliminary work. The other was a three-volume family saga, which would cover the decade 1937 to 1947. 'When people wrote about that time,' she observed, 'it was largely in terms of the battles fought; family life was merely a background. I thought it would be interesting to do it the other way round. England had changed so much during the war, but this hadn't been much written about. Martin said immediately, "Do that one." '[10] And so she began what would eventually become the Cazalet Chronicle.

She also took on all the work she could find. For a week in May at Lumb Bank, once home to Ted Hughes, she taught fiction for the Arvon Foundation with fellow novelist Nell Dunn, who was also in the women's group. She and Nell Dunn agreed that their students could be divided into those who really wanted to write, and those who wanted to be writers: the latter only wanted to know how to get published. In May she covered the Chelsea Flower Show, and the TV adaptation of *Something in Disguise* was broadcast in June and July. She also had a gardening column in *Woman's Journal*.

In March the following year (1983), Jane went on an Arts Council tour of the north with fellow novelists Penelope Lively and Paul Bailey. As well as addressing small audiences in draughty public libraries, they were expected to go and talk to schoolchildren. Jane had not realized this was part of the package, and as she had little experience of schools or children, her visits were not a success. After one or two she said, 'Look, I'm terribly sorry, I'm just no good at this.' Their Arts Council minder was forced to agree, and from then on she was let off schools.

Penelope Lively's diary provides a vivid description of Jane at that time. For one evening in Burnley, 'Jane wore décolleté black lace and emeralds which I hope the Burnley audience of twenty-three appreciated'; while at another reading in a pub in Northwich, 'Jane in paste and pearls this time, and frothy white blouse, telling improper stories over prawn cocktails.' In Blackpool they had an audience of about a hundred: 'half school parties of 17 year olds and the other half local elderly ladies, so an odd mix of punk hairstyles and neatly netted grey curls . . . Not back till 1 am again – all wilting somewhat by now, even Jane, though she revives in the evenings and talks copiously and trades bawdy jokes with Paul . . . I liked Jane Howard a lot, who I'd only met briefly once before.'[11]

Later that month, Jane's fourth and last grandchild – Ben – was born to Nicola and Elliott. Jane spent several weekends with them, as well as with Ann and Jonathan Clowes. In April she went to York to collect the Yorkshire Post Literary Prize, and the following month she was offered what seemed to her a huge sum of money to write a biography of the Queen Mother, then in her early eighties. Ruth, Lady Fermoy, lady-in-waiting to the Queen Mother, was very keen that Jane should take up the project, and a congenial lunch was arranged with the prospective subject. But further talks revealed that Jane would not be given access to the Royal Archives, so there seemed no point in doing it. When she told Jonathan, he agreed at once. Jane was grateful for the way he 'never tried to persuade me or make me feel I was making a mistake'.[12]

Jane's divorce from Kingsley came through in September 1983; but however much she disliked living alone, the relief of not being with him was considerable. She was now free to travel, and over the next few years she visited Thailand, Greece, India and Jordan. Best of all was being able to see old friends and make new ones, without having to worry about Kingsley's reactions. She was also able to see a lot more of Dosia, who had been so good to her after her operation. Neither she nor her second husband, Andrew Verney, had got on with Kingsley.

She tried to see more of Jill Balcon. 'Please come,' she wrote. 'We have seen so little of each other in the last three years and I feel that if we don't do something about it we shall never catch up with the consequent alienation.'[13] She tried again in December. 'I'm prepared to do whatever would suit you . . . but I really feel that if we don't get some time together we shall start to lose what has been a very long friendship.'[14] She could not see that Jill had never really got over Jane's betrayal with Cecil, and had no particular desire for more of her company.

Jane had met Bill and Shirley Letwin at Lemmons, and they were one of the few couples who continued to ask her to dinner on her own. They had her for Christmas in her first year in Delancey Street, and the following year they came to her. It was through the Letwins that Jane met the writer Sybille Bedford, who evidently took a shine to her.

'She used to say me, "I think we could have a very lovely time, because I do know how to love," said with great conviction.' And although she had very little money, she loved good food and wine. 'She started . . . asking me out to dinner, and I didn't realise about her financial circumstances at all. She was tremendously generous. We went to several restaurants in the King's Road, and to Chez Moi in Addison Avenue. They were good restaurants and she ordered quite expensive wine . . . I just thought, this is what she does.'[15]

Jane invited her to dinner at Delancey Street, where she entertained regularly. One dinner included Pat Kavanagh and Julian Barnes,
who had held their wedding reception at Gardnor House in 1979,
before Jane left Kingsley; Martin Amis and his girlfriend Antonia
Phillips, who were married the following year; Jenner Roth and her
husband, Terry Cooper; Laurie Lee; Liz and Wayland Young; as well
as Monkey and Ursula. But although Jane was always a generous hostess who went to a huge amount of trouble for her guests, she did
expect to be paid for in restaurants: Sybille Bedford was a case in
point – but just because someone asks you out to dinner and chooses
the wine doesn't mean you can't share the bill.

Another friend who found this out was Fay Maschler, whose
marriage to Tom was in its final stages. Jane was very sympathetic.
They spent whole evenings talking about what shits men were; but
they also threw several informal supper parties together, to which
they invited as many single men as they could find and enough
women not to make it look obvious. Jane was warm and gregarious,
she knew a lot of people and seemed enviably well travelled. Fay was
also impressed by her knowledge of music, theatre and literature – but
she did have her blind spots. Fay was and still is the *Evening Standard*'s
restaurant critic, and she often invited Jane to dinner when she was
reviewing. But they also went out to restaurants on occasions when
Fay was off duty, and Jane always expected her to pick up the bill.

Fay was also amused by the fact that although she was younger than
Jane's daughter Nicola, Jane always behaved as though they were the
same age – and even assumed they were the same shape. Jane had put
on a good deal of weight since leaving Kingsley: she had always loved
her food, and comfort eating was irresistible. At one point she even
visited a plastic surgeon, Philip Lebon, to see whether he might be
able to give her a tummy tuck but she never pursued the matter. She
discovered a shop called Forgotten Women which started at size
eighteen, and suggested that Fay might like to see what they had.
She also looked out 'shroud-like cardigans for me, out of mail
order catalogues'.[16]

Jane also had an idea that she would like to live in a big house with
some female friends; and when Fay thought about buying a house in
Notting Hill, she seized on the idea and said she would like to move
in too. Fay was told to make sure there was a big garden, and the

house should be spacious enough so that she could have the whole of the ground floor – 'because of course I shall need to get in and out of the garden'. The Notting Hill idea was quietly dropped.

Rosie Plush had accompanied Jane all the way through her marriage to Kingsley, and done much to console her when it was over. But she was now almost fifteen years old, and very ill. In early 1984 Jane forced herself to have Rosie put down; and as the vet gave her a lethal injection, Jane held the dog in her arms until she had stopped breathing. One of the letters of condolence came from the novelist Brigid Brophy, with whom she had campaigned for Public Lending Right a year or two before. 'Be assured you did the right thing at the right time in the right way . . . Try, however, to oblige yourself to attend to the fact that you gave her a sweet life, sweetened by your friendship with her, which was always so touching for a third party like me to observe . . . Thank you for letting me know.'[17]

Jane doubted whether she could ever replace Rosie Plush. Her expectations of dogs were as high as her expectations of people, but the dogs never let her down so it was worth trying again. After a suitable period of mourning she bought another King Charles spaniel, Darcy, who was black with ginger eyebrows. Jane described Darcy as a great beauty, who was very conscious of her looks and dignity; and she proved as loyal and true a friend as Rosie.

That spring Jane went on a British Council lecturing tour to Turkey with Faith Pullin, with whom she shared a great admiration for the novels of Elizabeth Taylor. They visited Ankara and Izmir, where Jane gave a talk called 'What are Novels For? The Uses of the Novel'; and on 8 April, in Istanbul, she took the opportunity to meet the man who had taken a film option on *Getting It Right* – the American director Randal Kleiser. Kleiser was a seasoned director whose most celebrated film was the musical *Grease* (1978), starring John Travolta. He was very enthusiastic about the book, and wanted Jane to write the screenplay. That summer he stopped in London and they discussed it further; he wanted to shoot the film in England, and would be in touch once he had found a producer.

At the same time, Jane had been contacted by a young film producer called Jonathan Cavendish (who went on to make the *Bridget Jones* films, among many others). Cavendish had been much inspired by

The Irish RM series for Channel 4, which was based on *Some Experiences of an Irish RM*, written at the turn of the last century by two women who concealed their gender by calling themselves E.O. Somerville and Martin Ross. It recounted the fictional experiences of a retired English army officer who becomes a Resident Magistrate in the west of Ireland.

Jonathan Clowes put Cavendish in touch with Jane, and he asked whether she would be willing to write the script. She was, and when she had done a preliminary treatment they went to Ireland with the director, Peter Sykes, to visit Edith Somerville's home village of Castletownshend, near Skibbereen in the far south-west of County Cork. This was Jane's first time in Ireland. She was delighted by the village on its steep slope, at the top of which was Drishane, where Edith Somerville had lived. However, further research showed that the lives of Somerville and Ross didn't generate enough drama to sustain a film; so Jane wrote a script loosely based on their relationship, called *The Attachment*.

The film was never made – the last £250,000 of the money eluded them; but Jane and Jonathan Cavendish, and his wife Lesley whom he married a year or so later, became friends and remained so. He remembered going to see her for the first time at Delancey Street: she was then in her early sixties, he in his mid-twenties. Cavendish was impressed by her thick mane of hair and the strength of her face; yet despite the age difference, 'I found myself having to lead the conversation – she seemed very raw and uncertain.' She began inviting him to dinner parties, and at one point, asked whether he would like to accompany her to a party in Oxford. Jonathan mentioned this to his mother, and was very amused when she warned him that tongues would start wagging: 'Jane has a reputation, you know.'[18]

Yet Jane was a very different person from when that reputation was forged. No man would be interested in an old bolter, she told herself, and this seemed to be turning into a self-fulfilling prophecy. Once he knew her better, Jonathan Cavendish told her that she was still a very attractive woman and there was no reason why she should not find another man, but her desolate expression was not helping: 'You must put the lights on,' he said, 'try to flirt a little!' But Jane didn't know how. 'Teach me how to flirt,' she said – but it was too late to start. Jane's literary agent, Ann Clowes, was struck by the difference between her and Doris Lessing whom she also represented. Doris was a radical who looked the world in the face, and met it head-on; she was happy to lead a single life, and so she engaged with people easily, men and women alike. Jane's approach was more complicated. For much of her life she had only to stand in a room, and men would be drawn towards her like flies to honey. Those days were long gone; but she could make an effort and be very funny and entertaining, could almost flirt – especially with a good-looking man who was being equally engaging.

Through Selina Hastings, Jane had met Tony Scotland, who had worked in television and radio and was then a freelance writer; and his partner, the musician Julian Berkeley. The first evening they met, Tony and Jane hit it off at once: 'we were both really working at it,' as he put it; and at the end of dinner, Tony and Julian gave her a lift home. They waited till she had let herself in; and as she did so she glanced back at Tony: 'It was an incredibly tragic look, as if I had *abandoned* her and those huge eyes were saying, "Is this really goodbye?"'[19]

Soon after she left Kingsley, Jane told John Julius Norwich that the saddest thing was feeling that 'I'll never lie in a man's arms again.'[20] She missed human contact to such a degree that she took to having a massage once a fortnight. A masseuse would come to the house, and while she was there Jane was not to be disturbed, and the telephone was taken off the hook. Her then lodger remarked that she was very serious about her massages, to which Jane replied, 'You must realise how important they are to me: it's the only time now that anyone touches my body.'[21]

In the autumn of 1984 Jane was asked to be one of the judges of the Society of West End Theatres Awards, which were about to be renamed the Oliviers. She went to over twenty plays that season, which provided her with many opportunities for an evening à deux – but no lasting relationship emerged. Jane took Jonathan Cavendish to the awards dinner, where the Best New Play went to Michael Frayn for *Benefactors*.

To everyone's astonishment the Amis–Kilmarnock ménage was still in one piece, and they began looking for a larger house. Jane had hoped that once Kingsley 'felt safe with his household arrangement with

Hilly, we might become friends'.[22] Given what he said about her in interviews following the split, it is amazing that she harboured such illusions at all. Any lingering hopes in that direction were extinguished by Kingsley's first novel since the divorce, *Stanley and the Women*. This can be read not so much as a message in a bottle, as a sustained howl of rage against Jane: not only through the characters of Stanley's ex, Nowell Hutchinson and his current wife, Susan Duke, but through womankind in general. And yet what drives the plot forward is not what women do, but what happens when an almost-adult child goes mad. Kingsley was always a semi-detached parent, but he did care for the chaotic Sally; and this novel is also about the point when a child can no longer be reached, when parents become powerless and professionals take over.

Hilly, Ali, their son Jamie and Kingsley moved to 194 Regents Park Road in 1985. Julian Barnes felt that Kingsley's arrangement with the Kilmarnocks meant that

> his whims were much more indulged. He had Hilly to run after him, he had Lord Kilmarnock . . . I remember once going to the pub, and then we settled in to Kingsley's sitting room, and Ali came in with a tray and gave us our supper . . . and just before the door closed Kingsley very deliberately said, 'Not bad for a boy from Norbury, eh, to have his supper brought to him by a *peer of the realm*!' When the door was shut I asked him, 'Are you turning Ali into a Monkey figure?' In other words, are you making him the butt of your jokes; and he looked rather taken aback . . . I once asked Hilly how she was doing and she replied, 'Oh not bad, dear! Down to about thirty tranks [tranquillizers] a day!'[23]

Jane spent much of 1985 and 1986 on the script of *Getting It Right*. She enjoyed working with Randal Kleiser, with whom she went to stay in New York and Los Angeles; but she hated the first producer, Charles Evans, who she felt did not treat her with the importance she deserved. 'We had meetings in his office about the script and then were put into a fusty little room with no air conditioning for hours to do our homework, with a plate of wizened sandwiches for lunch.' Jane's idea of lunch was a proper meal, preferably in a restaurant – not a sandwich. 'He treated me like an impoverished secretary who, at any minute, he might sack. He didn't last long.'²⁴ The next was much nicer, but left to run Disneyland in Paris; and the third, Jonathan Krane, saw the picture through. The film, which appeared in 1989, had an impressive cast: Lynn Redgrave in a Ziggy Stardust wig played Joan, and Helena Bonham Carter was Minerva. Peter Cooke appeared as Mr Adrian and John Gielgud played Minerva's father; but he lacked the coarseness required to portray a hard-nosed seat-belt salesman with social ambitions.

Jane had wanted the part of Gavin to go to Daniel Day-Lewis, who in 1985 had two film successes: *My Beautiful Laundrette*, and *A Room with a View*. Knowing Jane's connection with the family, Randal Kleiser said that asking Daniel would be seen as nepotism.²⁵ The part went instead to Jesse Birdsall, who did not make quite enough effort to disguise either his good looks or his physical confidence. Randal assured her that the film had acquired cult status in America (the whole film can be seen on YouTube, which might be an indication), but Jane felt that it had not done well in England because 'anything extreme in the way of behaviour was cut out. Americans could not take more than a pastel degree of realism then.'²⁶ She was perhaps unaware of films such as *Platoon*, *The Shining* and *Rambo*, all of which celebrate 'extreme behaviour' of one sort or another; but it was not only British audiences who were disappointed by the film's lack of edge. The *New York Times* complained that its tone was 'mannerly and polite, when it might more profitably be rude'.²⁷

In 1986 Kingsley Amis won the Booker Prize for *The Old Devils*, while Jane and Fay Maschler joined forces to write a cookbook. They felt that although many cookbooks will suggest menus for big events such as the Golden Wedding or the Hunt Breakfast, theirs would give the reader ideas for those specific social scenarios that home cooks are faced with. They included menus for a Ladies' Lunch, an After-Theatre Supper and a Funeral Tea; but they also came to the rescue if you were contemplating Weekend Entertaining, Invalid Cooking, or a Budget Dinner; and what you might feed Dull People, Greedy People or the Abandoned Man. There was even a section on the most daunting scenario imaginable: preparing a meal for a celebrated cook; that chapter was entitled, Jane Grigson to Dinner.

It was a clever idea for a cookbook, and being more than just recipes meant that the book looked as happy on a bedside table as it did in the kitchen. They had great fun inventing the scenarios, and their very different styles of cooking led to a fine variety of recipes. Jane had learned to cook at Seer Green just before the war, and her cooking was very much of its time: there was a lot of butter, cream, game and hard work. Fay's recipes tended to be simpler, with a greater emphasis on vegetables. Both were inspired by cooks like Madhur Jaffrey and Claudia Roden, who were bringing Indian and Middle Eastern food into the mainstream. As for Jane, who had spent so many years on the thankless task of cooking for Kingsley, it was a liberation to make whatever she wanted, however authentic and foreign. As Fay observed, 'cooking for him must have been a torment'.[28]

To publicize the book, they decided to face their own challenge and have Jane Grigson to dinner – an event that was to provide a large colour feature in *Homes & Gardens* magazine. Jane Grigson was accompanied by the novelist Paul Bailey, who had been a friend since Jane did the Arts Council tour with him and Penelope Lively; and the other guests were a couple she had recently met with Paul and Marigold Johnson: the historian Roy Foster, and his wife Aisling, a novelist and a formidably good cook.

The guests had been invited for eight; but at seven fifteen Jane rang the Fosters, sounding distinctly on edge. She wanted them to come at once, so they hurried round to Delancey Street to find Jane 'in a terrible mood'. The photographers had already been there for some time, so the dishes were wilting even before the guests had arrived. There were Greek mezze of various sorts, a roasted *poulet de Bresse* with butter and herbs eased under the skin, and home-made orange and raspberry jellies which were melting under the hot lights.

Jane thought the photographers would leave once the guests arrived; but they stayed on to photograph the diners and the meal itself. 'Why can't they just go!' she hissed. Roy Foster described how everyone drank too much out of nerves while 'Jane Grigson sat through it all like a Buddha, saying almost nothing; so when Jane [Howard] was saying all the foodie things like how she had bought the chicken specially from the butcher in Mount Street, and how one should always loosen the skin and stuff butter underneath, Jane Grigson just smiled serenely.'[29]

That October Jane spent a weekend in Oxford with a young English don called Fram Dinshaw, and his wife, the novelist Candia McWilliam. It was through them that she met Jonathan Burnham. He is now the Senior Vice-President and Publisher of HarperCollins in the US, but in 1987 he had just graduated from Oxford. He was about to move to London to take up a job with Chatto & Windus, and needed somewhere to live.

It was perfect timing. Since Mrs Uniacke's retirement a year or so ago, Jane had been renting out her basement flat and her last lodger had just left. Jonathan Burnham came to see it in January but it was more than he could afford, so she showed him the large top-floor room, which had a bathroom but no kitchen. He moved in, but the arrangement meant they would have to share a kitchen and a front door.

'At first we weren't supposed to cross each other's flight paths,' he remembered, 'but we ended up sharing, and sometimes cooking together.' To begin with, all went well. They knew many of the same people, and since he worked in publishing there was always plenty of book talk, and plenty of gossip. There was also music.

'We had a piano in Delancey Street that was actually winched up in front of the house and dropped off on my floor . . . Jane was very insistent that there be a piano, and since I played quite seriously she encouraged it. I remember playing in the evenings, with the sound presumably filtering down . . . I think she liked the sense of music in a house as part of its fabric.' Jane never played the piano herself, but she listened to a lot of music at that time, 'especially Mozart Piano Concertos, and she particularly loved Scarlatti'.[30] There were also long conversations in her sitting room, when she proved herself a very good listener and a wise friend, who took his emotional ups and downs as seriously as she took her own.

At the same time, a curious tension began to build.

She could exert a tacit emotional pressure that was very unnerving. If she asked what I was doing that evening and I said I was going out, she'd put on a face like a Greek tragic mask and say, 'Oh . . . I suppose I'll be alone again.' She could not bear being alone; and although the break from Kingsley had happened years before, she acted as though the wounds were very, very raw and she was still recovering from this massive emotional trauma.[31]

Another source of great unhappiness was the way she seemed to have been dropped by literary London. Jonathan was invited to any number of publishing parties, 'and she was always very keen to know who was there ... She had a big complex about her position as a writer, and was bitterly hurt that Margaret Drabble didn't include her in her edition of *The Oxford Companion to English Literature.*' Jonathan felt she deserved better, and believed it was her upper-middle-classness that kept her out of the literary scene: 'She never made a secret of the fact that she admired Mrs Thatcher.'

She tried to spend as few evenings alone as possible. As well as old friends like Dosia Verney, Nina Milkina, Liz and Wayland Young and Geraint and Winnie Jones, she was good at making new friends from a younger generation. Among them were the biographer Selina Hastings, daughter of Jack and Margaret Huntingdon; her goddaughter Alexandra St Aubyn, known as Minky; and Patricia and Mark Wyndham, whom she met at the Midhurst Book Fair they used to organize in aid of cancer research.

She valued her friends and put a lot of effort into keeping in touch – particularly if they were ill or in trouble: as Selina Hastings put it, 'Jane was a wonderful foul-weather friend.'[32] When Anne Norwich's divorce from John Julius came through, Jane made a point of coming to comfort her. 'She was not only a wonderful shoulder to cry on, she was full of practical advice: for example, when you go back to the house to collect furniture, remember to take things like towels and blankets too.'[33]

When Tanya Hobson became ill with cancer in the summer of 1987, Jane often went down to Hampshire to cook and keep her company. She died the following year, and soon afterwards Tanya's daughter Charlotte came to see Jane, who was her godmother. Charlotte was then seventeen and had just lost her mother – but Jane was the one who burst into tears.

Jane was particularly anxious about Sargy. His marriage to Frances was very happy, and they now had three children; but in 1979 both his retinas had detached. He lost all use of his right eye; and despite twelve operations on the left eye, his sight was slowly fading. Nicola's husband Elliott Starks was one of his students at the Camden Arts Centre, and in 1987 Elliott presented Sargy with his first white stick: both he and Jane felt he could no longer do without one. 'It was done with the utmost tact,' wrote Sargy, 'and I knew they were right. Later it struck me as wonderfully ridiculous and funny that I was turning up to teach a painting class with a white stick.'[34] Yet while Sargy could make a joke of it, there is no greater catastrophe for a painter. He would come round and have tea with Jane, in between the classes he still taught at the Camden Arts Centre. They were heart-breaking teas. Jane remembered him saying that he wished he were blind already, rather than have to go through the anguish of waiting for it to happen.

In the summer of 1989 Jane finished the first volume of the Cazalet Chronicle, *The Light Years*. It had had a very long and difficult gestation, for Jane had never written about her family before; and this book had to set the foundations for (as she then thought) two more Cazalet novels. Sybille Bedford gave her some much needed support in the early stages.

'At one point – mutually and miserably engaged upon the slow torture of producing novels, we swapped manuscripts* because we discovered that we shared the horrible anxiety that what we were engaged upon writing was probably *no good* at all.' Sybille, said Jane, encouraged her 'with the utmost generosity (she is one of the most *entirely* generous people I have ever met – all the time, in every imaginable way).' The novel Sybille had been struggling with was *Jigsaw*. 'I did my best to persuade her how good it was . . . but Sybille was not so easily convinced.'[35]

When Jane had finished *The Light Years*, she asked Jonathan Burnham to read it through and edit it, which he did – but there was almost nothing to do. Perhaps it was Sybille's influence, but all he picked up was a small point of continuity. 'She was very disappointed: "*Surely* there must be something else?" but there wasn't.' He was amazed how she had plotted it all out in her head: 'She was not the sort of writer who went in for huge wall charts – just small slips of paper, on which she had the chronologies of her various characters.'[36]

The projected three volumes of the Cazalets had been bought by Fanny Blake at Macmillan, who had edited some of Jane's novels in

---

* 'Swapping manuscripts' is rather misleading: what they actually did was read their manuscripts to each other over the telephone.

paperback at Penguin. When she took delivery of the typescript, her reaction was the same as Burnham's: 'It was utterly engrossing, and I couldn't find *anything* that needed changing. I wanted to edit it, wanted to look as though I was doing my job – but there was nothing to do.'[37]

The whole extended family of Howards, and the houses they lived in in London and Sussex, are the springboard for the Cazalet Chronicle; and the main purpose of *The Light Years* is to introduce them and set the plot lines. Jane's grandparents, Alexander and Frances Howard, are almost unchanged. In the novels he is William Cazalet, head of the family timber business and known as 'the Brig', just as he was in real life; while her grandmother, known as 'the Witchy', becomes 'the Duchy'. The Howard grandparents had three sons and a daughter, as do Jane's Cazalets. Their daughter Ruth becomes Rachel Cazalet: like Ruth she never married, but sustained a lasting relationship with a woman.

The three sons marry, to make three Cazalet couples: Hugh and Sybil, Edward and Villy, Rupert and Zoe. Hugh and Sybil have such a polite and affectionate marriage that they cannot bear to cause each other a moment's discomfort, and so only tell the other what they think he or she would like to hear. Sybil spends the summer in a state of advanced pregnancy – she is carrying twins, but only one will survive.

While Hugh and Sybil and Rupert and Zoe are mainly fictional, Edward and Villy (short for Viola) are the only couple to be closely modelled on real people: Jane's parents, David and Kit Howard. She treats them with sympathy and understanding. Villy can't help not liking sex any more than the charming Edward can resist other women. Nor can he see the damage he's doing. When Edward, like Jane's father, makes a lunge at his fifteen-year-old daughter Louise, he has no idea of the horror, shame and confusion he has inflicted on her.

Rupert is the youngest of the three brothers, and the only one not to work in the family timber business: he wants to be a painter, but works as a schoolmaster. His first wife has died before the novel opens and his new wife, Zoe, is a very young and selfish beauty who resents her stepchildren, Clary and Neville. When a flirtation with her mother's doctor ends in rape, Zoe is appalled to find herself pregnant. All the other Cazalet wives rejoice, but Zoe sinks into deep depression – she loves Rupert, but knows the child is not his. Her miscarriage brings profound relief, and from then on she begins to grow up.

The first child of all three couples is a girl: the eldest, Louise, is the daughter of Edward and Villy; Polly is Hugh and Sybil's; and Clary is Rupert's. All three girls have other brothers and sisters, and their shifting alliances and quarrels take up much of the book; but Louise, Polly and Clary are the most important figures because, as Jane admitted, they are facets of herself. Over the course of the Chronicle, Louise's life mirrors Jane's: she goes to acting school, marries a glamorous older man, has a child too young, has affairs, becomes used by the world. Polly, both kind and pretty, is much more likely to find happiness. Louise and Polly are the figures of experience and innocence, but to these she has added one more avatar: Clary, who from a very young age knows that her task is to become a writer.

In the bleak times after leaving Kingsley, Jane drew great comfort from writing *The Light Years*. She immersed herself in the world of a long adolescence that, for all its miseries (lack of maternal love, bullying at school, her father's advances) had been very intensely lived. Her original idea was that the Cazalet trilogy would examine how domestic life in England was changed by the war, but this happens anyway without analysis as the story moves forward. Jane is far more interested in the fabric of married life, in the everyday details of clothes, food and the running of a pre-war household. She is also preoccupied by the way children interact with each other and with adults, and she develops this using a child's acute perception. There are an awful lot of Cazalets to take in – eighteen on the family tree – as well as a smattering of other relatives; but because the novel is so well constructed, Jane can take her time unfolding all these interconnected stories.

In the summer of 1989 Peter Scott died. Jane had not seen him for many years, but they had remained on good terms and she was very touched that he left her something in his will – not a huge amount, but enough to buy a beautiful cashmere rug. She spent that Christmas with Nicola, Elliott and Ben in Gloucestershire, and then returned to Delancey Street. She had never really liked the house, and as the winter dragged on, she began to realize that there was less and less to hold her there. Even the garden depressed her.

Part of the problem was that her road had become a one-way street, and parking became much harder. When she returned late after an evening out she would have to park a long way from the house. The walk home in the dark made her nervous. And for someone who depended so much on her friends, there were other unwelcome changes. Dosia and Andrew Verney left London for Pewsey in Wiltshire, and Sargy and Frances were also moving. British Rail were thinking of running the Channel Tunnel rail link through their garden in Lyndhurst Grove, Peckham, and were willing to pay well over the asking price for it. Jonathan Clowes became ill, and he and Ann decided to move to Villefranche in the south of France in April 1990. They reduced their client list and kept a London office; but they would not be able to return to England for a year, and Jane knew she would miss them desperately. London suddenly looked drained.

The shortcomings of her tiny garden at Delancey Street were thrown into relief while she worked on an anthology of gardening. One of the first passages in the book is by the philosopher and scientist Francis Bacon, describing his ideal garden, which he felt needed about thirty acres. She was fascinated by the magical and medicinal uses that plants were put to, and delighted by non-gardeners' views of gardening. She included Dr Johnson mocking Pope's grotto, Pope satirizing topiarists and Addison on tulip enthusiasts. But she had great respect for gardeners too, and not just the Vita Sackville-Wests and Gertrude Jekylls. She applauded the energetic optimism of Elizabeth von Arnim, a great example of the just-do-it school of horticulture.

Jane put Delancey Street on the market in the spring of 1990 and began house-hunting. She was looking for a spacious flat with a big garden, but that combination was rare in north London. She found a large house in Dartmouth Park with a quarter of an acre of derelict ground; it could have been made into three flats, and she found two friends who were interested. Together they offered the asking price, which was accepted; but after having had it expensively surveyed they were gazumped. It was very frustrating, particularly since she had now accepted an offer for Delancey Street and would have to pack up the house in July, just as *The Light Years* was being published. The furniture went into storage, and until she found a house she would stay with Monkey in Foxham Road. Since the last days at Gardnor House, when they had both been so miserable, their relationship had steadily improved, and Monkey was happy to be able to provide Jane with a roof after all the years he had lived with her.

He was also able to provide some much needed support when the reviews appeared on Sunday, 22 July. 'Golly! Jolly Dull' was the title of Nicci Gerrard's review in the *Observer*. However, she did say that 'buried beneath the comforting suet of detail are kernels of another, more vital story: the secret lies by which domestic peace is maintained; the self-sacrifice that props up a marriage; the shadow of war falling across adolescents, darkening their emerging sexuality. Perhaps these quick, bitter hints will flavour the next volume.'[38]

D.J. Taylor in the *Sunday Times* was unimpressed, and points out that Jane's 'occasional attempts to affect the thought processes of the lower orders are a touch patronising'.[39] There is some truth in that last charge, despite Jane's bohemian credentials. She had had affairs and abortions, she was neither racist nor homophobic, and in marrying Kingsley she had married out of her class. And yet Jane seemed unable to shake off a certain attitude, probably absorbed when she was taught How to Handle Servants as part of the domestic science course at Seer Green before the war. She tries hard to present the Cazalets' cook, maids and chauffeur as real people with real concerns, but never quite succeeds. They all say 'ever so' too often, a shilling is always a bob, they know their place and they talk in proverbs and clichés:

> 'What did I tell you, Mrs Cripps? There's many a slip between cup and lip.'
>
> 'It just shows you never can tell,' she agreed. She was rolling thin strips of bacon round blanched prunes for angels on horseback after the pheasant. 'Would you fancy another drop scone, Mr Tonbridge?'[40]

Jonathan Burnham had also noticed this 'us and them' divide in the way Jane was with Mrs Uniacke, who came to see her for tea from time to time after her retirement. Jane saw Mrs Uniacke as a great friend and ally, but she spoke to her with that studied politeness that used to so annoy Kingsley, and talked about her as though she were part of another species. After one visit, Jane remarked that 'She always wears her funny little hat when she comes.' And Jonathan couldn't help saying, 'She *is* a real person, you know.' I asked him if, when he was editing *The Light Years*, he had mentioned the us–and–them dimension to Jane. He replied that he had not: it was so ingrained in the book that it would have been almost impossible to eradicate, and she probably would not have seen why she should: after all, that's the way it was in the late 1930s.

After the dismissive reviews in the Sunday papers, Jane O'Grady's in the *Times Literary Supplement* on 27 July was healing balm. She wrote that 'the need for realism, and for enough characters to develop or die in the next three or four volumes of the saga, inevitably results in an overcharged canvas'; but the three main marriages were 'excellently drawn', and like many people – the book went to number nine in the *Sunday Times* bestseller list – she found *The Light Years* 'enjoyable and engrossing'.[41]

Yet while the Cazalet servants remained to a certain extent formulaic, Jane is an acute observer of those who, in the eyes of the world, might be seen as of little consequence: secretaries and clerks who have been badly treated by life, and can't afford to let the wounds show. One of the most poignant characters in the Cazalets is that of Villy's old governess, Miss Milliment, whom Villy brings out of an impoverished retirement to teach Louise and Polly. Miss Milliment is a portrait of Miss Cobham, Jane's own governess. In the social hierarchy, Miss Milliment – just like Jane Eyre, ninety years before – inhabits a very uncomfortable position. She is not a servant, since her father was a vicar and she is educated; but she is invited out of the schoolroom for lunch with the family only on Fridays. (Villy's mother Lady Rydal thinks it quite unnecessary to give her a glass of sherry before the meal, although Villy – who is very kind to Miss Milliment – always does.)

Miss Milliment is ugly, old and fat, her only home a cheerless room in a south London boarding house. She has nothing to look forward to but loneliness and penury, yet she remains resolutely cheerful and will not allow herself any self-pity.

She is invited to join the family towards the end of the summer holidays of 1938, by which time war looks increasingly likely. But

ELIZABETH JANE HOWARD

if this appalling prospect is averted, Miss Milliment makes herself a
promise. She will let go of all she has left of the one man who ever
loved her: a lock of hair and a few letters, written before he died fight-
ing on the Western Front. As the family celebrates the fragile peace
brokered by Chamberlain with the Munich Agreement, Miss Milliment
walks into the woods and buries her most treasured possessions. It is
one of the saddest and most beautiful passages that Jane ever wrote.

19

The Final Disillusion

Writing about her country childhood through the prism of
the Cazalets almost certainly contributed to Jane's desire to
escape London; although she had no particular reason to consider
settling in East Anglia until one presented itself. Sargy and Frances
Mann had moved to the market town of Bungay, Suffolk, in May
1990. They now had four children, of whom the youngest was seven
months old. Sargy was in his early fifties and almost blind, while
Frances's life was dominated by cooking, laundry and the demands of
a baby. Neither of them had any intention of giving up painting.

The River Waveney flowed beside their garden and the broad
meadow beyond, with alders overhanging the river. It was a beautiful
spot: Sargy took over and enlarged the studio that stood close to the
water, and in early September they invited Jane's daughter Nicola and
her husband Elliott to come and spend the weekend.

Nicola and Elliott were at that time thinking of moving from
Gloucestershire; and as the house next door to the Manns' was on the
market, they thought they'd have a look at it. Bridge House was set
well back from the road, on its own driveway, while the garden at the
back looked on to the same riverside meadow. It was a little too big
for Nicola, but she thought it was worth mentioning to Jane; and Jane
came up to see it at the end of the month with her god-daughter
Minky St Aubyn, whom she thought had a good eye for houses.
They were met at Diss by Frances, who drove them the sixteen miles
to Bungay.

Jane loved the place on sight, and Minky felt the same. The house,
apparently dating from 1688, was mainly mid-eighteenth century. It
still had its lovely windows and shutters, pretty fireplaces, and the
original doors and door furniture. A bow window had been added on
to the sitting room in 1840, but nothing had been spoilt. Jane did not

know then that the property included the large meadow that ran beside the river, and a third of the island that lay in midstream.

She put in an offer straight away, but back in London she was assailed by a flurry of second thoughts. She consulted Jenner, and together they went to Bungay in October to see the house again. As Jane showed her round her face was alight with excitement, and Jenner suddenly realized how important the country was to her friend and how much she had missed it. 'Of course she was delighted to be next to Sargy and Fran, but she was enchanted by the garden and the meadow and the island. She knew at a glance what she wanted to do to the house, and it became a great project – Jane loved a project.'[1] It was also the ideal combination of town and country. Jane could stroll out into the garden and the meadow, and hear nothing but the river and the birds; while a brief walk up Bridge Street took her straight into the town's market square, with its shops, pubs and the graceful domed Buttercross.

She bought the house, but she could not take vacant possession until mid-December. She was grateful to Monkey for putting her up in Foxham Road, but it was rather cramped. Jane had to sleep in the sitting room and had little more than a dress rail for her clothes. There was no place to work, but Jenner and Terry lent her a room in their house which she turned into a temporary study; and here she continued writing the next volume of the Cazalets, called *Marking Time*.

'I felt then as though I were marking time until an unknown and new life began. Most days I dreaded it – dreaded being definitively lonely, cut off from so many of my friends.'[2] Another severance from her old life came with one last and completely unexpected meeting with Kingsley.

It took place at the Savile Club, at a party to launch a new Macmillan edition of William Cooper's *Scenes from Provincial Life*. Nick McDowell, who was working in the publicity department, asked the author, whose real name was Harry Hoff, whether he was sure about inviting both Kingsley and Jane. Harry Hoff said it would be fine so Nick, who was new to literary London, left it at that. On the evening of the party Nick and Jane were standing at the top of the Savile Club stairs as Kingsley made his entrance, wearing bedroom slippers. 'Jane went white, she was rooted to the spot; and Kingsley said, "Hello, love," and passed on. Poor Jane was terribly upset.'[3]

★

That September she visited New York and Boston, supposedly to promote *The Light Years*; but beyond giving her a good dinner, she found that her publishers had done little else. This was not unusual: in-house publicity only swings into action for serious bestsellers, otherwise authors in the United States are expected to make their own promotional arrangements. But coming on top of the lukewarm reception the book had received in England, Jane felt the lack of transatlantic interest more keenly than she should have done.

Luckily, she was too excited about the new house to brood for long. On 12 December, with Minky's help, Jane moved to Bridge House. They drove in separate cars, laden with her belongings; and the removal men came with the furniture in the early afternoon. Minky stayed that night, but she had to leave the next day. The second night would be the first that Jane spent alone at Bridge House, with only Darcy for company. Not long after they had turned in Darcy was violently sick, and evidently needed to go outside too. Jane had to find her way downstairs in the dark, fumbling for light switches – but the house felt friendly and she was not afraid: it was a good sign.

The joy of having a proper garden again, and a meadow, made up for the wrench of moving away from so many friends; and now she had an opportunity to try out some of the ideas that had arisen in the course of compiling *Green Shades: An Anthology of Plants, Gardens and Gardeners*, which came out in 1991. Yet she had perhaps pinned too many hopes on the proximity of Sargy and Frances. She built a fantasy based on a rose-tinted vision of Lemmons where, she told herself, everyone had been happy. They would all live, eat and entertain together, and separate only to work – it would be like an artists' colony. It never occurred to her that Sargy and Frances, still raising their children and absorbed in their own life and concerns, might not share her dream.

In her books, she can pinpoint the exact moment when someone starts to deceive themselves. Take this example from the second Cazalet volume, which she was working on at the time. A pregnant girl called Angela, who has been heartlessly dumped by her married lover, is walking across Kensington Gardens for one final meeting with him:

In spite of everything that had happened, she could not help feeling excited and happy at the prospect of meeting him, and during this walk she moved from being afraid – from dreading – what he might be going to say to her, to wondering what he might say, and eventually to *imagining* what he might say which, of course, became what she wanted to hear. I shall remember this day all my life, she thought, and, more dramatically, I am walking towards my fate.[4]

Jane knew how easily a fantasy can distort reality, and yet she could not see herself doing it. The Manns did all they could to make her welcome and help her settle in. They had her round regularly to lunch and dinner, introduced her to their friends, and very much enjoyed her company, but at the same time they made it clear that they needed their privacy. Jane could have spared herself several misunderstandings and the occasional confrontation had she not been so easily carried away by her imagination.

There was an enormous amount of work to be done to the house. A proper staircase had to go in – previously there had only been a spiral one – as well as new bathrooms and a kitchen. There was no dining room, so Jane decided she would build a sunny conservatory which would link the kitchen and the garden. She planned on doing a lot of weekend entertaining, so it was very important that the house should be not only pretty but extremely comfortable so people would want to come again. Luckily, she had some money – about £100,000, which was the difference between the purchase of Bridge House and what she had made on the sale of Delancey Street – but the builders would not be able to start till March.

That Christmas, the first at Bridge House, Monkey arrived ahead of the other house-guests. They sat in the sitting room which was painted dark green, until Monkey suddenly sprang to his feet saying he couldn't stand the gloom any longer. He went out and bought an industrial tub of white paint and some brushes, and over the next few hours they painted two big rooms and a long corridor. On Christmas Day they all went round for drinks and presents with Sargy and Frances – the start of a happy tradition, only broken in the last two months of Jane's life when the Manns went round to her.

When the builders arrived early that spring, Jane was obliged to move out, and stayed with friends. On her return in early April she found that the builders had done almost nothing and she still had no bedroom and no kitchen; so while she could work at home, she took her meals with the Manns and slept at their house. It is ironic that although Jane had a heartfelt understanding of a child's perspective in her books, she was unaware of just how much work four children can be. 'It was a long two weeks,' admitted Frances. 'I was always behind with everything that had to be done, and it was rather depressing hearing Jane at breakfast saying, "What's for dinner?" when I hadn't even thought about lunch . . . I once made the mistake of saying "cauliflower cheese", and she looked horrified.'[5]

Things were more or less straight by the summer; and as Macmillan had decided that they were going to publish *Marking Time* in November, the text had to be ready by August. Fanny Blake had left Macmillan to go back to Penguin, and Jane's new editor was Jane Wood. She described how they worked together:

> The thing about Jane is that she plots her novels very well, in her head. But she needs constant reassurance, and she is easily set back or discouraged. Some authors like to get as far as a first draft before letting any fresh eyes on the work, but not her . . . I used to go and spend the weekend and we would talk the next chapters through; and by the time I came again she would have another fifty pages for me to look at.[6]

Wood was particularly worried by the first chapter, in which most of the adult Cazalets are gathered around the wireless waiting for the announcement of war on 3 September 1939. She thought, and Jane agreed, that it would be a good idea to have a short introductory passage outlining the characters and the story so far.

In *Marking Time*, the second volume of the Cazalet Chronicle, the war is beginning to bite and the 'bitter seeds' she had planted in *The Light Years* are starting to grow.

Hugh, the eldest Cazalet brother, is to run the business with his reluctantly retired father; he worries about his wife Sybil, who is not well. Sybil has cancer, but can't bring herself to tell Hugh because he'd be so worried. Edward finds a desk job with the RAF, guarding

Hendon aerodrome – giving him the perfect excuse to see more of his voluptuous mistress, Diana. He can't often come home at weekends, he says, and Villy thinks he is being overworked. The youngest brother, Rupert, joins the navy. His wife, Zoe, is pregnant again, but she is also being much nicer to her stepdaughter Clary.

Louise begins to suspect that her mother doesn't like her very much; but she's more interested in the good opinion of her new friend, Stella Rose. Stella invites her to spend the weekend with her cultivated, Viennese family; but the weekend is ruined for Louise when they go to the theatre, and she sees her father and Diana in the audience – it's clear that they are very intimate. After his assaults Louise has avoided her father; but when he follows her to her room one evening and tries to kiss her again, she confronts him with what she saw. Her father slinks away, abashed; and for the first time, Louise feels sorry for her mother.

As Isobel Armstrong wrote in the *Times Literary Supplement*: 'The adolescent girls live in a world of secrets, of information withheld from them . . . The novel's achievement is to show that concealment, in this dissolving social order, is as frightening and common as it was in the Victorian family.'[7] Polly in particular hates the way adults lie to children: she overhears worried talk about her mother, but they won't include her; and later on, as she sees her parents not talking for fear of upsetting each other, it seems to her an appalling waste of love.

Louise's acting experience closely follows Jane's; and like Jane's, it is curtailed partly by the war, and partly by a man. At a party in London she meets Michael Hadleigh, a successful portrait painter who has joined the navy. Michael is a thinly disguised Peter Scott, and his formidable mother, Lady Zinnia, wants him to marry and beget an heir as soon as possible.

New characters emerge from the gang of cousins. Polly strikes up a friendship with her cousin Christopher, the son of Villy's sister Jessica. Much of his misery is due to the fact that he has been bullied all his life by his unsuccessful father. Christopher becomes a conscientious objector; but he is so shunned by those he works with that he suffers a nervous breakdown, and is taken in by the Duchy. His sister Angela has removed herself from her parents more successfully. Dismissing their authority she moved to London, and falls hopelessly in love with a man in the BBC who secures her a job as a continuity announcer; but when he finds out she is pregnant, he drops her flat. (The passage quoted on p.282 describes the moment before their final meeting in Kensington Gardens.)

For Clary the war becomes horribly real when, in the summer of 1940, Rupert goes missing in France. As the months go by the rest of the family tacitly assume that he is dead, but Clary refuses to give up hope. The book ends in December 1941. Pearl Harbor forces Christopher to rethink his position as a pacifist, while for the family, there is at last news of Rupert: he is still alive and in hiding in France. The news is months old, but Clary's faith has been vindicated. Around the same time, Diana's husband Angus is killed in action – and she too is pregnant with a child she knows is Edward's: the time has come, she thinks, to separate him from Villy.

Abortion, betrayal, illness, incest, death, nervous breakdown, lesbian love – *Marking Time* is not short on drama; but it's the texture of the days that keeps it all remarkably grounded. Roy Foster wrote to tell Jane that *Marking Time* 'cast the same hypnotic spell as *The Light Years*, and that's saying something. The dazzling surface parade, the dark undertows beneath, really constitute an achievement.'[8]

There are moments when Jane's writing, as if hypnotized by the slow passage of time, drifts into neutral. The novelist Candia McWilliam described the Cazalets as a good example of 'the nourishing nature of a sort of automatic writing'.[9] Yet Jane's acute perception is never far away and, if the reader isn't careful, easy to miss. As her god-daughter Charlotte Hobson put it, 'Jane's brilliance was sort of hidden in plain sight.'[10] 'Whatever you think of its unputdownability quotient,' wrote Nicolette Jones in the *Sunday Times*, 'by the end . . . you feel as though you had lived through every minute of the period that *Marking Time* describes.'[11]

Once the house was as comfortable as she could make it, Jane launched into a heroic programme of weekend entertaining. Her very first guests were Selina Hastings and P.D. James, who had a house in Southwold, a town rich in little curio shops which Jane loved. Others included Fay Maschler, Wayland and Liz Young, Jonathan and Lesley Cavendish, Nell Dunn, Penelope Lively, Ronnie and Natasha Harwood, John Julius and Mollie Norwich, Jonathan Burnham, her editor Jane Wood, Mark and Patricia Wyndham, and Jonathan and

Ann Clowes, who were still based in France although their year in tax exile was now over. Another regular visitor was Drue Heinz, who always came with her grey parrot, Inigo. The Wyndhams had a narrow-boat, the *Colby*, and thanks to them Jane was able to renew her delight in canals and waterways.

Jane was supposed to be working on the third volume of the Cazalets, *Confusion*; but she was putting so much energy into the garden and the meadow and having people to stay that not much work was done. In 1993 alone, she had house-guests for thirty-five weekends of the year – and Jane believed that a weekend meant not only people to stay, but more guests for dinner on Saturday and Sunday lunch. These often included Sargy and Frances; while other dinner guests included the poet Anthony Thwaite and his wife Ann, the biographer, who lived a few miles away at Low Tharston; and Neil Powell, another poet who lived almost next door and edited the *PN Review*. Her neighbours, Laurence and Jocelyn Magnus, were impressed by the number of younger friends she knew – many of them drawn from people who worked at Macmillan.

Her principal help in the house came from Dawn Fairhead, who cleaned for Sargy and Frances; and when she met Jane, 'We hit it off at once because I was a dog person, and fell immediately for Darcy.'[12] At that stage Jane could do a lot for herself, particularly in terms of cooking and shopping; so Dawn did the cleaning and laundry. (To give an idea of the laundry generated by her entertaining, Jane found it worthwhile to install the sort of professional steam iron that does sheets.) Jane did most of the gardening in the early days; but the heavy work was done by Dawn's husband David, and in the meadow by David Evans. He had beautiful old tractors, and was particularly notable for cutting and baling hay.

Every year, Jenner Roth would organize a three-day residential workshop for the dozen or so members of the women's group; and Jane suggested that instead of spending money on a hotel, 'the residential', as it was known, should be held at Bridge House. This became an annual event, as was the painting group that was established a few years later. The core members of this group were Ann Clowes, Patricia Wyndham, Anne Norwich, Elfin Ebury and Jackie Hume (who, as Jackie Gomme, had been Jane's secretary when she directed the Cheltenham Literary Festival). They would come up for a week in June to paint in the meadow, with help and advice from Frances.

Jane never really conquered her fear and dislike of being alone; and as so many of her weekend guests remembered, the moment they said they ought to be getting home Jane was begging them to stay a little longer. 'Must you really go? *Can't* you stay till Monday?' No amount of bleating about the long drive back and the early start next day ever did much good as Jane's eyes brimmed with tears. She dreaded the summer holidays, when everyone was away; but the *Sunday Times* sent her off to write travel pieces on Bali, India, China, Sicily and the Seychelles – a holiday on which she took her god-daughter Minky.

There were frequent trips to London, where she stayed with Selina Hastings or Catherine Freeman in Primrose Hill, or Patricia and Mark Wyndham in Chiswick. However, she was not the sort of guest to whom one could give a spare key and a towel and then let them get on with it. Her hosts were expected to keep her company over coffee and drinks, drive her round London, sometimes give a dinner in her honour. This is what Jane did for her friends when they came to Bungay for the weekend; but to expect the same level of attention in mid-week London was pushing the bounds of hospitality. Jenner Roth was perhaps the only friend of Jane's who was not afraid to say no to Jane, and Jane respected her for it. But most of her acquaintance had been brought up like the Cazalets, where the tyranny of good manners overrides every other impulse.

Confusion, the third volume of the Cazalet Chronicle, was published in October 1993. Jane told Roy Foster that she wanted to convey 'the *utter confusion* of the young – that pendulum that swings between a kind of arrogant excitement and chaotic uncertainty as to the meaning of anything. My own confusion nearly annihilated me, but perhaps that was partly the war.'[13]

It is also a book of betrayals and self-deceptions. Villy, who had been nursing an infatuation for a young musician whom she thinks of as Lorenzo (real name Laurence Clutterbuck), is overjoyed when he invites her to dinner; but when she finds herself in a squalid bedsit, she realizes that the last thing he wants is the sublime platonic romance of her imagination.

Louise has married Michael Hadleigh who is now in the navy, and is living in the Gloster Hotel in Cowes – just as Jane did with Peter Scott. Sometimes she enjoys playing the part of Mrs Michael Hadleigh, the child-bride of a glamorous and brilliant man. But beneath that glittering tip is an iceberg of boredom, loneliness and resentment – especially of the way she's been pressured into having a baby too soon. She toys with the idea of confiding in her friend Stella, but 'she was afraid it might clear things up in a way that she might find unendurable'.[14]

Polly and Clary move to London, where they live with Polly's father Hugh. There has been no more news of Clary's father Rupert, who is still in hiding in France; but the two girls come to rely on his best friend Archie Lestrange. Archie represents men as, in Jane's experience, they so rarely were: kind, considerate, protective and selfless. Polly finds herself in love with him, despite the fact that he is so much older, as well as being lame and nearly bald; and, ever truthful, tells him so. With equal honesty, Archie tells Polly gently that he does not love her; but almost without knowing it, his feelings for her cousin Clary are growing.

Louise falls in love with a cousin of Michael's called Hugo Wentworth, giving Jane the chance to relive the joy and guilt of her affair with Wayland Young. Jane's narrative method of telling the story from the viewpoints of various characters usually makes her a very compassionate novelist. But compared to the sureness with which she can get inside Edward, Hugh or Archie, she finds the mind of Michael Hadleigh almost impenetrable. He comes across as generally decent, but sexually confused and emotionally infantile.

Since their lives and circumstances mirror each other's so exactly, it is impossible not to see Michael Hadleigh as a portrait of Peter Scott. Yet she makes little attempt to sketch out the pressures he lived under, nor his sadness at what was happening to their relationship. Jane never denied her share in the failure of her first marriage; but part of her could never forgive Peter for being more interested in the war than in her.

The book got to number eight in the *Sunday Times* bestseller list (the top spot that winter was occupied by Roddy Doyle's *Paddy Clarke Ha Ha Ha*), and the three Cazalet books were selling well. Nicolette Jones, who had reviewed *Marking Time*, enjoyed its sequel but even she felt that 'it does go on a bit';[15] while in the *Times Literary Supplement*, J.K.L. Walker wrote that, although she had failed to convey the danger, fear and depression that the war brought to civilians, on another level it was 'a flawless, busy, yet ultimately sentimental performance, a superior Boots novel'.[16]

This was partly due to the way in which the novels were marketed. Macmillan had commissioned jackets showing family houses in rural settings that glowed with a warm nostalgia – designed to attract the largely female readership that enjoyed what had recently become labelled as 'Aga-sagas'. In many respects the Cazalet Chronicle, with its prosperously conventional family and Home Counties setting, was an easy target for that particular shot. Yet the reviewers absorbed more from the cosiness of the covers than they should have done, for the Cazalet Chronicle cannot be dismissed so easily.

What Jane reveals about the way death is handled in a family like hers, and the impact it has on young children who are given no opportunity to express their grief; the moment when Polly suddenly realizes the utter loneliness and misery of her younger brother; the gap between Louise's expectations of marriage and the reality; the ease with which people deceive themselves, how mortified they feel afterwards; and the sheer scale and textured depths of the novels: all these show that Elizabeth Jane Howard was at the height of her powers.

One reader who recognized this was Hilary Mantel, who had been a fan for many years. In a letter to Jane she said:

I teach a little bit you know, and tend to stay in touch for years with students, and read successive drafts of their MS – and I'm always telling people to sit down with your novels and take them apart to see how you make strong but dynamic structures – you are more adept than any author I can think of at switching between time schemes, or from one narrative to another. You leave the reader poised, always, wanting more. I say to people 'open a gap between what your reader has and what he desires' . . . I so vividly remember reading you for the first time – how Mrs Fleming sank obediently to the situation – and carrying you home from the public library with the glee of a brigand who has taken a prime hostage. It always does seem odd to be writing to you, and proposing to share tea and buns.[17]

Yet whatever the merits of the novels, the real family called Cazalet couldn't help feeling extremely resentful at the way that Jane had so casually hijacked their name. Jane said she had wanted her family to have a Huguenot past, and picked 'Cazalet' without doing any further research. Had she done so, she would have discovered that the name she had given the character based on her charming but irresponsible father was also the name of a High Court judge. 'I did happen to meet Elizabeth Jane Howard on one occasion,' wrote Sir Edward Cazalet. 'She was very much on the defensive . . . She simply said that people would not think it referred to me.'[18] Jane was very lucky that he chose not take the matter further.

Every year Jane bought bulbs for the meadow, by the hundred. Penelope Lively was once staying with Jane when they arrived, and they all had to be taken out of their bags and turned the right way up until they could be planted. Penelope was pressed into bulb-turning duty, and recalled that by the end of the evening they had covered almost every horizontal surface in two rooms. February brought the Seville oranges, and Jane made vast quantities of marmalade. As the year progressed she made chutney and jam, while into her freezer went stews and fish pies for the weekend as well as things that don't freeze quite so well, like game terrines.

She was very pleased with her conservatory dining room. It had big Welsh dressers filled with Victorian crockery and baskets of fruit, and a plumbago that gradually took over the glass roof space. At her broad, green-painted table with its border of vines she could easily sit twelve, and in later years she installed a wood-burning stove in the corner for chilly nights. Pots of cymbidium orchids, scented geranium, stephanotis and purple oxalis sat on a broad ledge drinking up the sun, and the doors opened on to a terrace which was one of the most beautiful features of the house.

Selina Hastings recalled that it 'was paved with what looked like ancient gravestones, but they were actually the York stone slabs on which monumental masons practised their engraving. So you had these wonderful worn stones, seventeenth, eighteenth century, etched with exquisitely engraved calligraphy, and in between them grew moss and tiny campanula plants which bloomed a vivid blue.'[19] Jane and her guests would have lunch there in summer, looking down the length of the garden to the meadow.

Jane had a large collection of paintings by Sargy, and several by Frances; as well as works by Michael Ayrton, Stephen Andrews, Graham and Julie Giles, Sophie Tute and Michael Fell. There were also a number of drawings by Peter Scott of herself and Nicola, family portraits, Victorian genre paintings, while almost every rug and cushion had been stitched by Jane. The overall effect was generous, colourful, richly textured and crammed with shelf after shelf of books. Fiction she kept in her study, behind the huge desk that had been made to her specifications. History and music were in the sitting room, biography ran the length of a long corridor, and every bedroom had its well-stocked bookcase. For the first time in her life, Jane was rich enough to live the way she wanted. She cleared the meadow and planted a great many trees and shrubs, bought books and beautiful clothes and collected antique gold jewellery.

Although she had originally planned the Cazalets as a trilogy that spanned the Second World War and two years either side of it, the end of *Confusion* takes the reader only up to the end of the war. The Cazalets needed another volume in which to complete their various stories, and Macmillan were keen for her to write it, but the company had undergone a number of changes. In 1994 she heard that her editor, Jane Wood, was leaving to go to Orion.

Jane was terribly upset, feeling that she could not change editors in midstream with the Chronicle still unfinished. It would risk losing the tone of the books, and the energy and rhythms that she had built up over years of close collaboration with Jane Wood. She told Macmillan that she could not possibly work with anyone else, and they agreed to engage her on a freelance basis.

In early March 1995 Jane did an event at the King's Lynn Festival with Louis de Bernières. She was accompanied by Wayland and Liz Young's daughter, Louisa, who was about to publish her first book: a biography of her grandmother, Kathleen Scott. 'I had made friends with Jane through that,' she wrote, 'and she invited me along to the festival and I found myself heaving with envy of her and Louis.' Listening to them made Louisa decide that she really wanted to be a novelist.[20]

Louis de Bernières went on to spend several weekends with Jane, and was astonished by the quantity of people she entertained. 'I think the main motive for this manic entertaining was her fear of loneliness,' he said, 'and she also told me that it was one of the reasons she had had so many lovers in her youth.'[21] Later on, it was Jane who found the house near Bungay where de Bernières still lives.

Mark and Patricia Wyndham had exchanged their narrow-boat for a spacious Dutch barge, the *Wilhelmina*; they invited Jane and Monkey to join them for a holiday on the Burgundy Canal. Jane's birthday, 26 March, fell while they were still in France, and the Wyndhams decided to take her out to a restaurant to celebrate. Jane looked forward to this outing with childlike anticipation, and could not hide her disappointment when she found it was a pretty simple place with a few tables and a short menu that catered for the locals. Once again, her imagination had streaked ahead of what might reasonably be found within walking distance of an industrial canal, in a remote stretch of rural France. But she and Monkey were excellent company nonetheless, and Patricia said she would always remember the night they asked Jane to read her ghost story, 'Three Miles Up', which is set on a canal. 'I've never been so frightened in my life,' said Patricia. 'We were all *terrified*, including Jane.'[22]

Jane had turned seventy-two. She had trouble walking, felt tired all the time, and feared she might have piles. Her doctor told her that she would need an operation to replace a bit of blocked artery in her leg; but when she had the piles investigated, the specialist decided to take a tissue biopsy immediately. It was intensely painful, and Jane knew that he would not have done it unless he had suspected something more serious.

It was early September, and she had to wait ten days for the result: ten days of anguish, during which – like most people who find themselves in this situation – she found herself contemplating pain and death in a way she had never done before. Yet on the ninth day, as she walked from the town back to her house, her mood suddenly lifted: 'as though, without warning, I'd emerged from a heavy fog into clear sunlight. I felt extraordinarily, irrationally happy. Whatever happened, it would be alright.'[23] With that release came a readiness to accept the results, whether good or bad. It was bad: she had cancer of the colon.

The operation on her leg was postponed, and she would begin a course of radiotherapy in January.

Not long after that, Martin Amis rang to tell her that Kingsley was dying. After a bad fall in Wales, he had sustained a cracked vertebra. This required painkillers, which began to conflict with his daily battery of pills for blood pressure, gout, cardiac irregularity, constipation and swelling of the legs – not to mention his daily intake of a bottle or more of whisky. Now aged seventy-three, even Kingsley's iron constitution was wearing out. Jane had always hoped that they might return to some sort of amicable relationship, but Kingsley had been too deeply shaken by her defection. She asked Martin whether she might see Kingsley once more before he died, but he did not think it would be a good idea. Kingsley died on 25 October 1995. The funeral was private but Jane did go to the memorial service a year later, at St Martin-in-the-Fields. She was touched when Martin asked her to sit with him and his second wife, Isabel Fonseca.

A few days after Kingsley's death, on 29 October, Jane was Sue Lawley's castaway on Radio 4's *Desert Island Discs*. (It was her second time as castaway on the show, the first having been in 1972.) The programme had been pre-recorded; and in the opening moments, Jane remarked that 'falling in love uses the same sort of love as writing books', and said she did not have the energy to do both at the same time. Sue Lawley was interested in this idea and kept coming back to it in between the discs (which included Nina Milkina playing Chopin, an aria from *Ariadne auf Naxos*, Scarlatti's Sonata in B Minor and Haydn's Trumpet Concerto). By the end of the programme the listeners were in no doubt that Jane, despite being a successful novelist and living in a big house with a lovely garden, was fundamentally lonely. 'I feel so old,' she said, 'but I would love to have a loving companion, someone I could be interested in and care for.' Even at the time her friends thought that it was unwise of her to have made such an admission, which made it clear she lived alone and was emotionally vulnerable. But Jane had better things to think about. In early November she published the last of the Cazalet Chronicle, *Casting Off*.

At the end of the last volume Rupert was on his way back to England, torn between his family obligations and his love for Michele, the woman who had sheltered him in France for months. He confides in his friend Archie, just as his wife Zoe did after her affair with Jack

Greenfeldt. All the Cazalets confide in Archie, since they find it very hard to reveal their emotions to each other – sometimes with good reason. Zoe is occasionally tempted to confess her affair, but 'Telling Rupert about Jack would put him further into the past than she was ready for.' It takes a long time to let go of love, even when you know the beloved is dead.

When Villy hears from Edward that he's leaving her for Diana, it is Archie to whom she pours out her rage and despair. Villy had no idea that as he bought her new house, he knew he was never going to live in it; and what made it even worse was that he had asked their daughter Louise to meet Diana, and consulted her about how best to break the news.

Louise is playing the part of being married to Michael, but she feels nothing for him any more and nothing but guilt for her son. She tries to find small acting or radio jobs where she can, but the failure of her marriage infects everything. Polly and Clary, meanwhile, have moved into two rooms above a poulterer's (Jane's first house in Blandford Street). Polly is working for an interior decorator, and finds she has a talent for it; while Clary is working at a small literary agency run by Noel and Fenella Forman. Noel is based on Robert Aickman, whose commanding selfishness Clary mistakes for genius, as does his wife. But when Clary gets pregnant, Noel wants nothing more to do with her.

Once again, Archie comes to the rescue. It is he who arranges the abortion, and he who looks after her during the depression she sinks into afterwards. Yet as she gets better, he resents the way she sees him as a father figure: she must grow up and take control of her life, before he can reveal that he has loved her for months, perhaps years.

Of the three girls, Polly is the one whose path will always run smooth. Through her work she meets and falls in love with a shy, funny man called Gerald, who turns out to have a monstrously large house, a title and no money. Luckily Polly finds a set of watercolours by J.M. Turner in his attic, so she will be able to do up the house, and fill at least one wing of it with happy children. This is the sort of life that Jane might have had, had she not been so possessed by ambition: Polly has all her warmth and home-making qualities without the drive to do more.

The book ends with Polly and Gerald's wedding; but despite the air of celebration, the uneasy currents have not gone away. Edward and Diana's marriage, though barely begun, is heavy with disappointment. Villy's bitterness is making the two children still at home with her anxious and miserable. Louise has left Michael, but has no idea how she is going to live; and Archie and Clary will have to find a new way of being together, if their relationship is going to work.

Over the course of the four Cazalet books the stories become richer, the emotional fault lines between the characters develop lives of their own, and Jane's own writing gains in depth: she can articulate states of being with enviable insight. Hilary Mantel described the novels as 'panoramic, expansive, intriguing as social history and generous in their story-telling. They are the product of a lifetime's experience, and come from a writer who knew her aim and had the stamina and technical skill to achieve it.'24

The Cazalets, and her appearance on *Desert Island Discs* in October 1995, had generated a lot of letters from readers and listeners. One of them was from a man who said that he had fallen in love with her voice as he listened to the radio, and he would very much like to have tea with her. Then came a second letter, in which he wondered whether she had received his first and said he quite understood if she did not want to have tea with him. Jane replied saying that she was not well, so tea would have to be postponed till March. He wrote back immediately, and soon a correspondence developed.

A crucial point in their relationship came in late 1995. 'I was standing by my bedroom window looking at the place under the beech tree where soon the snowdrops would appear, and wondering whether this was the last year I should see them, when the telephone rang. It was him.'25 They did not talk long, and Jane said she could not remember whether it was then or later that she told him she had cancer. It was probably then, because otherwise why would she have seen the moment as important. The letters continued in the new year as she was having radiotherapy, five days a week for three weeks.

Then she had a letter saying that he loved her. She replied that this was silly, because he didn't know her at all. But the letters continued, about three times a week, and although there were not many details, he seemed to have had a sad life. He had parted from his wife and was living on his own. She told him she could not write as often as he did, since she was starting a new novel.

His name was Malcolm Shane: not his real name, but there are good reasons for still withholding it. He kept telling Jane how beautiful she was. She wrote back to say that too was nonsense, since she was fat with white hair – not at all as she appeared on the book jackets. Nevertheless she was enjoying this literary flirtation, and enjoyed being courted. She showed some of Malcolm's letters to Jane Wood: 'They were very reverential, respectful, intelligent – he'd certainly done his research.'[26] He had read all her novels, as well as biographies of Peter Scott and Kingsley Amis.

Jane was due to have the postponed vascular operation on her leg in early April 1996, and as she had initially said she would meet Malcolm in March, they arranged a date. The problem was that he lived very far away, in Orkney, and he didn't have much money. By now she had told several of her friends about Malcolm, and how excited and fluttery she felt at the prospect of meeting him. They urged her to be sensible. Meet him somewhere neutral like a London hotel, they said; after all you don't know Malcolm, you might not even like him. But Jane felt daunted by the prospect of tea in London. Both of them would feel awkward and shy, it would be a disaster. Instead she decided to have him to stay at Bridge House for a weekend, with other guests.

They arranged that he would come to Suffolk for the weekend of 15–18 March. Selina Hastings came to visit early that month, and found herself having to drive Jane on Saturday to Harleston for a shopping expedition. She bought some waterproof mascara, since she knew she would be moved to tears when she saw him; and a froth of silky lingerie, nightgowns and petticoats which she referred to as her trousseau. 'It was the most exhausting day,' said Selina. 'She had to try everything on for my approval, and she was so excited, like a seventeen-year-old.'[27]

Dawn Fairhead came in every weekday, and as the meeting with Malcolm approached she saw that Jane's anticipation was becoming more anxious. She turned to Dawn at one point and said, 'Supposing he wants to make love to me? What should I do?' Dawn replied, 'Well, you never really forget what to do, do you . . . it's like riding a bicycle.'[28] In fact there was no doubt in Jane's mind that they would have sex. It was now sixteen years since she had left Kingsley and there had been no sex for some years before that.

★

Jane had invited Jane Wood and her fiancé, Edward Russell-Walling, to stay for the Malcolm weekend; but since they could not come till the Saturday she had invited Nick McDowell to keep her company that Friday evening.

Malcolm arrived, having driven in a hired car from Stansted. Jane wrote that 'We had a glass of wine together before Nick joined us for dinner.' Nick had brought his six-year-old daughter Anna, and was putting her to bed. Jane noticed that while Malcolm wasn't particularly good-looking, it was clear that he possessed enormous charm. She could see that he was nervous, because his palms were sweaty when they shook hands. Over dinner he was quiet, but he'd had a long journey and was probably very tired. Nick felt that Malcolm seemed quite harmless: 'He was entirely bland and invisible: he had no presence.' As for Jane, Nick felt that 'she was nervous – she knew she was taking a risk and was conscious of it'.[29] Jane Wood and Edward Russell-Walling had similar reactions: 'We thought him somewhat dull and limited, and not nearly good enough for Jane, but we didn't doubt that he loved her.'[30]

As soon as Nick had retired, Jane told Malcolm that 'there is something we have to get out of the way,' and led him upstairs. 'As is my wont when afraid of something, I plunged in and invited him to share my bed. It was clear at once that this was his element. But, less like other people I'd known, he made no sudden conquest, said we needed time – or rather, I needed time to get to know him. This remark, which had never been made to me before, enchanted me.'[31]

He left on the Monday morning and their letters resumed: Dawn noticed from the envelopes that he had beautiful writing, and that Jane 'would wait for the postman like a schoolgirl'.[32] Jane invited him to stay again, after the operation on her leg in early April. This time he would stay for ten days, so they could get to know each other better.

Nicola came to visit Jane a few days before Malcolm's second visit, and heard from Frances that she and Sargy were worried about him. Jane was still recovering from the operation, so it was Nicola who went to collect Malcolm from Norwich airport. 'How's Jessica?' he said when they were in the car, meaning Jane – which was not a good start. In her diary Nicola noted: 'I do hope he's OK really, it's difficult to say. She needs him though. I hope he won't abuse it.'[33]

Jane too noticed Nicola's wariness. She could see that Malcolm was making great efforts to be nice to her, and that she wasn't impressed. He showed Nicola the programme for a horse show in Somerset, where he and his second wife used to live (not the one he had recently left, that was his third). She had died in a riding accident that day, he said, and he had written her name on the cover. The programme was a few years old, but Nicola was instantly suspicious. Fatal accidents involving horses are rare, and very much discussed. She and Elliott kept horses and knew the riding community in the West Country well, yet she had no recollection of any fatal accidents in the recent past. Nicola said nothing, but made a note of his wife's name.

A few days after Nicola had returned to Gloucestershire, Jane had a serious fall on the York stone slabs outside her conservatory. She fell on her bad leg, splitting open the wound from the operation, and could not move until rescued by Frances and her daughter Susanna.

The doctor said she would have to remain more or less bedbound until the wound had had a chance to heal. Malcolm, who had been out when she fell, now came into his own. 'I was in a good deal of pain,' wrote Jane, 'and he delighted in looking after me – cups of tea, and doing the shopping. He suggested coming to live in Bungay and buying a cottage. I felt what he really meant was that he wanted to live in my house with me, and something somewhere in me told me that this was a bad idea.'[34]

Yet wherever the warning bells were coming from, Jane was not yet willing to listen to them. 'I enjoyed sex with him, and we talked together very companionably,' she wrote. 'It felt extraordinary to be *having* a sex life.'[35] Yet there were odd things about him. Although he was only sixty-two, he seemed to have no job or occupation, not even a hobby. 'All he wanted to do, he said, was look after me. This sounded both nice and not quite right.' Malcolm lived in a council house in Orkney, and admitted to some credit card debt which Jane paid off for him. She also paid his air fares, but didn't mind since he was doing the travelling.

Dawn didn't much like him: 'He was a bit too touchy-feely, putting his arm round you, that sort of thing.'[36] Jane had another friend staying for a few days who obviously didn't like him either, and the feeling was mutual: they both came to tell Jane that the other was drinking in secret. Jane did not take this too seriously – in front of her, Malcolm drank wine and beer and not much of either.

He stayed for over a month, from 25 April to 27 May; and during this time, much to Jane's discomfiture, he proposed. Jane told him that she didn't want to be married to anyone ever again, and he seemed to accept it; but he continued paying court to her.

Jane had invited Selina, Monkey and her old friend Susan Allison for a weekend in May. It was the first time Selina had met Malcolm, whom she described as 'big, red, beefy, with too much chest hair and a Scottish accent'. At one point during lunch he slipped out, making no excuses, and returned twenty minutes later with four single roses wrapped in cellophane. He gave one to Susie, one to Selina, and presented the last two 'to the most beautiful woman in the room'. Selina and Susie found this display of gallantry positively embarrassing and so did Jane, but she was touched and delighted nonetheless. After lunch the three guests, with heavy-handed tact, left the house to go for a walk; and as they were walking Monkey said, 'It's so sad, I have lost my sister.'[37]

At this stage, anyone who told Jane that Malcolm was not her intellectual equal was accused of being a snob: 'I didn't give a damn about his class, it made no difference to me. But in one way it did. It made me both defensive about and protective of him.'[38] Yet whether she was willing to admit it or not, she was embarrassed. Not only that, she did not quite trust him.

Jane had to go to London one day during his second stay, to give a talk. 'She didn't want to parade him at the literary event,' said Monkey, 'nor did she want to leave him in the house alone, so she asked me to give him dinner. He was just under six foot tall, and burly – you wouldn't have wanted to get into a fight with him.'

Malcolm spent the entire evening singing Jane's praises and saying how much he wanted to marry her, 'which I found very dull. I also noticed that he did not ask a single question about me, and gave away very little about his own life. I found myself thinking, Is this man going to be around every time I go and see Jane?'[39] Meanwhile, Jane's family were sufficiently worried about Malcolm to start doing some background checks.

★

When Malcolm left at the end of May, Jane noticed that she did feel a certain relief. 'I wondered whether – like Elizabeth Taylor's very good story about meeting someone to whom she's written for years and finding she's unable to bear him through a lunch – we might be better on paper,' she wrote. 'But no, as soon as he was away I thought of when he'd be back. "You like me in bed," he said one day, and it was true. What he didn't know was how unusual this was for me.'[40]

As she was going on holiday with Nick McDowell and Sarah Raphael in Greece that August, she invited Malcolm to come again for ten days in July. While they were together, she rang Nicola to say how good it felt to have him back.

But one evening Malcolm proposed once more, as if he had no recollection of her very firm refusal the first time. Jane told him emphatically that it was out of the question: she was never going to marry again, and the subject was closed. Malcolm became very angry. *Why* wouldn't she marry him? Wasn't he good enough for her and her posh friends? He worked himself into such a rage that he hit her and then stormed out of the house. Jane was terrified. She locked all the doors, stuck a chair under the handle of her bedroom door which had no lock, and barely slept. He was out all night.

The following morning, a journalist came to do an interview. Malcolm turned up while they were still talking, and Jane told him to come back later. When Malcolm returned that afternoon, he was very charming and repentant; and of course, she took him in. He left on 10 July.

Jane did tell Nicola that he had become 'drunk and nasty' at one point during his visit, but by then other disturbing facts about Malcolm were starting to emerge. Elliott had discovered that no one had ever died in a fatal accident at the Chew Magna Horse Show. 'That was his big mistake, telling me about how he and his dead wife had lived in Chew Magna and how she had died at that horse show,' said Nicola. 'Had he told us she had been killed in a motorbike accident, we might never have found out.'[41]

Alerted by Nicola, Jane's brother Robin had hired a private detective to look into Malcolm's past. He had found out that Malcolm's last wife had died not in a riding accident, but of a cerebral haemorrhage: and in people under fifty, the most likely cause of this is an injury to the head. He had had three children, not one as he claimed; and two of his wives – the one who had died, plus the current one from whom he was separated – had reported his violence against them to the police. The detective talked to several people who had known him, and their voices were unanimous: stay well clear of him, and don't mention our names.

Nicola felt that Monkey would be the best person to tell her. Jane was due to come to London on 12 July, before going on holiday with the McDowells a day or so later. Monkey thought that it would be better for her to digest the news away from home, among people who would look after her. She was going to stay the night with Selina, but Monkey asked her to come round first. He sat her down, made some tea, and said, 'I've got something rather awful to tell you.'

'She listened very, very quietly,' he said, 'and I had the feeling that while she was obviously very shaken, it did not come as a complete shock.'[42] After she had heard the truth from Monkey, Jane went to spend the night with Selina and they talked for a long time, till Jane was exhausted with weeping. 'Half of her was aghast and horrified and humiliated,' said Selina; 'the other, desperately mourning the loss of the man in her life.'[43]

Before she left, Jenner and Terry drafted a letter for Jane to send to Malcolm, which she did. She told him that she now knew certain things about him that made her never want to see or hear from him again, and she was lodging a copy of the letter with her solicitor.

Nick McDowell and Sarah Raphael gathered her up and took her to the island of Ios, with their two little daughters. 'Inevitably ours was a household geared towards small children,' said Nick. 'But Jane behaved with grace and forbearance, and only after the girls were in bed did she begin to talk.' He really admired the courage with which she faced the humiliating truth. At the same time, 'it was extraordinary to me that someone as powerful as Jane could lose all power, as soon as a man came along who was interested in her.'[44]

While she was away, Colin reinforced the door to her bedroom and fitted strong bolts on it. It was impossible to make the whole house impregnable, but at least she could lock herself in her bedroom and know she was safe till help came. When she returned home, she put aside her novel in progress and began a new one: it was to be called *Falling*.

20

Love All

JANE WROTE THAT during the sleepless nights on Ios, 'I went back to the naive conviction I'd had with Jim Douglas-Henry which had been my undoing: that people didn't tell lies about love. How long it had taken me to recognize that this was a fallacy! I have said earlier that I am a slow learner – and here I was, at seventy-four [*sic*], having to discover this all over again.'¹ She felt so sad, and such a fool – but Malcolm would not have been able to manipulate her so well if he hadn't been good at it.

Friends were sympathetic and supportive. Selina took her to Ireland soon after she got back, and they stayed with the Fosters and Catherine Freeman. Catherine remembered Jane sitting by the fire, and telling her sadly that Malcolm was the best lover she had ever had. 'I can't say how dreadful your news is,' wrote Ann Clowes from France. 'Please come here when you get back from Ireland and stay as long as you like. It might be a good idea to be away from Bungay when Malcolm has his ticket [Jane had booked his flights for a visit in late August] in case he turns up . . . You must hurt so much that you have a pain. It is one of life's dirtiest tricks. We must just be glad Nicola had the courage of her convictions and determination to find out.'²

When I began researching this book, there was one question I kept asking myself: How can anyone who writes so well about love and deception, who sees people's motives so clearly in her novels, make so many mistakes in their personal life? Now I see that the question put the cart before the horse. It was *because* Jane lived at such an intense emotional pitch; because she rushed headlong into things without considering the risks; because she could not control her impulsive imagination: all these made her the novelist she was.

I also thought about what Jenner Roth told me, when I asked her what she meant when she described Jane as 'a bottomless pit of neediness'. After a long pause she said, 'To receive love, you have to have something to put it in,' and she brought her hands together into a bowl, as if she were holding water. I asked what that love-holding bowl was made of. 'It's made of touch, and saying sweet things, and hugging and intimacy – all the things Jane did not get as a child. So if you don't know how to make that bowl, or if it's broken, when love comes along you have nowhere to put it, it just trickles away. That's why Jane could never have enough love, why she was constantly searching for more.'[3]

This was what made her so vulnerable to people like Malcolm. 'He was very cunning,' wrote Jane Wood. 'He'd read her books; he was quite literate, his letters were well expressed. He was no fool. He knew which buttons to push to win Jane's affection. His most telling weapon was to convince her of his love.'[4]

Jane Wood asked Jane to compile an Anthology of Marriage: it would be part of a series that included Childhood, Friendship and First Love. Jane appreciated the irony – after all, she had never been very successful at marriage herself. But she had thought and read about it a great deal, and the selection is not only about joy and companionship: it also explores the terrors of the wedding night; the treacherous reefs that lie in wait for husbands sent out shopping for their wives; the unspoken misunderstandings that grow into chasms of silence and sadness, and the exhaustion of loss and grief.

Towards the end of that blighted year, Jane decided to rent two little houses on the island of Nevis in the Caribbean in January 1997. Jim and Pam Rose, the Wyndhams, and Monkey and Minky would join her, and she looked forward to it eagerly; but as time went on she was in more and more pain. Biopsies revealed that while the cancer in her colon had not returned, the course of radiation had created a number of ulcers that would have to be removed, sooner rather than later; and this meant that while everyone else went on holiday to Nevis, Jane could not.

It was a long operation, a slow recovery, and she had to learn how to live with a colostomy; but by mid-February she was well enough to accept another travel commission from the *Sunday Times* – this time to the Maldives and she asked Nicola to join her. Nicola was a keen scuba diver, and accepted with pleasure, although they were both a little nervous at the prospect: they had never spent two weeks alone together. But this was Jane's way of thanking Nicola for her crucial role in unmasking Malcolm, and they both remembered the holiday as a breakthrough in their relationship. The warmth between them grew, and Nicola showed Jane how to swim with a mask and snorkel. Jane had always had a horror of putting her head underwater, but with Nicola to help her, she was introduced to the brilliance and beauty of the tropical reefs.

Back home she settled down to write *Falling*, which was based on her experience with Malcolm. Jane usually found writing very hard, but as her editor Jane Wood observed, '*Falling* didn't seem to cause as much grief as some. I think writing the book was in some sense cathartic . . . I don't remember much agonised reliving of the events that inspired the novel, more a feeling of letting them go.'[5] Her health, however, was not improving. Jane often tried to give up smoking but because she thought it helped her concentrate, she smoked while she worked. This led to bouts of asthma and bronchitis (which were particularly bad in the winter) and she was increasingly troubled with arthritis, which meant that she could do less and less gardening. Another problem was that although Jane drank in moderation, she had always been a greedy eater, and from the time she came to Bungay she more or less gave up trying to lose weight. By the late nineties, she could not stay on her knees in the garden for long even with a kneeler. But having people for the weekend meant preparing the same lavish meals she had made at Lemmons, and standards never slipped. Nicola once remarked that whatever the dish, from kedgeree to a game terrine, Jane's version was always the most complicated and demanding.

She was still doing a prodigious amount of entertaining, and from 1998 onwards, Zachary and Alice Leader become frequent visitors. Zachary was then working on Kingsley's letters, and would go on to write his biography. Jane grew very fond of his wife Alice – although Alice felt she only wanted one side of her. 'I published two novels and a book of stories for teens and she never read them . . . she didn't want me as a novelist, I was always supposed to be dear sweet Alice.'[6]

All her friends were invited every year, and she urged the younger ones to bring their children. Children were always welcome, she wrote in *Slipstream*, especially if they enjoyed playing adventurous games on the island; but Jane expected them to be in bed by seven, and not be seen again until the following day. She did not approve of them eating with the adults in the evening, so many friends with young children preferred not to come at all.

In early 1999 Jane met Verity Lambert, who had optioned the Cazalet Chronicle for a series of television plays. She came down to Bungay for the night with her co-producer, Joanna Lumley. Joanna had read *The Light Years* as she was filming *A Rather English Marriage* with Tom Courtenay and Albert Finney, and then devoured the rest. Her acting commitments meant that she wouldn't have much to do with the practicalities of getting the project up and running, but Verity hoped that her name would bring the series to the attention of the higher echelons of the BBC. Jane remembered a night heady with excitement and champagne, casting and recasting, discussing what would be left out and what was essential. At about one in the morning, an exhausted Joanna went to bed and left them to it – but Verity and Jane, both inveterate night-birds, carried on for several more hours.

At the end of the month Jane visited Sri Lanka with friends, where she realized 'how feeble I'd become'. She couldn't go for walks, let alone climb the 1,200 steps to the citadel of Sigiriya. When they got to the villa on the south coast, she was laid up by another serious bout of asthma.

She finished *Falling* on her return home, in the spring of 1999, just before having an operation that reversed the colostomy she had had for almost two years. Louis de Bernières made one of his frequent attempts to get her to give up smoking:

> Jane if you are to be replumbed, you've got to pack in the weed . . . I know that it's a beloved friend, and even an entire lifestyle (it certainly was in my case), but I am sure that you must have been through worse bereavements before. What people never tell you is that if you quit smoking, you can drink twice as much hooch without getting a hangover. It's worth it.[7]

Falling was launched that September, and was hailed as one of the most psychologically perceptive of all her books. Anne Norwich's partner was Dr Peter Dally, one of the most respected psychiatrists of his day. He read *Falling*, and told Anne it was one of the best portraits of a psychopath he had ever come across.

Henry Kent is a middle-aged man who preys on women; and when the story opens he is living in a squalid boat on a canal and running out of money. He notices that a woman in her fifties has bought a nearby cottage – a successful playwright called Daisy Langrish. Henry Kent comes to her door posing as a gardener, who might bring some order to the abandoned and overgrown garden. Daisy agrees, and soon he is helping her move in, lighting the fire, and making himself useful in a thousand different ways. Jane wanted to explore the mind of someone who 'lies about love': so Henry speaks for himself, in the first person – the reader is inside his head. Most women, he says, have been badly mistreated by men, and that is why they need him. What he gives them is 'affection, cherishing and *loving* which cannot be assumed, but once present needs constant expression. Women need not only to be loved; they need to be told so.'[8] Henry deliberately attunes himself to Daisy, to the point where he can sense what she is thinking even before she knows it herself. The way he cultivates her dependence on him and how he plans to handle the suspicions of her friends have to be expressed so that the reader can see how he is always in control of the situation. This makes Henry a more articulate version of Malcolm, and every bit as dangerous.

The book alternates between Henry and Daisy but while Henry's narrative is told in the first person, Daisy's is told mostly in the third: reinforcing the idea of Henry as predator, Daisy his prey. Daisy is old enough and intelligent enough to hold Henry at a distance at first. But she cannot see that she's being played like a fish on a line: sometimes Henry lets it out, sometimes he reels it in, but she is never off the hook. As he becomes a familiar presence around the house and garden, she is touched by his consideration and thoughtfulness. She begins to soften; and when she falls on the garden path in the rain and has to spend days with her leg up, he becomes indispensable – and that is the moment he moves in.

Jane builds the sexual tension slowly. Henry lies beside her at night, melts the shyness of her body, and tells her he loves her long before they have sex. At this point Daisy is talking in the first person through her diary, and Jane's voice breaks through: 'It was some hours later during that timeless night that I recognised and could accept his unconditional love, and then, for the first time in my life, I felt free to be nothing but myself. Years slipped away from me until I was ageless, without shame.'[9] In bed, Henry has the ability to hold himself back almost indefinitely; so when he does finally make love to her – three-quarters of the way through the book – Daisy is in ecstasy. And yet she knows that her friends are unimpressed by him, and that in front of them he seems dull.

It is Daisy's friends, and her daughter Katya, who rescue Daisy by looking into Henry's past and revealing that the stories he told about his life were a succession of self-serving lies. He has ruined the lives of three women they know of, and probably many more. Henry is confronted, and put on a train with a one-way ticket to Edinburgh. He has no money beyond a few pounds in his pocket, which he spends on vodka. Long before journey's end, he has identified his next victim. 'I caught her eye and smiled, but said nothing . . . I would wait because I knew that in the end she would be the first to speak.'[10]

David Evans, who looked after Jane's garden and the meadow, came in for some serious ragging in the Chequers pub after the publication of *Falling*: everyone winked and dug him in the ribs, and accused him of being the model for Henry Kent.[11] Jane probably never knew about this, but she was very gratified by the letter she received from Sybille Bedford, to whom she had read the first chapter over the telephone.

> Just to repeat: your opening of FALLING is BRILLIANT. Strong, immediately captivating. What a complex male voice is there revealed, incisive, consciously devious (wicked, possibly evil) as well as self-deceiving. What you read me has the clarity and subtle steel of Choderlos de Laclos (of *Les Liaisons Dangereuses*, which I dare guess you have not even read, meaning the novel, not the adapted play; hence no influence, yet in your own voice [there are] marks of that cruel insight . . . Such power. The reader, this reader, longs for more.[12]

She also received a visit from the woman who was Malcolm's last wife, Linda, who had read an interview with Jane about *Falling* and guessed that the man in question was Malcolm. The story she told Jane was chilling. She and Malcolm had lived briefly in Chew Magna before moving to Orkney, where she had a house. Soon after they moved to Scotland Malcolm said they ought to go and see his mother in Edinburgh. A cup of tea was offered, and Malcolm went to make it; and while he was in the kitchen his mother leaned over and said in a whisper, 'You should keep away from my son: he's a dangerous man.'

Linda worked for the NHS, and had a car and a small boat with which to commute to the mainland. Malcolm didn't do much, but he went everywhere with a large carrier bag full of letters. He seldom left the house without this bag, and she was never allowed to look at what it contained: it was his private correspondence. But who could he be writing to?

One day Malcolm left the house without the bag, and Linda seized her moment. Knowing he would be furious if he found her reading his letters, she took the car and drove a short way down the road to a spot where she had a good view in all directions, and started to read them. The letters were all from well-known women, actresses and writers with whom Malcolm was in correspondence; and he had annotated the margins with remarks such as 'too fat' or 'married' or 'not enough money'. Horrified and fascinated, she read on. On hearing footsteps she looked up, and saw that Malcolm was running towards the driver's side of the car with a large stone in his hand. Linda lunged over to the passenger side in a panic, and scrambled out of the car – but as she threw open the door, all the letters were caught by the wind. Malcolm dropped the stone and started scrabbling for them, which gave Linda the chance to run as hard and fast as she could. Linda said she had never run so fast in her life. Further down the road she stopped a rubbish-truck, whose driver gave her a lift to the police station. She went to stay with her sister, and when she finally plucked up the courage to go home, she saw that Malcolm had taken the boat and fled. He never came back. Linda had come to see Jane to assure her that she was not the only one, that others too had been fooled. 'I think it was very good of her to come, and brave of her to tell me,' said Jane.[13]

A few months later Jane had a postcard from New York, from Malcolm himself. He had evidently read *Falling*. 'Dear Daisy,' it read. 'Here for adventure with the lady on the train. Best wishes, Hal.' She never heard from him again; but in 2002 she received a letter from a woman called Wendy Barr in Orkney, telling her that Malcolm was dead. Miss Barr had been his next-door neighbour and in a later letter told Jane that every night he would come back to his house so drunk that she could hear him falling about.

'You are too nice a person to let someone like Malcolm hurt you,' she wrote. 'He was very plausible, and you have got him spot-on in *Falling* – his "kindness to women" ploy. He was the same towards me – appeared so concerned /understanding etc.'

Meanwhile, the process of adapting the Cazalet Chronicle for television inched forward. The idea had been sold to the BBC, and in early 2000 Verity commissioned an experienced adapter, Douglas Livingstone, to do the cutting and write the scripts – a daunting task since the Chronicle has an enormous cast and covers three decades. The BBC originally said it wanted to do six plays for each of the four books, which Jane thought would be about right; but almost immediately, the heads of drama began to reduce that number. In September she had a letter from Joanna Lumley, whom she had seen at the launch party for *Falling*.

'I'm so sorry if I sounded gloomy about the BBC commissioning only six of the episodes of the Cazalet Chronicle,' wrote Joanna. What she meant was that at this stage the BBC wanted six episodes to cover the first two books, and had not yet come to a decision about the last two. 'They make me so angry. Maybe I shouldn't have said anything until it's official . . . But all is far from lost, or even depressing. We must wait for their decision: rather like waiting for sheep to tango.'[14]

Eventually the BBC decided that while the first two books of the Cazalets should be covered in six episodes, the last two books should have twelve – so eighteen episodes were commissioned in all. In the spring of 2000 the scripts were ready. Jane attended the read-through, 'at which sixty-two people sat round an enormous table to read, with Suri Krishnamma the director, Joanna and Verity and me at one end, and two of the BBC drama heads by our side.' They had a strong cast: Hugh Bonneville played Hugh Cazalet and Stephen Dillane played Edward; while Lesley Manville was an excellent Villy, and Anna Chancellor, Diana. Ursula Howells, who had played May Browne-Lacey in *Something in Disguise*, was the Duchy.

Shooting began in the autumn of 2000. Joanna felt that there should have been a 'class coach' on the set, for neither Verity nor the director were familiar with the Home Counties world and there was little care in getting small details right: men didn't stand up when the Duchy entered a room, the wine was not decanted, potatoes were plonked on to people's plates rather than served round. Jane was particularly exasperated by the net curtains on the windows of Home Place: 'In the *country*? But why, when there's nobody to look in?'[15]

At about the same time Peter Salmon, who had been Controller of BBC1, was replaced by Lorraine Heggessey. She was against *The Cazalets* from the start, evidently believing that it was this kind of backward-looking, class-riddled nostalgia that kept the BBC in the past, when it should be forging into the future.

The first six episodes of *The Cazalets* were scheduled to go out in the autumn of 2001; but then Verity was told that they would be going out that summer, at 9 p.m. on Friday evenings – a notorious black hole in the schedule, when viewing figures would be at their lowest. The first went out on 22 June, just as the summer holidays were about to start; and with one interruption for the men's semi-final at Wimbledon on 3 July, it ran till the 27th. The ratings were, of course, nothing like they would have been on Thursday in term-time, and this gave the BBC the opportunity to axe the last twelve episodes. This was bitterly disappointing for everyone concerned; but Jane had never had much to do with the production, beyond an advisory role at the beginning; and she was already absorbed in a new project.

The idea of her writing a memoir had been suggested even before Kingsley's death, but when it was first mooted she felt there were too many people still around who would be upset by it. Yet she herself had already appeared in several biographies. Sean Day-Lewis's biography of his father had appeared in 1980, and Kathleen Tynan's of her husband Kenneth came out in 1987. Of her famous husbands, Elspeth Huxley on Peter Scott was published in 1993, and Eric Jacobs on Kingsley Amis in 1995, shortly before Amis died. Valerie Grove on Laurie Lee appeared in 1997, and David Cesarani's *Arthur Koestler* was published the following year. (Jane did not appreciate being lumped with 'Koestler's Women' in a newspaper serialization.) She had talked to all the authors mentioned, and at length to Zachary Leader whose

Letters of Kingsley Amis appeared in 2000, as did Martin Amis's memoir, *Experience*.

By the end of the 1990s the time had come, she felt, to 'set the record straight': she wasn't just a wife, mistress or stepmother in the lives of various literary figures. She had her own identity, her own experience of those relationships, and her own recollections – which were very different from theirs.

That was the starting point, but as she began writing other motives emerged. 'I have found that writing is often my chief means of communicating with myself,' she wrote in the preface. 'I write to find things *out*, as much as, and sometimes more than, to tell them to other people.' The book was called *Slipstream* because 'I feel,' she wrote, 'as though I have lived my life in the slipstream of experience; and that often I have had to repeat the same disastrous situation several times before I got the message.'[16]

Jane consulted Jane Wood throughout the writing process. 'She agonised about how much to tell,' said Jane Wood, 'but then decided that if she was going to do it, she shouldn't hide anything even if people were hurt by certain revelations.'[17]

Yet Jane Wood did not edit the book: she was primarily a fiction editor, and she worked for Orion. To please Jane, Macmillan had agreed that Wood should work on the Cazalet books but they made it clear that Jane's memoir, her first book of non-fiction, would be edited in-house. Her new editor was Jeremy Trevathan, who was the partner of Jane's old friend, the novelist Paul Bailey. He recalled that 'The parts of *Slipstream* that she was most churned up about were her abandonment of Nicola, and her affair with Cecil Day-Lewis. I think she also felt that those would be the events on which she would be judged . . . One thing she kept saying (of her younger self) was, "You see, I could never talk to anyone." '[18] This was more of a plea for sympathy than any objective recollection of the truth: Jane was never short of friends, and seldom shy of talking about her problems.

The book, published in 2002, was hailed as unusually candid, and courageous. In the *Sunday Times* Humphrey Carpenter was very sympathetic, feeling that Jane had been almost forced into her first marriage and never really recovered.[19] In the *Times Literary Supplement*, Sarah Curtis wrote that 'The reader may be irritated by the sense of resentment that creeps into the narrative from the beginning, but increasingly fascinated by the puzzle of the personality she honestly reveals.'[20]

Part of the puzzle can be explained by the passage of time. When Jane was young, girls were raised to believe that boys were better at everything; and as they grew up, to believe that they were not really a part of the world unless they were married. Men took their God-given privilege for granted: feminists and women with professions were jokes rather than equals, and any woman who objected to the inequality was not facing facts. Yet by the time Jane's third marriage was over, the relationship between the sexes had changed dramatically. Men like Kingsley Amis bitterly resented having to share their world with women who could be doctors and judges, who had power and autonomy, who could enter a pub without a male escort and join institutions that had hitherto been their exclusive preserve.

It was only as her marriage to Kingsley was breaking up that Jane recognized the part that women could play in her life, as friends, therapists and teachers of how to live without a man. It was through them that Jane said she finally learned to listen to other people, to understand why she kept making the same mistakes, and to come to terms with the damage done by her mother's coldness. It is impossible to overemphasize how much Jane felt she had benefited from the years of therapy with Jenner Roth and the women's group. By the time Jane came to write *Slipstream*, she felt infinitely more in control of her life that she had in the last few years at Lemmons. At the same time the episode with Malcolm had shown that her yearning for male company, admiration and sexual intimacy was as strong as ever, and that she would never shake off her emotional vulnerability.

This was borne out by Annabel Turner, who had begun helping her with administrative and secretarial work the year before. Jane received a great deal of fan mail after *Slipstream*, and she asked Annabel to help her answer it. Most people just wanted to express their appreciation; but Annabel felt that there were one or two others who were trying to get closer.

I'm not saying they were stalkers exactly, but it felt as if they were trying to set up a friendship or a correspondence that Jane might find it hard to retreat from; so I would write something grateful and reserved, and Jane would say, 'Don't you think we should be a bit more encouraging?' She liked the idea of them getting in touch again. Of course she didn't want another Malcolm, that was too terrible and humiliating . . . But she couldn't shake off her romantic nature: never gave up hope that she might yet find Mr Darcy.[21]

A similar tale was told by Jacqui Graham, who had been Jane's publicity agent since *Falling*, and had arranged that Jane should attend a *Daily Mail* lunch in November at the Savoy to publicize *Slipstream*. Here she was introduced to Anthony Wedgwood Benn, whom she had never met – which was hardly surprising, since he had spent most of his working life on the far left of the Labour Party. Yet within minutes she had taken a shine to him, and asked him to come to Bungay for the weekend. He gave her a look of astonishment, and left soon after.

One person who was not happy with *Slipstream* was Roy Foster. He and Aisling were visiting her one weekend, when 'Jane asked me if I'd read the book and I told her straight, I'd found it disappointing: "*I* don't want to know about all the men you've been to bed with," I said. "I'm more interested in your work, and in you as a writer – there's almost nothing about that!" – "You don't like my book, I think I'm going to cry," she said. At that point I think I was supposed to put my arms around her and fold her to my manly bosom, but I didn't.'[22]

Later Jane wrote him a letter saying, 'I think you are quite right. I didn't include enough about writing – largely because I didn't think it would interest people, although why I should [make] such a distinction between the possible interest in life as opposed to work I cannot now see.'[23] Yet the fact remains that in *Slipstream* Jane isn't thinking about her work. It rates a few mentions here and there, usually about how difficult she found it; but the question that absorbs her is why she made so many mistakes in her relationships. This seems justifiable in a book that calls itself a memoir, rather than an autobiography. A memoir is selective, and thus entitles the author to concentrate on one aspect of a life.

Jane had been made a CBE in 2000; but while it was gratifying to have her work recognized, it didn't make writing any easier. She still owed Macmillan the novel she had dropped when she started *Falling*, but picking up the threads only revealed knots that had never been untangled. Annabel came twice a week, and while there were fewer house-guests a weekend was still a big event, at which more people came to Saturday dinner and Sunday lunch.

She talked about herself with a mixture of diffidence and disarming candour; but her conversation could also be funny, astringent and wildly unpredictable. She told one lunch party that a woman's vagina never grows old, being as responsive at eighty as it was at eighteen – a remark guaranteed to leave everyone floundering for what to say next.

In April 2004 Jane did a Radio 4 *Bookclub* programme with Jim Naughtie, on *Falling*. First Naughtie and Jane talked about the book, and then a studio audience asked her questions about it. At no point did Jane mention Malcolm's name; but the programme drew a sharp complaint from his sister, who refused to see his dark side. What she saw was a well-known writer making capital out of an affair that had gone wrong, and she was indignant that Jane continued to refer to Malcolm as a 'conman' and a 'psychopath' in public, causing distress to his family. She also reminded Jane that Malcolm's family had been considerate enough to return Jane's own letters to him, unread and uncopied, when they were found among his possessions after his death.

Ann Clowes replied on Jane's behalf, saying that at no point in either *Falling* or *Slipstream* had Jane mentioned Malcolm's name, and he was not being used in some callous way to promote her book. Jane had experienced some very unpleasant sides to Mr Shane, and she was entitled to describe them in a reasonable way however painful this might be for the family. However, she was grateful for the return of her letters.

One of the many people who read and enjoyed *Falling* was Tristram Powell, whose parents Anthony and Violet had been friends of Kingsley and Hilly. Powell felt that it would make a very good television drama. Jane was happy for him to do it, but she did not write the script. That was the work of Andrew Davies, with whom Powell had worked on the TV adaptation of Kingsley's *The Old Devils*. After that everything fell neatly into place, for Davies's daughter then worked for Yorkshire Television. Henry Kent was played by Michael Kitchen, with whom Powell later worked on *Foyle's War*; Penelope Wilton took the part of Daisy Langrish, and the film was broadcast on 6 March 2005. Both actors were excellent while the relationship grew and they were essentially acting solo, but there was very little sexual chemistry between them. At one point when they are in bed, Michael Kitchen is heard saying, 'I love getting women to the point when they are desperate for sex, and I so enjoy the power of withholding it,' but this is undercut by Penelope Wilton looking at him as though he were about to give her a parking ticket.

Jane had started her novel in progress, which she called *Percy*, in the late 1990s. She put it down to do the *Anthology of Marriage* and then came the Malcolm episode, *Falling*, bouts in hospital and *Slipstream*. Picking it up after such a long time was, not surprisingly, immensely difficult.

She wrote to her editor Jeremy Trevathan:

> I have to tell you that I am in a frightful mess about this novel, and need someone to talk to about it in order to try and sort myself out . . .
> It isn't that I'm having a bloc exactly, but for various reasons – having started it so long ago and worse, having shown it to one person who said I was trying to write two novels at once, I started it all over again cutting out the second subject as it were, and now that feels wrong and I don't know what the hell I am doing. Swimming in treacle up a hill in a fog and dreading each session . . . It isn't that there is an awful lot of MS but the two versions make it an unsimple read. I would like to talk to you about that before trying to assemble it.[24]

There are several drafts, fragments and notes about *Percy* in Jane's archive. From the notes alone, it seems that one of her themes was the way a small town can be taken over by someone rich coming in from outside, who is determined to shake the place up and inaugurate an arts festival. Lists of characters indicate that the festival was going to be a much larger component in the book, which eventually came out in 2008 under the title *Love All*.

As walking or standing became increasingly difficult, Jane expected her house-guests to pull their weight. 'That's when she would tell me to start doing the cooking for all these people,' remembered Alice Leader. 'Selina and Monkey and I had to do everything, cooking and laying the table and washing up.'

But if this was hard on the guests, it was often hard on the hostess too. Tamasin Day-Lewis and Jonathan Burnham came down for one weekend and as Jane's legs were particularly bad at that time, the two of them – both excellent cooks – did all the shopping and cooking on their own. Jane sat in her study, listening to distant chatter and gales of laughter drifting in from the kitchen and feeling increasingly aggrieved. It took her a long time to walk to the conservatory dining room for meals, and Tamasin remembered that while every dish Jonathan cooked was greeted with rapture, everything she cooked was judged not up to the mark. The final straw was when Tamasin and Jonathan cleaned out and tidied her kitchen cupboards: they had hoped she would be pleased, but she was outraged.

Monkey installed a small lift in a corner of her study so she could avoid the stairs, and she spent more and more time in this room: either at her desk, or in a big chair by the fire where she read. Another dog came into her life. Eddie was a beautiful female lurcher with haunted eyes and a pale coat, whom Annabel had adopted from someone who couldn't cope with such a large animal. Eddie was too big for Annabel's household too, but luckily Jane was willing to take her on. Darcy had died in 1998 and she had been dogless ever since, and Eddie – as well as looking like a film star – thirsted for love. The dog slept with her at night, and Jane said it was like sharing the bed with a set of golf clubs.

Jane had lost her brother Robin in the spring of 2003. He had meant the world to her when they were children and she always remained fond of him, but they did not see each other that often and he was nothing like as close to her as Monkey. The death of Sybille Bedford, however, in February 2006, was a bitter blow. Jane never forgot the help she had been on the first volume of the Cazalets, and the fourth volume – *Casting Off* – is dedicated to her. Jane went to Sybille's memorial service in June; and the following month she set off to spend two weeks in France.

Jane was now eighty-three, so it was a bold move to organize a holiday in France for a large group of friends. She had taken a property in the Languedoc near Carcassonne, consisting of two houses and a swimming pool. Monkey, Nicola and their cousin Kay Howard came, as well as Tristram Powell and his wife, Selina, Jacqui Graham, Penelope Lively, Pam Rose, Jane's editor Jeremy Trevathan and his partner Paul Bailey. She had looked forward to it, as usual, with unclouded anticipation and her imagination had told her it was all going to be wonderful: with all her friends around her and a pool to swim in every day, she would regain strength and health.

But tensions arose between Monkey and Paul Bailey: Paul felt that Monkey should be prouder and more open about his sexuality. He was also outraged (as many people were) by the vehemence of Monkey's far-right opinions, and his casually racist remarks that might have raised an eyebrow in the 1960s, but were no longer tolerable. Jane could not forgive Paul for his antagonism to Monkey, even when Paul shared the last of his heart pills with her brother since Monkey had run out. She also resented the fact that Paul was very funny and entertaining. He kept his end of the table in a roar, and generally stole the limelight.

At the same time Jane did not have the energy to get in and out of the pool every day; and because she had trouble walking – she leaned heavily on a stick – she often felt left out. She enjoyed pottering around the local market; but did not join the people who went off to Montaillou or Carcassonne, and wished they had stayed by the pool with her.

Two new friends came into Jane's life in the late 2000s. One was Janet Hodgson, a young woman who came to live with her as a cook-companion. No money was involved in the arrangement: Jane wanted a friendly, creative person to share her house and in return, Janet would cook two or three lunches or dinners a week. Janet rented out her flat in Highbury, moved into the spacious top-floor flat at Bridge House, and hoped to use the coming months to write a cookbook.

Janet was fascinated by Bridge House: as she put it, 'You couldn't have put it together unless you had lived like that all your life.'[25] Janet loved talking to Jane, who taught her a great deal; and because she had never experienced the kind of life Jane led, she felt rather like an anthropologist observing everything. But as time went on, she was expected to cook more and more. Every morning Jane would say, 'What shall we have today?' Janet had to do the shopping and cook-ing, often for lunch or dinner guests; and since Jane insisted on recipes that were very time-consuming and required a lot of washing up, there wasn't much time left over to write her cookbook. Instead, Janet asked whether she could do some filming, and Jane agreed. The footage Janet took on her little digital cine-camera is a vivid glimpse of Jane as she was towards the end of her life: making marmalade, doing the rounds of the meadow on her mobility scooter, and talking about books, and love and Kingsley Amis.

Another friend whom she saw a great deal of at this time was Dom Antony Sutch, a Catholic monk who had been headmaster of Downside School and was a frequent contributor to 'Thought for the Day' on Radio 4. He had left Downside, and was now the parish priest at the church of St Benet's in Beccles.

Dom Antony particularly valued their conversations, which were very serious on big subjects; and although Jane said she was desperately lonely, 'to someone not in the literary world like me, it seemed she knew everybody'. At the same time she felt she had been used by many people, especially men, who had never recognized or acknowledged her achievements and talents.

They came together one evening in the autumn of 2007, to watch a programme on television by Kate Blewett called *Bulgaria's Abandoned Children*. Tony Scotland had a strong connection with Bulgaria, and in 1999 he had been so moved by the plight of orphaned children in state care homes in the Balkans that he had set up a charity called the Bulgarian Orphans Fund. He had been a consultant on Kate Blewett's film, which focused on the severely disabled children who lived in that St Petka Home at Mogilino in northern Bulgaria. Tony urged Jane to watch it – if she could bear to. He warned her that some scenes were extremely distressing.

Father Antony recalled that 'After about fifteen minutes, I said, "I really don't think I can take much more of this." Whereupon Jane turned to me and said, "Antony, they have to live in this hell twenty-four hours a day, seven days a week, three hundred and sixty-five days a year; and the least *you* can do is be with them for an hour or so." She was absolutely right, of course.'

Dom Antony was particularly grateful to Jane a few years later, when a complaint about his conduct at Downside created a scandal. The police cleared him of all charges, but the damage was done. He was forced to give up his ministry in Beccles and found himself shunned by many, but not by Jane. 'She was a wonderful friend and did everything she could,' he said. 'Her steadfast loyalty meant a very great deal to me, especially when everyone else was running for cover.'[26]

Jane worked regularly, from ten thirty to one thirty every day; but with Jane Wood she had grown accustomed to a good deal of support, so Jeremy Trevathan went to visit her over a number of weekends while she was writing Love All. She had started to use a computer, thinking of it as a highly strung typewriter. She would print out her work at the end of each session, plus the occasional paragraph or two which was glued or stapled into the text. When Jeremy came down they would go over what she had done, resulting in more handwritten notes over the pages. He asked if all the corrections were being kept on the computer, and she assured him they were.

She finished the book in early 2008, and Jeremy came down to Bungay with a disc on which to download it all. 'She showed me to the computer and I asked for the name of the file the script had been saved to. She didn't understand and alarm bells started to ring for me!' It emerged that the text had been saved 'to hundreds and hundreds of individual, dated files', but there was no clue as to where each one should come in the novel. Jeremy could not afford to show his dismay. Jane was not well at the time, and 'I honestly felt that she wouldn't be able to cope if I told her the script was unacceptable as it was.'

All the individual files had to be scanned and put in order, and the corrected copy with its glued and stapled additions and handwritten addenda was incorporated – an editorial nightmare. There were also chunks of unfinished text throughout, marking as yet unwritten linking sections. Jeremy sketched them in, and over another couple of visits to Bungay he showed Jane where they were and she corrected them. Yet the whole exercise had shaken her faith: not in the computer, but in an editorial process of a complexity she had never encountered before. Jeremy, too, was not used to dealing with such a fragmented typescript; and it was 'only some years later that I heard she had taken it into her head that Paul and I had rewritten the text without her permission'.[27]

Yet whatever the difficulties Jane experienced in the process, Love All is unmistakably hers – even though it has almost no sex and no erotic undercurrents, which makes it unique among her novels. She described it as an exploration of 'how you live without love – or the consequences of living without love', hence the wonderfully elliptical title. It is also a meditation on the nature of love: how can you tell the difference between true love and infatuation, desire or wishful thinking? Can it grow out of friendship, or affection, or loneliness and yearning for a mate, or is it something else entirely? The characters in this novel are incarnations of various states of mind more than they are real people. But although she had spent a lifetime exploring what love is or is not, her recent encounter with Malcolm had shown that she was still very unsure of the answers.

Persephone Plover, Percy for short, lives with her old Aunt Floy and a cat called Marvell, in a house remarkably similar to the one in which Jane and Kingsley lived in Maida Vale. Floy is a garden designer who has just received a commission to restore the gardens of Melton, a country house that has been bought by a self-made tycoon called Jack Curtis. Percy, recovering from an unhappy romance, accompanies her to Melton where they are lodged in luxurious comfort in the great house, and made much of by their host.

Not far away live Thomas Musgrove and his sister Mary, who had lived at Melton as children. Thomas resents the fact that his father sold Melton and dreams of buying it back; but since his nursery garden business is barely scraping by, this is unlikely. Besides, he is haunted by a greater loss: that of his adored wife Celia, who died in a car accident some years before the novel opens. She left him with a daughter, Hatty, now eight years old. Thomas would not be able to manage, financially or emotionally, without his older sister Mary who is in her mid-thirties. It is she who runs the house, raises Hatty, holds down a part-time job and tries to keep her temperamental brother on an even keel – all on a shoestring budget. They have been joined by Celia's brother Francis, a painter, who helps Thomas with the nursery garden.

Since Floy is going to need a great many plants for Melton, she and Thomas strike up a good working relationship; and before long, Thomas finds himself falling in love with Floy's niece Percy. Jack too is very taken with her, and gives her a job as administrator of the cultural festival he is planning. He bought Melton as a place in which to display his money, but without anyone to share it with, he has become oppressed by its emptiness. He proposes to Percy, and is staggered when she turns him down. She sees that he doesn't really love her. 'I know you think you do,' she tells him, 'but it's the idea of it you want — not me.'[28]

Thomas is also becoming increasingly infatuated with Percy. When she and Floy go back to London after the Melton gardens are finished, he follows them on the pretext of starting a garden design course; but soon he is helping the elderly and increasingly frail Floy with her London commissions, and paying court to a reluctant Percy. Percy has already turned down his first proposal, but he begs her to think it over, and she says she will because she can't bear to give him a flat refusal.

Everything changes when Floy falls down dead in her garden one evening. It is the painter Francis, Thomas's brother-in-law, who helps Percy through the shock of unexpected death and the numb days that follow. (Thomas himself is unavoidably detained elsewhere.) And Francis proves far more of a comfort to Percy than Thomas, with his clumsy attempts at consolation.

Mary has rather enjoyed the weeks without Thomas; and Jack, lonelier than ever in his grand house, now turns his attentions to her. He sees her selfless kindness and strength, she sees his need for warmth, and they fall in love; but Mary cannot bring herself to tell her brother. When Thomas comes back from London, he's convinced it won't be long before Percy accepts him; but within days he receives a letter from her, turning him down. He is utterly distraught, and Mary explains to Jack that she cannot break the news of their engagement while he is in such a state. It is only when he attempts suicide that Mary realizes that she can either marry Jack or save her brother Thomas, but she cannot do both.

At the end of the novel, Francis and Percy have set up house together in London — not as lovers, but as friends: it seems so much more relaxed to live with warmth and affection, rather than the tension and drama of love. Francis is possibly gay, certainly a non-player sexually. Will their relationship last? We don't know, but it will do for now.

The book is filled with distorted, disappointed love. As the novel opens, Percy sees that her dream lover was just another married man looking for sex on the side. Jack's first wife saw him as a trophy, which is exactly how he saw her; while Mrs Fanshawe, his elderly secretary, nurses an unspoken passion for her boss that gnaws at her sanity. Rosalie, the single mother, is looking for a steady provider; while her parents are alienated from each other by penury and ill-health. There are also the scars inflicted by loss: Floy's only love died in the First World War, and she never had another; while Thomas lost Celia, and then Percy.

Percy and Francis try to sidestep the matter altogether, settling for a kind of sibling relationship. But Mary and Thomas are real siblings; and just like Elizabeth and Oliver in *Something in Disguise*, the sister is the one who does the real work of driving the engine, while trying to keep the brother from going off the rails. In *Persuasion*, Jane Austen's Mary Musgrove is a self-absorbed whinger, but in *Love All* we see her opposite: a woman with the same name, who never puts herself first and doesn't complain anything like enough.

Mary feels needed, and that gives her some satisfaction; but one of the most interesting aspects of the book is how finely Jane balances Mary's dilemma. The story is set in the 1960s, which, as Nicholas Clee observed in the *Times Literary Supplement*, is 'almost the last period when she could show a young woman torn between love and duty'.[29] Mary does love Jack: she sees that he values her qualities, and he can give her security, stability and love – things she will never get from Thomas. But Thomas, for all his maudlin self-dramatization and his breathtaking selfishness, cannot be abandoned. It's all very well for the reader to shout 'Mary, this is your last chance! Dump Thomas, scoop up Hatty (you'll have to rescue her at some point anyway) and for God's sake, marry Jack!' This is the response of the modern woman who feels no guilt about putting herself first; but Mary has been looking after her brother all her life, and she cannot let him down now.

Jane's mind was as sharp as ever, and she had not lost her appetite for work or entertaining; but she could no longer manage on her own in Bridge House and needed a live-in carer. Alice Leader knew just the right person, who had looked after her mother in Chicago. She was a fully trained Bulgarian nurse called Teodora Georguieva, Teddy for short – a pretty woman with a mass of auburn hair, a fiery character and a ready smile. What her English lacked in grammar it made up for in fluency, and she was accompanied by Mort, her orange Pomeranian dog.

The only flight Teddy could find that would take dogs in the cabin flew to Paris, so Frances Mann arranged to pick them up at Calais and drove them to Bungay. Jane looked forward to having a dog in the house again, since Eddie had died a year or two before; but while Mort was willing to make friends with Jane, he remained firmly attached to Teddy.

Although Jane saw Teddy's qualities, it inevitably took time to relinquish a certain independence and accept being looked after. 'She wants to treat me like an enormous expensive doll who can't even comb her own hair,' she wrote to Tony Scotland, 'but kindness is all.'[30]

In mid-July Jane heard that Jill Balcon had died. She had only come to Bungay once, and it had not been a great success. Jill was a very light sleeper and had objected to Jane playing the radio in the small hours. Jane was sad, and sorry that they could not have taken more comfort in each other as old friends; but she had other things to think about.

Jane had not forgotten the Bulgarian orphans, and in the summer of 2009 she organized a fund-raising lunch for Tony's Bulgarian Orphans Fund. This was a charity pared down to essentials: there were no costs or overheads, so every penny Tony raised was spent on buying what was needed for the children: building material to repair dilapidated buildings, bedding, medical supplies, food, clothes, school supplies – whatever was required was piled into his van and driven to Bulgaria, or bought on the spot.

Following Tony's example, Jane was determined that the lunch she organized would be entirely donated so that everything raised could go to the children. 'She got everyone involved,' remembered Laurence Magnus, 'and it was quite amazing how she could get people to do things. She identified so personally and passionately with the cause, that it was difficult for anyone to refuse her.'[31]

The day of the lunch was set for Monday, 3 August. Jane had asked her friend Prue Leith to give a talk, which attracted considerable interest. Prue Leith agreed to come on the Sunday and spend the night, as did Tony and Julian Berkeley; and Jane asked Janet Hodgson to come and cook Sunday lunch and dinner for them. Cooking for

Prue Leith was a daunting prospect, but she was very kind and complimentary about Janet's efforts although Jane, ever the perfectionist, was annoyed that Janet had not included any peppers among the roast vegetables. And Janet couldn't help a wry smile when Prue, praising Jane's magnificent achievement the following day, added that 'She also runs the best private hotel in Suffolk.'[32]

The lunch took place at Upland Hall (home of Laurence and Jocelyn Magnus), and was packed with people who had paid £50 a head to be there. John Groom the butcher had been particularly generous: he gave all the meat for the lunch, and he and his wife cooked it while Dawn Fairfield, Annabel Turner and others made mountains of salads and puddings, and Janet made industrial quantities of potato salad. Jane, who could no longer stand for more than a few minutes on her zimmer frame, was frustrated that she couldn't do more; but she still managed to make the Cumberland sauce, the mayonnaise and the chutneys.

The event was a huge success, and raised £5,000. By the time it was over everyone involved was exhausted, both emotionally and physically. Janet went for a swim in the river, thinking that Jane had probably gone to bed; but she found her at her desk, already at work on the long list of thank-you letters she wrote to everyone who had helped.

21

'I *Know* He's Going to Get Better'

THE LUNCH FOR the Bulgarian Orphans had been such a success that Jane repeated it the following year: this time her speakers were Ruth Rendell and P.D. James, in a discussion chaired by Melvyn Bragg. This too was well attended, but she thought people would get bored if she had a lunch every year; so in 2011 she persuaded the owners of the Fisher Theatre in Bungay to lend it to her for an afternoon. Unfortunately the only attraction was Jane reading her story for children, *Freddie Whitemouse*. Only twelve people turned up. Jane was disappointed, but undeterred. 'We will never read *anything* to *anybody* between two and four in the afternoon again,' she told Tony as they left the theatre.[1]

She did one final lunch in 2012, with Sue MacGregor talking to William Nicholson and Penelope Lively; and the very last fundraiser for the Bulgarian Orphans that she tried to stage was an auction. This proved too ambitious. None of the people she could draw on had any experience of auctions, so it dwindled into an unpublicized raffle with only one prize – an ornate shell mirror made by Jane herself – which raised far more than expected. Altogether, the events Jane organized in her late eighties raised almost £28,000, which is a tribute to her courage, tenacity and refusal to take no for an answer.

I think I must have bought some tickets for the raffle of the shell mirror. I could hardly say no. In February 2013 I had suggested myself as her biographer, and both Patricia Wyndham and Monkey had backed my petition. I had written two biographies, and was not completely unknown to Jane. With my parents Anne and John Julius I had once lunched at Lemmons as a teenager, where my clearest memories are of Sargy who was wonderful company and treated me like an adult. I also remember Jane and Kingsley coming to dinner with us. She was beautiful with a sad expression, and he was very red in the face and never stopped talking. I heard next day that they didn't leave till about two in the morning. Since then, I had news of her from time to time from my mother, who was a regular member of the painting group. In fact it was she who had said, when I finished my last book, 'Why don't you do Jane?' and the more I read, the more I wanted to write her life.

Jane was rather flattered at the thought of a biography, and she invited me to stay for a weekend the following month. It would be the first of five long weekends I spent at Bungay that year. My previous subject had been extremely reluctant to talk about his lovers, so I could not get over the frankness and honesty with which Jane told me about hers. 'I think you're obsessed with my sex life,' she said sadly at one point. I blushed furiously and changed the subject. I wasn't obsessed really, just fascinated. As time went on she would say, 'Haven't you got some early chapters ready by now? I do want to read your book before I pop off, you know.'[2]

To my great relief her attention was diverted by a far more significant event: the final volume of the Cazalet Chronicle, *All Change*, which was coming out in November. The supposedly last volume of the Cazalet Chronicle had been published in 1995, but Jane had never really let go. Many of the characters were portraits of the people she had grown up with and they lived in places she had known and loved, while Louise, Polly and Clary were reflections of herself. In her imagination they *had* become her family, as much as Monkey and Nicola and Elliott, her four grandchildren and eleven great-grandchildren. No wonder she was still preoccupied with the Cazalets' loves and losses and betrayals, their money worries and extravagances, and she wanted to write at least one more book about them.

Maria Rejt was to be her new editor. Maria was publishing director at Macmillan, and in 2010 she was asked to head a new imprint called Mantle, that would very much reflect her taste and style. She was a keen fan of Jane's. 'I remember being shown into her study, and her sitting there working at her computer . . . She had the most beautiful, mahogany, deep dark voice. And she was quite nervous which surprised me, although she was incredibly easy to talk to.'[3]

Jane seems to have had no trouble immersing herself again in the Cazalets as characters, but she admitted that it was 'absolute hell from a continuity point of view. You keep on having to remember what you called someone's chauffeur fifteen [*sic*] years ago.'[4]

The novel came out in November 2013, Jane's ninetieth year, and it was dedicated to Hilary Mantel and her husband, Gerald McEwen. Jane had always appreciated the way Mantel had been such a champion of her work, standing up for her against those who dismissed her books as 'women's fiction'; and this was her way of saying thank you. The literary world was much more enthusiastic about the prospect of another Cazalet novel in 2013 than it had been in 1990, when *The Light Years* came out to a distinctly lukewarm reception. Part of this was due to the light-speed of social and technological change, so that the world of fifty years ago seems almost as distant as the world a century earlier – and the comfortable world of the Cazalets had become almost unimaginable.

There was no doubt that the books were held in considerable esteem and affection; and the BBC provided a tremendous drum-roll for the last volume by putting on a forty-five-part adaptation of *The Cazalets* for Radio 4 which ran for months. To celebrate the launch, a lunch was organized at the Black Dog Restaurant in Bungay on 6 November. Nicola and Elliott were there, and Sargy and Frances; while a mini-bus from London brought her editors Maria Rejt and Jane Wood, friends including Selina Hastings, Ann Clowes and Jenner Roth, several journalists and of course Monkey. Jacqui Graham recalled that 'he was on wonderful form that day, enchanting . . . Jane asked him to sit next to her when she started to get a little weary.'[5]

Jane was enormously cheered and gratified by the attention that *All Change* was receiving. In a long interview entitled 'The Page-Turner who Turned the Heads of Literary Giants', she told Jane Clinton that her publishers 'had wanted to put *The Last Cazalet* on the cover, but I said it might not be the last one. I might want to write another one. I easily might not, but I'd like the choice.'[6]

All Change begins in 1956, nine years after *Casting Off*. The Duchy is dying and the world she knew is dying with her – although not as fast as one might think. After her death, her only daughter Rachel stays on at Home Place with three devoted servants to look after her, although, like her, they are too old to embark on a new life. Rachel's lover Sid thinks that, at last, Rachel is free of family duties and can live with her; but Sid herself has cancer, and once again Rachel takes on the role of nurse. Sid's death is one of the most moving passages in the book, but there is one final loss that Rachel will have to face.

In the last four volumes, money was scarcely a problem for the Cazalets. The family timber business provided comfortable incomes for them all, for what seemed like very little effort – but in fact the firm has been losing money for years. Edward sees what should be done, but can't persuade his elder brother Hugh to make the slightest change in the management of the business. This is the first time they have disagreed so violently, and both brothers find it very upsetting. Each tries to enlist the support of their youngest brother Rupert, but he is even less of a businessman than they are. Hugh, who thought he would never get over the death of his wife Sybil, is happily married again and finds comfort there; but Edward is far from happy with the grasping Diana. She has obliged him to buy a country house on which she has spent vast sums of money, and he is seriously in debt; while the lavish dinner with which she tries to impress Rachel and Sid was described by one reviewer as 'a wonderful piece of cut-glass venom'.[7]

Edward's first wife Villy lives in London, in the house he bought before abandoning her for Diana. Villy, eaten up with rancour, has never let their son Rolly – now eighteen – meet That Woman, so he barely knows his father. But she has given a home to Miss Milliment, the old governess: an act of kindness that becomes a terrible weight of responsibility, as Miss Milliment drifts into dementia.

Louise has given up acting. She makes money modelling, and broods over the selfishness of her rich lover Joseph Waring – a portrait of Michael Behrens – who will never marry her. Polly, the one who got it right, lives in the country with her adoring, titled husband and has babies. So does Clary; but she and Archie are both frustrated by their penny-pinching existence. During the course of the book their marriage is sorely tested, but holds fast.

The firm's bankruptcy hits Hugh with a terrible force: he feels 'as though he had been put in charge of a whole small world, and let down every single person in it'. Rachel is told that Home Place, which had been bought in the firm's name, will have to be sold. It's a bitter blow, coming so soon after Sid's death; but she is determined that the whole family will gather for one last, magnificent Christmas together.

Death and the process of dying is much in evidence, which is perhaps not surprising as Jane approached her own end. But she was still absorbed by the everyday fabric of family life. It seems odd that she, who didn't want much to do with children in her own life, should devote so much space in her novels to their teatimes and bath-times, their squabbles and complaints and winsome ways. Even when their mercilessly innocent remarks bring the adults up short, some readers find these passages overlong. Yet she is not so much observing the children as reliving, with extraordinary clarity, what it's like to be a child: something that the impatient reader has, perhaps, largely forgotten.

Writing in *The Spectator*, Nicola Shulman revelled in the fact that in order to appreciate the last Cazalet novel properly, she gave herself the treat of rereading the previous four. 'Howard has lost none of her insight, none of her comedy, and none of that rare . . . ability to magic us into a room with the characters,' she wrote. She also observed that Jane 'has made this past her element, and through her we experience it as natives, not tourists'.[8] In the *Sunday Times*, Lucy Atkins observed that 'Painful events . . . are underpinned by deep family love and loyalty. This is cumulatively reassuring, without becoming dim-witted or simplistic, largely because Howard is such an acute observer of human behaviour.'[9]

By now Jane could barely walk. It took her a long time to get from the study to the dining room on her zimmer frame, wincing with pain at every step. She needed extra oxygen, which was delivered through what she called her 'whiskers' – thin transparent tubes under her nose. Everything was more of an effort; but her mind was clear, and she had already embarked on another novel exploring the Seven Deadly Sins ('I've done them all') of which she had written about 160 pages. But in late November, something happened that shook her to the core.

Monkey had not been feeling well for some time. He had diabetes, and had told Patricia Wyndham one evening at the theatre that although he ate very little, he felt permanently bloated. On the week-end of 22–24 November he was admitted to hospital in great pain. They performed an emergency operation, after which he was taken into intensive care. A biopsy revealed that he was suffering from gastric lymphoma, but as his heart was not considered strong enough to cope with a course of chemotherapy, he was put into an induced coma. Jane was told he was in hospital, but not how serious the situation was. Her instinct was to get to London as soon as possible to see him, but Nicola persuaded her to wait until he was a little stronger.

Nicola and Elliott had moved to Bungay from Cheltenham in 2011, so as to be closer to Jane. In time they bought a little house a few hundred yards away, but they occupied one of the bedrooms at Bridge House so as to be on hand if anything happened in the night. Teddy was still looking after Jane, but she was planning to go back to Bulgaria.

Jane was very glad of Nicola and Elliott's company, and their quiet, practical kindness. On 27 November Nicola drove her to Norwich to record an interview with Jim Naughtie for the *Today* programme. At one point in the interview, Naughtie used the word 'frisky' to describe her turbulent youth. 'I wasn't the only frisker,' replied Jane. 'Frisky was quite popular in those days. Wars always make people pretty unfaithful.'

Looking back on the interview later, Jim Naughtie said that 'She talked about her famous, and famously stormy, marriage to Kingsley Amis and said, "You know, I refuse to hate Kingsley." It seemed to me . . . that there was almost nothing that she regretted, and I think that's rather an admirable way to pass into your nineties and to fade away.'[10]

Her appearance on the *Today* programme was the last time she was heard live on the radio; and at the end of the interview she sent a message to Monkey in hospital, hoping he would get better. By the time she had returned to Bungay, Jane was exhausted. She could not stop thinking about Monkey and, on a lower level of anxiety, she was apprehensive at the prospect of Teddy's departure and the arrival of a new carer.

Teddy had been with her for almost five years, and their relationship seemed to veer between affectionate banter and moments of intense irritation. Annabel Turner, Jane's secretary, was convinced that 'Teddy really loved Jane, and the fact that they both added such drama to each other's lives was a good thing for both of them. I think Teddy brought Jane back to life at least three times, and it was tough love: Teddy made her walk to the end of the corridor and back despite the moans, building her up and taking no nonsense.' Some people were shocked that Teddy still allowed Jane the occasional cigarette, but Teddy was defiant. 'She can't *walk*, she can't *dance*, she can't *fuck*, and now you say she can't *SMOKE*?'[11]

The last time I saw Jane was in early December 2013, and she had asked my mother Anne to come too. She could no longer leave her bedroom, and divided her time between her bed and a chair by the window. 'I *know* Monkey's going to get better,' she told us, 'I *know* he's going to get better because if he doesn't, I don't think I can face it.' Soon after we had left, on 5 December, Frances came in. It was she who broke the news to Jane that Monkey had died in hospital, without regaining consciousness.

The letters of condolence began pouring in, for Monkey had been very much loved: not just by his friends but by his family, and especially the young cousins who had used his house as a base, sought his advice and relished his eccentric company. Jane answered every letter, and they brought her great solace: the stories and jokes people told her about Monkey kept him alive for her.

Around mid-December the new carer, Eva Major, took over Teddy's duties with a gentle professionalism that made the change-over much easier than Nicola had feared. On the 19th, Jane went into Bungay on her mobility scooter to buy Christmas presents, and she spent Christmas with Nicola and Elliott and their son Ben. Nicola felt that it was in the days after Christmas, at the sad tail-end of the year, that Jane began to feel just how empty life was without her beloved brother. Once she had answered all the letters, there seemed to be nothing left to do. She was often ill in the winter, and by New Year's Day she was so weak that she could no longer swallow properly, so she couldn't take any painkillers or medication: it was obvious that she was sinking rapidly.

That night she had a visit from Dom Antony Sutch. They talked a bit and then she said, ' "You know I don't believe in God; but will you give me absolution?" She didn't mean absolution from sin, in a Christian understanding of the word. I think what she wanted was to be allowed to go. To be told that there was nothing left to do.'[12]

Jane watched an animal programme on television with Nicola in the late morning of 2 January, but she was very tired; and when Nicola went up to her room after lunch she was asleep. Nicola was waiting for two community nurses, who were coming to help Jane get changed and make the bed. When they arrived Nicola went over to rouse her mother, but found that she was no longer breathing. She had slipped away quietly between one moment and the next. In her life, she had never found the great lasting love she had spent so much time searching for. But she died in her own bed, in her own house, with her daughter close by – which is as good an end as anyone can hope for.

∼

The death of Elizabeth Jane Howard was announced on the *Six O'Clock News* that night. The following morning, every national paper had a short article announcing her passing in its main pages, as well as a full-page obituary. There were of course many mentions of her husbands and lovers, and photographs of her with Kingsley. But they all recognized her candour and her courage, and the fact that she had produced a body of work that was not only enjoyable, but rich in humanity and worthy of attention. She would have been delighted by Martin's tribute in the *Mail on Sunday*: 'I was a semiliterate truant who read Harold Robbins and the dirty bits in Lady Chatterley. Only my "wicked" stepmother made me what I am today,' read the stand-alone headline above his warm but clear-eyed tribute to her efforts to complete his haphazard education.

In her lifetime, Jane was eclipsed by Kingsley Amis. Her stories about the experience of love and the conflicting demands of a woman's life could not compete with the raw energy of his voice, and her books were dismissed as 'women's fiction'. Luckily women's voices have become much stronger since then, and their lives and concerns are taken more seriously. If you go into a bookshop today you are likely to find more books by Elizabeth Jane Howard than by Kingsley Amis.

Now that would have surprised her.

Acknowledgements

IN GIVING ME the opportunity to write her life, Elizabeth Jane Howard bestowed a great gift; so my first and most heartfelt thanks must go to her. I had five long interviews with Jane at her house in Bungay, Suffolk, over the course of 2013. She enjoyed the process of being interviewed and talked simply and easily about her life, more diffidently about her books. She was justly proud of what she had achieved, yet I felt it had come at a great cost. Her hands were always busy as we talked, with knitting or embroidery; and occasionally she lifted her eyes from her work to give me a glance of such startling intensity that I felt she was looking straight through me.

Jane's daughter Nicola Starks and her husband Elliott have been extremely generous with their time and hospitality, and their assistance on many different points in the project has been invaluable. I deeply regret that I only had two interviews with Jane's brother Colin ('Monkey') Howard, before his death in December 2013. He was enchanting company, frank and funny, and he had known Jane for longer than anyone else. The observations of her stepson, Martin Amis, were vital to the story of her marriage to his father Kingsley Amis. I am very grateful for his help, and permission to quote from his father's novels and letters.

Ann Evans, Jane's literary agent, was tremendously patient under sporadic bombardments of emails; as were Jane Wood, Jacqui Graham, Selina Hastings, Patricia Wyndham, Kate Hopkinson and Nick McDowell. I had wonderful talks with Peter Stanford, who gave me permission to quote from his interviews with Jane; and Louisa Young, who gave me permission to consult the Peter Scott and Kennet Papers in the Cambridge University Library. I am indebted to Cecil Day-Lewis's literary executor, David Whiting, for permission to quote from his letters and poems; to Chris Fletcher, Head of Special

Collections at the Bodleian Library, Oxford, and Oliver House of the Weston Library, for access to the Papers of Cecil Day-Lewis and Jill Balcon, and those of Stephen and Natasha Spender. I would also like to thank Denise Anderson of the Special Collections at Edinburgh University Library, who arranged for me to consult the papers of Arthur Koestler. The letter to Jane from Koestler is reprinted by permission of Peters Fraser & Dunlop (www.petersfraserdunlop.com) on behalf of the estate of Arthur Koestler. My chapters on Jane and Kingsley's marriage owe an immeasurable debt to the work of Zachary Leader.

All Jane's papers, like those of Kingsley Amis, are in the Huntington Library in San Marino, California. At the Huntington Library I thank Steve Hindle, Sue Hodson and, above all, Gayle Richardson, the archivist who had catalogued Jane's papers. Gayle's 'Finding Aid' for the Papers of Elizabeth Jane Howard proved to be an invaluable work of reference, and Gayle was the greatest possible help – both at the research stage and during the writing. While working at the Huntington, I was the guest of Terry and Dennis Stanfill. Their house, with its beautiful Italian garden, was twenty-five minutes' *walk* from the Huntington; and their kindness and warmth made my weeks of research infinitely more comfortable, companionable and fun than I could ever have expected.

I would also like to thank Annunziata Asquith, David Astor, Josie Baird, Peter and Adrian Baird, Ariane Bankes, Michael Barber, Julian Barnes, Helen Benckendorff, Julian Berkeley, Louis de Bernières, Drusilla Beyfus, Fanny Blake, Jonathan Boyd, Jonathan Burnham, Antonia Byatt, Jonathan and Lesley Cavendish, Sir Edward Cazalet, Dr Hugh Cecil, Rupert Christiansen, Nicholas Clee, Richard Davenport-Hines, Tamasin Day-Lewis, Kate Douglas-Henry, Tony Ellis of the King's Lynn Festivals, Dawn Fairhead, Lara Feigel, Sarah Smyth and Lyndsey Fineran of the Cheltenham Festivals, Aisling Foster, Professor Roy Foster, Antonia Fraser, Catherine Freeman, Reg Gadney, Derek Grainger, Valerie Grove, Teodora Georguieva, Selina Hastings, Lexi Hopkinson, Judith Howard, Kay Howard, Mark Howard, Ruth Howard, Jan and Philip Hulme, Jackie Hume, the late P.D. James, Professor Edmund Keeley, Joy Law, Alice Leader, Jeremy and Petra Lewis, Kristin Linklater, Magnus Linklater, Penelope Lively, Michael Llewellyn-Smith, Joanna Lumley, Nick McDowell, Laurence and Jocelyn Magnus, Sargy and Frances Mann, Susanna Mann, Hilary Mantel, Alexandra Martyn of the Ageas Salisbury Arts Festival, Fay Maschler, Georgina Morley, Mavis Nicholson, Mollie Norwich, Justine Picardie and Liz Pearn of *Harper's Bazaar*, Neill Powell, Tristram Powell, Sue Prideaux, Faith Pullin, Maria Rejt, Pam Rose, Jenner Roth, Lawrence Sail, Alysoun Sanders of the Macmillan Archive, Tony Scotland, Al Senter, Christopher Sinclair-Stevenson, Hugh Sprattling, Peter Stanford, Dom Antony Sutch, Ann and Anthony Thwaite, Jeremy Trevathan, the late Ion Trewin, Anabel Turner, William and Caroline Waldegrave and Hywel Williams.

Almost everything I know about writing I learnt from two outstanding historians: my father John Julius Norwich, and my husband Antony Beevor. Their skilful editing has strengthened the book immeasurably. Felicity Bryan, my agent, and my editor Roland Philipps, have given me unfailing support and encouragement. I also want to thank Sara Marafini for another stunning jacket, Caroline Westmore for her patience in guiding me through the mysteries of digital editing, and Rosie Gailer the publicity director, for her tireless efforts – as she puts it – to keep my dance card full.

Lastly I want to salute my mother, Anne Norwich, whose originality and intellectual curiosity have been an inspiration all my life. It was she who suggested I write this book, and for that idea – and so much else – I am profoundly grateful.

Illustration Credits

Notes

Abbreviations

AC: Artemis Cooper
AK: Arthur Koestler
CDL: Cecil Day-Lewis
EJH: Elizabeth Jane Howard
EJH followed by a number: Elizabeth Jane Howard Papers, 1925–2014, at the Huntington Library, San Marino, California
HFP: Howard Family Papers
KA: Kingsley Amis
KK: Kathleen Kennet
PS: Peter Scott
SS: *Slipstream*, EJH

Chapter 1: Dancing with the Ballets Russes

1. HFP, Kit Somervell to her parents, 27 December 1919.
2. HFP, Kit Somervell to her parents, 23 December 1919.
3. Ian Stewart, 'Maugham the Dramatist', *Country Life*, 11 October 1984, p.1070.
4. *SS*, p.14.
5. EJH 4186, Abandoned Novel, 2009, p.41.
6. HFP, Kit Somervell to her parents, 20 January 1920.
7. EJH 4186, Abandoned Novel, 2009, pp. 34–5.
8. HFP, Kit Somervell to her parents, 23 January 1920.
9. HFP, Kit Somervell to her parents, 28 January 1920.
10. HFP, Kit Somervell to her parents, 7 February 1920.
11. Kit to Arthur Somervell, 20 March 1920.
12. EJH, *The Light Years*, p.197.

Chapter 2: Family Life

1. Rowland Watson, *The House of Howard: The Story of an English Firm*, Country Life, London, 1952.
2. *SS*, p.23.
3. HFP, Kit Howard, notebook recording the progress of EJH and Robin Howard.
4. Ibid.
5. Ibid.
6. Ibid.
7. Ibid.
8. Ibid.
9. Ibid.
10. EJH 4202, 'A Chronicle: Writing Exercise for Therapy', 1976–7, p.9.
11. HFP, Kit Howard, notebook recording the progress of EJH and Robin Howard.
12. EJH to AC, interview, 18–20 March 2013.

Chapter 3: Lessons

1. HFP, Kit Howard, notebook recording the progress of EJH and Robin Howard.
2. EJH interviewed by Naim Attallah; *Asking Questions: An Anthology of Encounters with Naim Attallah*, Quartet Books, 1996.
3. *SS*, p.28.
4. Ibid., p.43.
5. EJH 1732, Edith Somervell to EJH, 29 October 1939.
6. *SS*, p.46.
7. 'A Voyage Round my Teacher', *Daily Express*, 8 September 1982.
8. *SS*, p.65.
9. Ibid., p.68.
10. Ibid., pp. 68–9.
11. Kay Howard to AC, 29 November 2014.

Chapter 4: Ambitions, Courtship and War

1. *SS*, p.73.
2. Ibid.

3. Marian McKenna, *Myra Hess,* Hamish Hamilton, 1976, p.120.
4. EJH 3623, Wayland Young to EJH, undated, *c.*2000.
5. *Romeo and Juliet,* Act II scene v.
6. *SS,* p.82.
7. Ibid., p.82.
8. Huxley, p.112.
9. Ibid.
10. EJH 2252, EJH to PS, 2 Lansdowne Road, 3 June 1940.
11. PS to KK, 11 June 1940, quoted in Huxley, p.115.
12. EJH 2253, EJH to PS, 2 Lansdowne Road, 16 June 1940.
13. Quoted in Young, p.258.
14. *SS,* p.88.
15. Huxley, p.119.
16. EJH 2262, EJH to PS from the Beacon, 14 September 1940.
17. EJH 2264, EJH to PS from the Beacon, 23 September 1940.
18. EJH 2265, EJH to PS from the Beacon, 29 September 1940.
19. EJH 2270, EJH to PS, from Instow House, 10 November 1940.
20. EJH 2421, PS to EJH, from HMS *Broke,* 12 December 1940.
21. EJH 2426, PS to EJH, 4 March 1941.
22. EJH 2276, EJH to PS, undated, winter 1940.
23. EJH 117, story by EJH about her experience with Seth Holt ('Richard'), typed on foolscap paper, with autograph corrections by PS.
24. EJH 2430, PS to EJH, 14 April 1941.
25. EJH 2403, Kit to PS from the Beacon, 15 May 1941.
26. EJH 2441, PS to EJH, 5 August 1941.
27. Elizabeth Young, Lady Kennet, to AC, 8 July 2013.
28. EJH 2280, EJH to PS, 14 January 1941.
29. Peter Scott Papers, Cambridge, A.126, TS of a letter from PS to EJH, from Avenue Hotel, Belfast, 16 February 1941.
30. Quoted in Huxley, p.128.
31. EJH 2451, PS to EJH, 24 October 1941.
32. Quoted in Huxley, pp. 128–9, KK diary entry, May 1941.
33. *SS,* p.97.
34. Quoted in Huxley, pp. 128–9, KK diary entry, May 1941.
35. *SS,* p.101.
36. EJH 3623, Wayland Young to EJH, undated, *c.*2000.
37. EJH 2308, EJH to PS from Stratford, undated, September 1941.
38. EJH 2310, EJH to PS from Stratford, 17 September 1941.
39. Ibid.

40. Dosia Verney interviewed by Sally Hardcastle for BBC Radio 4 profile of EJH, July 1987.
41. Quoted in Huxley, p.129.
42. Kennet MSS, 108/2, letter from KK to Bill Kennet, Fritton, 22 February 1942.
43. *SS*, p.114.
44. Peter Scott Papers, Cambridge, A.163, EJH to PS, TS, 8 February 1942.
45. Quoted in Huxley, p.132, KK diary entry, 2 April 1942.
46. Quoted in Huxley, p.133.
47. *SS*, p.115.

Chapter 5: Mrs Peter Scott

1. Quoted in Huxley, p.133.
2. EJH 2225, EJH to KK, 29 April 1942.
3. Peter Scott Papers, Cambridge, A.126, TS of a letter from KK to PS, 11 September 1941.
4. *SS*, p.122.
5. 'The Stresses of Divorce', *Whicker's World*, aired 22 April 1967.
6. EJH 2227, EJH to KK, from the Gloster Hotel, Cowes, 23 May 1942.
7. Kennet MSS, 108/2, KK to Bill Kennet, 2 May 1942.
8. Quoted in Young, p.260.
9. *SS*, p.140.
10. EJH 946, Kit Howard to EJH, 23 June 1942.
11. Peter Scott Papers, Cambridge, A.163, EJH to PS, 7 September 1944.
12. EJH 2232, EJH to KK, 6 July 1942.
13. EJH 2322, EJH to PS, 3 November 1941.
14. *SS*, p.125.
15. EJH 2230, EJH to KK, undated.
16. Peter Scott Papers, Cambridge, A.163, EJH to PS, 7 September 1944.
17. Ibid.
18. *SS*, p.132.
19. EJH 4202, 'A Chronicle', pp. 9–10.
20. *SS*, p.137.
21. Quoted in Young, p.262.
22. Kennet MSS, leather-bound volume of the letters of KK to Bill Kennet, undated.
23. *SS*, p.140.

24. Quoted in Young, p.262.
25. Quoted in Huxley, p.141.
26. EJH 2507, PS to EJH, 2 September 1944.
27. Kennet MSS, 108/2, EJH to PS, 7 September 1944.

Chapter 6: Guilt and Betrayal

1. Ann Clowes to AC, 25 September 2015.
2. *SS*, p.143.
3. Ibid., p.150.
4. Peter Scott Papers, Cambridge, A.163, EJH to PS, 7 September 1944.
5. Ibid.
6. *SS*, p.151.
7. EJH 3623, Wayland Young to EJH, undated, *c.*2000.
8. Huxley, p.144.
9. *SS*, p.151.
10. Ibid.
11. Ibid., p.158.
12. Ibid., p.157.
13. Ibid., p.158.
14. EJH 2383, EJH to PS, 29 March 1944.
15. EJH 2385, EJH to PS, 3 April 1944.
16. *SS*, p.163.
17. Peter Scott Papers, Cambridge, A.163. EJH to PS, 7 September 1944.
18. EJH 2508, PS to EJH, 11 September 1944.
19. PS to KK, 9 January 1945, quoted in Huxley, pp. 152–3.
20. *SS*, p.170.
21. EJH 144, speech, 'On Public Speaking', *c.*1985.
22. Colin Howard to AC, 11 April 2013.

Chapter 7: Making the Break

1. *SS*, p.178.
2. Ibid., p.182.
3. Ibid., p.183.
4. EJH to AC, interview, 22 May 2013.
5. EJH 1224, Robert Linscott to EJH, 1 July 1946.
6. *SS*, p.190.

7. Ibid., p.193.
8. EJH 1223, Robert Linscott to EJH, 3 June 1946.
9. Unsent letter from PS to EJH, quoted in Huxley, p.171.
10. Nicola Starks to AC, 2 July 2013.
11. Quoted in Huxley, p.164.
12. Elizabeth Young, Lady Kennet, to AC, 8 July 2013.
13. Ibid.
14. *SS*, p.200.
15. Colin Howard to AC, 11 April 2013.

Chapter 8: The Beautiful Visit

1. EJH 1241, Robert Linscott to EJH, 31 August 1948.
2. EJH 3511, EJH to Anthea Sutherland, 23 August 1948.
3. *SS*, p.205.
4. Ibid., p.199.
5. Ibid., p.229.
6. Ibid., p.209.
7. Pam Rose to AC, 14 May 2013.
8. *The Long View*, pp. 12–13.
9. EJH 315, Michael Behrens to EJH, undated, postmark 5 May 1949.
10. EJH 314, draft of a letter from EJH to Michael Behrens, undated, *c.* January 1949.
11. *SS*, p.202.
12. EJH 323, Michael Behrens to EJH, undated, *c.* summer 1949.
13. *SS*, p.223.
14. EJH 316, Michael Behrens to EJH, 28 September 1949.
15. EJH 2148, Robert Linscott to EJH, 25 January 1950.
16. EJH 1256, Robert Linscott to EJH, 24 August 1950.
17. Antonia White, *New Statesman and Nation*, 13 May 1950, p.550.
18. Julian Symons, *Times Literary Supplement*, 12 May 1950.
19. EJH 3333, CDL to EJH, 16 June 1950.
20. EJH, *The Beautiful Visit*, p.155.
21. Ibid., p.297.
22. Ibid., p.309.
23. Ibid., p.312.
24. Stanford, p.238.
25. *SS*, pp. 219–20.
26. EJH 2159, CDL to EJH, from Musbury, Axminster, Devon, undated.

27. Joy Law to AC, 15 October 2014.
28. Ibid.
29. *SS*, p.217.
30. Josie Baird to AC, 9 April 2013.
31. EJH 3520, EJH to Anthea Sutherland from Blandford St, 21 September 1950.
32. EJH, Glen Cavaliero Introduction to 'Three Miles Up', Tartarus Press, 2003.
33. EJH 1260, Robert Linscott to EJH, 20 June 1950.
34. EJH 1288, Robert Linscott to EJH, 1 November 1951.
35. EJH 3333, CDL to EJH, 16 June 1950.

Chapter 9: Between Courage and Despair

1. EJH 1268, Robert Linscott to EJH, 29 October 1950.
2. EJH, *All Change*, p.257.
3. EJH 4202, 'A Chronicle', p.10.
4. *SS*, p.218.
5. Nicola Starks to AC, 2 July 2013.
6. EJH 1305, Robert Linscott to EJH, 3 March 1953.
7. EJH 49, essay on writing, *c.*1957.
8. *SS*, p.236.
9. Ibid., p.462.
10. EJH 401, Paul Bowman to EJH, 10 August 1953.
11. EJH 404, Paul Bowman to EJH, 1 December 1953.
12. EJH 405, Paul Bowman to EJH, May 1954.
13. EJH 343, Michael Behrens to EJH, undated.
14. EJH to Jill Balcon, from 48 Blandford St, 21 May 1954, Cecil Day-Lewis Archive, Bodleian Library.
15. *SS*, p.246.
16. Ibid.
17. EJH 405, Paul Bowman to EJH, 18 May 1954.
18. *SS*, p.241.
19. EJH 334, Michael Behrens to EJH, 12 July 1954.
20. EJH 335, Michael Behrens to EJH, 16 July 1954.
21. EJH 1318, Robert Linscott to EJH, 29 December 1954.
22. *SS*, p.251.
23. Ibid., p.252.
24. EJH 338, Michael Behrens to EJH, Christmas 1954.

25. EJH to Jill Balcon, 17 July 1954, Cecil Day-Lewis Archive, Bodleian Library.
26. *SS*, p.251.
27. Arthur Koestler, diary note, 19 June 1955.
28. Colin Howard to AC, 11 April 2013.
29. Ibid.
30. Ibid.

Chapter 10: Literary Lovers

1. *SS*, p.261.
2. Scammell, p.435.
3. Ibid., p.420.
4. Ibid., p.432.
5. *SS*, p.269.
6. Ibid., p.265.
7. Scammell, p.436.
8. EJH to Arthur Koestler, undated, *c*. August 1955, Arthur Koestler Papers, University of Edinburgh.
9. Ibid.
10. *SS*, p.274.
11. Kate Hopkinson to AC, 26 November 2014.
12. EJH 1135, Arthur Koestler to EJH, 8 Montpellier Sq. SW7, *c*. July/August 1955.
13. Valerie Grove, *The Life and Loves of Laurie Lee*, Robson Books, 2014, first page of Preface.
14. Ibid., pp. 314–15.
15. EJH, 'Travel with your Loved One', *Brides & Setting Up Home*, early spring 1975.
16. *SS*, p.278.
17. EJH, 'Travel with your Loved One', *Brides & Setting Up Home*, early spring 1975.
18. Grove, *Laurie Lee: The Well-Loved Stranger*, pp. 212–13.
19. *SS*, p.281.
20. EJH 1196, Laurie Lee to EJH, 20 October 1972.
21. *SS*, p.282.
22. Romain Gary to Arthur Koestler, 3 February 1955, Arthur Koestler Papers, University of Edinburgh.
23. *SS*, p.290.

24. EJH interview with Peter Stanford, 23 March 2006.
25. EJH 2162, CDL to EJH, Sunday, postmark 11 December 1955.
26. EJH 2163, CDL to EJH, Tuesday, postmark 13 December 1955.
27. *SS*, p.291.
28. EJH 2164, CDL to EJH, undated, December 1955.
29. EJH 2108, CDL to EJH, Christmas 1955.
30. EJH interview with Peter Stanford, 23 March 2006.

Chapter 11: The Long View

1. EJH 2172, CDL to EJH, 15 January 1956.
2. EJH interview with Peter Stanford, 23 March 2006.
3. EJH 2172, CDL to EJH, 15 January 1956.
4. EJH 2186, CDL to EJH, 27 June [1956].
5. John Davenport, *Observer*, 4 March 1956.
6. Marigold Johnson, *Times Literary Supplement*, 23 March 1956.
7. EJH, *The Long View*, p.213.
8. Ibid., pp. 101–2.
9. Ibid., p.218.
10. Martin Amis to AC, 5 November 2013.
11. Stephen Spender, *New Selected Journals 1939–1995*, ed. Lara Feigel and John Sutherland, with Natasha Spender, Faber & Faber, 2012, pp. 225–7.
12. Ibid., p.311.
13. Ella Winter, *Observer*, 15 September 1957.
14. *Encounter*, vol. VII, no. 5, November 1956, p.35.
15. Stephen Spender to EJH, 28 July 1956, Stephen Spender Collection, Bodleian Library.
16. EJH 1547, A.D. Peters to EJH, 10 Buckingham St, Adelphi, WC2, 25 May 1956.
17. EJH 910, EJH to Elizabeth and Robert Linscott, 19 May 1956.
18. Ibid.
19. Kathleen Tynan, *The Life of Kenneth Tynan*, Weidenfeld & Nicolson, 1987, p.129.
20. EJH to AC, interview, 21 May 2013.
21. EJH 2150, Cyril Connolly to EJH, Quisisana and Grand Hotel, Capri, undated, *c*. late August 1956.
22. EJH 2627, from a note written by Jeremy Lewis as he was preparing the Cyril Connolly biography, and quoting a letter from EJH to Cyril Connolly of 31 August 1965.

23. EJH 2193, CDL to EJH, postmark 6 September 1956.
24. *SS*, p.299.
25. Ibid.
26. EJH 2194, CDL to EJH, 2 October 1956.
27. EJH 2197, CDL to EJH, 28 December 1956.
28. Nicola Bennett, *Speaking Volumes: A History of the Cheltenham Festival of Literature*, Sutton Publishing, 1999, p.42.
29. EJH 2197, CDL to EJH, 28 December 1956.
30. EJH 2203, CDL to EJH, undated, early 1957.
31. EJH 2199, CDL to EJH from Chicago, 7 March 1957.
32. EJH 2198, CDL to EJH, 6 Croom Hill, *c.* late 1957.
33. *SS*, p.291.
34. EJH 3147, 'Moods of Love' (poem), stanzas IV & V only, inscribed 'For Lizbie', *c.* July 1956.
35. EJH 3148, 'Moods of Love' complete printed proof sheets.
36. *SS*, p.300.
37. Ibid., p.299.
38. Kristin Linklater to AC, 28 January 2015.

Chapter 12: A Matrimonial Mistake

1. Jeremy Lewis to AC, 10 June 2016.
2. EJH, *The Sea Change*, p.205.
3. EJH interview with Peter Stanford, 25 April 2005.
4. *SS*, pp. 315–16.
5. EJH, *After Julius*, p.6.
6. *SS*, p.320.
7. Kate Douglas-Henry to AC, 12 June 2016.
8. EJH to AC, interview, 21 May 2013.
9. *Queen* magazine, May 1961.
10. Ibid., October 1960.
11. Ibid., July 1960.
12. Ibid., September 1961.
13. Ibid., October 1960.
14. Ibid.: *The Siege of Peking*, July 1959; *A Visit to Don Otavio*, September 1960; *Cider with Rosie*, November 1959.
15. Selina Hastings to AC, 31 May 2014.
16. Kristin Linklater to AC, 28 January 2015.
17. *SS*, pp. 321–2.

18. Kate Douglas-Henry to AC, 12 June 2016.
19. *Sunday Times*, 25 October 1959.
20. Marigold Johnson, *Times Literary Supplement*, 20 November 1959.
21. J.D. Scott, *Sunday Times*, 22 November 1959.
22. *Sunday Times*, 6 December 1959.
23. Paul Mason, *The Maharishi*, Element Books (UK), 1994, p.46.
24. Nicola Starks to AC, 2 July 2013.
25. Colin Howard to AC, 11 April 2013.
26. Olive Shapley, *Broadcasting a Life: The Autobiography of Olive Shapley*, Scarlet Press, 1996, p.163.
27. Kristin Linklater to AC, 28 January 2015.
28. EJH to AC, interview, 21 May 2013.
29. Kristin Linklater to AC, 28 January 2015.
30. Cyril Frankel, *Eye to Eye: A Memoir*, Bank House Books, 2010, p.54.
31. EJH to AC, interview, 17 June 2013.
32. *SS*, p.353.
33. Bennett, *Speaking Volumes*, p.42.
34. Jackie Hume (then Jackie Gomme) to AC, 2 April 2014.
35. Bennett, *Speaking Volumes*, p.44.
36. BBC, *Bookstand*, 28 November 1962, quoted in Josyane Savigneau, *Carson McCullers: A Life*, trans. Joan E. Howard, Women's Press, 2001.
37. *SS*, p.338.
38. Jacobs, p.255.

Chapter 13: Lucky Jane

1. *SS*, p.462.
2. Leader, *Life*, p.171.
3. Ibid., p.228.
4. Martin Amis to AC, 5 November 2013 and 29 April 2016.
5. Martin Amis, p.102.
6. Ibid., p.156.
7. Leader, *Life*, p.500.
8. EJH 2217, EJH to KA, 6 February 1963.
9. EJH 2118, KA to EJH, undated letter, 23 February 1963.
10. EJH 2122, KA to EJH, 7 March 1963.
11. EJH 2218, EJH to KA, 23 February 1963.
12. EJH 2120, KA to EJH, 25 February 1963.
13. EJH 2218, EJH to KA, 23 February 1963.

14. EJH 2117, KA to EJH, 11 February 1963.
15. EJH 2120, KA to EJH, 25 February 1963.
16. EJH 2124, KA to EJH, 24 March 1963.
17. EJH 2106, 'Waking Beauty', poem by KA for EJH.
18. Leader, *Life*, p.490.
19. EJH 2127, KA to EJH, 24 April 1963.
20. See Leader, *Life*, p.501.
21. Ibid., Notes to Chapter 20: 'Break-up', note 4, p.904.
22. Ibid., p.501.
23. *SS*, p.344. Jane wrote that Nicola 'turned more to her new mother-in-law than she did to me', although this was never the case; it was her stepmother, Philippa, who she was close to.
24. EJH 2220, EJH to KA, 19 May 1963.
25. Ibid.
26. Ibid.
27. *SS*, p.346.
28. Ibid.
29. For more on where the two scenes are in *One Fat Englishman* and *After Julius*, see Leader, *Life*, p.518. Jane's contribution to *One Fat Englishman* begins in Chapter 13, with 'Roger had steered them well round the corner of the house' and ends with what Leader calls 'two perfect Amisian sentences': 'Roger stood there a moment experiencing, unusually for him, a mixture of feelings. One of them resembled agitation.' Kingsley's contribution to *After Julius* begins in Chapter 12: 'As soon as Major Hawkes had grasped exactly what was entailed' and ends somewhere like 'Behind her she heard his long sigh, and the faint slap as his horizontally raised arms fell to his sides.'
30. KA to William Rukeyser, 26 August 1963, Leader, *Letters*, p.640.
31. Martin Amis, p.143.
32. EJH 2130, KA to EJH, 12 May 1963.
33. Leader, *Life*, p.349.
34. Mavis Nicholson to AC, 10 June 2015.

Chapter 14: *After Julius*

1. Leader, *Life*, p.530.
2. Martin Amis, pp. 144–5.
3. EJH to AC, interview, 17–19 June 2013.
4. *SS*, p.351.

5. An Evelyn Waugh Website by David Cliffe, Evelyn Waugh in his own Words (transcript of the *Monitor* interview), abbotshill.freeserve.co.uk

6. Mark Amory (ed.), *The Letters of Evelyn Waugh*, Weidenfeld & Nicolson, 1980, p.618.

7. Leader, *Life*, p.534.

8. EJH to Jill Balcon, 12 September 1964, Cecil Day-Lewis Papers, Bodleian Library.

9. *SS*, p.354.

10. EJH to Jill Balcon, 12 September 1964, Cecil Day-Lewis Papers, Bodleian Library.

11. *SS*, p.355.

12. *Daily Mail*, 30 June 1965.

13. Stanford, pp. 298–9.

14. Edmund Keeley to AC, 18 July 2014.

15. EJH 373, John Betjeman to EJH, 13 January 1966.

16. Kay Dick, *Sunday Times*, 7 November 1965.

17. EJH, *After Julius*, p.275.

18. EJH to AC, interview, 3 December 2013.

19. Fiona MacCarthy, *Guardian*, 5 November 1965; Kay Dick, *Sunday Times*, 7 November 1965; Marigold Johnson, *Times Literary Supplement*, 4 November 1965.

20. EJH 1187, Laurie Lee to EJH, 24 November 1965.

21. EJH 2207, CDL to EJH, Crooms Hill, *c.*1965.

22. EJH 373, John Betjeman to EJH, 43 Cloth Fair EC1, 13 January 1966.

Chapter 15: Stepmother

1. Neil Powell, *Amis & Son: Two Literary Generations*, Macmillan, 2008, p.278.

2. *SS*, p.357.

3. Leader, *Life*, p.547.

4. *SS*, p.358.

5. Leader, *Life*, p.573.

6. Frederic Raphael, *Sunday Times*, 20 March 1966.

7. Leader, *Life*, p.496.

8. KA, *The Anti-Death League*, p.190.

9. Martin Amis, p.97.

10. Leader, *Life*, p.547.

11. *SS*, p.358.

12. Martin Amis to AC, 5 November 2013.
13. Keeley, *Inventing Paradise*, p.96.
14. Sargy Mann to AC, 20 May 2013.
15. Martin Amis, p.215.
16. Sargy Mann quoted in Richard Bradford, *Martin Amis: The Biography*, Constable, 2012, pp. 51–2.
17. 'The Stresses of Divorce', *Whicker's World*, aired 22 April 1967.
18. Kingsley Amis, *Sunday Telegraph*, 2 July 1967.
19. EJH 97, private and confidential report on the visit to Prague, 1966.
20. Leader, *Life*, p.580.
21. *SS*, p.368.
22. Ibid.
23. Ibid., p.369.
24. EJH, 'The Real Tragedy of the South', *Daily Telegraph*, 7 April 1968.
25. EJH to AC, interview, 10–12 January 2014.
26. Leader, *Life*, p.584.
27. Ibid., p.588.
28. EJH to AC, interview, 10–12 January 2014.
29. *SS*, p.369.
30. Martin Amis, letter to EJH and KA, 9 January 1968, quoted in *Experience*, p.150.
31. Leader, *Life*, p.601.
32. Illustrated brochure for Gladsmuir, spring 1968.
33. Newspaper cutting, undated.
34. EJH to AC, interview, 22 May 2013.
35. Martin Amis, *Koba the Dread*, Jonathan Cape, 2002, p.6.
36. EJH to AC, interview, 17–20 June 2013.
37. *SS*, p.359.
38. Edmund Keeley to AC, 11 July 2014; also Leader, *Life*, p.612.
39. Julian Symons, *Sunday Times*, 9 November 1969.
40. William Trevor, *Guardian*, 6 November 1969.
41. EJH 1384, Olivia Manning to EJH, undated, *c.* winter 1969.

Chapter 16: Lemmons

1. Martin Amis, interview in the *Daily Telegraph*, 21 November 2009.
2. Gully Wells, *The House in France: A Memoir*, Bloomsbury, 2011, pp. 144–5.
3. Leader, *Life*, p.610.

4. *SS*, p.380.
5. Martin Amis, p.189.
6. Kingsley Amis, *Girl, 20*, Jonathan Cape, 1971, p.12.
7. Ibid., p.129.
8. Ibid., p.216.
9. Martin Amis, p.230.
10. EJH 4202, 'A Chronicle', p.17.
11. *SS*, p.378.
12. Ibid., p.383.
13. Mary Conroy, *Sunday Times*, 2 April 1972.
14. 'Botticelli comes to Berkshire', *Times Literary Supplement*, 24 March 1972.
15. Stanford, p.316.
16. Tamasin Day-Lewis, *Where Shall We Go for Dinner? A Food Romance*, Weidenfeld & Nicolson, 2007, p.61.
17. EJH, 'How Day-Lewis Wrote his Last Poem', *Sunday Times*, 30 July 1972.
18. *SS*, p.386.
19. Leader, *Life*, p.641.
20. KA, 'Death of a Poet, *Observer*, 28 May 1972.
21. Tamasin Day-Lewis, *Where Shall We Go for Dinner?*, p.60.
22. Ibid., p.66.
23. *SS*, p.388.
24. Leader, *Life*, p.635.
25. EJH 1203, Rosamond Lehmann to EJH, undated, early August 1972.
26. Stephen Spender to EJH, 4 August 1972, Stephen Spender Collection, Bodleian Library.
27. EJH to Stephen Spender, 21 August 1972, Stephen Spender Collection, Bodleian Library.
28. KA, *Memoirs*, p.309.
29. Leader, *Life*, p.659.
30. Tom Maschler, *Publisher*, Picador, 2005, p.161.
31. Ion Trewin to AC, 2 December 2014.
32. Antonia Byatt to AC, 16 January 2015.
33. *SS*, p.418.

Chapter 17: 'An Agonising Decision'

1. *SS*, p.391.
2. Ibid., pp. 395–6.

3. C.J. Driver, *Guardian*, 10 July 1975.
4. Robin Robertson, ed., *Mortification: Writers' Stories of their Public Shame*, 4th Estate, 2003.
5. *SS*, p.405.
6. Paul Johnson to AC, 22 October 2013.
7. *SS*, p.401.
8. EJH 4202, 'A Chronicle', p.15.
9. *SS*, p.402.
10. EJH 4202, 'A Chronicle', p.3.
11. Ibid., p.4.
12. Ibid., p.9.
13. Kate Hopkinson to AC, 11 January 2016 and 12 January 2016.
14. EJH 4202, 'A Chronicle', p.7.
15. Ibid., p.19.
16. Martin Amis to AC, 5 November 2013.
17. *SS*, pp. 406–7.
18. Martin Amis, p.217.
19. EJH 4202, 'A Chronicle', p.20.
20. EJH 606, Kay Dick to EJH, 14 July 1976.
21. EJH 4270, KA to EJH, Gardnor House, 16 September 1976.
22. EJH 4271, KA to EJH, 21 September 1976.
23. EJH 4202, 'A Chronicle', p.37.
24. Ibid., p.42.
25. Ibid., p.43.
26. Ibid., p.44.
27. Ibid., p.46.
28. Martin Amis, p.218.
29. *SS*, p.416.
30. Ibid., p.417.
31. Valerie Grove to AC, 13 June 2015; Valerie Grove in the *Evening Standard*, 13 February 1978.
32. KA, *Jake's Thing*, p.285.
33. *SS*, p.416.
34. Fay Maschler to AC, October 2014.
35. EJH to AC, interview, 18–20 March 2013.
36. Kate Hopkinson to AC, 26 November 2014.
37. KA to Bob Conquest, 20 February 1981, Leader, *Letters*, p.910.
38. KA to Philip Larkin, 29 September 1979, Leader, *Letters*, p.876.
39. *SS*, p.423
40. Joy Law to Zachary Leader, 27 December 2005.

41. Quoted in Leader, *Life*, p.680.
42. *SS*, p.424.
43. KA, *Stanley and the Women*, p.207.
44. EJH 2224, draft of a letter to KA dated 29 October 1980.
45. KA to Philip Larkin, 5 December 1980, Leader, *Letters*, p.905.
46. KA to Brian Aldiss, 15 December 1980, Leader, *Life*, p.908.
47. KA, *Stanley and the Women*, p.38.

Chapter 18: Introducing the Cazalets

1. EJH 4276, KA to EJH, 29 December 1980.
2. 'Misogyny and Madness', Michael Barber talks to KA, *Books Magazine*, May 1984.
3. *SS*, pp. 432–3.
4. EJH 3334, Daniel Day-Lewis to EJH, 18 March 2003.
5. EJH, *Getting It Right*, pp. 309–10.
6. Anne Duchêne, *Times Literary Supplement*, 14 May 1982.
7. EJH 752, Victoria Glendinning to EJH, 12 May 1982.
8. Nicholas Shrimpton, *Sunday Times*, 16 May 1982.
9. EJH 2053, Angus Wilson to EJH, undated, *c.*1982.
10. *SS*, pp. 433–4.
11. Penelope Lively, diaries, March 1983, courtesy of Penelope Lively.
12. *SS*, p.419.
13. EJH to Jill Balcon, 18 April 1983, Jill Balcon Papers, Oxford.
14. EJH to Jill Balcon, 19 December 1983, ibid.
15. EJH in conversation with Selina Hastings, 1 March 2008.
16. Fay Maschler to AC, October 2014.
17. EJH 454, Brigid Brophy to EJH, 24 January 1984.
18. Jonathan Cavendish to AC, 16 April 2014.
19. Tony Scotland to AC, 15 February 2016.
20. John Julius Norwich to AC, 18 September 2014.
21. Jonathan Burnham to AC, 30 October 2013.
22. *SS*, p.438.
23. Julian Barnes to AC, 12 September 2013.
24. *SS*, p.436.
25. EJH to AC, interview, 21 May 2013.
26. *SS*, p.437.
27. Vincent Canby, *New York Times*, 5 May 1989.
28. Fay Maschler to AC, October 2014.

29. Roy and Aisling Foster to AC, 9 October 2014.

30. Jonathan Burnham to AC 4 October 2015.

31. Jonathan Burnham to AC, 30 October 2013.

32. Selina Hastings to AC, 23 February 2013.

33. Anne Norwich to AC, 29 July 2014.

34. Peter Mann and Sargy Mann, *Sargy Mann: 'Probably the Best Blind Painter in Peckham'*, SP Books, 2008, p.104.

35. EJH 146, 'On Sybille Bedford', speech given by EJH on occasion of a birthday dinner for Sybille Bedford, 17 April 1991.

36. Jonathan Burnham to AC, 30 October 2013.

37. Fanny Blake to AC, 14 January 2016.

38. Nicci Gerrard, *Observer*, 22 July 1990.

39. D.J. Taylor, *Sunday Times*, 22 July 1990.

40. EJH, *The Light Years*, p.407.

41. Jane O'Grady, 'Carrying on as Usual', *Times Literary Supplement*, 27 July 1990.

Chapter 19: The Final Disillusion

1. Jenner Roth to AC, 2 June 2014.

2. *SS*, p.448.

3. Nick McDowell to AC, 11 December 2015.

4. EJH, *Marking Time*, p.381.

5. Frances Mann to AC, 12 October 2015.

6. Jane Wood to AC, 20 May 2014.

7. Isobel Armstrong, *Times Literary Supplement*, 8 November 1991.

8. EJH 4478, Roy Foster to EJH, 30 December 1991.

9. Candia McWilliam to AC, 25 February 2016.

10. Charlotte Hobson to AC, 23 April 2016.

11. Nicolette Jones, *Sunday Times*, 26 January 1992.

12. Dawn Fairhead to AC, 23 November 2014.

13. EJH to Roy Foster, 6 January 1992, courtesy of Professor Roy Foster.

14. EJH, *Confusion*, p.91.

15. Nicolette Jones, *Sunday Times*, 21 November 1993.

16. J.K.L. Walker, *Times Literary Supplement*, 29 October 1993.

17. EJH 2871, Hilary Mantel to EJH, *c*. November 1998.

18. Sir Edward Cazalet to AC, 8 April 2015.

19. Selina Hastings to AC, 6 February 2016.

20. Louisa Young to AC, 22 January 2016.

21. Louis de Bernières to AC, 14 November 2014.
22. Patricia Wyndham to AC, 4 December 2013.
23. *SS*, p.459.
24. Hilary Mantel, *Guardian*, 30 January 2016.
25. *SS*, p.461.
26. Jane Wood to AC, 20 May 2014.
27. Selina Hastings to AC, 31 May 2013.
28. Dawn Fairhead to AC, 23 November 2014.
29. Nick McDowell to AC, 17 October 2013.
30. Jane Wood to AC, 8 February 2016.
31. *SS*, p.463.
32. Dawn Fairhead to AC, 23 November 2014.
33. Nicola Starks, diary excerpt, 25 April 1996.
34. *SS*, p.464.
35. Ibid.
36. Dawn Fairhead to AC, 23 November 2014.
37. Selina Hastings to AC, 31 May 2013.
38. *SS*, p.465.
39. Colin Howard to AC, 11 April 2013.
40. *SS*, p.464.
41. Nicola Starks to AC, 23 November 2014.
42. Colin Howard to AC, 11 April 2013.
43. Selina Hastings to AC, 31 May 2013.
44. Nick McDowell to AC, 17 October 2013.

Chapter 20: *Love All*

1. *SS*, p.466.
2. EJH 2623, Ann Clowes to EJH, 1 August 1996.
3. Jenner Roth to AC, 2 June 2014.
4. Jane Wood to AC, 8 February 2016.
5. Ibid.
6. Alice Leader to AC, 23 July 2014.
7. EJH 2646, Louis de Bernières to EJH, undated.
8. EJH, *Falling*, p.4.
9. Ibid., p.277.
10. Ibid., final words, p.422.
11. Sargy Mann to AC, 22 November 2014.
12. EJH 2574, Sybille Bedford to EJH, 16 October 1996.

13. EJH to AC, interview, 30 July 2013.
14. EJH 2863, Joanna Lumley to EJH, 25 September 1999.
15. EJH to AC, interview,18 June 2013.
16. *SS*, Preface, p. xiii.
17. Jane Wood to AC, 20 May 2014.
18. Jeremy Trevathan to AC, 4 September 2014.
19. Humphrey Carpenter, *Sunday Times*, 20 October 2002.
20. Sarah Curtis, *Times Literary Supplement*, 15 November 2002.
21. Annabel Turner to AC, 22 November 2014.
22. Roy Foster to AC, 9 October 2014.
23. EJH to Roy Foster, 20 March 2003, courtesy of Professor Roy Foster.
24. EJH to Jeremy Trevathan, 1 July 2005, Macmillan Archives.
25. Janet Hodgson to AC, 11 June 2014.
26. Dom Antony Sutch to AC, 17 November 2014.
27. Jeremy Trevathan to AC, 1 March 2016.
28. EJH, *Love All*, p.265.
29. Nicholas Clee, *Times Literary Supplement*, 17 October 2008.
30. EJH to Tony Scotland, 8 December 2008, courtesy of Tony Scotland.
31. Laurence Magnus to AC, 22 November 2014.
32. Janet Hodgson to AC, 11 June 2014.

Chapter 21: 'I *Know* He's Going to Get Better'

1. Tony Scotland to AC, 15 February 2016.
2. EJH to AC, interview, 30 July 2013.
3. Maria Rejt to AC, 20 May 2014.
4. EJH interview with Selina Durrant, *Sunday Telegraph Stella Magazine*, 10 November 2013.
5. Jacqui Graham to AC, 5 March 2016.
6. EJH interview with Jane Clinton, *Sunday Express*, 17 November 2013.
7. Jennifer Selway, *Daily Express*, 15 November 2013.
8. Nicola Shulman, *The Spectator*, 23 November 2013.
9. Lucy Atkins, *Sunday Times Culture Magazine*, 3 November 2013.
10. Jim Naughtie on *The Last Word*, Radio 4, 3 January 2013.
11. Annabel Turner to AC, 22 November 2014.
12. Dom Antony Sutch to AC, 20 November 2014.

Bibliography

The Complete Works of Elizabeth Jane Howard

The Beautiful Visit, Jonathan Cape, 1950 (edn used in text: Pan Books, 1993)

We Are for the Dark: Six Ghost Stories (co-author Robert Aickman), Jonathan Cape, 1951

The Long View, Jonathan Cape, 1956 (edn used in text: Macmillan, 1994)

Bettina: A Portrait (co-author Arthur Helps), Chatto & Windus, 1957

The Sea Change, Jonathan Cape, 1959 (edn used in text: Jonathan Cape, 1973)

After Julius, Jonathan Cape, 1965 (edn used in text: Macmillan, 1994)

Something in Disguise, Jonathan Cape, 1969

Odd Girl Out, Jonathan Cape, 1972 (edn used in text: Macmillan, 1994)

Mr Wrong, Jonathan Cape, 1975

The Lovers' Companion, David & Charles (Canada), 1978

Getting It Right, Hamish Hamilton, 1982 (edn used in text: Pan Books, 1996)

Cooking for Occasions (co-author Fay Maschler), Michael Joseph, 1987

The Light Years, vol. I of The Cazalet Chronicle, Macmillan, 1990

Green Shades: An Anthology of Plants, Gardens and Gardeners, Aurum Press, 1991

Marking Time, vol. II of The Cazalet Chronicle, Macmillan, 1991

Confusion, vol. III of The Cazalet Chronicle, Macmillan, 1993

Casting Off, vol. IV of The Cazalet Chronicle, Macmillan, 1995

Marriage: An Anthology (ed.), Weidenfeld & Nicolson, 1997

Falling, Macmillan, 1999 (edn used in text: Pan Books, 2000)

Slipstream: A Memoir, Macmillan, 2002

Love All, Macmillan, 2008 (edn used in text: Pan Books, 2009)

All Change, vol. V of The Cazalet Chronicle, Mantle, 2013

Additional Sources

Amis, Kingsley, *The Anti-Death League*, Victor Gollancz, 1966

——, *Girl, 20*, Jonathan Cape, 1971

——, *Jake's Thing*, Jonathan Cape, 1978

——, *Stanley and the Women*, Hutchinson, 1984

——, *Memoirs*, Hutchinson, 1991

Amis, Martin, *Experience*, Jonathan Cape, 2000

Bellos, David, *Romain Gary: A Tall Story*, Harvill Secker, 2010

Day-Lewis, Tamasin, *Where Shall We Go for Dinner? A Food Romance*, Weidenfeld & Nicolson, 2007

Grove, Valerie, *Laurie Lee: The Well-Loved Stranger*, Viking, 1999

Humble, Nicola, *The Feminine Middlebrow Novel, 1920s to 1950s: Class, Domesticity, and Bohemianism*, Oxford University Press, 2002

Huxley, Elspeth, *Peter Scott: Painter and Naturalist*, Faber & Faber, 1993

Jacobs, Eric, *Kingsley Amis: A Biography*, Sceptre, 1996

Keeley, Edmund, *Inventing Paradise: The Greek Journey 1937–1947*, Farrar, Strauss & Giroux (New York), 1999

Leader, Zachary, *The Life of Kingsley Amis*, Jonathan Cape, 2006

——, (ed.), *The Letters of Kingsley Amis*, HarperCollins, 2001

Mann, Peter and Sargy Mann, *Sargy Mann: 'Probably the Best Blind Painter in Peckham'*, SP Books, 2008

Powell, Neil, *Amis & Son: Two Literary Generations*, Macmillan, 2008

Scammell, Michael, *Koestler: The Indispensable Intellectual*, Faber & Faber, 2010

Stanford, Peter, *C. Day-Lewis: A Life*, Continuum, 2007

Wells, Gully, *The House in France: A Memoir*, Bloomsbury, 2011

Young, Louisa, *A Great Task of Happiness: The Life of Kathleen Scott*, Macmillan, 1995

Index

Works by Elizabeth Jane Howard (EJH) appear directly under title;
works by others under author's name.
Titles of rank are generally not shown unless mentioned in the text.